THE ENCYCLOPEDIA OF REAL ESTATE FORMS & AGREEMENTS:

A Complete Kit of Ready-To-Use Checklists, Worksheets, Forms, and Contracts With Companion CD-ROM

The Encyclopedia of Real Estate Forms & Agreements: A Complete Kit of Ready-To-Use Checklists, Worksheets, Forms, and Contracts With Companion CD-ROM

Copyright © 2009 Atlantic Publishing Group, Inc.

1405 SW 6th Avenue • Ocala, Florida 34471 • Phone 800-814-1132 • Fax 352-622-1875

Web site: www.atlantic-pub.com • E-mail: sales@atlantic-pub.com

SAN Number: 268-1250

Library of Congress Cataloging-in-Publication Data

The encyclopedia of real estate forms & agreements : a complete kit of ready-to-use checklists, worksheets, forms, and contracts with companion CD-ROM.
    p. cm.
Includes index.
ISBN-13: 978-0-910627-10-8 (alk. paper)
ISBN-10: 0-910627-10-X (alk. paper)
1. Real estate business--Law and legislation--United States--Forms. 2. Real property--United States--Forms. 3. Vendors and purchasers--United States--Forms. I. Atlantic Publishing Co.
KF568.1.E53 2009
346.7304'370269--dc22
                2007028077

Printed in the United States

PROJECT MANAGER: Melissa Peterson • mpeterson@atlantic-pub.com
INTERIOR DESIGN: Antoinette D'Amore • addesign@videotron.ca
JACKET DESIGN: Jackie Miller • sullmill@charter.net
ILLUSTRATIONS: Holly Marie Gibbs • hgibbs@atlantic-pub.com

Printed on Recycled Paper

We recently lost our beloved pet "Bear," who was not only our best and dearest friend but also the "Vice President of Sunshine" here at Atlantic Publishing. He did not receive a salary but worked tirelessly 24 hours a day to please his parents. Bear was a rescue dog that turned around and showered myself, my wife, Sherri, his grandparents Jean, Bob, and Nancy, and every person and animal he met (maybe not rabbits) with friendship and love. He made a lot of people smile every day.

We wanted you to know that a portion of the profits of this book will be donated to The Humane Society of the United States. *–Douglas & Sherri Brown*

The human-animal bond is as old as human history. We cherish our animal companions for their unconditional affection and acceptance. We feel a thrill when we glimpse wild creatures in their natural habitat or in our own backyard.

Unfortunately, the human-animal bond has at times been weakened. Humans have exploited some animal species to the point of extinction.

The Humane Society of the United States makes a difference in the lives of animals here at home and worldwide. The HSUS is dedicated to creating a world where our relationship with animals is guided by compassion. We seek a truly humane society in which animals are respected for their intrinsic value, and where the human-animal bond is strong.

Want to help animals? We have plenty of suggestions. Adopt a pet from a local shelter, join The Humane Society and be a part of our work to help companion animals and wildlife. You will be funding our educational, legislative, investigative and outreach projects in the U.S. and across the globe.

Or perhaps you'd like to make a memorial donation in honor of a pet, friend or relative? You can through our Kindred Spirits program. And if you'd like to contribute in a more structured way, our Planned Giving Office has suggestions about estate planning, annuities, and even gifts of stock that avoid capital gains taxes.

Maybe you have land that you would like to preserve as a lasting habitat for wildlife. Our Wildlife Land Trust can help you. Perhaps the land you want to share is a backyard— that's enough. Our Urban Wildlife Sanctuary Program will show you how to create a habitat for your wild neighbors.

So you see, it's easy to help animals. And The HSUS is here to help.

THE HUMANE SOCIETY
OF THE UNITED STATES.

2100 L Street NW • Washington, DC 20037 • 202-452-1100
www.hsus.org

DISCLAIMER

The forms, contracts, and other legal documents within this book are intended for reference only. Atlantic Publishing Group, Inc. is not in the business of providing legal or real estate advice. Forms provided in this book are not state specific, and anyone seeking forms for a particular state should contact their state's real estate board or a legal professional. Readers are encouraged to seek professional legal advice if they have questions on the details of a contract or are uncertain about the laws in their state. The contracts within this book may not be suitable for all real estate situations, and readers should seek the advice of a legal professional to ensure the contract meets their needs.

TABLE OF CONTENTS

Chapter 2: Basic Real Estate
Purchasing Forms and Agreements 61

Chapter 3: Contractor/Subcontractor Forms,
Agreements, and Checklists 107

Chapter 5: Commercial Real Estate Forms   171

Chapter 6: Lease Agreements   219

Chapter 7: Residential Lease/Purchase Agreements   293

Chapter 8: Rental Agreements, Applications, and Forms   299

Chapter 9: Landlord Forms   337

Chapter 10: Late Payment Forms   349

CHAPTER 1

Basic Real Estate Forms & Agreements

AGREEMENT FOR PURCHASE & SALE OF REAL ESTATE I

Date: _____

Seller: _____

Address: _____

City: _____ State: _____ Zip: _____

Buyer: _____

Address: _____

City: _____ State: _____ Zip: _____

This Agreement is hereby made as of this date by and between the abovementioned Seller and Buyer.

1. Property

Both parties listed above hereby agree that the Seller will sell and the Buyer will buy the following property, which is located in _____ County and _____ State. The address is known by the following address: _____.

This sale will also include the following personal property, fixtures, and appliances:

_____

The following items are excluded and, unless listed below, all other items will be included whether or not they are affixed to the property or structures.

_____

The Seller specifically warrants that the property, improvements, building or structures, the appliances, roof, plumbing, heating, and/or ventilation systems are in good and working order. This clause shall survive closing of title.

2. Purchase Price

Total purchase price to be paid by the Buyer will be $_____ and will be payable as follows:

A non-refundable earnest money deposit of	$_____
Balance due at closing	$_____
Owner financing from the Seller	$_____
New loan	$_____
Subject to existing loans	$_____

The sale price is subject to an appraisal to be completed by Buyer and/or an agent of Buyer's choice.

3. Deposit

The Buyer's deposit will be held in escrow by the agent of the Buyer's choice. If default of this Agreement shall occur, Seller will retain the deposit as his/her compensation without any further contact between the parties.

4. New Loan

This Agreement is conditional upon the Buyer's ability to obtain a new loan in the amount due to the Seller at time of closing, a total amount of $_____. Buyer must provide to the Seller written proof of a loan commitment on or before the following date: _____ (month) _____ (day), _____ (year).

5. Seller Financing

Buyer shall execute a promissory note in the amount of $_____. In the event of default, a recourse shall be against the property, and there shall be no personal resource against the Borrower. As a security for presentation of the promissory note, the Buyer shall provide the Seller with a mortgage, deed of trust, or other routine security agreement, which shall be secondary to a new first mortgage not to exceed $_____.

6. The Closing

The Closing will be held on or about _____ (month) _____ (day), _____ (year), at the time and place designated by the Buyer. Buyer will also choose the escrow, title, and/ or closing agent. The Seller hereby agrees to convey the title by a general warranty deed.

7. Possession

The Seller will surrender the possession of the property in clean condition and free of all personal effects and debris on or before _____ (month) _____ (day), _____ (year). In the event that the possession is not delivered at closing, the Buyer has all rights to withhold proceeds from the sale in the amount of $_____ as security. The Seller will be responsible for damages in the amount of $_____ per day for each day that the property is occupied beyond the date listed above. This clause shall survive the closing of the title.

8. Execution in Counterparts

This Agreement may be executed in counterparts and by faxed signatures. This Agreement will be effective as of the date of the last signature.

9. Inspection of the Property

This Agreement is subject to a final inspection and approval of the property by the Buyer in writing on or before _____ (month) _____ (day), _____ (year).

10. Access to the Property

The Buyer will be entitled to the property's key and have access to show partners, lenders, inspectors, and/or contractors prior to closing. The Buyer may also place appropriate signage on the property prior to closing for prospective tenants and/or assigns.

Date of Signing By All Parties: _____

_____   _____
Seller   Seller

_____   _____
Buyer   Buyer

AGREEMENT FOR PURCHASE & SALE OF REAL ESTATE II

Date: _____

Seller: _____

Address: _____

City: _____ State: _____ Zip: _____

Buyer: _____

Address: _____

City: _____ State: _____ Zip: _____

The abovementioned parties are in agreement that the seller shall sell and that the buyer shall buy the property described below in accordance with all of the terms and conditions that follow.

Legal description of the property, including location (county and state): Refer to attached Exhibit A.

Street address: _____

Personal property that is part of the transaction: _____

Total purchase price: $ _____

1. Payment.

Payment shall be made as follows:

The deposit is to be held in escrow by _____, subject to a mortgage assumption in favor of _____ with an interest rate of _____% per annum with an approximate balance of $_____, payable in monthly installments of $_____. Mortgage and note in the principal amount of _____ shall have interest at _____%, according to the terms in attached Exhibit B, Cash, certified check, or cashier's check in the amount of $_____ shall be paid at closing, subject to prorations and adjustments.

2. Financing.

New Financing.

The purchaser must obtain a firm commitment for a loan if any portion of the purchase price is to be financed by a third party at an interest rate of not more than ____% in a minimum principal amount of $_____within _____ days of this agreement date. Buyer shall apply for and make all reasonable effort to obtain afore-mentioned loan. This agreement may be canceled by either party in the event that buyer fails to obtain said loan or waives buyer's rights.

Existing Mortgage.

Seller is to provide a mortgagee statement describing the interest rate, remaining principal, payment method, and containing an assurance that the mortgage is in good standing. The buyer may rescind this agreement if mortgagee approval of the buyer is required and not provided, or if the mortgagee charges any fee in excess of $100 or requires an interest rate increase, unless the seller opts to pay this excess or increase. Each party agrees to pay half of any such fee that is not more than $100. Buyer shall make an earnest effort to be approved. Seller shall be credited with any escrow deposits held by mortgagee.

Purchase Money Mortgages.

In the event of default, any purchase money note and mortgage will allow grace pe-riod of 30 days for a first mortgage and 15 days for a second mortgage. The purchase money mortgage and note will guarantee the right of full or partial prepayment without penalty. In the case of resale property, interest adjustment or acceleration shall not be provided for. The seller may borrow clauses from mortgages and mort-gage notes of other private parties located in the same county. The owner of the encumbered property shall be required by the mortgage to keep any prior liens and encumbrances in good standing and shall be forbidden from accepting any future advances or modifications under prior mortgages. At the seller's option, all personal property being transferred shall be subject to the mortgage lien and documented by a recorded financial statement.

3. Evidence of Title.

At the seller's expense, the seller shall, within 21 days from this agreement date or within 30 days of closing, whichever occurs first, provide the buyer with either:

An abstract of title that has been prepared by a reputable title company, be-ginning with the earliest public records of the property or with a later date, if this is customary in the county where the property is located. A marketable title reasonably free from defects shall be conveyed by the seller, subject only to encumbrances, liens, and qualifications or exceptions drawn out in this agreement and discharged by the seller by closing. Marketable title shall be de-termined according to the law. The abstract shall become the buyer's property upon this transaction's closing, subject to the retention right thereof by first mortgagee until paid in full.

Or

A commitment of title insurance, with the title policy premium of the fee owner to be paid at closing by the seller. A qualified title insurer is to issue the commitment of title insurance and agree to issue a policy in the buyer's name for an amount equal to the purchase price, thereby ensuring that the buyer is receiving title to the property subject only to encumbrances, liens, or excep-tions or qualifications set forth in this document and those which the seller shall discharge by closing.

Upon receiving evidence of the title, the buyer shall have 30 days to examine an abstract or 5 days to examine a title commitment. Buyer shall notify seller in writing within 3 days of any defects found therein. From receipt of such notice, seller shall have 120 days to remove such defects. Otherwise, buyer may either accept original title or be refunded all funds paid therein, thereby releasing both parties from all terms of this agreement. Seller shall use all means available to prevent such an event.

At closing, the seller shall provide the buyer an affidavit attesting to the absence of any potential liens on the property and attesting that there have been no improvements made to the property for the 90 days prior. If such improvements have taken place within said time, seller shall provide all related waivers or releases of lien and a statement that all related bills have been or will be paid by closing.

4. Acceptance Time and Effective Date: _____

5. Deadline for Execution of this Offer: _____

If the abovementioned deadline is not met, the buyer has the right to be refunded the deposit, thus voiding the offer. The date when both parties have signed this offer shall be the effective date.

6. Closing Date: _____

7. Limitations, Easements, and Restrictions.

The Buyer agrees to comply with: prohibitions, restrictions, reservations, zoning, and other governmental requirements; restrictions, covenants, and matters appearing on the plat or common to the subdivision in which the property is located; recorded public utility easements, as long as these easements are contiguous throughout property lines and follow local governmental standards; taxes for the closing year and subsequent year; and any purchase money mortgages or assumed mortgages.

8. Leases and Occupancy.

Seller is the only party in occupancy. Terms of any intended rental or occupation of the property after closing shall be listed herein. Seller shall, no less than 15 days before closing, provide copies of all tenant leases to buyer, along with all related occupancy information, which the buyer may confirm with tenants. At closing, seller shall provide all original leases to buyer. If buyer is to assume occupancy prior to closing, buyer accepts all related risks and responsibilities therein at time of occupancy and accepts property as is unless noted otherwise in writing.

9. Survey.

The property may be surveyed by the buyer at the buyer's expense. If a certified survey performed by a registered surveyor shows that the property does not begin or end as was indicated to the buyer, or that improvements are not contained within the property, or any other violations to this agreement are found, such shall be treated as a defect of title.

10. Termites.

Within 10 or more days before closing, the buyer may have improvements inspected by a certified pest control agent at the buyer's expense to make a determination as to the presence of any visible termite presence or damage. Within 7 days of written notice of a termite problem, buyer shall have said damaged inspected and correction estimated by a licensed general or building contractor. In such case, seller shall pay for treatment and repair up to 1.5% of the purchase price. If such costs exceed that maximum, buyer may cancel this agreement by providing written notice to seller not more than 5 days after receiving the repair estimate. If buyer instead agrees to proceed, seller will credit buyer for aforementioned 1.5%. All wood-destroying organisms that must be reported under any current state pest control act shall be considered "termites."

11. Egress and Ingress.

The seller agrees that there is adequate egress and ingress to the property to allow for the use set out in herein.

12. Time is of the Essence.

Time is of the essence of this contract. Weekends and legal holidays shall not be counted against any references toward 6 days or fewer. Any deadline falling a weekend or legal holiday shall be extended to 5 p.m. the next business day.

13. Closing Documents.

Assignments of leases, deed of mechanics lien affidavit, and any corrective instruments necessary to perfecting the title shall be provided by the seller. Mortgage, security agreement, financing statements, mortgage note, and closing statement shall be provided by the buyer.

14. Expenses.

Seller shall be financially responsible for intangible tax on and recording of purchase money mortgage to seller, recording costs of any corrective instruments, and state documentary stamps that must be affixed to the instrument of conveyance. Recording costs for the financing statements and deed, as well as documentary stamps to be affixed to any notes secured by the purchase money mortgage, shall be the financial responsibility of the buyer.

15. Proration of Real and Personal Taxes.

Taxes shall be prorated based on the current year's tax and date of occupancy, with allowance for maximum allowable discount and homestead or other exemptions, and with each party paying his/her share. If such figures are unavailable, taxes will be prorated in accordance with taxes of the previous year. If the closing year has brought new improvements, and the prior year's taxes are being prorated, an agreement to include the improvements shall be reached by both parties. Otherwise, an informal assessment shall be requested of the county property appraiser. Receipt of tax bill may constitute adjustment of proration.

16. Special Assessment Liens.

Seller shall be responsible for payment of any special assessment liens in existence at closing. Buyer shall assume responsibility for payment of any pending liens. Seller shall be responsible for payment of the assessment of the improvement.

17. Personal Property Inspection and Repair.

Seller warrants that all cooling, heating, plumbing, and electrical systems, in addition to all machinery and major appliances, are in working condition at date of closing. Buyer may pay for licensed inspection of such and shall submit written report of same to seller by closing. Seller shall be financially responsible for such repairs using escrow funds at closing. Buyer waives right to pursue any such repairs not reported prior to closing. With reasonable notice, seller shall provide access for such inspection.

18. Loss Risk.

Restoration costs shall be the seller's responsibility if any damages that occur to the improvements do not exceed 3% of the assessed valuation and closing shall proceed with the aforementioned cost escrowed. If restoration costs exceed the abovementioned 3%, the buyer may either cancel the agreement and be refunded any related deposits or accept the property as-is, along with either the aforementioned 3% or any insurance monies payable.

19. Maintenance.

The personal property included in this contract, in addition to real property, including landscaping and any pool, shall be maintained by seller from effective date until closing date. The buyer or buyer's agent shall have access to inspect the property to verify said maintenance before closing.

20. Closing Procedures and Proceeds of Sale.

As soon as the payment clears the bank, the title deed will be recorded and the buyer shall take over any expenses involved in showing that the buyer holds clear title and that no encumbrances or changes since the last date of evidence have made the title unmarketable by the seller. The seller's attorney or other agreed-upon escrow agent shall hold the cash proceeds of sale in escrow for no more than 5 days after closing. If seller's title is not marketable, buyer shall have 5 days to provide written notice of same to seller, giving seller 30 days to correct said defect. If seller fails to timely cure such defect, all funds hereunder paid shall, upon and within 5 days of written demand, be returned to buyer and buyer shall leave the property and return ownership of the property to seller by special warranty deed. Buyer's failure to request refund in a timely manner constitutes forfeiture of claims against seller and acceptance of title as is. The closing requirements of any lending institution from which the purchase price is to be obtained take precedence over any such requirements contained herein. At closing, seller may require from said lending institution commitment to disperse mortgage proceeds even despite any title defect for which the buyer is responsible. The escrow and closing procedure stipulated by this contract may be waived if the attorney, closing agent, or title agent follow some other procedure that protects buyer and seller against adverse applicable matters and complies with the laws of this state.

21. Escrow.

Escrow agents who receive funds related to this purchase agree to immediately deposit and hold such funds and to disburse them, subject to clearance according to the terms and conditions herein. Failure of funds to clear shall not excuse performance by buyer. If there are doubts about the buyer's duties or liabilities under this contract, the escrow agent has sole discretion to hold funds related to this purchase until both parties agree on their disbursement, or until a judgment of a court of competent jurisdiction determines the rights of each party. When the rights of each party have been determined, the escrow agent may terminate all liability by depositing all the funds related to this agreement with the clerk of the court of the county with jurisdiction over the dispute, accounting for any funds delivered out of escrow, and notifying all the parties of this action. In the event that the parties to this contract engage in legal proceedings involving the escrow agent in its role as escrow agent, or that the escrow agent initiates legal proceedings related to this contract, the escrow agent shall be entitled to a reasonable attorney's fee and related costs, to be paid in favor of the prevailing party. The escrow agent will not be liable to any party or person for misdelivery of funds subject to escrow to buyer or seller, except when the misdelivery is attributed to a willful breach of this contract or to negligence on the part of the escrow agent.

22. Attorney Fees and Costs.

This entire agreement is subject to the laws of the state of _____. Both parties agree to submit to the personal jurisdiction and venue of a court of subject matter jurisdiction located in _____ County in the state of _____, thereby waiving right to jury trial. In the event of such litigation, the prevailing party's costs arising from the litigation shall be paid by the other party. An action filed more than one year after the date when the cause(s) of the action accrued will not be entertained by the above-mentioned court or any court of competent jurisdiction, even if damages were calculable at the time when they accrued.

23. Default.

If the buyer fails to carry out the terms of this agreement within the specified time, the seller is entitled to retain the deposits paid by the buyer as liquidated damages, consideration for the execution of this agreement, and in full settlement of any claims. Once this occurs, all parties shall be released from the terms of this agreement. If the seller fails, refuses, or neglects to carry out the terms of this agreement for any reason other than the seller's inability to correct defects in the title after diligent effort, the buyer may seek specific performance of the terms of this contract by the seller or receive a refund of deposits without waiving any legal rights to sue for damages resulting from breach of this agreement.

24. Contract Not Recordable, Persons Bound, and Notice.

This agreement is not to be made public record. The terms of this agreement shall be equally binding on both parties, and on their heirs and successors. Wherever the singular person is used in this text, plural shall also apply, and wherever one gender is used, it includes both genders. Notice given by or to the attorney representing either party shall be the same as notice given directly by or to the party represented by the attorney.

25. Prorations and Insurance.

Buyer's and seller's portions of assessments, taxes, interest, rent, insurance, and other revenues and expenses of the property shall be determined as of closing. Buyer shall have the option of taking over any existing insurance policies on the property, if they are assumable, in which case the insurance premiums shall be prorated. To cash at closing, the final cash amount will be adjusted to reflect the buyer's and seller's shares of the abovementioned expenses. In the event that the buyer occupies the property before closing, all prorations in this agreement calculated "as of closing" in this agreement shall instead be calculated as of "date of occupancy," unless otherwise provided herein.

26. Notice on Radon Gas.

Radon is a naturally occurring radioactive gas that, when accumulated in a building in high enough quantities, may present health risks to those exposed over time. Levels of radon exceeding state and federal guidelines have been found in buildings in this state. You may obtain more information on radon and testing at your county public health unit.

27. Conveyance.

Title to the property will be conveyed by the seller to the buyer only by statutory warranty deed in accordance with the aforementioned limitations, easements, or as otherwise accepted by the buyer. At the buyer's request, personal property of the seller will be conveyed through an absolute bill of sale with warranty of title, subject to any liens provided for in this agreement.

28. Other Agreements.

No previous oral agreements, representations, or contracts shall be enforceable against either party unless they are incorporated in this agreement. Changes or modifications to this agreement will not be binding or valid unless they are executed in writing and agreed to by both parties.

29. Handwritten or Typewritten Provision.

Handwritten or typewritten provisions inserted or attached as addenda and signed by both parties shall control all conflicting provisions.

30. Contractual Procedures.

Unless explicitly not allowed by law, service of process of any litigation arising herein may be obtained through certified mail, return receipt requested; both parties waive any rights to object to the service method.

SPECIAL CLAUSES. SEE ATTACHED ADDENDUM 1.

Date:

_____   _____
Buyer   Witness

_____   _____
Seller   Witness

Exhibit A shall contain the legal description of the property.

Exhibit B shall pertain to the amount and payment of the purchase price, as follows:

1. Consideration.

The total purchase price of $_____ is based on a capitalization rate of ___%. If the projected net operation changes prior to or on the day of closing, the purchase price shall be adjusted accordingly.

2. Manner of Payment.

The purchase price shall be paid in accordance with the following:

Upon execution of this agreement, a check shall pass to seller from buyer, in the amount of $_____. Additional amounts demanded by seller, up to the total cash down payment of $_____ plus expenses shall be due to the seller. If additional funds are required, the seller shall take back secondary financing of the balance for ____ years at ____% interest. Both parties acknowledge that the seller is using the buyer's money for the purchase and construction of the property and shall pay interest of ____% APR on this money to the buyer. Interest shall accrue and be payable at closing.

The purchase price is to be allocated for tax purposes in accordance with the following: _

_____

3. Changes to Tenant's Lease.

This Property is being sold subject to the conditions and terms of the tenant's lease, attached as "Exhibit C," and incorporated in this contract by reference. Certain provisions in this lease call for fluctuations in the cost of improvements, as requested by the tenant, who will then remit the increased rent to the landlord.

Seller Initials: _____
Buyer Initials: _____

SPECIAL CLAUSES ADDENDUM

Date: _____

_____
Buyer

_____
Seller

1. Inspections.

From acceptance date of this agreement, buyer shall have 30 days to have the following inspections completed and approved, and 60 days to have the property appraised: plumbing inspection, roof inspection, electrical wiring inspection, air conditioning and heating systems inspection, structural inspections, and termite inspection. In the event that said or any other inspections performed on behalf of buyer are not acceptable to buyer, the same shall may opt to cancel this agreement and have any funds on deposit with escrow agent, plus any accrued interest, refunded to buyer.

2. Deposit.

Within 3 days of acceptance of this agreement by seller, buyer shall deposit with an escrow agent a certificate of deposit for $_____, which shall be returned to buyer at closing. Pursuant to this contract, all escrow deposits shall be the buyer's property.

3. Addendum in Addition.

This addendum is in addition to the above agreement of sale and purchase.

4. Debris and Personal Property.

The Seller will surrender the possession of the property in clean condition and free of all personal effects and debris on or before _____ (month) _____ (day), _____ (year). Seller agrees to leave the property free and clear of all trash and any other miscellaneous debris.

Closing Company Name and Address:

_____

The abovementioned company shall handle closing and prepare title insurance for the seller, with all standard closing costs appropriated in accordance with this contract.

_____   _____
Buyer   Witness

_____   _____
Seller   Witness

SUPPLEMENT TO AGREEMENT FOR PURCHASE & SALE OF REAL ESTATE: SPECIAL CLAUSES

Date: _____

Buyer: _____

Seller: _____

This addendum is a supplement to the above described agreement of sale and purchase.

At closing, seller shall pay the buyer $_____ cash in exchange for a mortgage deed and promissory note under these terms and conditions:

Any institutional financing obtained by the buyer shall take precedence over this mortgage and purchase money note. Any later buyer shall be able to assume this mortgage and purchase money note.

If the seller chooses to sell the mortgage and purchase money note referred to in this addendum, the buyer shall have the first right of refusal of any bonafide written offer. The buyer must reject or accept the written offer within 5 days after it is presented by the seller, with closing no more than 30 days later.

For contractual purposes and valuation under IRS guidelines, the value of improvements on the property shall be $_____ and the improvements on the value of the land shall be $_____. All personal property on the premises shall have a total value of $_____.

The seller confirms that no other leases exist aside from those referenced in this agreement, the conditions and terms of which are below:

The seller attests to the following and acknowledges that the buyer has executed this agreement based on the representations in this document. If any of these representations or warranties prove to be inaccurate, the buyer has been damaged against the outstanding balance under the mortgage and purchase money note given herein to the seller by the buyer:

Date: _____

_____   _____
Buyer   Witness

_____   _____
Seller   Witness

EXCHANGE AGREEMENT

Date: _____
First Party: _____
Address: _____
City: _____ State: _____ Zip: _____
Second Party: _____
Address: _____
City: _____ State: _____ Zip: _____
First Property: _____
Address: _____
City: _____ State: _____ Zip: _____
Second Property: _____
Address: _____
City: _____ State: _____ Zip: _____

1. First Property.
First Party will deliver to the Second Party the First Property contingent on Second Party obtaining a trust deed loan to provide the First Party with a $_____ monthly payment including interest of _____ % APR.

The Second Party will either take title subject to or assume total encumbrances on the following loans:

First Loan: $_____   Monthly payment $_____
Interest rate _____%
Second Loan: $_____   Monthly payment $_____
Interest rate _____%
The sum total of First Property is $_____, and includes the following personal property: _____.

2. Second Property.
Second Party will deliver to the First Party the Second Property contingent on First Party obtaining a trust deed loan to provide the Second Party with a $_____ monthly payment including interest of _____ % APR.
The First Party will either take title subject to or assume total encumbrances on the following loans:

First Loan: $_____   Monthly payment $_____
Interest rate _____%

Second Loan: $_____   Monthly payment $_____
Interest rate _____%
The sum total of Second Property is $_____, and includes the following personal property: _____.

3. Terms of Exchange.
The First Party and Second Party will execute terms of exchange that are either cash payment, or money note secured by a trust deed on said Property, in the amount of $_____ payable in monthly payments of $_____, including interest at _____% APR, all due _____ years from closing date.
First Party will deliver the additional following property to Second Party:
_____with a total equity of $ _____.
Second Party will deliver the additional following property to First Party:
_____ with a total equity of $ _____.

4. Adjustments.
The differences in loan balances disclosed in beneficiary statements shall be adjusted at closing by cash, in the carryback note, or in total value.

5. Assignment of Leases.
First Party and Second Party each assigns all existing leases and rental agreements to the other Party at time of closing.

6. Proration.

All taxes, insurance premiums (if applicable), interest, and all other related expenses and payments will be prorated based on the closing date. Grantees will either furnish new insurance policies or assume existing insurance policies.

7. Termination of Agreement.

First Party and Second Party may terminate this agreement within _____ days of acceptance by submitting in writing to the other Party reasonable cause for termination, which may or may not include: inspection of the Property for title and physical conditions sufficient to establish equity, inspection of income and expense statements and leases on the property to be received (these documents are to be submitted for inspection within 3 days after acceptance), or approval of a natural hazards disclosure statement on the property. See any additional terms and conditions in attached addendums.

8. Acceptance of Offer.

This exchange will be revoked if a written acceptance of this offer is not delivered within _____ days of date of this agreement to the _____ Party or real estate agent named below. Brokers may extend performance dates by one month at their discretion.

9. Escrow and Closing.

Both Parties will deliver signed instructions to _____ (escrow or closing agent) as soon as reasonably possible after acceptance, with each Party paying its customary or escrow closing charges, and with all documents required for closing handed to escrow or closing agent within _____ days.

10. Delivery of Possession.

Possession of Property and all keys and access codes shall be delivered to each Party on closing. If one of the Parties is unable to convey a marketable title within a reasonable time, or if Property is destroyed prior to transfer of title, then upon demand, all funds and documents deposited into escrow by the other Party shall be returned to him/her.

11. Title.

The title will be fully vested in each Party to whom the Property is delivered. Each title shall be free of liens and encumbrances other than those specified in this agreement and shall be subject to all existing conditions, restrictions, covenants, reservations, and easements of record. The Title insurance shall be obtained from _____ (Title Insurance Company), and will be paid by _____ (grantor or grantee).

12. IRC Section 1031, Tax-Free Exchanges.

Both Parties reserve their right to assign, and agree to cooperate in effecting an Internal Revenue Code Section 1031 tax-free exchange transaction prior to closing.

13. Brokerage Fees.

First Party will pay $_____ on closing to (Broker) _____, and Second Party will pay $_____ on closing to (Broker) _____. Should either Party wrongfully prevent the change of ownership under this contract, that Party will pay all brokerage fees.

Executed by First Party

Date: _____

First Party

Witness

Witness
Executed by Second Party
Date: _____

Second Party

Witness

Witness
ADDENDUM I
Special Clauses:

AFFIDAVIT AND MEMORANDUM OF AGREEMENT FOR PURCHASE AND SALE

Date: _____
State of _____, County of _____
Seller: _____
Address: _____
City: _____ State: _____ Zip: _____
Buyer: _____
Address: _____
City: _____ State: _____ Zip: _____

On this day, the Buyer and Seller below personally appeared before me, the undersigned authority, and, being first duly sworn, deposed and said that:

1. An Agreement for the Purchase and Sale of the real property described in the attached Exhibit "A" was entered into by and between the _____ (Buyer) and _____ (Seller), on this date _____ (month) _____ (day), _____ (year).

2. The closing of the purchase and sale of the property described in the attached Exhibit "A," as set forth in the signed Agreement, is to take place on _____ (month) _____ (day), _____ (year).

A copy of the Agreement for Purchase and Sale of the property can be obtained by contacting

Address: _____
City: _____ State: _____ Zip: _____
Tel: _____

Seller   Buyer

This instrument was prepared by: _____

State of _____, County of_____

Sworn to and subscribed before me, a Notary Public, for the State of
_____, County of_____

This _____ day of _____ 20_____

By: _____

Notary Public

My Commission Expires: This _____day of _____, 20 _____

EXHIBIT "A"

Description of Real Property.

AGREEMENT AS TO DIVISION OF EXPENSE FOR ADJOINING LINE

Date: _____

Owner A: _____

Address: _____

City: _____ State: _____ Zip: _____

Owner B: _____

Address: _____

City: _____ State: _____ Zip: _____

The Parties are owners of adjoining tracts of land. _____ (Owner A) owns lot number _____ in _____ District and _____ Section of _____ County. _____ (Owner B) owns a portion of the lot number _____ in the same District and County. The line between the adjoining tracts is in dispute and in order to settle and establish the line between adjoining tracts, the Parties hereby agree to the following:

1. _____ as surveyor may run and establish the line by starting at a _____ common to the corners of _____, _____, and _____, _____ (south or north) of the disputed line, and run the line there from, allowing the usual magnetic variation, in a _____ (north or south) direction to the _____ (north or south) line of the lots Numbers _____ and _____.

2. The aforementioned line run as above shall be staked out and marked by _____. The line must be accepted by both Parties as the true and correct dividing line between the tracts of land owned by both parties.

3. Both parties hereby agree that any expenses incurred by the running of the line shall be paid in equal portions by both Parties.

_____   _____

Owner A   Owner B

_____   _____

Witness   Witness

AGREEMENT AS TO OVERHANGING EAVES

Date: _____

Owner A: _____

Address: _____

City: _____ State: _____ Zip: _____

Owner B: _____

Address: _____

City: _____ State: _____ Zip: _____

This Agreement made on the above date between Owner A of _____ and Owner B of _____.

Owner A is the owner of a dwelling house abutting against the _____ wall of the dwelling owned by Owner B, situated at _____ (street), _____ (city), _____ (state). Owner A has affixed to the _____ side of the dwelling an iron gutter or pipe which conveys rain water from the roof of Owner A's house onto the eaves of Owner B. As of this date, disputes have arisen between both owners respecting the rights of Owner A to affix the gutter. It is now hereby agreed to the following by both parties:

1. The gutter/pipe shall be deemed to have originally affixed and may remain affixed with the express license and consent of Owner B to the intent that neither Owner A nor any person who claims under or through Owner A shall acquire any right of eavesdrop or any easement or other right in respect to the gutter/pipe.

2. Owner A is required to pay Owner B for any damages or injuries that may occur to Owner B's dwelling due to the gutter/pipe being affixed.

3. Owner A also agrees that within _____ days after service of a notice in writing that Owner B may require Owner A to take down and remove the gutter/pipe and make good on all damages occurred by the gutter/pipe.

_____   _____

Owner A   Owner B

This instrument was prepared by:

State of _____

County of _____

Sworn to and subscribed before me, a Notary Public, for the State of _____

County of _____

This _____ day of _____ 20_____

By: _____

Notary Public

My Commission Expires: This _____day of _____, 20 _____.

AGREEMENT FOR EXCHANGE OF PROPERTY

Date: _____

Broker: _____

Address: _____

City: _____ State: _____ Zip: _____

Owner: _____

Address: _____

City: _____ State: _____ Zip: _____

This Agreement is effective as of the date above by and between the aforementioned Broker and Owner.

1. Purpose

The Owner of the property at the address listed above, described as follows: _____ _____, which the Owner wishes to exchange said property for property owned by _____, at the following address _____ (address), _____ (county), _____ (state), described as _____.

2. Broker to Negotiate Exchange

The Owner understands that if the Broker listed above secures an acceptance of the proposition to exchange the properties on terms that are acceptable to the Owner, then within _____ days of said acceptance the Owner is required to provide a certificate of title and a _____ Deed conveying a good and sufficient title to the first property as described above.

3. Broker Commission

The aforementioned Broker is entitled to a commission of _____% of any money given to the Owner pursuant to the exchange of deed in excess of $_____. The Broker is guaranteed a minimum commission in the amount of $_____.

4. Term

The agency will continue for a term of _____ months to pay the Broker a commission as set forth above in the event that the Owner takes ownership of the property.

5. Governing Law

It is hereby agreed that the laws of the State of _____ will govern this Agreement.

6. Dispute Arbitration

Under the terms of this Agreement, any and all disputes are subject to arbitration. Either of the Parties may make a claim for arbitration by filing such request in writing with the other party no more than _____ days after the dispute occurs. From there on out, the arbitration shall be conducted by _____ according to the requirements of this Agreement and the laws of the State mentioned in Section E.

7. Broker Covenants

The Broker also agrees to act as the Owner's fiduciary in regards to any negotiations and to deal with the Owner. Broker also must make full disclosures to Owner of all material matters relating to any negotiations.

In Witness Whereof, each party hereby agrees and executes this Agreement on _____ (month) _____ (day), _____ (year) at the following location _____.

Owner _____

Broker _____

AGREEMENT FOR SALE OF INTEREST OF BUYER

Date: _____

Seller: _____

Address: _____

City: _____ State: _____ Zip: _____

Buyer: _____

Address: _____

City: _____ State: _____ Zip: _____

1. Purpose

The Seller purchased, by way of a contract in writing, the following property: _____ from _____ on _____ (date) for $_____ (purchase price). The Seller paid a deposit of $_____. The Seller hereby agrees to sell this property to the Buyer for $_____, a price which has been agreed upon by both Parties.

2. Deposit

The Buyer will pay the Seller a $_____ deposit for the purchase of the afore-mentioned property. Once this deposit has been paid to the Seller, Seller agrees to release and convey all rights and interest of and in the property, free from all charges and encumbrances, to the Buyer.

3. Payment

The Buyer also agrees that upon taking the conveyance of the property, he/she will pay the residue in the amount of $_____ to the original seller in accordance with the previously mentioned contract.

4. Costs and Expenses

The Buyer agrees, at his/her own expense, to effectually indemnify the Seller from and against any and all losses, expenses, damages, and any other costs regarding the convey-ance of the property and from and against any actions taken on account or in respect to the aforementioned contract.

5. Nonperformance

It is also further agreed to by both Parties that if the contract shall not, for any reason whatsoever, be performed, this contract will become void and any deposit money paid by the Buyer will be repaid to the Buyer by the Seller. Seller will also repay to the Buyer all expenses and costs incurred as well as all losses and damages sustained by the Buyer.

6. Damages
For the due performance of this contract, both the Buyer and Seller hereby bind themselves to each other in the punitive amount of $_____, which shall be recovered as liquidated damages between them.

_____   _____
Buyer Signature   Seller Signature

ENTIRE SETTLEMENT OF CLAIMS AND PROPERTY RIGHTS AGREEMENT

Date: _____
Party A: _____
Address: _____
City: _____ State: _____ Zip: _____
Party B: _____
Address: _____
City: _____ State: _____ Zip: _____

It is hereby agreed to by both parties that this instrument is a complete and final memorandum to the agreement both parties signed on _____ (date) concerning all issues in connection with the division of the community property of both parties and all rights and claims of each party. Both parties understand in or to the separate property of either of them, and of each and every claim of every character one against the other, and that no agreement exists between the parties other than as specifically set forth in this agreement, and it is covenanted and agreed by each of the parties with the other that he or she will not assert or claim against the other any right or claim in or to any property of the other, except under the terms of this agreement, and except as provided by the terms and provisions of this agreement, and will not assert against the other except as otherwise specifically provided in this agreement, any claim for alimony, maintenance or support, costs, attorneys' fees or any other claim by reason of their marital relationship or otherwise, or in any action for divorce or separate maintenance, or in any other action or proceeding involving the marriage state or any obligations of it wherever brought.

_____   _____
Party A Signature   Party B Signature

ADDENDUM FOR ATTACHMENT TO STANDARD CONTRACT

Date: _____
Purchaser (Buyer): _____
Address: _____
City: _____ State: _____ Zip: _____
Seller: _____
Address: _____
City: _____ State: _____ Zip: _____

1. This Addendum is a part of the Agreement for Purchase and Sale of Real Estate.

Executed by and between the Buyer and Seller. Buyer and Seller agree that this addendum is executed concurrently with the previously mentioned Agreement for Purchase and Sale of Real Estate.

As of the date of signing of this agreement, the Seller represents and warrants to the Buyer that:

2. Title.

The Buyer will acquire title and entire right to the property listed in the Agreement. Title must be free and unencumbered, clear of all liens, liabilities, agreements, leases, judgments, claims, rights, easements, restrictions, and any other matters that might affect the title, except for the exceptions permitted by this Purchase and Sale Agreement, the tenant leases, and the continuing contracts.

3. Consents.

The Seller confirms that it has acquired, or will acquire before the closing date, all consents and permissions connected to the transactions set forth in the Purchase and Sale Agreement and required under the covenants, agreements, encumbrances, laws, or regulations.

4. Utilities and Access.

The Seller certifies that the property has a proper water supply, storm and sewer facilities, phone connections, electricity, fire protection, ingress from and egress to highways at the current curb cuts; and other necessary public utilities.

5. Hazardous Substances.

The Seller hereby certifies that the property has not been used in part or any way to treat, deposit, store, dispose of, or place any hazardous substances, as defined by 41 USCA Section 9601(14); nor has the Seller authorized any other person or entity to treat, deposit, store, dispose of, or place any hazardous substance, as defined above, on the property, or any part of the property; and to the best knowledge of Seller, no other person or entity has ever treated, deposited, stored, disposed of, or placed any hazardous substance, as defined above, on the Property; or any part of the Property. Should a release or threatened release of a hazardous substance be discovered on the Property, whether or not the Seller was in any way responsible for such release, which makes the Buyer liable in any way under the Comprehensive Environmental Response, Compensation, and Liability Act of 1980, 42 USCA Section 9607, or under any other statutory or common law, the Seller agrees to indemnify and hold harmless the Buyer from any such liability that may be imposed or occur.

6. Soil Conditions, Encroachments, Flood, and Mudslide Hazards.

To the best of the Seller's knowledge, there are no hazardous or detrimental soil conditions on the property, the building does not encroach onto adjoining land or onto any easements, and improvements from adjoining land do not encroach onto the Property. The location of the building is in compliance with all applicable setback requirements, and the site is not located in an area that has been identified as having special flood or mudslide hazards by an agency or department of the federal government.

7. Completion and Operation of the Building.

At this time, the building located on the property is not yet built and will not be completed before the closing date. The Seller guarantees that construction of the building will be carried out according to the plans and specifications approved by the Tenant, which are attached to this document. Construction will be completed following a good standard free of any material defects, and carried out at all times according to the approved project plans and specifications, in compliance with all federal, local, and state laws, ordinances, rules, regulations, and orders in existence on or before the Closing Date.

8. Licenses, Permits, and Zoning.

Before the Closing Date, all building permits and all other notices, licenses, permits, certificates, and authority, including notice that all punch list items have been completed to the satisfaction of the Buyer, required in connection with the construction, use or occupancy of the Property, shall be delivered to the Buyer.

9. Certificates of Occupancy.

Before the Closing Date, valid and final Certificates of Occupancy will be issued for the building and each part and portion of the building, except for those areas occupied by tenants who, under the laws of the State of _____, must obtain their own Certificates of Occupancy. The Seller affirms that to the best of its knowledge such tenant(s) have obtained Certificates of Occupancy and that as of the Closing Date, no part of the Property will have been leased without obtaining such certificates.

10. Notices; Requests.

No government agency, or employee or official of a government agency, has given any notice to the Seller that it considers the construction on the Property or the operation or use of the Property to be out of compliance with any law, ordinance, regulation or order, or that any investigation has been or might be initiated respecting any possible non- compliance. There are no unpaid expenses or outstanding invoices from any person, entity, or authority, including, but not limited to, any tenant, lender, insurance carrier, or government authority, for the cost of repairs, restorations, or improvements to the Property.

11. Maintenance; HVAC.

Each part and portion of the Property and the Property as a whole are in good condition and repair. The structure of the building is sound and adequate for the needs of its present tenants. The Seller will continue to maintain the building from the date that this Addendum until the Closing Date. The heating and air conditioning systems are in good condition and working order and adequate for all requirements of the existing tenancies.

12. Liens.

At all times before and up to the Closing Date, the Seller shall keep the Property free and clear of all liens, claims, or demands (including, but not limited to, mechanic's liens) in connection with labor or materials provided for work performed on the Property or any portion of the Property on or before the Closing Date. If any such lien is filed, the Seller must secure its release within thirty (30) days after the notice of its filing by bonding or other appropriate means. Seller shall pay, at or before the due dates, all assessments, bonds, and special assessments that constitute a lien or encumbrance against the Property as of the closing date. These payments do not constitute a waiver of responsibility for any new liens incurred according to the preceding section of this paragraph.

13. Right of Set-Off.

Buyer reserves the right, in its own exclusive judgment, to deduct payment for any damage or injury sustained by the Buyer as a consequence of any inaccuracies or misrepresentations by the Seller in this Agreement from the balance of the Promissory Note given at closing by the Buyer to the Seller as partial payment of the purchase price. The Buyer may choose to either deduct the amount for damage or injury from the outstanding balance of the Promissory Note, or from the sequential monthly payments due to be made under the Lease Agreement. The Seller maintains the right, within twenty-one (21) days of receiving formal notification that the Buyer intends to exercise this right of set-off, to object to such a set-off by filing an action for declaratory relief challenging the Buyer's grounds for exercising this right of set-off.

Besides the provisions listed in this Addendum, the Purchase and Sale Agreement shall remain fully enforceable and otherwise considered unchanged.

Buyer and Seller both initial below:

_____   _____
Seller   Buyer

BUYER'S PURCHASE CONTRACT

Date: _____

Seller: _____ Social Security Number: _____-_____-_____

Address: _____

City: _____ State: _____ Zip: _____

Buyer: _____ Social Security Number: _____-_____-_____

Address: _____

City: _____ State: _____ Zip: _____

Purchaser: _____

The Seller agrees to sell and the Purchaser agrees to buy the real estate property listed below, including all improvements and personal property as stipulated below:

Street Address_____,

_____ (City), _____ (County),

_____ (State), _____ (Zip).

Legal description of Property:

_____.

The following personal property is included:

_____   _____

_____   _____

The purchase price will be paid as follows:

    Deposit: $_____

    Cash to Seller at Closing: $_____

    Existing Loans and Liens: $_____

    New Loan to Seller at Closing: $_____

    Purchase Price: $_____

1. Deposit.

A deposit must be made to either a licensed Title Company or attorney within 48 hours of the Seller's acceptance.

2. Loans.

The Purchaser will take title subject to the following loans on terms agreeable to the Purchaser:

    a. Loan to _____

Balance $_____

Interest rate: _____ %, Monthly Payment $_____

Loan Number _____

Date of last payment: _____

Loan current through _____

b. Loan to _____

Balance $_____

Interest rate: _____ %, Monthly Payment $_____

Loan Number _____

Date of last payment _____

Loan current through _____

Other liens: _____

Any overstatement of the above amounts of loans and liens will be added to note to Seller. Any understatement will be deducted from the balance due to the Seller at Closing.

3. Payment of Balance.

Balance due to the Seller in the amount of $ _____ shall be paid as follows: _____ with an interest rate of _____%.

4. Date of Closing and Title Transfer.

The closing of this sale will occur at _____ (location) on or before _____ (date).

5. Title.

Seller(s) agrees to transfer the title free and clear of all encumbrances except those listed in this Agreement. Seller will pay any state taxes or stamps required to record deed and mortgage. Seller is responsible to furnish title insurance in the amount of the purchase price, verifying that no encumbrances or exceptions exist except for those already noted in this Agreement.

6. Prorations.

Purchaser's and Seller's portions of loan interest, property taxes, insurance, and rents will be prorated based on the Closing Date.

7. Security Deposits.

Seller will give any security deposits made by existing tenants to Purchaser at closing.

8. Impound Accounts.

All impound accounts for taxes and insurance are included in the purchase price and shall be transferred to Purchaser at closing. Seller will be charged for any deficiency in these accounts on the date of closing.

9. Inspection.

Purchaser will have complete access to inspect the Property and submit a written list of necessary repairs to the Seller. Seller will pay costs of performing these repairs.

10. Insurance.

Seller must insure Property and maintain it in its current condition until Closing. If damage occurs to the Property before closing, the Purchaser may opt to close and collect the insurance proceeds from the Seller.

11. Appliances.

Seller agrees that the house and all the mechanical systems of the Property are in good working order at closing. Ownership of appliances and other personal property will be transferred to Buyer at Closing by presentation of a Bill of Sale free of encumbrances.

12. Defaults.

In the event that Purchaser defaults on this contract in any way, Seller shall retain deposit. In the event the Seller defaults on this contract, the Purchaser may pursue all remedies allowed under law and Seller agrees to be responsible for all costs incurred by Purchaser in pursuing these remedies.

13. Assignees and Successors.

The terms and conditions of this contract shall bind all successors, heirs, administrators, trustees, executors, and assignees of the Seller and Purchaser.

14. Other Terms and Conditions.

_____

The Seller and Purchaser both have read and agreed to the aforementioned terms and conditions of this agreement.

_____   _____
Seller   Seller

_____   _____
Purchaser   Purchaser

AGREEMENT TO EXTEND TIME PERIOD OF OPTION

Date: _____
Seller: _____
Purchaser: _____

In consideration of the additional sum of $_____ to be paid to the Seller listed above by the Purchaser, the time period of that specific option from the Seller to the Purchaser dated, _____ is hereby extended to _____ (date). This extension shall apply to all provisions and conditions of the option. The extension shall also adapt to the Purchaser and the Purchasers heirs, assigns, and nominees.

In Witness Whereof, each party hereby agrees and executes this Agreement on _____ (month) _____ (day), _____ (year) at the following location _____.

_____   _____
Seller   Purchaser

AGREEMENT TO PURCHASE PROPERTY THROUGH A BROKER

Date: _____
Real Estate Agent(s): _____
Address: _____

City: _____ State: _____ Zip: _____
Buyer: _____
Address: _____
City: _____ State: _____ Zip: _____
Property Address: _____
City: _____ State: _____ Zip: _____

Total Purchase Price: $ _____
Deposit Amount: $_____
Offer Ending Date: $_____

The above is my offer and agreement to purchase, through you, the property listed above. I will immediately make you the cash deposit offered, _____% of the purchase price offer, if you accept this offer. Noninterest bearing, this deposit shall not be considered money in earnest. Both parties may demand specific performance.

In the event that I can receive a good, merchantable title to the abovementioned property, I shall accept and pay the purchase price balance at closing.
I shall, on demand, pay your commission of sale and any costs related to your collection of said claim in the event that I breach this contract after its acceptance. This offer shall remain in effect until the abovementioned ending date.

_____   _____
Purchaser   Date

The offer above is accepted.

You, _____ and _____, shall be paid _____% commission for the sale indicated above.

AGREEMENT TO PURCHASE AND SELL A BUSINESS

Date: _____
Seller: _____
Business Address: _____
City: _____ State: _____ Zip: _____
Buyer: _____
Address: _____
City: _____ State: _____ Zip: _____

This Contract is made and entered into on the above-listed date by and between the aforementioned Seller and Buyer.

WHEREAS, the Seller is the title-holder of a business known as _____
_____, with its primary office positioned at
_____; and

WHEREAS, the Seller manages the abovementioned business involving the retail sales of _____ and other various items, and in combination therewith, has developed a status and following and has amassed specific assets more fully explained hereafter; and

WHEREAS, the Buyer has articulated an interest in the purchase of the business of the Seller; and

WHEREAS, the Seller desires to sell to Buyer, and Buyer wishes to buy from Seller the _____ under the terms and conditions herein set forth.

NOW, THEREFORE, in contemplation of the shared assurances and conditions herein contained, intending to be lawfully bound hereby, the parties do hereby concur as follows:

1. Sale of Business.

The Seller agrees to sell to the Buyer and the Buyer agrees to purchase and obtain from the Seller, all of the right, title, and interest of the Seller in and to the retail sales business, _____, including without limitation, all inventory and stock-in-trade, a list of which is attached as Exhibit "A" hereto; certain equipment, a list of which is attached as Exhibit "B" hereto; office equipment, furniture, computers, software, signage, shelving, cabinets, supplies, and all other items of concrete property located in the Seller's place of business and used in combination with the business of the partnership of the Seller, a schedule of which is attached as Exhibit "C" hereto; and the good will of the Seller, and together with the customer records and customer files and the manufacturer records and manufacturer files that the Seller has maintained in conjunction with the operation of the sole proprietorship.

2. Acquisition Price.

The total purchase price to be paid by Buyer to Seller shall be ($_____) _____Dollars.

3. Payment.

The Buyer shall compensate to the Seller upon the implementation of this Contract the figure of _____ ($_____) Dollars, against the acquisition price (the "Acquisition Price"), with the balance of the Acquisition Price ($_____) to be paid by the Buyer to the Seller at the Closing as follows:

    a) _____ dollars ($_____) by certified funds, cashier's check, wire transfer, or other satisfactory means of payment; and

    b) A Note, which is attached as Exhibit "D" hereto, to the Seller from the Buyer for _____ dollars ($_____), which shall be secured by a security interest in the supply on-hand at the store at_____ _____, as proved by a Security Agreement, which is attached as Exhibit "E" hereto, and a Financing Statement, which is attached as Exhibit "F" hereto. The period of the Note shall be ten (10) years with a two (2) year balloon compensation from the date of Closing. If the Buyer pays the residual major balance in full within twelve (12) months from the date of Closing, then the Seller shall discount the residual major balance then owed by five percent (5%). The first payment due on the Note shall be sixty (60) days after the date of Closing.

4. Distributions.

The Seller and the Buyer hereby agree that the Acquisition Price shall be owed as provided herein, and that the following portions are fair and realistic and the product of the negotiation between the Seller and the Buyer of the terms and conditions of this sale:

Inventory	$___,000.00
Fixtures, Signage, & Processors	$___,000.00
Goodwill, Trademark	$___,000.00
Non-compete Agreement	$___,000.00
Total	$___,000.00

5. Amity.

At the Closing, the Seller shall relocate all of the Seller's good will to the Buyer with regard to the Seller's operation of the partnership, including the trade name _____ and the domain name **www.**_____**.com**. The Seller shall further allocate to the Buyer, at the Closing, all of the right, title, and interest of the Seller in and to the telephone number employed by the Seller with appreciation to the Seller's partnership.

6. Seller Assistance & Training.

The Seller has agreed and hereby agrees to help and teach (e.g. traveling to (location:_____) with the Buyer to assist with the buying) the Buyer with respect to the function of the business known as _____ following the date of Closing for a period of three-hundred sixty (360) days, and shall attempt to make the purchase by the Buyer as easy as possible. The Seller shall attempt to make acquainted the Buyer with all facets of the business of the Seller's clientele so as to build on the best possible relationship between the Buyer and the clientele of the Seller.

7. Guarantees.

The Seller hereby guarantees and signifies to the Buyer, which contracts and accounts shall continue to exist the Closing, that the Seller is the sole owner of the partnership and the assets thereof, free and apparent of any and all liens and hindrances and free and free of the claims of any person. Except as herein provided, the Seller makes no other guarantees and all other contracts, express or implied are hereby disclaimed.

THE SELLER HEREBY EXPRESSLY DISCLAIMS ANY AND ALL OTHER STATE OR IMPLIED GUARANTEES AND ANY CONFIRMATIONS OF FACT OR ASSURANCES MADE BY THE SELLER SHALL NOT BE CONSIDERED TO CREATE ANY EXPRESS GUARANTEE THAT THE PHYSICAL PROPERTY SHALL CONFORM TO ANY SUCH AFFIRMATION OR PROMISE. ANY ACCOUNT OF THE PHYSICAL PROPERTY IS FOR THE SOLE PURPOSE OF RECOGNIZING THE PHYSICAL PROPERTY AND SHALL NOT BE CONSIDERED TO CREATE AN EXPRESS GUARANTEE THAT THE PHYSICAL PROPERTY SHALL CORRESPOND TO THE DESCRIPTION. NO AFFIRMATION OR ASSURANCE, OR ACCOUNT, SHALL BE DEEMED PART OF THE COVENANT BETWEEN THE PARTIES HERETO. THE SELLER FURTHER HEREBY EXPRESSLY DISCLAIMS ANY INDIRECT GUARANTEE OF MERCHANTABILITY, AND FURTHER HEREBY SPECIFICALLY DENIES ANY GUARANTEE OF FITNESS OF THE PHYSICAL PROPERTY FOR ANY SPECIFIC REASON, AND THE PARTIES HERETO AGREE THAT THERE ARE NO GUARANTEES THAT EXTEND BEYOND THE REQUIREMENTS OF THIS PARAGRAPH. THE PHYSICAL PROPERTY IS SOLD "AS IS" AND "WHERE IS."

8. Accounts Receivable.

The Seller shall retain all accounts receivable from the operation of (…), apart from the items on lay-a-way at the time of Closing, which the Buyer shall be entitled to receive any remaining payment(s) due on that merchandise from the date of Closing and thereafter. The Seller shall be entitled to collect all accounts receivable at any and all times following the Closing. The Buyer shall completely help with the Seller with respect to the Seller's hard work to amass all accounts receivables due the Seller.

9. Transfer Papers.

The Seller shall move title to the partnership and the assets thereof to the Buyer, pursuant to a Bill of Sale and a Transfer, copies of which are attached as Exhibits "E" and "F" hereto.

10. Legal Responsibilities.

The Seller shall pay all business debts and any other legal responsibility linked with the operation of the partnership at or prior to the Closing. Any business debts or similar liabilities materializing after the Closing that are lawfully the liability of the Seller shall be paid by the Seller immediately upon presentation thereof.

11. Lease of Building Contingency.

Prior to Closing, if the Buyer, after realistic good-faith efforts, has not been able to negotiate a new five (5) year lease with an optional five (5) year postponement between the Buyer and Landlord for _____ dollars ($_____) per month for the first five (5) year term plus the realistic rate of utilities attributable to_____ _____, then this Agreement shall be null and canceled and the Buyer's deposit money of $_____ shall be refunded by _____, 20__.

12. Financing Eventuality.

Prior to Closing, if the Buyer, after realistic good-faith attempts, has not been able to obtain a personal loan for at least _____ dollars ($___,000) so as to enable the Buyer to comply with provision a) of Paragraph 3 herein, then this Covenant shall be worthless and annulled and the Buyer's deposit money of $_____ shall be reimbursed by _____, 20__.

13. Further Declarations and Shared Cooperation.

Each of the parties hereto hereby gives the other with all declarations that they will equally cooperate in all compliments at any and all times hereafter, and that they will further implement and transport to each other all documents realistically asked for to validate and record the proper and convenient sale of the accounting practice of the Seller and the transition herein contemplated.

14. Control of Business.

The Seller shall continue to control the business of the partnership in the standard course in every regard through the date of the sale.

15. Mass Sales Compliance.

The Seller shall fulfill with all mass sales necessities with respect to the sale of the partnership of the Seller to the Buyer as provided herein.

16. The Closing and Closing Date.

The closing date (the "Closing Date") shall occur on _____, 20___. The Closing shall be held at the offices of_____.

17. Non-compete Agreement.

In thoughtfulness of the agreements and activities on the part of the Buyer herein contained, the Seller hereby agrees that they will not, openly or indirectly, for their own account or for the account of others, engage in the retail sales of (type of business being bought and sold here), for a period of five (5) years following the Closing, in (County name) or in any county neighboring thereto.

18. Notices.

All notices and communications required by this Contract shall be made in writing and shall be delivered to each party's address as listed on this contract. The mailing of a notice by registered or certified United States mail, certified or return receipt requested, postage prepaid, shall constitute delivery. A notice or demand shall be deemed constructively made at the time it is personally delivered. If a communication is given by mail, it shall be conclusively deemed given five days after its deposit in the United States mail addressed to the party at the address given at the beginning of this Contract.

19. Titles.

Titles and headings contained in this Contract are for reference reasons only and shall not affect in any way the meaning or interpretation of this Contract.

20. Execution in Complements and Counterparts.

This Contract may be executed in counterparts or by two or more complements, each of which shall be considered an original and all of which together shall comprise one and the same instrument. If executed by faxed signatures, this Contract will be effective as of the date of the last signature.

21. Heirs and Assigns.

This Contract shall be binding upon and inure to the benefit of heirs, executors, administrators, successors, and assigns of the respective parties.

22. Prior Agreements.

This Contract represents the entire agreement between the Buyer and Seller, and there are no agreements, understandings, restrictions, warranties, or representations between the parties, written or oral, other than those included in this Contract.

23. Adjustments and Amendments.

An alteration or modification to this Contract may be made at any time, by means of a written document signed by Buyer and Seller.

24. Costs.

Each of the parties shall be responsible for any costs it incurs in association with this Contract and its preparation and implementation.

25. Governing Law.

This Agreement (including its interpretation, application, validity, performance, and breach), shall be governed by, construed, and implemented in accordance with the laws of the State.

26. Survival of Responsibilities.

All agreements and responsibilities set forth herein of the parties hereto shall continue to exist at closing and any termination of this Contract.

IN WITNESS WHEREOF, the parties hereto have set forth their hands and seals on the date indicated.

_____

Buyer Signature

_____

Buyer's Witness Signed

_____

Buyer's Witness Printed

_____

Seller Signature

_____

Seller's Witness Signature

_____

Seller's Witness Printed

CONTRACT ASSIGNMENT

Date: _____

Assignor: _____

Assignee: _____

The above listed Assignor, who executed a contract dated _____
_____ between:

_____ (Contractor)

and

_____ (Contractee)

regarding the property described as _____ hereby assigns all rights to said contract to the aforementioned Assignee in exchange for a payment of $_____.

The Assignee hereby agrees to fulfill all terms, conditions, and contingencies of the aforementioned Contract and to perform as required in good faith and within any time periods established by said Contract on the following date: _____.

_____   _____

Assignor   Assignee

_____   _____

Witness   Witness

PURCHASE CONTRACT ADDENDUM

Date: _____

Seller: _____

Property Address: _____

Because the aforementioned Seller has requested to stay in the above listed property after the date of closing, a sum of $_____ will therefore be held in escrow at the time of the closing by the closing agent or other assign as the Buyer has appointed, until the time at with the Seller vacates the property and leaves it in a neat and clean condition as defined below.

The Seller agrees to vacate the property within _____ days after the date of closing. If the Seller does not vacate the premises by this date, then a charge of $_____ per day will be assessed and deducted from the escrow account. Seller will also forfeit all monies in escrow. Seller will then be considered a Tenant in Sufferance, thereby giving the Buyer full rights to evict the Seller.

The "neat and clean" definition is as follows: any and all trash must be removed from the interior and exterior of the property. Property should be left clear of any possessions of the Seller.

If Seller does not leave the property in Neat and Clean condition, the Buyer will have any clean up completed at the Seller's expense and will be deducted from the escrow account.

If the Buyer is forced to take legal action against the Seller in order to enforce this Agreement, the Seller will hereby be responsible for any and all legal fees and costs associated with such action.

_____
Seller

_____
Buyer

CONTRACT TO SELL LAND THROUGH A SERIES OF CONVEYANCES

This agreement, made _____ [date] between _____ and _____, Seller(s), and _____, Buyer(s), provides that:

1. Property.
The sellers agree to sell and buyers agree to buy real property in the County of _____, State of _____, described as follows: _____.

2. Survey.
Sellers will have the property surveyed at their own expense by a registered professional who will furnish a mutually satisfactory survey to the buyer.

3. Purchase Price.
The purchase price of the land is agreed to be $_____ per acre, acreage to be determined by the survey. Acreage upon contract date is believed to be: _____.

4. Conveyance.
Buyer will acquire title to, and sellers shall convey the property in parcels, according to the following terms:

a) Buyer's deposit of the sum of $_____ into escrow upon signature of this agreement; sellers shall as soon as practicable convey to buyer a parcel with area equal to _____ percent of the total area of the land. The particular location of the parcel will be mutually agreed upon by all parties. At the time of such conveyance buyer will pay the balance of the purchase price of _____ percent portion over and above the initial deposit of $_____, and this first escrow shall close. It is understood the portions being surrendered are not undivided interests in the whole of the land, but rather parcels within the land which is being conveyed as a whole.

b) Buyer is to acquire at least _____ percent of the remainder of the whole parcel of land in each of the _____ years following the conveyance described in section (a) above, paying for them at the rate specified in this contract. The buyer may, if he so chooses, accelerate acquisition in any manner after one year from the agreement set forth in section (a), providing that further that payment is made by an exchange transaction as set forth in this contract.

5. Interest.

Buyer shall pay an interest rate on unpaid portions of the total purchase price for all the land at the sum of _____ percent per annum.

6. Transfer of Possession.

After execution of this agreement sellers shall remain in possession of all of the property without rental or any payment to buyer for a period of _____ days. Buyer will then take possession of all of the property without any additional payment to sellers, and buyer will acquire all rights incident to its possession, including the right to lease, receive rental, and conduct operations or business as allowed by local laws.

7. Title and Title Insurance.

Sellers hereby make all conveyances by good and sufficient grant deed and state that the property is free and clear of all encumbrances except easements of record that are already noted. Title insurance policies shall be paid for by: (select one) buyer_____ seller _____. Sellers shall pay for all revenue stamps and any broker's fees or other commissions that are due on this transaction. Current taxes will be prorated as of the date first written above, with the buyer paying all recording fees. Other expenses shall be handled and paid for in accordance with usual practice in _____ County, _____.

8. Heirs and Assigns.

This agreement is binding upon the successors and assigns of the sellers and the assigns of buyer.

Signed,

_____   _____
Seller   Date

_____   _____
Seller   Date

_____   _____
Buyer   Date

_____   _____
Buyer   Date

CONTRACT OF OFFER AND ACCEPTANCE

Date: _____

Seller: _____

Address: _____

City: _____ State: _____ Zip: _____

Purchaser: _____

Address: _____

City: _____ State: _____ Zip: _____

Address of Property: _____

City: _____ State: _____ Zip: _____

Legal Description of Property: _____

Following are the terms of this offer:

1. Additional Items.

Anything presently attached to the premises, including fixtures, window coverings and related hardware, storage, storm protection, screens, covers, heating and/or cooling systems, garage door mechanisms, transmitting devices, ventilation, shades or awnings, and vegetation, in addition to the following individually listed items:

_____

_____

Upon closing, all aforementioned personal property items are to be transferred to purchaser by delivery.

2. Deposit.

Purchase Price: $ _____

Initial Deposit: $ _____ Payable To: _____ Check Type: _____

The check, properly endorsed by payee, is to be deposited by _____, Broker, upon acceptance of this offer. Within _____ days of acceptance of this agreement, the deposit is to be increased to 10 percent of the purchase price (20 percent if unimproved). If this offer has not been accepted by _____ (date), this offer shall be void and initial deposit shall be returned.

3. Payment.

Subject to prorating, the purchase price is to be paid as follows [strike through any subparagraphs that do not apply:

Payment shall be made in certified check, cashier's check, or cash at closing.

Unless the Purchaser has obtained and given Seller written notice of another mortgage commitment within _____ days of this agreement, the Purchaser agrees to pay the existing trust deed or mortgage, so long as it is not in default at closing.

Existing Mortgage or Trust Deed Date:

County of Register:

Document Number:

Current Note Holder:

Remaining Balance: $_____

Interest per Annum on Remaining Principal: _____%

Number of Installments per Year:

Amount of Each Installment: $_____

Final Payment Due Date:

a) Assumption of Mortgage.

An assumption agreement satisfactory to the legal note holder must be signed by both Seller and Purchaser. The maximum purchaser assumption expense shall be $_____ and any balance shall be paid by the seller. The Owner shall remain obligated to the legal note holder if required.

b) Trust Deed.

If permission cannot be obtained from the legal note holder for the Purchaser to assume the debt or to obtain another mortgage commitment as outlined above, Purchaser shall take the title subject to the trust deed or mortgage (unless this is specifically prohibited by the mortgage document, in which case the deposit shall be returned to the purchaser and the contract will be null and void). The amount of money due will be adjusted a closing to reflect the principal balance due on the note.

c) Legal Documents.

Documents will be prepared by the Seller's attorney in a manner acceptable to the Purchaser. If the attorneys representing the Purchaser and the Seller cannot agree about the manner in which the documents are to be drawn up, a trust deed shall be prepared by the Seller's attorney using an appropriate _____ [bank or trust company] legal form, or the _____ & Co. printed legal form for an agreement for warranty deed, installment. Purchaser must provide a credit report to seller within _____ days of signing this agreement. Seller must notify Purchaser within _____ days from the date this agreement was signed that Seller will accept the purchase money note and mortgage or agreement for warranty deed, installment. If Seller gives Purchaser written notice of its unwillingness to accept the note and mortgage or agreement, this contract shall be null and void, and the deposit shall be refunded to the Purchaser. Failure by the Seller to deliver any notification to the Purchaser within the specified time shall be deemed acceptance of the said note and mortgage or agreement. If Purchaser fails to furnish Seller with a credit report within the specified time, this contract shall become null and void at Seller's discretion.

d) New Mortgage.

This offer is contingent on the Purchaser being able, within _____ days of acceptance of this agreement by Seller, to secure a mortgage commitment in the amount of $_____ with interest at _____% per annum or less, to be amortized over _____ years with commission for such loan not exceeding _____%. Purchaser will pay for flood hazard insurance if required by mortgagee. Purchaser must notify seller in writing within _____ days if a mortgage commitment under the terms set out above cannot be obtained. If the Seller does not receive such written notification, it will be understood that Purchaser has secured such a mortgage commitment or has agreed to purchase Property without mortgage financing. If Seller receives written notice that purchaser has not been able to secure a mortgage, Seller has the option, within _____ days of the notice, to secure a mortgage commitment under the same terms. Purchaser agrees to provide all necessary credit information to Seller and to sign an application and the customary papers necessary for the securing of mortgage commitments. If neither Purchaser nor Seller is able to secure a mortgage commitment on the terms listed above, this contract shall be null and void and the deposit shall be refunded to the Purchaser.

4. Conveyance of Title and Escrow Payout.

When title has been accepted by Purchaser, the closing or escrow payout shall be performed according to the terms of this agreement. Title shall be conveyed to Purchaser by a stamped recordable warranty deed including a release of dower and homestead rights; or by means of another appropriate deed and payment of purchase price, including any deposit and delivery of any purchase money mortgage; or by delivery of an agreement for warranty deed installment.

5. Restrictions on Title.

Title received by purchaser will be subject to general taxes for the year _____ and subsequent years; any special taxes or assessments for incomplete improvements; and installments of any special tax or assessment for improvements now completed but not due by date when agreement was signed. Purchaser accepts compliance with zoning and building laws and ordinances; building lines and building and liquor restrictions of record; easements for private roads; public utility easements; public roads and highways; recorded covenants and restrictions regarding occupancy and use; any party wall rights and agreements; and any mortgage or trust deed, as described above. [This subparagraph unnecessary if agreement for warranty deed, installment is provided for.]

6. Title Commitment.

Seller must provide Purchaser a title commitment for an owner's title insurance policy issued by a title insurance company licensed to do business in the state of _____, in the amount of the purchase price, no fewer than 5 days before Closing. This title insurance policy shall cover real estate title beginning with the date that this agreement was signed, showing title in the intended grantor. Title insurance will be subject to the conditions and stipulations and standard or general exceptions contained in the policy issued by that company; any title exceptions listed in this agreement; and liens or encumbrances that may be removed when the Seller uses money from the payment for Property at Closing to make the payments necessary to remove them. A delay in the Seller's delivery of commitment for title insurance because purchaser's mortgagee is late in recording mortgage and bringing down title shall not constitute a default under this agreement. Every title commitment provided by the Seller under this agreement shall be deemed evidence of good title, subject only to exceptions contained in documents pertaining to the commitment. For any part of the Property that was registered in the office of the registrar of titles of _____ County on the date of this agreement, the Seller may either tender the title commitment required in this agreement, and a currently dated registrar of title's special tax search; or display the owner's duplicate certificate of title or a certified copy and tender a currently dated registrar of title's special tax search and a currently dated registrar of title's federal tax lien search. Seller shall also furnish an affidavit of title covering the date of Closing, subject only to the title exceptions permitted by this agreement, and sign customary ALTA forms. Existing mortgage and lien debts are to be paid by seller out of sale proceeds.

7. Defects in Title.

If the title commitment reveals exceptions or defects in the title other than those referred to in this agreement, Seller shall have 30 days from the date the title commitment is delivered to purchaser to have these exceptions removed. If Seller is unable to have these exceptions removed within 30 days, Purchaser may elect either to terminate this contract or, by giving notice to seller within 10 days after the end of the 30-day period, to take title as is, reserving the right to deduct liens or encumbrances of a definite or ascertainable amount from the purchase price. If purchaser does not elect to do this, this contract shall become null and void with no further action, and the deposit shall be refunded to the purchaser.

8. Proration.

The following items shall be prorated based on the date when purchaser takes possession of Property: Real estate taxes (based on most recent estimates); any insurance policies requested by and assigned to purchaser; any rents; water taxes, and other proratable items, including flood hazard insurance. Purchaser shall assume fire and extended coverage insurance policies (except for homeowner's insurance policies) at closing. If Property in this agreement has increased in value since last available tax assessment because of improvements, both parties agree to reprorate when the tax bill for _____ [year] becomes available.

9. Escrow and Delivery of Possession.

Possession Delivery Date: _____

Amount of Purchase Price to be Held in Escrow: $_____

Escrow Holder: _____

Possession shall be achieved on the date that the Seller has vacated the premises and delivered the keys to Purchaser or Broker(s). Escrow is to be paid to the purchaser at the rate of $_____ per day for each day possession is withheld beyond that date. The balance remaining in the escrow account after delivery of possession shall be paid to Seller. Seller agrees to remove all debris from premises by possession date.

10. Default.

The deposit and this contract shall be held by _____ on behalf of both parties. If the Purchaser defaults, broker's commission and any incurred expenses shall be paid out of the deposit money, and the balance shall be paid to Seller. At Seller's discretion, forfeiture of the deposit may be considered full settlement of all damages. If the Seller defaults, the Purchaser may elect to accept a refund of the deposit and by doing so, release the Seller from all obligations under this contract. If improvements on the premises are destroyed or damaged prior to closing, this contract, at the discretion of the Purchaser, will become null and void.

11. Survey.

Seller is responsible for providing, prior to closing, a survey by a licensed land surveyor showing that the location of the buildings is within the plot lines and that there are no encroachments of buildings from adjoining properties. As long as all existing improvements and encroachments appear on this survey, purchaser shall bear the cost of any later survey that may be required by purchaser's mortgagee or desired by purchaser.

12. Mortgage.

Purchaser may place a mortgage on this property and apply proceeds toward purchase. Flood hazard insurance required by mortgagee will be paid for by purchaser.

13. Notices; Requests.

No government agency, or employee or official of a government agency, has given any notice to the Seller that it considers the construction on the Property or the operation or use of the Property to be out of compliance with any law, ordinance, regulation or order, or that any investigation has been or might be initiated respecting any possible non-compliance.

14. Real Estate Settlement Procedures Act of 1974.

Seller and Purchaser will execute all documents and supply all information so that any federal lender can issue its commitment and close the transaction according to the requirements of the Real Estate Settlement Procedures Act of 1974.

15. Communications.

All notices and communications required by this Agreement shall be made in writing and shall be delivered to each party's address as listed on this contract (or at any other address designated by written notice as the address to which such communications should be delivered) by personal service or by regular, certified, or registered mail.. The mailing of a notice by registered or certified United States mail, certified or return receipt requested, postage prepaid, shall constitute delivery. A notice or demand shall be deemed constructively made at the time it is personally delivered. If a communication is given by mail, the week day (except for legal holidays) after the date of mailing shall be deemed the date of delivery.

16. Closing.

Closing shall take place on _____
(Date) at the office of:

Name: _____

Address: _____

At request of either party, closing can occur in escrow with the title company issuing the title commitment by deed and money escrow. Seller and Purchaser will share costs equally.

17. Broker's Commission.

Seller shall pay a broker's commission of _____% to _____.

Purchaser: _____
            Signature

Seller: _____
            Signature

EXCLUSIVE RIGHT OF SALE CONTRACT

Date: _____
Owner: _____
Address: _____
City: _____ State: _____ Zip: _____
Agent: _____
Address: _____
City: _____ State: _____ Zip: _____

This Agreement grants exclusive right to abovementioned licensed Agent to find buyers for abovementioned Owner's Property, described in Exhibit "A," attached.

1. Owner's Guarantee.

Owner guarantees that it is the exclusive owner of Property and has lawful authority to sell and convey it. Owner guarantees that Property is free of any encumbrances and not subject to limitation of any kind. Owner gives exclusive right to Agent to advertise and sell Property at the agreed-upon price and terms set forth in Exhibit "B," attached to this contract, or at a lower price if accepted by Owner, without regard to purchaser's race, creed, color, or place of national origin.

2. Term.

The term of this Agreement shall be _____years, beginning on the date of this Agreement, and ending on the _____day of _____, unless both parties agree to extend the ending date.

3. Owner's Agreement.

Owner agrees to pay prorated taxes, insurance, rents, and interest on encumbrances if applicable, at closing. Owner will pay all current liens, before or at closing time. Owner warrants that the Property description, Exhibit "A", is accurate and agrees to indemnify and hold the Agent and any and all others relying on the Property description, harmless as to any errors it might contain. Owner agrees to follow customary procedures to secure a merchantable title for the closing in the event that Agent finds a purchaser for the Property. Owner agrees to provide purchaser with a sufficient Franchise Agreement, and any and all other necessary documents, free and clear of all encumbrances. Owner agrees not to lease the Property, or any portion of it, during the term of this Agreement.

4. Agent's Agreement.

Agent agrees to use its best efforts to secure purchasers for the Property, including advertising in local publications, supplying complete information to and assisting cooperating agents in any closing transactions on the Property, and taking all reasonable precautions to protect Owner and Property during the term of this Agreement.

5. Commission.

At Closing, Owner agrees to pay to the Agent a commission of _____% of the purchase price for the Property, regardless of whether Agent, any cooperating agent, any third party, or Owner affects the sale of the Property. If, within 60 days after the termination this Agreement, the Owner agrees to sell the Property to a purchaser to whom the Property was submitted during the term of this Agreement, Owner agrees to pay the commission to the Agent. Agent may represent and receive commissions from both parties in any exchange of the Property.

6. Prospective Purchaser.

If any prospective purchaser contacts the Owner, Owner agrees to provide Agent with the name, address, and telephone number of said prospective purchaser within 24 hours of initial contact. Owner agrees that Agent will handle all future contacts.

7. Deposit.

All money paid as a deposit or binder in regard to the Property is authorized to be handled by any Agent, cooperating agent, or authorized escrow agent, in accordance with the laws of the State of _____. In the event that a sale is not completed and the deposit is forfeited by the purchaser, agent may retain 50% of any deposit, or a sum equal to agreed-upon commission that Agent would have received from the sale, whichever is less, as compensation.

8. Agent's Guarantee.

This Agreement does not guarantee a sale of the Property. Agent guarantees to apply its best efforts to sell the Property during the term of this Agreement.

9. Authority of Agent.

Agent may use Owner's name in connection with marketing or advertising the Property. Owner gives Agent the authority to solicit and obtain any and all information concerning the Property and any liens and encumbrances on the Property. Owner agrees to execute all documents required for this purpose.

10. Severability.

If any provision in this Agreement is found to be unenforceable under the law, the remaining provisions shall continue to be valid and subject to enforcement in the courts without exception.

11. Prior Agreements.

This document contains the entire agreement between the Owner and the Agent. No prior agreements, verbal statements or understandings pertaining to any of the matters in this Agreement shall be effective for any purpose.

12. Amendments.

Any modifications or amendments to this Agreement must be made in writing and signed by both parties.

13. Governing Law.

This Agreement, and all transactions carried out in connection with it, shall be governed by, construed, and enforced in accordance with the laws of the State of _____.
Should litigation result from this Agreement, Owner and Agent agree to reimburse the prevailing party for reasonable attorney's fees, court costs, and all other expenses, whether or not taxable by the Court as costs, associated with the litigation, in addition to any other remedy to which the prevailing party may be entitled. No action shall be entertained by said Court or any Court of competent jurisdiction if filed more than one year from the date that the cause(s) of action actually accrued, regardless of whether damages could be accurately calculated at that time.

14. Heirs and Assigns.

The agreements contained in this contract are binding upon the Owner and Agent and their respective heirs, successors, legal representatives, and assigns.

15. Recordation.

It is expressly agreed that this Agreement will not be recorded in any form in the public records of any county.

16. Assignment.

Neither party may assign this Agreement without the express written consent of the other.

Signed, sealed, and delivered in the presence of:

_____   _____
Owner   Owner's Witness

_____   _____
Agent   Agent's Witness

EXHIBIT "A" (Description of Property)

CONTRACT MEMORANDUM FOR PURCHASE & SALE OF PROPERTY

Date: _____

Landlord: _____

Address: _____
City: _____ State: _____ Zip: _____
Tenant: _____
Address: _____
City: _____ State: _____ Zip: _____
Property: _____

This is a Memorandum of the unrecorded Contract for Purchase & Sale of Property (hereby referred to as Contract), which was made between the Seller and Buyer for the purchase and sale of the property ("Property") listed above and described in Exhibit "A" attached to and made a part of this Contract.

The Seller has agreed to sell, and Buyer has agreed to buy, the Property according to the terms stated in the Contract, which are included in this Memorandum by this note. Unless provided for in the Contract, from this date forward, the Seller will have no right to enter into any new contracts, agreements, or leases regarding the Property to the Buyer, oral or written, without the prior written consent of the Buyer.

This Memorandum is not a comprehensive synopsis of the Contract. Provisions of this Memorandum shall not be used in interpreting the Contract. In the event of a disagreement between this Memorandum and the Contract, the Contract will take precedence.

IN WITNESS WHEREOF, the Seller and Buyer hereby agree to and execute this Memorandum on the date specified above.

_____   _____
Seller   Seller's Witness

_____   _____
Buyer   Buyer's Witness

STATE OF_____ COUNTY OF_____

The foregoing instrument was acknowledged before me this _____ day of _____,
20_____, by _____ as Seller and _____ as Buyer.

_____
Notary Public
My Commission Expires: _____

NON-EXCLUSIVE RIGHT OF SALE AGREEMENT

Date: _____
Owner: _____
Address: _____
City: _____ State: _____ Zip: _____
Broker: _____
Address: _____
City: _____ State: _____ Zip: _____

The Owner employs the Broker to sell certain real and personal property of the Owner; and the Broker accepts such employment and agrees to use his/her best efforts to find a buyer for the property of the Owner.

1. Broker's Qualifications.

The Broker is licensed as a real estate broker in the State of _____ and maintains an office, properly equipped and staffed by employees suitable to render the services contracted for in this Agreement.

2. Owner's Guarantee.

The Owner warrants that he/she is the legal owner of the property ("Property"), situated in the County of _____, State of _____, described in Exhibit "A", attached to and made a part of this Agreement, and has legal authority to sell and convey the Property. Owner warrants that Property is free of all liens and encumbrances; except taxes accruing subsequent to 20 ___ (Year), conditions, restrictions, easements, limitations, and zoning ordinances of record, if any, and the encumbrances described in Exhibit "B," attached to and made a part of this Agreement. Owner agrees to pay prorated taxes, insurance, rents, and interest on encumbrances if applicable, at closing. Owner will pay all current liens, before or at closing time. Owner warrants that the Property description, Exhibit "A," is accurate and agrees to indemnify and hold the Broker and any and all others relying on the Property description, harmless as to any errors it might contain. Owner agrees to follow customary procedures to secure a merchantable title for the closing in the event that Agent finds a purchaser for the Property.

3. Price.

Owner gives the Broker the right to sell the Property at the price and under the terms specified in Exhibit "C," attached to and made a part of this document, without regard to the race, creed, color, or place of national origin of any purchaser. The Broker may sell the Property at a lower price and upon different terms with the written consent of the Owner.

4. Broker's Guarantee.

Broker will list Property of the Owner and use his/her best efforts to find a purchaser. Broker will advertise the Property in local newspapers or other publications, and by other methods as he/she deems necessary. Broker will advertise the Property through the local multiple listing service, at the Broker's sole expense. Broker agrees to inspect the Property and obtain complete information about it. Upon request, Broker agrees to supply complete information to and assistance to cooperating brokers in any closing of a transaction on the Property. Broker agrees to take all reasonable precautions to protect the Property of the Owner during the term of this Agreement.

5. Term.

This Agreement shall be in effect for a term of _____ months, beginning on the date of execution of this Agreement by both parties, and ending on _____, 20 _____ (date), unless the parties agree to extend it or terminate it early according to the conditions set forth in this Agreement.

6. Property Description.

The Owner hereby guarantees that the property description, attached to this Agreement as Exhibit "A," is correct in all respects, and agrees to indemnify and hold the Broker and any and all others relying on this description, harmless as to any errors contained in it.

7. Title and Closing.

If the Broker finds a purchaser for the Property, the customary procedures for providing a marketable title, and for the closing of transactions of this nature, shall be followed. The Owner agrees to deliver to the purchaser a good and sufficient Warranty Deed, clear of all liens and encumbrances excepting those listed in this Agreement and those specifically enumerated in the attached Exhibit "B," which the purchaser assumes as a part of the purchase price.

8. Leases and Encumbrances.

The Broker is authorized by the Owner to solicit and obtain any and all information concerning the property and all mortgages and other encumbrances on it. The Owner agrees to provide any and all documents required for obtaining such information. The Owner agrees that he will provide full details to the Broker in writing if during the term of this Agreement, or any extension of it, the Property or any portion of the Property is leased, mortgaged, or otherwise encumbered.

9. Commission.

If the Owner agrees to sell the Property to a purchaser to whom the property was submitted by the Broker, any cooperating broker, or any third party, other than the Owner, during the term of this Agreement, or within sixty (60) days after the termination of this Agreement, the Owner agrees to pay to the Broker, at the time of closing, a commission of _____ percent (%) of the sales price for the Property. The Owner grants Broker permission to represent and receive commissions from both parties in any exchange of the Property.

10. Sale by Owner.

It is expressly understood that if the Owner secures a buyer for the property and closes the sale solely through the Owner's efforts, the Owner may enter into a contract for the purchase of the Property and conclude a sale without the obligation to pay a commission of any amount to the Broker, any cooperating broker, or any third party. If the Property is sold in this manner, Owner agrees to reimburse the Broker at the time of closing for any and all documented, reasonable out-of-pocket expenses incurred by the Broker during the term of this Agreement. The Owner agrees to provide the Broker with the name, address, and telephone number of any such prospective buyer, and the exact circumstances under which the prospective buyer learned about the Property, within _____ (___) hours of initial contact with any such prospective buyer.

11. Termination.

This Agreement may be terminated by either party before a contract for sale and purchase is executed, by the submission of written notice to the other party. If Owner terminates this Agreement, the Owner agrees to reimburse the Broker for any and all documented, reasonable out-of-pocket expenses relating to this Property incurred by the Broker prior to termination of the Agreement. If the efforts of the Broker, any cooperating broker, or any third party, other than the Owner, results in a sale of the property to any buyer during the period from the cancellation until the original expiration date of this Agreement, the cancellation shall be deemed void and the Owner will pay the Broker the agreed upon commission as set forth in this Agreement.

12. Deposit.

The Broker, any cooperating broker, or any authorized escrow agent, is authorized to accept and hold, on behalf of the Owner, in accordance with the laws of the State of

_____, any and all money paid as a deposit or binder in regard to the Property. If deposit is forfeited, the Broker may retain as compensation either fifty (50%) percent of the deposit, or a sum equal to the commission which would have been paid to the Broker if the sale had gone forward, whichever is less.

13. Sale is Not Guaranteed.

This Agreement in no way guarantees a sale of the Property; the Broker does guarantee that it will make its continued best efforts to sell the Property during the term of this Agreement.

14. Use of Owner's Name.

The Broker (may) (may not) use the name of the Owner in connection with marketing or advertising the Property either before or after any sale.

15. Lockbox.

The Broker (may) (may not) use a lockbox system to allow the Broker and cooperating brokers to access the property. The Owner understands that use of a lockbox system may expose the property to possible damage and/or theft, and the Owner expressly indemnifies the Broker, any cooperating broker, and any associated person or entity from all liability in connection with any loss resulting from the use of a lockbox system.

16. Severability.

If any provision in this Agreement is found to be unenforceable under the law, the remaining provisions shall continue to be valid and subject to enforcement in the courts without exception.

17. Prior Agreements.

This document contains the entire agreement between the Owner and the Agent. No prior agreements, verbal statements, or understandings pertaining to any of the matters in this Agreement shall be effective for any purpose.

18. Amendments.

Any modifications or amendments to this Agreement must be made in writing and signed by both parties.

19. Governing Law.

This Agreement, and all transactions carried out in connection with it, shall be governed by, construed, and enforced in accordance with the laws of the State of _____.
Should litigation result from this Agreement, Owner and Agent agree to reimburse the prevailing party for reasonable attorney's fees, court costs, and all other expenses, whether or not taxable by the Court as costs, associated with the litigation, in addition to any other remedy to which the prevailing party may be entitled. No action shall be entertained by said Court or any Court of competent jurisdiction if filed more than one year from the date that the cause(s) of action actually accrued, regardless of whether damages could be accurately calculated at that time.

20. Heirs and Assigns.

The agreements contained in this contract are binding upon the Owner and Agent and their respective heirs, successors, legal representatives, and assigns.

21. Recordation.

It is expressly agreed that this Agreement will not be recorded in any form in the public records of any county.

OWNER: _____   _____
Witness: _____   _____

Witness: _____   _____
BROKER: _____   _____
Witness: _____   _____
Witness: _____   _____

EXHIBIT "A"
(LEGAL DESCRIPTION OF PROPERTY)

The Property to which this Agreement pertains is located at:
Address: _____
City: _____ State: _____ Zip: _____
and described as:

_____

The following Personal Property is included:

_____

EXHIBIT "B"
SCHEDULE OF ENCUMBRANCES
AGAINST THE PROPERTY

1. **Mortgage Loan Number** _____,
in favor of: _____,
Address: _____
City: _____ State: _____ Zip: _____
executed by _____
on _____ (date) in the original principal amount of
$_____, with interest thereon at the rate of _____
(_____ %) percent per annum, and payable as principal and interest in monthly installments of $_____. This Mortgage (is) (is not) assumable.

2. **Mortgage Loan Number** _____,
in favor of: _____,
Address: _____
City: _____ State: _____ Zip: _____
whose address is _____, executed by
_____ on _____
(date) in the original principal amount of $_____, with interest
thereon at the rate of _____ (_____ %) percent per annum, and
payable as principal and interest in monthly installments of $_____. Said Mortgage
(is) (is not) assumable.

3. **Mortgage Loan Number** _____,
in favor of: _____,
Address: _____
City: _____ State: _____ Zip: _____
whose address is _____, executed by
_____ on _____
(date) in the original principal amount of $_____, with interest
thereon at the rate of _____ (_____ %) percent per year, and

payable as principal and interest in monthly installments of $_____. This Mortgage (is) (is not) assumable. 4.

There are no other liens or encumbrances against the Property, except:

_____

EXHIBIT "C"
PRICE AND TERMS ACCEPTABLE TO OWNER

1. The Owner will accept a gross sales price for the Property in the amount of $ _____.
2. The Owner (will) (will not) assist in financing the purchase of the Property by taking a Purchase Money Note and Mortgage, in an amount and according to the terms set out below, or in an amount and according to terms agreed to by the Owner, as a portion of the Sales Price:

_____

3. Additional terms of sale, if any, required by Owner:

_____

SELLER'S STANDARD REAL ESTATE SALES AGREEMENT

Date: _____

Seller: _____

Address: _____

City: _____ State: _____ Zip: _____

Buyer: _____

Address: _____

City: _____ State: _____ Zip: _____

Land: _____

Lot: _____ Block: _____ Unit: _____ Phase/Section: _____

Subdivision: _____ Recorded in Plat Book: _____ Page: _____

Address: _____

City: _____ State: _____ Zip: _____

This Agreement for purchase of the abovementioned real estate includes all light fixtures, mechanical, electrical, plumbing, air-conditioning, and any other systems or fixtures as are attached to the property; all trees, shrubbery, and plants now a part of the property; all the improvements on the property, and all appurtenance to the land and these items. For the purposes of this Agreement, real estate, and all these inclusions will be collectively referred to as the "Property." The full legal description of this Property is recorded with the Clerk of the Superior Court of the County in which the Property is located and is part of this Agreement by reference. Seller certifies and represents that it has the authority and capacity to convey the Property with all improvements.

Seller and Buyer agree to carry out this transaction according to the following terms and conditions, as set down in this Agreement. If there is a conflict of terms or conditions, any addendum will take precedence over the original terms set down in this Agreement.

1. Conveyance.

Conveyance of the Property will be by warranty deed, with all covenants, easements, and restrictions of record.

2. Purchase Price.

Buyer will pay for the Property the following sums included in the purchase price, which includes the following:

Deposit $_____

Additional deposit $_____, on _____

Purchase money loan to seller, including discount points, on terms set forth below $_____

Proceeds, of Buyer's new loan, to lender other than Seller, on terms set forth below $_____

Lender_____

Balance due at closing, which does not include Buyer's closing costs or any prepaid items, in U.S. currency or cashier's check $_____

Total purchase price $_____

All fixed equipment including carpeting, floor coverings, range, range hood, dishwasher, drapery hardware, ceiling fans, attached lighting fixtures, mailbox, fence, plants, and shrubbery as now installed on the property, are included in the purchase price, along with these items:

_____

3. Financing.

Only with consent of Seller, Buyer will provide a negotiable Promissory Note of Borrower to Seller for balance due, which shall secure debt on the property by a deed or mortgage, of $_____ per _____ for_____ months, bearing an annual interest rate of _____%, and excluding property taxes and hazard insurance, but including loan discount point(s), a _____% prepayment penalty.

If Buyer does not secure financing, deposit shall be forfeited to Seller as liquidated damages. Within five days of the date of agreement of the Acceptance, Buyer will apply for financing and provide any and all credit, employment, financial, and other information required by the lender. If Seller so chooses, Buyer shall reapply for a loan to an alternate institution, in the event the lender denies the original loan application, or Seller shall have the option to serve as an alternative source for financing. Seller shall have the right to terminate this Agreement, should the mortgage loan, without continued contingencies other than those covered in this Agreement, not be approved within thirty (30) days of the date of said Agreement's acceptance. In such case, the Buyer shall return to Seller all title evidence and surveys Seller had earlier provided.

4. Closing Costs.

Buyer is responsible for paying all closing costs, to include loan origination fees, title insurance and loan insurance, attorney's fees, cost of overnight delivery or courier, fees for appraisals, surveys, document preparation and recording, transfer tax, intangibles tax, funding fees, costs for credit reports, and Wood-Destroying Organism reports, and any other costs associated with the funding or closing of this Agreement. All of the following will be prorated as of the date of the closing: taxes, rentals, condominium or association fees, monthly mortgage insurance premiums, and interest on loans.

5. Closing.

The closing of the transaction and the delivering of the deed shall occur on or before _____, unless Buyer cancels Agreement or other situations cancel the Agreement. At Closing Seller must provide a marketable title, according to evidence and survey, subject to the customary exceptions included in title insurance commitments, such as current taxes, zoning ordinances, survey, easements of record, and restrictions.

6. Title Insurance.

Within five (5) days of this Agreement, Seller will deliver to Buyer or closing attorney a title insurance commitment for an owner's policy in the amount of the purchase price, and expenses related to correcting defects in the title, including but not limited to legal fees, discharge of liens, and recording fees.

7. Survey.

Within ten (10) days of acceptance of this Agreement, Buyer or closing attorney, may, at Buyer's expense, obtain a new staked survey showing any improvements now existing thereon and certified to Buyer, lender, and the title insurer.

8. Defects in Title.

After receiving title commitment and survey, Buyer shall have seven (7) days to notify Seller of any defects, as exposed through title evidence or survey, who, at Seller's expense, shall have thirty (30) days to repair defects and allow the continuance of said transaction.

9. Pest Inspection.

Buyer may order a Certified Pest Control Firm to inspect the property to determine whether any visible, active wood-destroying organism infestations or visible, existing structural damage from wood-destroying organisms to the improvements are present. "Wood-Destroying Organism" is any arthropod or plant life that damages a structure similar to the Property concerned in this Agreement. Should the abovementioned organisms be discovered on the Property, Buyer shall inform Seller by written notice, who will then have seven (7) days after receiving written notice, to have a licensed building or general contractor inspect and estimate the abovementioned organism damages, and pay any and all costs to treat and repair all structural damage, up to 1% of the purchase price of the Property.

10. Condition of Property.

Buyer has inspected and accepts the Property in its current condition, unless otherwise specified herein. Seller agrees to deliver the Property in its current condition except as otherwise specified herein. Seller certifies that it has no knowledge of latent defects to the Property, or of any facts materially affecting the value of the Property except the following:

_____.

11. Default.

If the Buyer fails to perform its obligations under this Agreement, Seller shall retain all of Buyer's deposit as liquidated damages and settlement of any claim, and Seller and Buyer shall be relieved of all obligations under this Agreement. If Sellers defaults on this Agreement, Buyer may receive $_____ in return for its deposit. Should any litigation arise out of this Agreement, the prevailing party shall recover all costs, including reasonable attorney's fees, in addition to any damages awarded by the court.

12. Prior Agreements.

No previous oral or contractual agreements exist between Buyer and Seller except those included in this Agreement.

13. Amendments and Modifications.

Changes to this Agreement must be made in a written document signed by both parties.

IN WITNESS WHEREOF, all of the parties hereto set their hands and seals the day and year first above written. Signed, sealed, and delivered in the presence of:

_____   _____
Seller   Seller's Witness

_____   _____
Buyer   Buyer's Witness

CHAPTER 2

Basic Real Estate Purchasing Forms and Agreements

SIMPLE AGREEMENT FOR PURCHASE & SALE OF REAL ESTATE

Date: _____

Buyer: _____

Address: _____

City: _____ State: _____ Zip: _____

Seller: _____

Address: _____

City: _____ State: _____ Zip: _____

1. The Property.

The parties hereby agree that Seller will sell and Buyer will buy the following property, located in and situated in the County of _____, state of _____.

Legal description: _____

_____

Address: _____

City: _____ State: _____ Zip: _____

The sale shall also include all personal property and fixtures, except: _____.

Unless specifically excluded, all other items will be included, whether or not affixed to the property or structures. Seller expressly warrants that property, improvements, building or structures, the appliances, roof, plumbing, heating and/or ventilation systems are in good working order. This clause shall survive closing of title.

2. Purchase Price.

The total purchase price to be paid by buyer will be $_____, payable as follows:

Non-refundable deposit	$_____
Balance due at closing	$_____
Owner financing from seller	$_____
New loan	$_____
Subject to existing loans	$_____

Sale price is subject to appraisal by buyer and/or agent of buyer's choice.

3. Deposit.

The buyer's earnest money shall be held in escrow by agent of buyer's choice. Upon default of this agreement, seller may retain entire sum of earnest money as his sole remedy without further resource between the parties.

4. New Loan.

The agreement is contingent upon buyer's ability to obtain a new loan in the amount of $_____. Buyer is not required to accept any loan with interest rate exceeding _____percent amortized over _____ years or pay any closing costs or points exceeding $_____. Buyer shall provide seller with written proof of a loan commitment on or before _____, 20 ___.

5. Seller Financing.

Buyer shall execute a promissory note in the amount of $_____. In the case of default by the buyer, recourse shall be against the property and there shall be no personal resource against the borrower. As security for performance of the promissory note, buyer shall provide the seller a mortgage, deed of trust, or other customary security agreement, which shall be subordinate to a new first mortgage not to exceed $_____.

6. Closing.

Closing is to be held be on or about _____, 20_____, at a time and place designed by buyer. Buyer shall choose the escrow, title, and/or closing agent. Seller agrees to convey title by a general warranty deed. Parties agree to pursue satisfactory closing with all due diligence.

7. Possession.

Seller shall surrender possession to the property in clean condition, and free of all personal items and debris on or before _____, 20_____. (Possession date) In the event possession is not delivered at closing, buyer shall withhold proceeds from the sale in the amount of $_____ as security. Seller shall be liable for damages in the amount of $_____ per day for each day the property is occupied or otherwise unavailable to buyer beyond the possession date. This paragraph shall survive the closing of title.

8. Execution of Terms.

This agreement may be executed in counterparts and will be accepted by facsimile signatures. This agreement is in effect as of the date of the last signature.

9. Inspection.

The completion of this agreement is subject to the final inspection and approval of the property by the buyer in writing on or before _____, 20_____.

10. Access.

Buyer shall be in possession of a key or suitable key code and be entitled to access to show partners, lenders, inspectors, and/or contractors prior to closing as needed. Buyer may place an appropriate sign on the property before closing for prospective tenants and/or assigns.

Seller	Date
Seller	Date
Buyer	Date
Buyer	Date

REAL ESTATE SALE CONTRACT: COMMERCIAL OR INDUSTRIAL PROPERTY

Date: _____

Purchaser: _____

Address: _____

City: _____ State: _____ Zip: _____

Seller: _____

Permanent Address: _____

City: _____ State: _____ Zip: _____

1. Purchaser's Agreement.

Purchaser agrees to purchase, under the terms of this Agreement, for the price of _____ dollars (_____$), the real estate located at:

Address: _____

City: _____ State: _____ Zip: _____

commonly known as _____,

and with approximate lot dimensions of _____ × _____, together with the following property presently located on it: _____

_____.

2. Seller's Agreement.

Seller agrees to sell the real estate and the property described above, for the price and according to the terms set forth in this agreement, and to convey marketable title to it to the Purchaser or the Purchaser's agent, by a recordable _____ deed, with release of dower and homestead rights, if any, and a proper bill of sale. The bill of sale will be subject only to:

(a) previously recorded covenants, conditions, and restrictions;

(b) private, public and utility easements, and easements for private and public roads and highways, if any;

(c) any party wall rights and agreements;

(d) existing leases and tenancies listed in Schedule A attached to this document;

(e) special taxes or assessments for improvements not yet completed;

(f) installments of any special tax or assessment for improvements already completed but not due by date when agreement was signed;

(g) any mortgage or trust deed as described below;

(h) general taxes for the year _____ and subsequent years;

3. Down Payment.

Purchaser has made a down payment of $_____to be applied to the purchase price, and agrees to pay or satisfy the balance of the purchase price, plus or minus prorations, at the time of closing as follows: *(Delete any of the following language that is not applicable.)*

(a) The payment of $_____.

(b) A down payment of $_____ with the balance payable as follows: $_____ as set forth in writing by the Purchaser (grantee), in a document granting full prepayment privileges without penalty, which shall be secured by a part-purchase money mortgage (trust deed). Both of these documents shall be attached as Schedule B to this agreement, or, in the absence of this attachment, shall be identified as forms No. _____ and _____, prepared by _____. These documents shall be accompanied by a security agreement and an assignment of rents, to be attached to this agreement as Schedules C and D.

The Purchaser agrees to provide a credit report and any financial statements required under the Uniform Commercial Code in order to make the lien created under them effective. Purchaser shall provide seller with an American Land Title Association loan policy issued by the _____ Title Insurance Company, insuring the mortgage (trust deed).

(If no Schedule B is attached to this document and the blanks above are not filled in, the note shall be secured by a trust deed, with both the note and trust deed set forth on the standard legal forms used by the _____*[name of bank or trust company].*)

(c) A mortgage or trust deed of record obtained by the Purchaser securing a debt of $_____ bearing interest at the rate of _____% a year. The Purchaser will pay an amount equal to the difference between the amount due on the debt at the time of closing and the balance of the purchase price.

4. Survey.

Seller will provide Purchaser, at Seller's expense, with a current plat of survey of the above real estate certified by the surveyor as having been carried out in compliance with the _____ Land Survey Standards.

5. Closing.

The closing will take place at _____ (time) on _____ (date), or on a specified later date and time if the conditions in paragraph 2 of the Conditions

and Stipulations are in effect, at the offices of _____
Address: _____
or of the mortgage lender. Seller must provide a marketable title at Closing. Any change to date and time of Closing must be mutually agreed upon in writing by both parties.

6. Broker's Commission.
Seller agrees to pay a broker's commission of _____ % as set forth in the broker's listing contract, or as follows: _____.

7. Deposit.
_____ shall hold the deposit on behalf of both parties.

8. Notices.
The Seller warrants that no government agency, or employee or official of a city, village, or other government agency, has given any notice to the Seller or its beneficiaries or agents that it considers the construction on the Property or the operation or use of the Property to be out of compliance with any law, ordinance, regulation or order, or that any investigation has been or might be initiated respecting any possible non-compliance. There are no unpaid expenses or outstanding invoices from any person, entity, or authority, including, but not limited to, any tenant, lender, insurance carrier, or government authority, for the cost of repairs, restorations, or improvements to the Property.

9. Duplicate Original.
A duplicate original of this contract, duly executed by the Seller and his or her spouse, if any, shall be provided to the Purchaser within _____ days from the date of this contract. If this duplicate original is not provided by the due date, at the Purchaser's discretion this contract shall become null and void and the deposit shall be refunded to the Purchaser.

This contract is subject to the conditions and stipulations set forth on its reverse side, which are hereby made a part of this contract.

Signature of Purchaser: _____
Printed name of Purchaser: _____
Signature of Seller: _____
Printed name of Seller: _____

[Reverse Side]
CONDITIONS AND STIPULATIONS
1. Survey.
Seller shall provide to Purchaser or Purchaser's agent, no less than five days before the closing date, the plat of survey of the above real estate, certified by the surveyor as having been carried out in compliance with the _____ Land Survey Standards (if required under the terms of this contract).

2. Title Commitment.
Seller shall provide to Purchaser or Purchaser's agent, no less than five days before the closing date, a title commitment for an owner's title insurance policy issued by the

_____ Title Insurance Company in the full amount of the purchase price, covering title to the real estate on or after the date of this contract, and showing title in the property subject only to the general exceptions contained in the title insurance policy; any title exceptions set forth in this Agreement; and title exceptions associated with liens or encumbrances which, under the terms of this contract, the Seller may discharge by payment of money using the funds received at Closing. The title commitment shall be conclusive evidence of good title. Seller also shall provide Purchaser with an affidavit of title in customary form, valid at the date of closing and certifying that the Seller holds title subject only to the exceptions set forth in this contract, and any exceptions or survey defects, for which the title insurer commits to extend insurance coverage as specified below.

3. Defects in Title.

If the title commitment or plat of survey (if required under the terms of this contract) reveals that title is unmarketable either because of unpermitted exceptions or survey defects, the Seller will have 30 days from the date of its delivery to correct these survey defects, have the exceptions removed from the commitment, or to obtain a commitment from the title insurer to insure against any loss or damage resulting from these exceptions or survey defects. In such a case, the closing will take place 35 days after delivery of the title commitment, or on the Closing date expressly specified in the first page of this contract, whichever is later. If the Seller fails to remove the exceptions or correct the survey defects, or to obtain the title insurance within the specified time, the Purchaser has two options: a) to void this contract; or b) after giving notice in writing to Seller within 10 days after the expiration of the 30-day period, to take title as is, with the right to deduct liens or encumbrances of a specified or ascertainable amount from the purchase price. If Purchaser does not choose to take title, this contract shall automatically become null and void.

4. Prorations.

Rents, premiums for insurance policies assignable to Purchaser, water and other utility charges, fuels, prepaid service contracts, general taxes, accrued interest on mortgage indebtedness, if any, and other similar items shall be prorated according to current rates and based on the time of closing. If the amount of the current general taxes is not available, the adjustment for taxes will be based on the amount of the most recent available tax figures. All such prorations are final unless otherwise specified in this contract. Existing leases and assignable insurance policies will then be to the Purchaser at Closing.

5. Manner of Payment.

All payments required in this contract to be made at the time of closing shall be by certified check or cashier's check, payable to Seller.

6. Stamp Tax.

Seller will be responsible to pay any stamp tax imposed by law on the transfer of the title, and to provide a completed real estate transfer declaration signed by the Seller or the Seller's agent according to the requirements of the Real Estate Transfer Tax Act of the State of _____.

7. Uniform Vendor and Purchaser Risk Act.

The provisions of the Uniform Vendor and Purchaser Risk Act of the State of _____ shall apply to this contract.

8. Termination of Contract.

If this contract is terminated by the Seller, the deposit will be returned to the Purchaser. If Purchaser brings about the termination of this contract, at the Seller's discretion, after written notification to the Purchaser, the deposit will be forfeited to the Seller and used to pay the Seller's expenses and the broker's commission; the balance, if any, may be retained by the Seller as liquidated damages.

9. Closing by Escrow.

If the Seller or Purchaser notifies the other party in writing not less than 5 days before the closing date, this sale can be closed through an escrow with _____ *[bank or trust company]*, in accordance with the usual deed and money escrow agreement used by _____ _____ *[bank or trust company].* Any special provisions required by this contract must be inserted in the escrow agreement. Upon the creation of such an escrow, it will take precedence over anything previously stated in this contract and payment of the purchase price and delivery of the deed shall be transacted through the escrow. This contract and the deposit shall be deposited in the escrow. The cost of the escrow shall be divided equally between Seller and Purchaser. (Strike paragraph if inapplicable.)

10. Time is of the Essence.

Time is of the essence of this contract, particularly for all provisions in which performance is a factor.

11. Notices.

All notices and communications required by this contract shall be made in writing and shall be delivered to each party's address as listed on this contract. The mailing of a notice by registered or certified mail, return receipt requested, shall constitute delivery.

ASSIGNMENT OF CONTRACT

Date	Property
Assignor	Assignee

The undersigned Assignor, having executed a contract on this date between the above-mentioned Assignor and Assignee, hereby transfers and sets over to Assignee all rights, title, and interest held by the Assignor in and to the following described property in exchange for compensation in the amount of $ _____:

Street Address_____

Unit Number_____

City and State_____

Zip Code_____

Assignee agrees to fulfill all terms, conditions, and contingencies of said Contract and to perform as required in good faith and within any time periods established by said Contract.

Signed this _____ day of _____, 20_____.

_____

Assignor's Signature

_____

Assignor's Printed Name

_____

Assignee's Signature

_____

Assignee's Printed Name

DUE-ON-SALE ACKNOWLEDGMENT

WHEREAS, _____ as Seller and

_____ as Purchaser have entered into a certain purchase and sales agreement on the date herewith, the parties fully understand, acknowledge, and agree as follows:

1. Both Seller and Purchaser are fully aware that the mortgage(s) deeds of trust securing the property located at _____ contain(s) provisions prohibiting the transfer of any interest in the property without satisfying the principal balance remaining on the underlying loans and/or obtaining the lender's prior written consent (i.e., a "due-on-sale" clause), and that this transaction may violate said mortgage. Seller specifically understands that completely at this time, and that this loan will remain in Seller's name and may continue to appear on Seller's credit report.

2. Seller and Purchaser execute this disclosure form after having had the opportunity to seek legal counsel as to the legal and financial implications of due-on-sale clause. The parties agree and understand that if said due on sale clause is enforced by the holders of said mortgages, the entire balance due under said mortgage/deeds of trust will have to be paid off. In this event, Seller and Purchaser agree to take all reasonable steps to satisfy said lender, including both parties taking steps to obtain financing and/or Purchaser submitting an application to formally assume liability for said obligations. Purchaser understands that in the event that the underlying debt is not paid off, the lender holding the deeds of trust may foreclose the property, which will extinguish Purchaser's interest under the Installment Land Contract.

3. Seller and Purchaser hereby agreed to defend, indemnify, and hold all parties involved in this transaction harmless from any liability in the event that the holders of the mortgages and/or deeds of trust on the aforementioned property are called due and payable.

By: _____
Seller
By: _____
Purchaser
State of _____
County of_____
Sworn to and subscribed before me, a Notary Public, for the State of _____
County of _____
This _____ day of _____ 20____

By: _____
Notary Public
My Commission Expires: _____, 20 _____

PURCHASE CONTRACT ADDENDUM ALLOWING SELLER TO REMAIN ON PROPERTY AFTER CLOSING DATE

Date: _____

Seller has requested to remain on the property after the closing date of _____. For this reason, $_____ will be held in an escrow account on the date of closing by the closing agent or other appointee until the time that the Seller vacates the property and leaves it in a neat and clean condition as described below.

Seller hereby agrees to vacate the premises no more than _____ days after closing has concluded. If the Seller does not remove himself/herself from the premises by this date, a $_____ charge for every day over will be charged to the Seller and be deducted from the escrowed amount.

If the Seller still remains on the property after _____ days from the set date, any and all money that remains in the escrow account will be forfeited. Buyer will have complete right to evict the Seller as he/she is now considered to be a Tenant in Sufferance.

The "neat and clean" definition is as follows: Any and all trash must be removed from the interior and exterior of the property. Property should be left clear of any possessions of the Seller.

If the premises are not left in the "neat and clean" condition as described above, Buyer will have a cleanup performed at the Seller's expense and will be deducted from the escrowed amount.

If it comes to the point whereby the Buyer needs to proceed with legal action in order to enforce this agreement, Seller will be responsible for any and all legal costs and costs of the action taken.

_____
Seller Signature

DOWN PAYMENT ACKNOWLEDGMENT

Seller Name: _____

Purchaser Name: _____

Date: _____

Property Address: _____

City: _____ State: _____ Zip: _____

Amount of Down Payment: $_____

Date of Payment: _____

The abovementioned down payment has been received by the seller and will be credited toward the purchase price of the property listed above. The parties agree that this amendment to any previous agreement reached in regard to the indicated property is legally binding.

_____   _____
Seller Signature   Date

_____   _____
Purchaser Signature   Date

_____   _____
Witness Signature   Date

_____   _____
Witness Signature   Date

AFFIDAVIT AND MEMORANDUM OF AGREEMENT FOR PURCHASE AND SALE

This contract is for the purchase and sale of the real estate property located at: _____ , which will further be referred to as the "property," and was entered into by the Seller: _____ and the Buyer: _____, on this date: the day_____, 20__.

A duplicate of the agreement for purchase and sale of said real property may be obtained by contacting: _____

whose mailing address is: _____ ,

and whose telephone number is: _____.

Avowed to and described before me this _____ day of: _____, 20___.

(Seal)

NOTARY PUBLIC

STATE OF _____

My commission expires _____

BUYER (SIGNATURE):_____
SELLER (SIGNATURE): _____

AMENDMENT OF PURCHASE AGREEMENT

Date: _____
Buyer: _____
Seller: _____
Property Address: _____
City: _____ State: _____ Zip: _____

This is an amendment to the original Purchase Agreement, dated _____.

The following is a detailed description of all amendments to the original agreement: _____
_____

The buyer and seller are in agreement that this amendment is accurate and valid and that it is effective immediately. Any and all terms and/or conditions not specifically altered by this amendment remain in effect.

_____   _____
Seller   Witness

_____   _____
Buyer   Witness

ASSIGNMENT FORM

Assignor: _____
Address: _____
City: _____ State: _____ Zip: _____
Assignee: _____
Address: _____
City: _____ State: _____ Zip: _____

This form is a contract that is effective on _____ (date), between the above named Assignor and the above named Assignee.

The agreements below have been agreed upon and the receipt and sufficiency of the conditions are acceptable to all parties:
1. The above named Assignor gives to the above named Assignee all of the rights, title, and interest in the Assigned Property Below.
2. The Assignor assumes and grants the following the conditions:

   a.   This document has the ability to effectively assigned all necessary powers
        and rights;
   b.   The Assignor assures that they have never given these privileges or rights
        to any other Assignee for the before mentioned property; and
   c.   The Property being assigned to the Assignee does not have any debt or
        liens associated with it and no other third parties have right or interest in
        the property.

3.   This agreement supersedes any prior agreements concerning this subject matter.
     There cannot be any changes or amendments made to this agreement without
     both parties agreeing in writing.

4.   This Agreement shall ensure to the benefit of and be binding upon the respective
     heirs, executors, administrators, and assigns of each of the parties hereto.

IN WITNESS WHEREOF this Agreement has been executed by the parties hereto as of
the date first above written.

_____   _____
Witness   Assignor

_____   _____
Witness   Assignee

ASSIGNMENT OF CONTRACT FOR PURCHASE OF REAL ESTATE

Assignor: _____
Address: _____
City: _____ State: _____ Zip: _____
Assignee: _____
Address: _____
City: _____ State: _____ Zip: _____
Seller: _____
Address: _____
City: _____ State: _____ Zip: _____

As the assignor named above, I hereby transfer and assign to the Assignee named above
and his/her heirs, legal representatives, and assigns, all possible rights and interests I may
have in the contract between the Seller named above and myself for the purpose of selling
the real estate described below. This assignment is subject to the covenants, conditions,
and payments therein contained:
[Description of Real Estate]

As the assignor, I now authorize and empower assignee to be able to demand and receive
from the seller the deed promised to be given in the contract through the process of performing all the above-mentioned covenants, conditions, and payments. I therefore assign
all the powers I would have had to execute this covenant if I had not assigned these right
and interests to an assignee.

Dated_____, 20_____.

ACCEPTANCE BY ASSIGNEE

As the above listed assignee I hereby accept the contracted assignment. In my acceptance to the terms laid out above I agree to perform all obligations that would have been performed by the assignor. I understand that I will be under the same contract and will abide by the terms and conditions stated therein. This contract will indemnify the assignor against any liability arising from the performance or nonperformance of any contracted obligations stated therein.

Signature of Assignee _____

Dated_____, 20_____.

CONSENT BY SELLER

As the above listed Seller, I also agree to the assignment of the contract to the Assignee listed above.

Signature of Seller_____

Dated_____, 20____.

ASSIGNMENT OF LEASE AND CONSENT

Date: _____

Tenant: _____

Assignee: _____

Landlord: _____

This Assignment is made on the above-listed date by and between the Tenant, Assignee, and the Landlord all listed above.

Whereas by the Lease Agreement that was signed on _____ (date) and made between the aforementioned Landlord and Tenant, the Landlord had leased to the Tenant the Property located at _____ from _____ (start date) until the expiration of the Lease Agreement on _____ (expiration date) and was subject to the terms, conditions, and obligations contained within the Lease Agreement;

Also Whereas the Tenant hereby would like to assign to the aforementioned Assignee and the Assignee would like to receive, an assignment of all the Tenant's rights, title, and interest in and to the aforementioned Lease Agreement;

And Whereas in conformity with terms and conditions of said Lease Agreement, the Landlord must provide prior written consent to the Assignment desired by the Tenant of which the Landlord is ready and willing to provide;

WITNESSETH that in concern of the Property and for good and valuable consideration, the acceptance and adequacy of which is hereby acknowledged, all parties hereby agree to the following terms and conditions:

1. Tenant hereby assigns to the Assignee all of his/her lease hold interest in the Property, together with the remainder of the term of the Lease agreement and all benefits, advantages, and responsibilities that are derived from this agreement and to provide all the same to the Assignee, subject to the requirements of rental payments and execution of the covenants and conditions contained within the Tenant's Lease Agreement.

2. The Tenant hereby represents and warrants to the Assignee the following:

    a. Besides any act of the Tenant, the Lease Agreement is in good standing and all rental payments are current and up-to-date. Tenant represents that he/she has followed all conditions set forth within the Lease agreement.

    b. The Landlord has not given a notice to the Tenant for termination of the Lease Agreement, and neither has the Tenant given notice to the Landlord to terminate the Lease Agreement.

    c. The Tenant has full authority and rights to assign the Lease Agreement and his/her interest in the Property according to the intent of this Assignment.

    d. Subject to the rental payment due as described in the Lease Agreement, the Assignee has the right to enter and occupy the Property for the remainder of the Lease Agreement term as outlined above. Assignee may also renew the Lease Agreement for his or her own benefit, should Assignee and Landlord agree to renewal.

    e. The Tenant has not provided the Landlord with any written notice of intention to renew the Lease term.

3. The Assignee agrees herewith to all terms, conditions, and obligations of the Lease Agreement as if the Assignee had been the originating Tenant into the Lease with the Landlord.

4. The Landlord hereby agrees to this Assignment from the Tenant to the Assignee and hereby acknowledges that the Lease Agreement is in good standing and valid and that Assignee has the right to renew the lease. This consent of the Landlord is limited to the Assignee and Assignee is hereby prohibited from subletting the property without prior written consent from the Landlord. Landlord reserves the right to grant or reject the application for subletting.

IN WITNESS WHEREOF all parties hereby execute this Agreement as of this first date written above.

_____	_____
Landlord	Witness for Landlord
_____	_____
Tenant	Witness for Tenant
_____	_____
Assignee	Witness for Assignee

ASSIGNMENT INDORSED ON LEASE

Date: _____

Lessor: _____

Lessee (Assignor):_____

Assignee: _____

Address: _____

City: _____ State: _____ Zip: _____

The undersigned Lessee, described in the attached Lease Agreement, hereby assigns all rights, title, and interest in and to such Lease to _____,
_____'s heirs, executors, administrators, successors, and assigns.
Upon written consent to this assignment by the Lessor, Lessee guarantees that Assignee, or Assignee's heirs, executors, administrators, successors, or assigns, will fulfill all the
agreements and conditions required of the Lessee or Assignee in the attached Lease. In
the event that the Assignee fails to fulfill any of the agreements and conditions of the attached Lease, this assignment does not modify or limit in any way the obligations of this
Assignor (Lessee) under the Lease. The Lessor or Lessor's heirs, executors, administrators,
successors, or assigns retain the right to seek the same legal remedy against this Assignor,
including the confession of judgment for moneys due under the terms of this Lease, as
if this assignment had not been made. The Lessee (Assignor) waives all right to any and
all notice from Lessor, Lessor's heirs, executors, administrators, or assigns, of agreements
broken by Assignee; or for rent or moneys due from Assignee, Assignee's heirs, executors,
administrators, successors, or assigns; or of assignment made by Assignees or them.

The Lessee (Assignor) agrees that if the Lessor takes any remedy against the Assignee
or Assignee's guarantor, this shall not preclude the Lessor from taking the same remedy
against the Lessee (Assignor) at the same or different times. The Lessor shall be entitled to
only one satisfaction for any debts or obligations that may accrue under the terms of the
attached Lease, or any assignment, extension or renewal of the attached Lease, or from
any holdover after termination of the Lease, or which may arise from the breach of any
agreement in the Lease.

Date: _____ *(month, day, year)*

Signature of Lessor: _____

Signature of Lessee (Assignor): _____

Signature of Assignee: _____

WITNESS: _____

STATE OF _____, COUNTY OF _____

The foregoing instrument was acknowledged before me, this _____ day of
_____, 20 _____.

_____ Notary Public

My Commission Expires: _____

ASSIGNMENT OF OPTION
TO PURCHASE REAL ESTATE

Assignor: _____
Address: _____
City: _____ State: _____ Zip: _____
Assignee: _____
Address: _____
City: _____ State: _____ Zip: _____

For the Value Received, the Assignor above hereby assigns to the Assignee all of the rights and interest of the assignor in the Agreement dated _____ in which the Assignor was provided with the option to purchase from _____ of _____, real estate described as _____
_____

at the price of $_____ and under all the terms and obligations enclosed within.

The option to purchase begins on _____ (date) at _____ (time) and is available until _____ (date) at _____ (time).

The Assignor, by acceptance and signing of this Agreement, hereby grants to the Assignee all rights to accept or decline the option to purchase in good faith and grants the Assignee the rights to recover any moneys Assignor has deposited in order to receive the option.

_____
Assignor Signature

_____
Assignee Signature

NOTARY
State of _____
County of_____
Sworn to and subscribed before me, a Notary Public, for the State of _____
County of _____
This _____ day of _____ 20_____
By: _____
Notary Public
My Commission Expires: This _____day of _____, 20 _____

ASSIGNMENT OF REAL ESTATE
PURCHASE AND SALE AGREEMENT

Assignor: _____
Address: _____

City: _____ State: _____ Zip: _____
Assignee: _____
Address: _____
City: _____ State: _____ Zip: _____
Buyer: _____
Address: _____
City: _____ State: _____ Zip: _____
The Assignor (named above) and the Assignee (named above) have made this agreement
on _____ day of_____, 20_____.

WITNESSETH:
The Assignor has previously entered into a contract for Real Estate Purchase and Sale
Agreement in which the Seller (named above) and the Assignor was named as the Buyer.
This contract was executed on _____, by said Assignor and on_____, by the above
named Seller the purpose of selling real Property, which is located in _____ (County),
_____ (State), will be attached and referred to as Exhibit "A."

As the Assignor, I agree to assign, transfer, sell, and convey to the above named Assignee
all of my rights and interests provided by before mentioned Real Estate Purchase and Sale
Agreement; and, it is assumed that the Assignee desires to be assigned all of the rights
provided by the prior Real Estate Purchase and Sale Agreement;

It is agreed that the payment of _____ dollars ($_____) has been re-
ceived and is sufficient and I therefore assign, transfer, sell, and convey all of my rights and
interest in the property mentioned in the Real Estate Purchase and Sale Agreement.

By signing this agreement, the Assignee agrees to take on all my duties and obligations
mentioned in the Real Estate Purchase and Sale Agreement.

This Contract is binding and transfers all benefits to Assignee and its successors, heirs,
and assigns.

The Contract has been witness and has been signed, sealed, and delivered upon this
date.

_____
Assignor

_____
Assignee

AGREEMENT TO ACQUIRE PURCHASE OPTION

Date: _____
Broker: _____
Address: _____
City: _____ State: _____ Zip: _____
Customer: _____

Address: _____

City: _____ State: _____ Zip: _____

This contract is hereby in force and effect as of the date listed above by and between the aforementioned Broker and Customer.

1. Broker's Functions

The customer sanctions the dealer to act as _____ (His/Her) agent to get an option from _____, of _____ (Address), to purchase property located at _____ (Address), owned by _____ in fee simple and _____ (Unburdened by easements, or hampered only by the following easements: _____), at a price of _____ ($_____) or less.

2. Broker's Payment

The customer guarantees to pay the dealer a payment of _____ ($_____) or _____ percent for procurement of the stated option.

3. Conditions for Entitlement to Payment

The agreement to compensate dealer the payment is specifically conditioned on:

1. Ability of _____ to express a charge plain title;

2. A determination that the property does in fact obey the rules of the legal description set forth above; and

3. A determination that the property is in fact unfettered by easements other than as set forth above.

4. Failure to Implementation Alternative

Customer specifically comprehends and agrees that _____ (His/Her) failure to carrying out an option for any grounds other than an imperfection noted above will not damage dealers right to the payment established in this contract. The payment will remain owed _____ days after delivery to customer of the option.

5. Term of Contract

This contract shall end _____ days from the above written effectual date. They at that time must return the funds tendered pursuant to this agreement for use in procuring an option.

The broker has no right to a payment for any alternative completed after _____ days from the above written effectual date

6. Customer not to Hinder with Organization

The customer hereby consents that _____ (He/She) will not speak with or impede in any way during the term of this contract and agrees that dealers payment will be due and will be paid if any violation by customer of this agreement stops dealer from getting an option.

7. Governing Law

It is agreed that this contract shall be governed and imposed in agreement with the laws of the State of _____.

8. Broker's Agreements

a. Broker recognizes receipt of _____ ($_____) intended to obtain the option.

b. Broker additional agreements to act as the customer would with respect to negotiations dealing with _____.

c. Broker must keep a record of all activities pertinent to negotiations with _____ _____ and to keep such records for _____ years after this agreement.

In witness whereof, each group to this contract has caused it to be performed at _____ _____ (Location) on _____ (Date).

_____   _____
Broker Signature   Date

_____   _____
Customer Signature   Date

AGREEMENT FOR PURCHASE AND SALE OF A BUSINESS

Date: _____

Purchaser: _____

Address: _____

City: _____ State: _____ Zip: _____

Seller: _____

Address: _____

City: _____ State: _____ Zip: _____

This agreement is entered into on _____ (date) between _____ (Seller), doing business as _____, with its primary place of business at _____ _____,

AND _____ (Purchaser) residing at _____.

The Seller is the owner of a business known as _____ _____, with its principal office situated at:

Address: _____

City: _____ State: _____ Zip: _____

of _____ and other miscellaneous items, and in operating this business, has developed a reputation and following and has accumulated certain assets more fully described hereafter.

The Purchaser has expressed an interest in the acquisition of the business of the Seller; and the Seller desires to sell to Purchaser, and Purchaser desires to purchase from Seller, the _____ under the terms and conditions set forth in this Agreement.

In consideration of the mutual promises and conditions contained in this Agreement, and intending to be legally bound by it, the parties agree as follows:

1. Sale of Business.

The Seller agrees to sell to the Purchaser and the Purchaser agrees to purchase and acquire from the Seller, all of the right, title, and interest of the Seller in and to the retail sales business, _____, including, without limitation, all inventory and stock-in-trade, as listed in Exhibit "A" attached to this document; certain equipment, as listed in Exhibit "B" attached to this document; office equipment, furniture, computers, software, signage, shelving, cabinets, supplies, and all other items of tangible property located in the Seller's place of business and utilized in conjunction with the operation of the partnership of the Seller, as listed in Exhibit "C" attached to this document; and the good will of the Seller, together with the customer records and customer files, and the manufacturer records and manufacturer files that the Seller has maintained in conjunction with the operation of the sole proprietorship.

2. Purchase Price.

The total purchase price to be paid by Purchaser to Seller shall be _____ ($_____) U.S. dollars.

3. Payment of Purchase Price.

Upon the execution of this Agreement, the Purchaser shall pay to the Seller the sum of _____ Dollars ($_____), against the purchase price ("Purchase Price"), with the balance of the Purchase Price ($_____) to be paid by the Purchaser to the Seller at the Closing as follows:

a) _____ dollars ($_____) to be paid by certified funds, cashier's check, wire transfer or other acceptable means of payment; and

b) A Note, attached as Exhibit "D" to this document, to the Seller from the Purchaser for _____ dollars ($_____), which shall be secured by a security interest in the inventory on-hand at the store at _____ _____, as documented in a Security Agreement, attached as Exhibit "E" to this document, and a Financing Statement, attached as Exhibit "F" to this document.

The term of the Note shall be ten (10) years with a two (2) year balloon payment from the date of Closing. If the Purchaser pays the remaining principal balance in full within twelve (12) months after the date of Closing, the Seller shall discount the remaining principal balance then owed by five percent (5%). The first payment due on the Note shall be sixty (60) days after the date of Closing.

4. Allocations.

The Seller and the Purchaser hereby agree that the Purchase Price shall be allocated as provided in this Agreement, and that the following allocations are fair and reasonable and the product of the terms of this sale negotiated between the Seller and the Purchaser:

Inventory	$_____,000.00
Fixtures, Signage & Computers	$_____,000.00
Goodwill, Trademark	$_____,000.00
Non-compete Covenant	$_____,000.00
Total	$_____,000.00

5. Goodwill.

At the Closing, the Seller shall transfer all of the Seller's good will to the Purchaser with respect to the Seller's operation of the business, including the trade name _____ and the domain name www._____.com. Furthermore, at Closing the Seller shall assign to the Purchaser, all of the right, title and interest of the Seller in and to the telephone number utilized by the Seller with respect to the Seller's business.

6. Seller Assistance & Training.

The Seller agrees to assist and train the Purchaser with respect to the operation of the business known as _____ following the date of Closing for a period of three-hundred sixty (360) days, and shall endeavor to make the acquisition by the Purchaser as smooth as possible. The Seller shall familiarize the Purchaser with all aspects of the business of the Seller's customers so as to develop the best possible rapport between the Purchaser and the customers of the Seller.

7. Warranties.

The Seller warrants and represents to the Purchaser, both now and after the Closing, that the Seller is the sole owner of the business and its assets, free and clear of any and all liens and encumbrances, and free and clear of the claims of any person. The Seller makes no other warranties except any that might be set forth in this agreement, and all other warranties, express or implied, are hereby disclaimed.

The Seller hereby expressly disclaims any and all other express or implied warranties. Any affirmations of fact or promises made by the Seller shall not be deemed as any express guarantee that the tangible property will conform to any such affirmation or promise. Any description of the tangible property is for the sole purpose of identifying the tangible property, and shall not be construed as an express warranty that the tangible property shall conform to the description. No affirmation or promise, or description, shall be considered as part of the agreement between the parties hereto. The Seller further expressly disclaims any implied warranty of merchantability, and any warranty of fitness of the tangible property for any particular purpose, and the parties agree that there are no warranties that extend beyond the provisions of this paragraph. The tangible property is sold "as is" and "where is."

8. Accounts Receivable.

The Seller shall retain all accounts receivable from the operation of the business, except for items on lay-a-way at the time of Closing, for which the Purchaser shall be entitled to receive any remaining payment(s) due on that merchandise from the date of Closing and thereafter. The Seller shall be entitled to collect all accounts receivable at any and all times following the Closing. The Purchaser shall fully cooperate with the Seller with respect to the Seller's efforts to collect all accounts receivables due the Seller.

9. Transfer Documents.

The Seller shall transfer title to the partnership and the assets thereof to the Purchaser, by means of a Bill of Sale and an Assignment, copies of which are attached as Exhibits "G" and "H" to this document.

10. Liabilities.

The Seller shall pay all trade debts and any other liabilities incurred by the operation of the business at, or prior to, the Closing. Any trade debts or similar liabilities materializing after the Closing that are lawfully the responsibility of the Seller shall be presented to the Seller for immediate payment.

11. Lease of Building Contingency.

If, prior to Closing, the Purchaser, after reasonable good-faith efforts, has not been able to negotiate a new five (5) year lease with an optional five (5) year extension between the Purchaser and Landlord of the business premises for _____ dollars ($_____) per month for the first five (5) year term plus the reasonable cost of utilities attributable to_____, then this Agreement shall be null and void and the Purchaser's deposit money of $_____ shall be refunded by _____, 20___.

12. Financing Contingency.

If prior to Closing, the Purchaser, after reasonable good-faith efforts, has not been able to secure a personal loan for at least _____ dollars ($____,000) so as to enable the Purchaser to make the first payment at Closing in accordance with provision a) of Paragraph 3 of this Agreement, then this Agreement shall be null and void and the Purchaser's deposit money of $_____ shall be refunded by _____, 20____.

13. Further Assurances and Mutual Cooperation.

Each of the parties to this Agreement assures the other that they will mutually cooperate in all respects at any and all times hereafter, and that they will further execute and deliver to each other all documents requested, within reason, to substantiate and document the proper, expedient and convenient sale of the business of the Seller and the transition as set forth in this Agreement.

14. Conduct of Business.

The Seller shall continue to conduct the business as normal in every respect through the date of the sale.

15. Bulk Sales Compliance.
The Seller shall comply with all bulk sales requirements with regard to the sale of the business of the Seller to the Purchaser as provided for in this Agreement.

16. The Closing and Closing Date.
The Closing shall occur on _____, 20_____ ("Closing Date"), at the offices of_____, located at: _____.

17. Non-compete Covenant.
In consideration of the business being undertaken by the Purchaser under the terms of this Agreement, the Seller hereby agrees that they will not, directly or indirectly, for their own account or for the account of others, engage in a similar business, for a period of five (5) years following the Closing, in _____ County or in any county adjacent thereto.

18. Notices.
Any notice, communication, request, or reply (severally and collectively called "Notice") required or allowed by this Agreement to be made by either party to the other must be in writing and may be served by registered or certified mail, return receipt requested, or by delivering the notice in person to such party to the addresses set forth in opening paragraphs of this Agreement, or to any other address indicated in writing by either party. Notice sent by mail as described above shall be effective only when received by the party to be notified.

19. Paragraph Headings.
Paragraph headings contained in this Agreement are for reference purposes only and shall not be used in any way to interpret this Agreement.

20. Execution in Complements and Counterparts.
This Contract may be executed in counterparts or by two or more complements, each of which shall be considered an original and all of which together shall comprise one and the same instrument. If executed by faxed signatures, this Contract will be effective as of the date of the last signature.

21. Heirs and Assigns.
The agreements contained in this contract are binding upon the Owner and Agent and their respective heirs, successors, legal representatives, and assigns.

22. Prior Agreements.
This document contains the entire agreement between the Owner and the Agent. No prior agreements, verbal statements, or understandings pertaining to any of the matters in this Agreement shall be effective for any purpose.

23. Amendment and Waiver.
This Agreement may be amended or modified at any time and in all respects by an instrument in writing executed by Purchaser and Seller.

24. Expenses.

Each of the parties shall be responsible for any and all expenses incurred by them in connection with this Agreement, and in the consummation of the transactions contemplated
hereby and in preparation thereof.

25. Choice of Law.

This Agreement, the construction of its terms, and the interpretation of the rights and duties of the parties shall be governed by the laws of the State of _____.

26. Survival of Obligations.

All covenants and obligations of the Purchaser and Seller as set forth in this Agreement
shall survive Closing and any termination of this Agreement.

PURCHASER: _____

WITNESS: _____

SELLER: _____

WITNESS: _____

STATE OF _____, COUNTY OF _____

The foregoing instrument was acknowledged before me, this

_____ day of _____, 20 _____.

_____ Notary Public

(SEAL) State of _____

My Commission Expires: _____

ASSIGNMENT OF RENTS BY LESSOR WITH REPURCHASE AGREEMENT

Lease Date: _____

Assignor/Lessor: _____

Address: _____

City: _____ State: _____ Zip: _____

Assignee/Lessee: _____

Address: _____

City: _____ State: _____ Zip: _____

Property Description: _____

Both parties agree that all rent and related income that is or will be payable to the assignor
is hereby transferred to the assignee in accordance with the abovementioned lease.

The abovementioned lease and rental property, as well as all related rights and interests,
are owned by the assignor. Assignor therefore has the right to make this assignment. The
aforementioned lease is authentic and legally binding.

The following are the only claims, encumbrances, liens, or set-offs relating to the property
and any income it produces:

Balance of Unpaid Rent as of Date of Assignment: $_____.
Next Payment Due Date: _____.

Assignor shall continue to perform all lessor lease obligations. Assignee shall be held harmless in the event of any failure to uphold such obligations.

Assignor will partake in no transaction of any kind regarding the lease without assignee's prior written consent.

Assignee is hereby granted discretion regarding collection of rent and any other monies due under the lease. This includes the right to grant extensions.

The right to require the assignee to proceed against the lessee or seek out any other solution is hereby waived by the assignor.

Assignor hereby waives any right to security deposits that may be deposited with assignee until payment of all lessee debts under the lease have been made to assignee.

Direct proceeding or proceeding independent of lessee against assignor by assignee may take place. In the event that the lessee becomes no longer liable by reason other than complete payment, the liability of the assignor shall not be affected. The liability of the assignor shall also not be affected by any substitution of security, forbearance of acceptance, release, extension, or suspension or impairment of assignees rights or remedies against lessee.

Timely, due payment under the lease terms is hereby guaranteed by the assignor. Upon any default on the part of the lessee, the assignor shall, on demand, pay the total unpaid rent balance under the lease, thereby repurchasing the assigned rights.

Assignee is hereby appointed attorney-in-fact by assignor, with full rights to demand, enforce, and receive payment; to issue releases, receipts, and satisfactions; and to sue for any monies owed in the name of either the assignee or assignor.

Assignee is free to give notice of assignment at any time. Assignor shall immediately transmit any payment made to assignor under the lease to assignee.

Except in the event that there is payment in full of any obligation, the payment of which is secured by it, or assignee releases such obligation in writing, this assignment cannot be revoked and shall remain in effect.

_____   _____
Assignor   Date

_____   _____
Assignee   Date

ASSIGNMENT BY BUYER
SUBJECT TO SELLER'S CONSENT

Assignor: _____

Address: _____

City: _____ State: _____ Zip: _____

Buyer: _____

Address: _____

City: _____ State: _____ Zip: _____

Assignee: _____

Address: _____

City: _____ State: _____ Zip: _____

I, the Assignor/Buyer named above, agree to give the Assignee named above all of the right, title and interest and hold in and to and under a prior agreement made on _____ *[date]*. This agreement was between myself and the seller. This agreement is to abide by the express condition precedent that the written consent of the Seller names above.

I, the Assignor/Buyer, agree not to take any action that could in any way hinder or delay by direct or indirect without getting the permission of the Seller named above. I further agree to process any documents that may be necessary as requested by the Assignee above with the express purpose to effect the assignment and/or consent.

If the Assignee above decides to initiate any action in respect of the assignment, I now grant the irrevocable power and authority to initiate any proceeding or action under my name or anyone working on my behalf, with the understanding that any expenses incurred by any such action be at the expense of the above named Assignee. Further, it is agreed that the above named Assignee will be responsible for any costs incurred against myself in any such action.

I agree that my assignment to the above named Assignee is with the expectation that Assignee can reasonably carry out the terms of the agreement as set forth. The above named Assignee will accept they are able to perform all of the duties and obligations normally performed by myself and that if there rises an occasion that consent is not or cannot be obtained, a written notice needs to be sent to me and the assignee may perform these duties after 30 days have elapsed.

_____   _____

Assignee Signature   Date

_____   _____

Assignor Signature   Date

And if applicable,

_____   _____

Buyer Signature   Date

AGREEMENT TO EXTEND PERIOD OF OPTION

Date: _____
Seller: _____
Buyer: _____

The abovementioned parties agree that the period of option date is hereby extended from _____ to _____. This extension is made in consideration of the buyer's additional payment of $_____ made to the seller.

Location of Signing:
Date of Signing:

_____   _____
Seller   Witness

_____   _____
Buyer   Witness

CONTRACT FOR SALE OF INTEREST OF BUYER

Date: _____
Seller: _____
Address: _____
City: _____ State: _____ Zip: _____
Buyer: _____
Address: _____
City: _____ State: _____ Zip: _____

This Contract is hereby made on this date by and between the above-listed Seller and Buyer.

1. By a contract in writing signed on _____ (date), the Seller acquired from _____, for a purchase price of $_____, of which he/she paid a deposit in the amount of $_____, all that freehold domain situated at _____, and now in the occupation of _____ _____; and Seller has agreed to sell the same to Buyer, who by this contract agrees to acquire at the amount of $_____ all his/her right, benefit, and interest whatsoever of and in the property under or by integrity of the contract:

2. In respect of the deposit of the Buyer paid to the Seller in the amount of $_____, and in consideration of the contracts on the part of Buyer contained below, Seller further agrees with Buyer that, on compensation of the remainder of the acquired money as mentioned below, he/she will, at the request, costs, and charges of Buyer in all things, effectually discharge and cause to be communicated all his/her right and interest of and in the premises, under or by goodness of the before recited agreement, as also the fee-simple of the premises, free from all charges and burdens, unto Buyer, his/

her heirs or assigns, or as he/she or they shall direct, the drafts of such conveyance which have first been approved by the Seller's attorney.

3. Buyer further consents, on taking such delivery of the premises as provided above, to duly compensate the residue of the $_____ to the original seller, according to the above narrated contract; and will duly complete the contract on the part of Seller in all other respects, and compensate all costs and operating costs whatever of, attending, and incident to the acquisition, and to such deliveries and guarantees as provided above.

4. Buyer also agrees to at his/her own expense indemnify seller for all losses, damages, costs, and expenses whatever of and attending the conveyance of the estate and otherwise in respect of it, and also from and against all proceedings and other actions whatever on account or in admiration of it under or by good quality of the narrated contract.

5. In addition it is agreed that if the aforementioned contract shall not, for any reason whatever, be accordingly executed, this agreement shall become invalid, and the surplus of the deposit money compensated by Buyer as provided shall be reimbursed to him/her by Seller, together with all operating costs incurred, and all losses and damages sustained by him/her under or by virtue of this contract.

6. For the due presentation of this agreement each party obliges himself to the other of them in the punitive amount of $_____, which shall be recoverable as settled damages concerning them under or by virtue of this contract.

Location of Signing: _____
Date of Signing: _____

_____   _____
Seller   Witness
_____   _____
Buyer   Witness

PERCENTAGE ON REFERRALS CONTRACT

Date: _____

I, _____, (Agent) agree to pay _____ (Broker), _____ percent of a total sale of any property that _____ (Broker) transmits to my office as a listing to be sold. I agree to pay _____ percent only if the property that was sent to be listed was sold.

_____   _____
Agent Signature   Date

_____   _____
Broker Signature   Date

AGREEMENT TO SHARE REFERRAL COMMISSIONS

Date: _____

Broker: _____

Address: _____

City: _____ State: _____ Zip: _____

Sales Representative: _____

Address: _____

City: _____ State: _____ Zip: _____

The Broker and Sales Representative agree to the following terms and conditions:

Duration of Agreement: _____

Days Written Notice Required for Termination of Agreement by either Party:

_____

The Sales Representative will introduce everyone interested in buying property to the Broker.

When referral by the sales representative leads to a sale by the Broker, the Broker will pay the sales representative ____ percent (%) of Broker's commission.

Location of Agreement Signing:

_____

Broker Signature   Date

_____

Sales Representative Signature   Date

CONDOMINIUM PURCHASE AGREEMENT

Seller: _____

Address: _____

City: _____ State: _____ Zip: _____

Buyer: _____

Address: _____

City: _____ State: _____ Zip: _____

Condominium Location:

Unit:

Parking Space Number:

Agreement:

Buyer chooses the title to be listed in one of the following manners:
___ Sole Tenant
___ Joint Tenants with rights of Survivorship
___ Tenants in Common
___ Other _____

The above name Seller agrees to reserve the condominium for the Buyer for the consideration of the sum dollars.

The Buyer in return agrees that the above mentioned unit may not be built and be in the planning stage. Buyer agrees to take possession as long as the conditions for feasibility or approvability of the project, the dates of construction or occupancy, and the purchase price, closing, and other expenses of purchase are met.

The Buyer will have priority over other future Buyers in choosing the exact unit. The Buyer understands that the choice of unit must be made within three days of the Seller's written request of the Buyer's choice. The Buyer further understands that once a unit is chosen that all of the information about the unit, parking space, and actual location of the unit shall be added to this agreement. The Buyer shall initial the additions to the agreement about the location of the actual unit to be occupied.

The Buyer understands that if a unit is not chosen, the Buyer will forfeit any priority of choosing a particular unit in the future. The Buyer will be given a choice of whatever units are remaining. If a unit is not chosen within six (6) business days, the Buyer understands that the Seller may be eligible for relief set out in later in the agreement. It is understood that if a unit has not been chosen and none are available, this agreement can be terminated by either Buyer or Seller, and any monies shall be refunded to the Buyer should this agreement be terminated.

Once the construction of a project has begun, any monies that were paid to reserve a unit will be escrowed as a deposit for the chosen unit by the Seller. The Buyer agrees to buy the unit from the Seller under the terms of the Declaration of Condominium and By-Laws and will be recorded in the Public Records of _____ (County), _____ (State). In the event that the Declaration of Condominium or Amendments have not been recorded, then a Site Plan and detailed Plans and Specifications that illustrate the actual location of the Unit will be attached to this agreement and will be used as reference to this agreement. The Buyer will be provided a copy of the floor plan and the unit will be built in the location specified to the dimensions agreed upon. The unit will be known as the "Property." The other units in the same building will be referred to as the "units." The Buyer agrees that any furnishings or decorations in the property are the possessions of the Seller and are used for exhibition purposes. If the Buyer wishes to purchase the items, this needs to be worked out with the Seller. The Buyer understands that other details such as the exact location of the Building in its relationship to the property and the size and location of walks and driveways may not be exactly the same the Plans.

The Price of the property is stated below:

$_____ basic Property Price, and is described in further detail in Schedule "A," which is attached to this agreement.

$_____ Price of Additions requested by the Buyer, and are described in further detail in Schedule "B," which is attached to this agreement.

$_____ Price of Custom features requested by the Buyer, and are described in further detail in Cost of custom changes, more particularly described in Schedule "C," which is attached to this agreement.

$_____ Final Price will be paid by Buyer to Seller in the following manner:

$_____ Deposit amount paid by Buyer on the execution date in order to reserve the property.

$_____ Optional deposit made by the Buyer made on _____, 20__.

$_____ Deposit made before construction begins.

$_____ The amount that the Buyer will need to finance on their first mortgage.

$_____ The balance due at closing, including any credits, adjustments and prorations.

$_____ TOTAL PURCHASE PRICE

1. The Buyer agrees and understands that the Seller is seeking to create _____ (name of the property or complex). The Seller is seeking to create a community of financially responsible and congenial residents. The Seller has the right to reject the agreement under these stipulations. Buyer agrees to allow the Seller to investigate the Buyer through means such as ordering a credit report. Buyer will hold Seller harmless any liability on account of such investigation. The Seller may accept this agreement based upon the investigation but cannot discriminate based upon the Buyer's race, creed, color, sex, age, or national origin. The Seller agrees to refund any payments already made to the Seller should the Seller reject this agreement, and this agreement shall be null and void and neither the Buyer nor the Seller will be under any further obligations.

2. The Declaration of Condominium (Declaration) and the Bylaws of the Condominium (Bylaws).

If the Declaration, Bylaws, or Amendments thereto are not recorded with the Public Records of _____County, _____State by the date of this agreement, the Buyer agrees to allow the Seller to record them with the above mention County and State. Upon completion of the Declaration and Bylaws, the Seller will provide a copy to the Buyer. The Buyer understands that the Seller may make changes to the Declaration and Bylaws as permitted by law. Such changes may not make amendments to the terms of this contract by:

a. Altering the size of the Unit.

b. Increasing the Buyer's share of common expenses.

c. Increasing the purchase price of the property.

d. Reducing the Seller's obligations to pay common expenses on unsold units.

e. Decreasing Buyers' voting rights in the Condominium Association.

f. Otherwise materially altering the rights of Buyer or the value of the Property.

The Buyer agrees to allow the Seller to make minor changes that the Seller believes may improve the Unit, minor changes in the other units and minor changes to the common areas. None of these changes may alter the physical location or design of the Buyer's unit or reduce the total number of units. The Seller agrees to provide the Buyer with copies of any portions of documents, invoices, plans, or contracts regarding such changes.

The Declaration and the Association.
Various covenants and restrictions set out in the Declaration will be imposed on the Unit and all other units in the Condominium. As stated in the Declaration, each owner of a unit within the Condominium will be a member of the Condominium Association Inc., a non-profit Corporation (the "Association"). This Association governs all the common areas within the Condominium, including the Recreational Facilities, driveways, and landscaping. The Association also makes decisions regarding all additions to units, changes in exterior colors, and other matters affecting the appearance and operation of the Condominium. The Buyer understands that a fee will be paid to the Association. Upon signing this agreement the Buyer will receive a copy of the form of the Articles of Incorporation and Bylaws of the Association.

3. Fractional Interest.
The undivided interest in the condominium project shall be referred to as the "Fractional Interest." This interest includes the fee simple title in the land as more particularly described in the condominium Declaration. The Fractional Interest will be figured using the total number of (units) located in the project.

4. The Unit Chosen by the Buyer (The Unit).
The Seller will construct the condominium project on the land described above according the agreed-upon plans created by the Architect. These plans are subject to changes or modifications when deemed necessary by the Seller. The Seller will allow the Buyer access to a final approved copy of the plans at its office during reasonable business hours. The Buyer understands that the exact color of paint, tile, carpeting, floor covering, cabinets, and appliances may be altered if their manufacturers make alterations or design changes. The Seller may change or substitute materials or equipment for similar materials and equipment of equal or greater quality than that which may be shown on the plans or listed in the specifications.

(a) Standard Package is included in the base price and includes a refrigerator/freezer/icemaker, range, heating and air conditioning, water heater, dishwasher, garbage disposal, washer and dryer, along with any other items described in Schedule "A," which is attached to this agreement.

(b) Items that are not included in the base price may be purchased at an additional cost. The cost and description of all options are listed in Schedule "B" which is attached to this document.

5. Buyer's Choices.
Buyer shall submit to the Seller, in writing, his/her choice of colors, fixtures, and/or materials offered by Seller for the subject Unit within two weeks of the execution of this

agreement. The Buyer understands that if these selections are not submitted within the specified period, the Seller then has the right to use its own judgment in such selections.

6. Deletions.

Any deletions of carpeting, appliances, or other features pertaining to the Unit must be submitted by the Buyer in writing to the Seller within two weeks of the execution of this agreement.

7. Custom Changes.

The Buyer may select custom changes to the basic plan and submit these to the Seller for Seller's approval. The Seller shall review these changes and provide the Buyer a new estimated price within two weeks of the Buyer's submission. Both the Buyer and Seller must sign a written agreement detailing the changes before they are made. In the event that changes are made to this additional work, the contract price shall be modified only as set out in a written custom change order. If approved by both parties, the detailed changes should be included in Schedule "C," which will be attached to this contract.

(a) Custom Changes to the Structure of the Unit. If the Buyer is requesting a structural change to the unit, then a request must be submitted to both the Seller and the Condominium Association. The Buyer must submit a written request to the Seller and the Condominium Association along with two (2) copies of all necessary plans and specifications, including materials and colors. The Seller and the Condominium Association have 30 days to approve or deny the changes and must send a written decision to the Buyer by hand delivery or by certified mail. The Seller reserves the right to deny any changes to the structure of the unit. If the Condominium Association or the Seller does not send a reply during the 30-day period, the application for custom changes is assumed to be denied.

(b) Cost Advance Deposit. A non-refundable deposit will be required to cover the costs of any approved custom changes.

(c) Changes. If the Buyer wishes to make any changes to this agreement or to the construction of the Unit, the Buyer must notify and get permission of the Seller. Buyer cannot make, or have made on his behalf, any agreement or contract for any purpose whatsoever with any person(s) other than the Seller.

8. Recreational Facilities.

Recreational Facilities may be included in the Condominium; such facilities will be shown in the Plans.

9. Subordination.

The Buyer understands that all rights granted under the terms and conditions of this Agreement are subject and subordinate to the lien of any mortgage that is taken out to finance the acquisition of the land, the cost of construction, or other costs incurred during construction including the cost of services incidental to construction, and to any and all cash advances that may become a lien under the terms of such a mortgage or under any other agreement relating to land acquisition and building construction involved in this project. The Buyer agrees to execute and deliver any document required to evidence such subordination by any finance institution providing a mortgage. Buyer will appoint the

Seller the attorney-in-fact of Buyer and give Seller the power to execute and deliver any such document on behalf of Buyer if the Buyer refuses or fails to do so within a week of being given a request.

10. Closing and Title.

(a) At closing, the Seller will furnish the Buyer with an insurable fee simple title to the Unit, and an undivided interest in the common elements of Condominium Association. The following conditions apply:

(i) The provisions of the Declaration and By-Laws of the Condominium Association.

(ii) Ad valorem real property taxes for the year of closing, prorated from the date of closing.

(iii) All conditions, limitations, restrictions, reservations, and easements of record as of the date of closing. These conditions include those set forth in the Declaration and contained in the recorded plat of the Condominium, and all other matters now of record or hereafter granted by Seller. Conditions of record include matters of zoning or other restrictions imposed by governmental authorities regarding the use of the Property, so long as they do not prohibit use of the Property by the Buyer for residential purposes.

(iv) Liens or claims of lien for work, materials, or labor shall be furnished at the Buyer's request.

(b) At the time of closing, the Seller agrees to provide to any Lender of a Mortgage a title insurance commitment issued by a reputable title insurer and agent of Seller's choice. This title insurer must be licensed to do business in the State of _____. This title insurance will be paid for by the Buyer. The Lender will be provided a mortgagee title insurance policy in the amount of Lender's first mortgage. This is subject only to the exceptions permitted by this contract, the standard exceptions contained in title insurance policies, and those matters that will be discharged by the Seller at or before the date of closing and delivery of the deed. The Buyer will receive, at the Seller's expense, an owner's title insurance policy issued by a title insurer and agent selected by Seller insuring Buyer's title to the Property subject to the Permitted Exceptions.

(c) Any mortgages and liens that are encumbering the Property not of the Buyer's acts or at Buyer's direction, will be discharged or released at or prior to the closing. The Seller has the option to pay these from the closing fees, or from the proceeds of the sale.

(d) The Buyer has the right to remove anything from the deed that does not conform to the provisions of this Agreement and to which the Buyer objects, if it appears that any such objection to title is valid. The provisions that do not conform may be removed within sixty (60) days. During that period, the Buyer's obligations shall remain in full force and effect. The Seller agrees that Buyer's legally valid objection will require the Seller to bring any action or proceeding or incur any expense necessary to remove any such objection to title. Further, any attempt by Seller to cure such objection to title shall not be considered as the right to refuse delivery of the deed by the Buyer.

11. Agreement Not to Record.
Buyer understands that setting out either the existence or any terms of this Agreement among the Public Records of County, _____, shall be considered a default by Buyer under the terms of this Agreement.

12. Time for Closing and Expenses.
(a) The closing date shall be thirty (30) days or less from the date the construction of the entire Condominium Building is completed. This will be the date that the County _____ issues a Certificate of Occupancy for the entire Condominium Building. The Seller will notify the Buyer in writing five (5) days prior to the closing date.

13. Closing Fees.
(a) Ad valorem real property taxes on the Property for the year of closing shall be prorated at the closing.

(b) The following expenses and amounts will be paid by Buyer at closing:
(i) Any Lender's attorneys' fees, private mortgage insurance, title insurance for Lender, any charges for points, prepaid interest, taxes, and insurance, any escrow for taxes and insurance, or any other costs that are the result of the Buyer obtaining a loan including, without limitation, credit report fees, appraisal fees, and any other expenses, intangible taxes, and documentary stamp taxes on the mortgage and note.
(ii) Charges to County Clerk for recording the deed.
(iii) Utility deposits for the Unit.
(iv) Three (3) months of fees paid to the Condominium Association and to the Owners' Association. These fees will be based on rate from first of the month in which closing occurs.
(v) Attorney or broker fees employed by Buyer.
(vi) The fee of $_____ for a condominium unit survey.

(c) The Seller is responsible for all other standard and customary closing costs and expenses including any other fees mentioned in this agreement.

(d) Once the Buyer accepts the deed conveying the Property the Seller shall be released from every obligation under this Agreement, except those which survive the delivery of the deed because of law or because of any other obligation mentioned in this agreement.

14. Use of Premises.
The unit cannot be used for any purpose other than as a residence. Units may be rented or leased to tenants as long as they adhere to the Owners' Association and, if applicable, the condominium Association. This condition remains in force after closing. The Seller has the right to obtain an injunction preventing the Buyer from violating this clause.

15. Pre-closing Inspection.
Prior to the closing date, the Buyer may do a pre-closing inspection of the unit with the Seller or Seller's representative at an agreed-upon time. The Buyer may develop a list of items requiring completion, adjustment or repair. This list will be signed by both Buyer

and Seller. The list of items must be completed by the Seller in a reasonable time. Escrows cannot be held for any incomplete items at closing.

16. Trespass/Possession.
The Buyer cannot enter the property at any time during the construction of the unit or grounds without the express permission of the Seller. The Buyer cannot take possession of the premises until after closing. If the Buyer violates this provision, it can be deemed as a material breach of this Agreement, and the Seller can remove the Buyer from the premises by any lawful means.

17. Initial Managing Agent.
The Seller can assign a Managing Agent and the Buyer must enter into a management contract up to and including a period of five (5) years. The Seller can wield all powers of the Association and the Board and Officers of the Association until a Board is elected.

18. Default of the Buyer.
If Buyer does not make payments according to the schedule agreed upon, the Buyer can be considered in default, and the Seller has the power to terminate this agreement by written notice to Buyer. If the Buyer defaults, the amount owed to the Seller can be difficult to determine; however, the liquidated sum of the damages shall be paid in full by the Buyer. The amount of liquidated damages will be equal to or less than 15% of the total purchase price of the Property. The exception to this provision is if the Buyer has incurred additional expenses and costs due to any custom work, extras, or other improvements to the Property requested by the Buyer, in which case the Seller is entitled to these extra fees. If there are monies beyond the provisions above, the Seller will refund them to the Buyer.

19. Seller Unable to Perform.
The Seller will have sixty (60) days from the date established to perform and deliver the deed within the confines of this agreement. If the Seller cannot perform and deliver its obligation within the sixty (60) day period, the Seller will be obligated to return to the Buyer any payments made by Buyer. Upon refunding of the deposited monies to the Buyer, the rest of this agreement will be null and void.

20. Risk of Loss.
If there is any damage or loss in the Unit prior to the closing, the burden will be borne by the Seller. After the closing, the burden will be upon the Buyer.

21. Notice.
All deliveries of any item or notice between the parties concerning this agreement must be in writing and must be hand delivered, or deposited in the United States Mail, addressed to the other party at the address stated in this Agreement. All mail notices must be made by certified mail, postage prepaid, return receipt requested, and shall be deemed delivered when deposited in the United States mail.

22. Financing of the Property.

It is assumed that the Buyer intends to use a Lender to obtain a mortgage to purchase the property. If the Buyer does not seek to obtain a mortgage, then it is the Buyer's obligation to close the purchase itself. If the Lender does intend to secure a mortgage, then it is understood that the Buyer must obtain a commitment from a Lender for such financing at prevailing interest rates and terms at time of closing. This mortgage must be obtained on or before thirty (30) days from date hereof, unless extended by Seller in writing. The Buyer is obligated to deliver to the Seller a copy of the accepted loan commitment and once this commitment is made by the Lender, the Buyer is obligated to close. The Buyer is obligated to follow the guidelines set by the Lender, and if the Buyer does not follow these and cannot secure the loan, then the Buyer can be considered default. If, through good faith and due diligence, the Buyer is not able to secure the loan, then all monies deposited will be returned to the Buyer and this contract will be terminated without further obligation by either party. Buyer agrees to make application for obtaining a mortgage within five (5) days from the date of Seller's acceptance of this agreement.

23. Non-Assignability.

The Buyer understands that this agreement cannot be assigned without written approval by the Seller.

24. Effective Date.

The signature of the Sales Representative means that a deposit has been secured, but does not mean acceptance by the Seller. The Seller must sign this agreement for it to be in force and effect.

25. Disclosure of Counsel.

The Seller has used _____ as Counsel during the negotiation of this agreement. It is assumed that the Buyer has not, without previous knowledge of this, relied upon the advice of the same Counsel in the negotiation of this Agreement. This would be considered a conflict of interest, and the Buyer would be required to obtain other Counsel to represent him in these matters should a dispute arise.

26. Miscellaneous.

(a) The Buyer and the Seller agree that this Agreement is an all-inclusive document, and the Seller shall not be bound by any other agreements, verbal statements, or understandings pertaining to any of the matters in this Agreement. No part of this agreement can be altered or changed without the written acceptance by all parties.

(b) The Buyer agrees that once the Seller has accepted and delivered the deed and the tender of notice that the Unit is available for occupancy, the Seller will have fully complied with all the requirements of this Agreement, and none of the terms of this Agreement shall be further applicable.

(c) Both Buyer and Seller agree to execute any and all documents required to carry out the terms and intent of this Agreement.

(d) The Buyer and Seller understand that the section headings contained in this Agreement are included for convenience only and are not part of the agreement itself.

(e) The Buyer and Seller agree that the only valid waiver of rights will be signed by each party, even if there is a breach or failure to perform.

(f) This Agreement has been executed according to the laws of the State of_____.
The Parties hereby waive trial by jury and agree to submit to the personal jurisdiction and venue of a court of subject matter jurisdiction located in County, _____. In the event that any litigation arises from this Agreement, the parties agree that the other party will pay any costs that the prevailing party may incur including reasonable attorneys' fees. No action shall be entertained by said court or any court of competent jurisdiction if filed more than one (l) year after the date any such cause of action accrued, even if there were calculable damages at that time.

27. Deposit.
The money deposited to secure an interest in the property shall be held in escrow by _____, or another escrow agent designated by the Seller. The amount of the deposit will not exceed 10% of the purchase price and will be held until closing or until this Agreement is terminated according to the terms of the Agreement. It is understood that any deposit amount exceeding 10% of the purchase price will be used for construction purposes once construction of improvements has begun.

IN WITNESS WHEREOF, Buyer and Seller have executed this Agreement in manner and form sufficient to bind them as of the dates set forth below their respective signatures.

BUYER(S)

_____   _____

_____

Date: _____

BROKER

_____

_____

SELLER

_____ By: _____

_____ Acceptance Date: _____

SCHEDULE A
STANDARD PACKAGE SHEET
The following items are included in the standard package:
- refrigerator/freezer/icemaker
- range
- air conditioning and heating equipment
- water heater
- dishwasher

- garbage disposal
- washer and dryer
- _____
- _____

Base Price of Unit $_____

BUYER(S) _____   _____

_____   _____

SELLER

_____ by: _____

SCHEDULE B
ADDITIONAL ITEMS

Standard Package Price: $_____

Optional Items:

_____ $_____

_____ $_____

Total Cost of Optional Items: $_____

Total Purchase Price of Unit: $_____

BUYER(S) _____

SELLER _____ By: _____

SCHEDULE C
CUSTOM CHANGES

Standard Package Price: $_____

Total Cost of Optional Items: $_____

Total Cost of Custom Changes: $_____

Total Price of Unit: $_____

BUYER(S) _____

SELLER _____ By: _____

Seller: _____

Address: _____

City: _____ State: _____ Zip: _____

Buyer: _____

Address: _____

City: _____ State: _____ Zip: _____

Recitals:

Date: _____

Land: _____

Seller (A):_____

Borrower (B):_____

Since the giving of the deed, conditions that have arisen have made the redeeding to Seller (A) mutually advantageous to both parties. A will therefore release the mortgage that currently exists on the abovementioned property, return any notes that A currently holds against Borrower (B), including those with the property's first mortgage that amount to $_____. B, spouse joining, will convey the property to A by good and sufficient warranty deed.

Both parties agree to find a buyer for the property for the per-acre price of $_____, or under mutual agreement, a lesser per-acre sum of $_____, but not in excess of $_____.

After finding a purchaser, A, spouse joining, will convey to the purchaser the property and will pay to B the first monies received for the property, $_____ without interest, as a lien on the property of no more than $_____ only when the property shall have been sold.

This contract is binding to the heirs, administrators, representatives, and assigns of A, and they, or any one of them, will be obligated to pay $_____ to B whenever the property described shall have been sold.

It is agreed that all interest that B owes A to this date forthwith be canceled and that this contract shall continue for _____ years, and the sale and full settlement shall be made in that time.

_____
Seller

_____
Borrower

COUNTER OFFER

The Offer to Purchase real estate at _____,
signed by Buyer on _____ *(date)* has been countered. With the exception of the following _____, all terms and conditions are to remain unchanged. Seller agrees to sell and convey said property under the terms and conditions of this Seller's Counter-Offer. The representations and warranties set forth in this counter offer will remain in effect beyond the closing of this real estate transaction.

This Counter-Offer will expire on _____ *(TIME IS OF THE ESSENCE)* and it shall not become a binding agreement until a signed copy of the approved Counter-Offer has been either sent by United States Postal Service Certified Mail to the sellers address at __ _____ or hand delivered to the Seller.

Dated: _____
Seller(s) _____
Negotiating officer _____

The above Counter-Offer has hereby been *(accepted/countered)*. If countered, the terms and conditions set forth in the original Offer to Purchase shall remain intact and will not include any of the above-listed terms of this or any other Counter-Offer with the exception of the following_____.

This Buyer's Counter-Offer will expire on _____ *(TIME IS OF THE ESSENCE)* and it shall not become a binding agreement until a signed copy of the approved Counter-Offer has been either sent by United States Postal Service Certified Mail to the sellers address at _____ or hand delivered to the Seller.

Dated: _____
Seller(s) _____
Negotiating officer _____

If the Buyer's above Counter-Offer is accepted the Seller must sign. In the event that the Seller would like to Counter-Offer the above listed offer, Seller must do so on a new Counter-Offer form.

Dated: _____
Seller(s) _____
Negotiating officer _____

[Attach original Offer to Purchase]

HOME EQUITY PURCHASE CONTRACT

Date: _____
Seller: _____
Address: _____
City: _____ State: _____ Zip: _____
Buyer: _____
Address: _____
City: _____ State: _____ Zip: _____

I , _____(Seller), agree that on this day of _____ , 20__ , that I have received the sum of $_____ from _____ (Buyer) for the purpose of purchasing the following property:

Lot_____ Block _____ Book_____ Page_____

It is agreed the above property will be sold for $_____ and the Buyer will take the title only if the property is not burdened in the excess of:

1ST TD $____ PAYABLE $___ MONTHLY ____ % INTEREST _____ DATE
2ND TD $____ PAYABLE $___ MONTHLY ____ % INTEREST _____ DATE
3RD TD $____ PAYABLE $___ MONTHLY ____ % INTEREST _____ DATE

FULL PRICE $_____

The amount due to the seller may be deducted from the encumbrances listed above and is due _____, 20_____. Any taxes, judgments, assessments, bonds, and any other liens existing prior to the date of this Agreement will be deducted from the amount paid.

Impounds will be charged to the lending institution and not to the buyer. Any other amounts existing due to impound will be paid by the Seller. Seller agrees to create a Deed in favor of the Buyer according to local, federal, and state guidelines.

Buyer agrees that the Title and Loans are to be in his/her name. In the event that Title and Loans are not satisfactorily agreed upon, the Buyer may return the Title and Loans to the Seller without further liability, and this agreement will become null and void. The Seller has the option and ability to rescind this contract within five (5) Business Days from the stated date.

It is understood and agreed that the Buyer may be purchasing the property in order to resell it immediately. It is also understood the Buyer is purchasing the property under the current market value. In order to execute the agreement in good faith, the property mentioned above must have an appraisal value of at least $_____. This amount must be equal to or greater than the amount being paid to Seller. If it is less than the amount being paid to Seller, the difference will be deducted from the net amount owed to Seller.

The Buyer will pay both the Escrow charges and the Title fees.

The Seller will pay the cost of damages cause by termites and assessed by roof inspectors.

The Seller will agree to pay for the cost of any damage to the property that occurs after the date of this contract and is caused by the Seller and any other parties associated with the Seller.

The Seller agrees to clean the premises, remove all debris, and make sure that the property is in good repair before the Buyer takes over. It is also understood that the Seller cannot remove any real property.

The remainder of the cost of the property is due after the Title has been verified and the premises have been vacated.

The Seller will agree to allow the Buyer to take possession of the above mentioned property on or before_____.

The Seller will allow the Buyer to show the property to prospective buyers prior to taking possession of it.

This agreement has been signed, sealed, and delivered on the dates signed below.

_____
Seller

_____
Witness of Seller

_____
Witness of Seller

_____
DATE

_____
Buyer

_____
Witness of Buyer

_____
Witness of Buyer

_____
DATE

PROMISSORY NOTE A

$ _____

DATE: _____

This note is given a "Good Faith Deposit" as outlined in the attached Contract to Purchase Real Estate between _____
and _____ dated _____ relating to the property listed as _____.
When requested the undersigned, hereinafter called the Payer, promises to pay the amount of $_____ without interest, to _____ or his assigns, hereinafter call the Payee.

This note is to be payable immediately once the Payee and Payer agree to the conditions, contingencies, and inspections outlined in the said contract are met.

In the event that this note goes unpaid for any length of time and collection action is taken, the undersigning Payer agrees to pay the Payee of this note all legal fees associated with the collections efforts. These fees include, but are not limited to, cost of suit, including attorney's fees.

_____
Witness

_____
Buyer

_____
Witness

_____
Seller

PROMISSORY NOTE B

(For Delinquent Renters. This form is to be filled out at Landlord's office. This Note is legally binding, and nonpayment can result in legal action.)

FOR VALUE RECEIVED, _____of

ADDRESS _____ CITY _____

STATE _____ ZIP _____

Promise (s) to pay to the order of_____

The principal sum of _____ DOLLARS ($ _____), in US dollars, with interest commencing on this date at the rate of _____% per year. If Payment is not received within thirty days from the date of the signing of this agreement, interest shall be charged at a daily rate of $_____ per day.

All payments shall be payable at the offices of:

_____

or at any other location designated in writing by the holder of this note.

If at any point the Maker or Makers fail to make payment or otherwise comply with the terms of this agreement, the Maker or Makers are still responsible for the balance, including any and all interest and the entire amount still unpaid. If the Maker or Makers fail to make payment or break(s) the terms of this agreement, the holder has right to accelerate collection of debt. Should the holder choose to not act or exercise his right to mature the debt, this action does not constitute a waiver of his right to accelerate the debt at any time in the future.

If payment is not made within 5 days of the stated due date, a late fee of 15% of the installment (not to be less than $10.00) will be added. The holder is entitled to all costs of collection if this debt is not paid. If this note is collected through legal process, an Attorney/Collection fee of 15% of the balance (not to be less than $100.00) will be added. Each of the undersigned, whether principal, surety, guarantor, endorser, or other party, severally waives and renounces demand, protest, notice of demand, protest, and non-payment.

_____

Signatures

IN WITNESS WHEREOF,

State of _____

County of_____

Sworn to and subscribed before me, a Notary Public, for the State of _____ County

of _____

This _____ day of _____ 20_____

By: _____

Notary Public

My Commission Expires: This _____day of _____, 20 _____

PAYMENT SCHEDULE:
DATE DUE   AMOUNT   DATE DUE   AMOUNT   DATE DUE   AMOUNT

_____   _____   _____   _____   _____   _____

_____   _____   _____   _____   _____   _____

RECEIPT FOR NON-REFUNDABLE DEPOSIT

Date: _____
Buyer: _____
Seller: _____

This receipt for the sum of $_____ is for a non-refundable deposit that Buyer placed to purchase _____ by _____ from Seller, owner of above-mentioned property.

Buyer understands, acknowledges, and agrees that failure to pay to Seller the remaining $_____due by the abovementioned date, forfeits the abovementioned deposit.

Seller hereby agrees in consideration of payment of said non-refundable deposit to withdraw abovementioned property from the market until the abovementioned date and to transfer any relevant title to abovementioned property to Buyer upon receipt of the remaining amount due.

CHAPTER 3

Contractor/Subcontractor Forms, Agreements, and Checklists

BUILDING CONTRACT

Date: _____

Owner: _____

Address: _____

City: _____ State: _____ Zip: _____

Builder: _____

Address: _____

City: _____ State: _____ Zip: _____

This Agreement made between _____ (Contractor), and
_____ (Owner).

Owner is about to erect _____

On a site located at:

Address: _____

City: _____ State: _____ Zip: _____

and has employed _____, Architect, to prepare drawings
and specifications of the _____

Contractor is willing to erect _____ conforming to the drawings and specifications attached to this contract and signed by Contractor, Owner, and Architect, and in accordance with the conditions, and for the consideration set forth below.

The parties agree as follows:

1. The Contractor agrees:

A. **Contractor's Responsibilities.** To furnish all the materials and perform all of the work for the erection of a _____ building on the premises of Owner at Address: _____
City: _____ State: _____ Zip: _____
in accordance with the plans and specifications prepared by _____, Architect, signed by Owner and Contractor, and attached to and made a part of this contract.

B. **Start and Completion Dates.** To commence work on or before _____ (date), and to finish the whole of the building and deliver up the building complete in every respect according to the drawings and specifications, and to the satisfaction of the Architect, on or before _____ (date), unless that date shall be extended as provided in the terms of this agreement, or endorsed on this contract and signed by the parties; in such case, on or before the extended date.

C. **Notices and Permits.** To give all requisite notices to the proper authorities, obtain all official inspections, permits, certificates, and licenses required by the work undertaken by the Contractor, and pay all proper and legal fees.

D. **Bond.** To provide a bond covering the faithful performance of the contract and payment of all obligations arising under the contract, in the form prescribed by the Owner and with surety approved by the Owner. If the bond is required by instructions given previous to the submission of bids, the premium shall be paid by Contractor; if subsequent to submission of bids, it shall be paid by Owner.

E. **Insurance.** To maintain insurance to protect Contractor from claims under workers' compensation acts and from any other claims for damages for personal injury, including death, which may arise from operations under this contract, whether such operations are carried out directly by the Contractor or by any subcontractor, or anyone directly or indirectly employed by either of them. Certificates of insurance will be filed with Owner, and will be subject to Owner's review and approval for adequacy of protection.

F. **Hold Harmless.** To indemnify and keep Owner harmless against all loss, costs or damage arising from injury to persons or property occurring during the performance of the contract, together with any and all attorney's fees incurred by Owner on account of the injuries.

G. **Access.** To provide proper facilities to enable Owner and Architect, and their representatives, to have access to and inspect the work during its progress.

H. **Alterations to Plans.** That Owner may make any alterations, deviations, additions, or omissions from the plans and specifications, or either of them, which he [she] shall deem proper and Architect shall advise, by a written order signed by Architect and approved by Owner, without affecting or making void this contract. In all such cases, Architect shall value or appraise the cost of such alterations, and add to or deduct from the amount agreed to be paid to Contractor any excess or deficiency resulting from such alterations.

Further time may be allowed for completion of the work caused by the alterations or deviations, as the Architect judges reasonable.

I. **Termination of Employment.** Owner, on receipt of a signed report from the Architect verifying that sufficient cause exists to justify such action, may, without forfeiting any other right or remedy, and after giving _____ days' written notice to the Contractor, terminate the employment of Contractor and take possession of the premises and of all materials, tools, and appliances on the premises, if:

a) The Contractor enters bankruptcy, makes a general assignment for benefit of his [her] creditors, or if a receiver is appointed because of Contractor's insolvency.

b) Except for situations in which extension of time is allowed by Owner and Architect, the Contractor persistently or repeatedly refuses or fails to supply enough properly skilled workers or proper materials to complete the work at hand.

c) The Contractor does not pay subcontractors, suppliers of materials, or labor in a timely manner, or persistently disregards laws, ordinances, or the instructions of the Architect, or substantially violates any provision of the contract.

2. The Owner agrees:

A. **Payment.** To pay the Contractor for the fulfillment of the terms of this contract, subject to additions and deductions provided for in the contract, as follows:

_____

_____

If the quantities originally specified are changed so that application of the agreed unit price to the quantity of work performed creates a demonstrable hardship to Owner or Contractor, the contract shall be equitably adjusted to prevent such hardship.

B. **Scheduled Payments.** Owner shall make payments as provided in the contract, as follows:

On the _____ day of each month: _____% (percent) of the total value, based on contract prices, of labor and materials incorporated in the work, and of a reasonable amount of materials stored at the work site up to the _____ day of that month, as estimated by Architect, minus the aggregate of previous payments.
Upon substantial completion of the entire work: a sum sufficient to increase total payments to _____% (percent) of the contract price _____. (Here you can insert any provision made for limiting or reducing the amount retained after the work reaches a certain stage of completion).

Final payment shall be due _____ days after substantial completion of the work, provided the work is fully completed and the contract fully performed.

If after the work has been substantially completed, the Architect certifies that full completion is materially delayed for some reason beyond the control and responsibility of the Contractor, Owner shall, on receipt of certificate of Architect, and without terminating the contract, pay the balance due for the portion of work that has been fully completed and accepted. This payment shall be made according to the terms and conditions governing final payment under this agreement, except that it shall not constitute a waiver of claims.

C. **Fire Insurance.** Owner will purchase and maintain fire insurance on the entire structure on which the work of this contract is to be done and on all materials, in or adjacent to and intended for use on the structure, to at least _____ percent (____ %) of the insurable value of the structure. The loss, if any, is to be made adjustable with and payable to Owner as trustee.

3. It is further agreed between the parties as follows:

A. **Authority of Architect.** The work shall be executed under the supervision and direction of the Architect, _____, and the Architect's decisions relating to the performance of this agreement shall be final and binding on the parties except as otherwise provided in this agreement.

B. **Final Inspection.** Upon receiving written notification from Contractor that the work is ready for final inspection and acceptance, Architect shall promptly inspect the work. When Architect finds that the work is acceptable and fulfills all the terms of the contract, Architect shall promptly issue a final certificate, signed by the Architect, stating that the work provided for in this contract has been completed and is accepted by him/her under the terms and conditions of the contract, and that the entire balance due to the Contractor and noted in the final certificate, is due and payable. Before Architect issues this final certificate, Contractor shall submit evidence satisfactory to Architect that all payrolls, material bills, and other debts connected with the work have been paid.

C. **Release of Liens.** Before receiving either final payment or any part of the retained percentage, Contractor, if required, must furnish Owner with a complete release of all liens arising out of this contract, or in its place, receipts in full. If required, the release or receipts should be accompanied by an affidavit that to the Contractor's full knowledge, the releases and receipts include all labor and material for which a lien could be filed. If any subcontractor refuses to furnish a release or receipt in full, Contractor may instead substitute a bond satisfactory to Owner, to cover the payment of any lien. Contractor shall reimburse Owner for any payments that the Owner may be compelled to make in discharging any liens, including all costs and a reasonable attorney's fee, that remain unsatisfied after all payments are made.

D. **Extensions for Delays Beyond Contractor's Control.** If progress of work is delayed at any time by causes beyond Contractor's control, such as any act or neglect of Owner or Architect, or of any employee of Owner or Architect, or by any other contractor employed by Owner, or by changes ordered in the work, or by strikes, lockouts, unusual delay in transportation, unavoidable casualties, or by delay authorized by Architect pending arbitration, or by any cause which according to the Architect's determination justifies the delay, then the date of completion shall be extended at the Architect's discretion. No extension shall be made for delay occurring more than _____ days before a claim is made in writing to Architect. If a cause of delay is ongoing, only one claim is necessary.

E. **Arbitration of Disputes.** If any dispute or difference arises between Owner or his [her] Architect and Contractor, with respect to any matter arising out of, or relating to, the contract, which the Architect does not have the authority to determine, the difference or dispute shall, immediately after it has arisen, be referred for final determination to two competent persons as arbitrators, one chosen by Owner and the other by Contractor, and to an umpire named by the two arbitrators, and the award of the arbitrators, or of their umpire if they disagree, shall be final and conclusive, provided the award is made in writing signed by the arbitrators and their umpire, and ready to be delivered to Owner and Contractor, within _____ months after such a referral is arbitrators or their umpire shall recommend in a written notice under their signature. The costs and charges attending such a referral shall be under the discretion of the arbitrators or their umpire, and shall be paid as they, he or she by their, his or her award, shall direct.

F. **Assigns and Sublets.** This contract may not be assigned or sublet as a whole by either Owner or Contractor without the written consent of the other. Contractor shall not assign any moneys due or to become due to him/her under this contract, without the previous written consent of Owner.

OWNER: _____

CONTRACTOR: _____

WITNESSED BY: _____

STATE OF _____, COUNTY OF _____

The foregoing instrument was acknowledged before me, this _____ day of _____, 20 _____.

_____

Notary Public

(SEAL) State of _____

My Commission Expires: _____

[Annex plans and specifications]

AGREEMENT FOR INDEPENDENT CONTRACTOR

This Agreement is entered into as of the _____ day of _____, 20( ), between _____ [company name] ("the Company") and _____ [service provider's name] ("the Contractor").

1. Independent Contractor.

The Company engages the Contractor as an independent contractor to perform the services set forth as described in this agreement, and the Contractor hereby accepts all the terms and conditions of this Agreement.

2. Duties, Term of Contract, and Compensation.

The Contractor has previously submitted an estimate, attached as Exhibit A, which details the Contractor's duties, term of engagement, compensation and provisions for payment of compensation. Changes to this agreement can be made only in writing. The agreement may also be supplemented with estimates for services to be rendered by the Contractor and agreed to by the Company. All amendments and supplements will be made a part of this document to be used for reference. All amendments and supplements are to be initialed by both parties.

3. Expenses.

During the term of this Agreement, the Company will reimburse Contractor for all reasonable and approved out-of-pocket expenses incurred in connection with the performance of the Contractor's duties under this Agreement. The Contractor shall be promptly reimbursed upon submission of a bill detailing these expenses. Contractor will not be compensated for time and expenses for traveling to and from Company facilities under this agreement.

4. Progress Reports.

Consultant may be required to provide, on a monthly basis, project plans, progress reports, and/or a final results report. When project is completed, Consultant will submit a final results report to the Company in a form and containing the information and data that is reasonably requested by the Company.

5. Confidentiality.

The Contractor acknowledges that in carrying out the responsibilities required by this Agreement, he/she may have access to various trade secrets, inventions, innovations, processes, information, records and specifications owned, used, or licensed by the Company and/or used by the Company in connection with the operation of its business. These include, without limitation, the Company's business and product processes, methods, customer lists, accounts, and procedures. The Contractor agrees not to disclose any of these either directly or indirectly, or to use any of them in any manner, either during the term of this Agreement or at any time after the end of this Agreement, except as required in the course of this engagement with the Company. All files, records, documents, blueprints, specifications, information, letters, notes, media lists, original artwork/creative, notebooks, and similar items relating to the business of the Company, whether prepared by the Contractor or otherwise coming into his or her possession, are the exclusive property of the Company. The Contractor agrees not to keep any copies of the foregoing without the Company's prior written permission. Upon the expiration or termination of this Agreement, or at any time requested by the Company, the Contractor shall immediately turn over to the Company all such files, records, documents, specifications, information, and other items in his or her possession or under his/her control. The Contractor further agrees not to disclose information about his/her retention as an independent contractor or the terms of this Agreement to any person without the prior written consent of the Company and shall at all times preserve the confidential nature of his/her relationship to the Company and of the services he provides.

6. Conflicts of Interest; Non-hire Provision.

The Contractor warranties that he/she is free to enter into this Agreement. The Contractor's signature below represents that this engagement does not violate the terms of any agreement between the Contractor and any third party. During the entire term of this agreement, the Contractor agrees to devote his/her productive time, energy, and abilities to the performance of his/her duties under this Agreement at the level required to complete the Contractor's duties under this Agreement successfully and on time.

7. Right to Contractual Employment.

The Contractor is expressly free to perform services for other parties while performing services for the Company under this Agreement. The Contractor agrees that for a period of six months following any termination, the Contractor shall not, directly or indirectly hire, solicit, or encourage any employee, consultant, or contractor of the Company to leave the Company's employment. Within one year of his/her leaving Company's employment or contractual engagement, the Contractor will not hire any employee, consultant, or contractor who has left the company.

8. Right to Injunction.

All parties to this Agreement acknowledge that the services rendered by the Contractor under this Agreement and the rights and privileges granted to the Company under the Agreement are of a special, unique, unusual, and extraordinary character that gives them a peculiar value, the loss of which cannot be reasonably or adequately compensated by damages in any action at law. It is further acknowledged that the breach by the Contractor of any of the provisions of this Agreement will cause the Company irreparable injury and damage. The Contractor expressly agrees that the Company is entitled to injunctive and other equitable relief to prevent or correct a breach of any provision of this Agreement by the Contractor. Resort to such equitable relief, however, shall not be considered a waiver of any other rights or remedies granted to the Company under this Agreement for damages or under law. The various rights and remedies of the Company under this Agreement or under law shall be construed to be cumulative, and not one of them shall be exclusive of any other or of any right or remedy allowed by law.

9. Merger.

The merger or consolidation of the Company into or with any other entity, or the merger of the Contractor with another company shall not terminate this Agreement.

10. Termination.

The Company may terminate this Agreement at any time by providing 10 working days' written notice to the Contractor. If the Contractor materially breaches provisions of this Agreement, is convicted of a crime, fails, or refuses to comply with the written policies or reasonable directive of the Company, or performs acts of serious misconduct in connection with performance of this Agreement, the Company at any time may terminate the engagement of the Contractor immediately and without prior written notice to the Contractor.

11. Independent Contractor.

The Contractor is and will remain an independent contractor in his or her relationship to the Company and is not an employee, partner, or agent of the Company for any purpose.

The Company shall not be responsible for withholding taxes with from the Contractor's compensation, and the Contractor has no claim against the Company for vacation pay, sick leave, retirement benefits, Social Security, worker's compensation, health or disability benefits, unemployment insurance benefits, or employee benefits of any kind.

12. Insurance.
The Contractor will carry liability insurance, including malpractice insurance, if required for any service that he or she performs for the Company, and will provide insurance policy information upon request.

13. Successors and Assigns.
All of the provisions of this Agreement are binding upon and for the benefit of the parties to this Agreement and their respective heirs, successors, legal representatives, and assigns.

14. Choice of Law.
This Agreement, the construction of its terms, and the interpretation of the rights and duties of the parties to it, are subject to the laws of the state of _____.

15. Arbitration.
Any controversies that arise out of the terms of this Agreement or its interpretation shall be settled in _____ (location) in accordance with the rules of the American Arbitration Association, and the judgment upon award may be entered in any court having jurisdiction thereof.

16. Waiver.
A one-time waiver by one party of breach of any provision of this Agreement by the other shall not be construed as a continuing waiver.

17. Assignment.
The Contractor shall not assign any of his or her rights, or delegate the performance of any of his or her duties under this Agreement, without first obtaining the written consent of the Company.

18. Notices.
All notices and communications required by this Agreement shall be made in writing and shall be delivered to each party's address as listed on this contract. The mailing of a notice by registered or certified United States mail, certified or return receipt requested, postage prepaid, shall constitute delivery. A notice or demand shall be deemed constructively made at the time it is personally delivered. If a communication is given by mail, it shall be conclusively deemed given five days after its deposit in the United States mail, addressed to the party at the address given below:

Contractor: _____

Address: _____

City/State/Zip: _____

Company: _____

Address: _____

City/State/Zip: _____

DUTIES: The Contractor will perform the following duties:

_____

TERM: The term of this contract shall begin with the execution of this Agreement and shall continue in full force and effect through _____ (date) or the earlier satisfactory completion of the Contractor's duties under this Agreement. The Agreement may be extended only by a written agreement signed by both parties.

COMPENSATION: (choose A or B)

A. As full compensation for the services rendered under this Agreement, the Company shall pay the Contractor at the hourly rate of $_____ per hour, with total payment not to exceed $_____ without prior written approval by an authorized representative of the Company. Compensation is payable within 30 days of receipt of Contractor's monthly invoice for services rendered, supported by reasonable documentation.

OR

B. As full compensation for the services rendered pursuant to this Agreement, the Company shall pay the Contractor the sum of $_____, to be paid as follows: ___

_____

19. Modification or Amendment.

No modification, amendment, or change of this Agreement shall be valid unless made in writing and signed by both parties.

20. Unenforceability of Provisions.

If any provision of this Agreement, or any portion thereof, is determined to be invalid and unenforceable under state or local law, the remainder of this Agreement shall nevertheless remain in full force and effect.

IN WITNESS WHEREOF the undersigned have executed this Agreement as of the day and year first written above. The parties agree that facsimile signatures shall be as effective as if originals.

Company

By: _____

Title _____

Contractor

By: _____

Title _____

SAMPLE INDEPENDENT CONTRACTOR FORM

Date:	Contractor:

I hereby declare that I am an independent contractor. I understand that as an independent contractor, I alone am responsible for any costs related to my actions, health, taxes, insurance, transportation, and any other tasks that may be involved with the work I am doing as an independent contractor.

I agree I will not hold anyone else responsible for claims or liabilities that may arise from the work performed as an independent contractor or from any cause related to the work done. I hereby waive any rights I have to hold anyone liable for any reason as a result of this work.

Contractor Signed: _____

Witness Signed: _____

Witness Name: _____

SAMPLE SUBCONTRACTOR BID SHEET

Name: _____

Address: _____

Address of job that is up for bid (fill in your address): _____

Date: _____

Amount of Bid: _____

Workman's Compensation Insurance Company Name: _____

Agent's Name: _____

Certificate Number: _____ Expiration Date: _____

(Attach copy of insurance card)

References: (list name, address, and telephone contact number for each reference)

1. _____

2. _____

3. _____

Work to be performed: _____

Materials you will supply: _____

Materials homeowner will supply: _____

Signature: _____ Date: _____

Signature: _____ Date: _____

CHANGE ORDER FORM

Date:	Job Location:
Customer:	Contractor:

This change order is part of the contract between the above mentioned customer and contractor for the job located at the abovementioned location. These changes are hereby part of the original contract and require written authorization before any additional alterations.

The changes are as noted below (please be specific in details):

_____

_____

The changes described above will change the original contract to $ _____ amount. This is an ❑ increase/ ❑ decrease of $ _____. Payment is to be made by: _____.

The aforementioned parties hereby agree that these will be the only changes made to the original contract and no additional revisions are to be made without additional written authorization signed by both customer and contractor. No verbal agreements will be considered valid authorization. This change order constitutes the entire agreement between both parties to the alteration of the original contract.

Customer Signed: _____
Customer Signed: _____
Contractor Signed: _____

CONTRACTOR INVOICE SAMPLE

To:	Invoice #:	Job ID #:
Owner's Name & Address:	Project Address:	
Owner Phone #:	Owner Fax #:	
Contractor Submitting Invoice:		

Payment Is:	❑ Down Payment ❑ Progress Payment ❑ Final Payment
Payment Amount:	$_____
Payment Due Date:	___/___/____
Start Date of Work Performed:	___/___/____
Completion Date of Work:	___/___/____
Type of Job:	❑ Contract ❑ Daily Worker

Worked to be performed or work completed description:

_____

Please note below any labor provided or furnished equipment:

_____

_____

_____

Contractor Signed

AGREEMENT BETWEEN CONTRACTOR AND OWNER

Date: _____

Owner: _____

Contractor: _____

This Agreement is hereby made and entered into as of the date above by and between the Owner and Contractor listed above.

The Owner and Contractor, for the reasons listed within this Agreement, hereby agree to the following:

1. Contractor agrees to provide all material and labor needed to perform the work listed below as shown by the drawing and described in the specifications prepared by _____ _____, which were provided by the Owner.

    _____

    _____

2. Owner hereby agrees to pay the Contractor for the abovementioned materials and labor, a total of $_____ to be paid via _____ (payment method) and on _____ [date(s)].

3. Contractor agrees that the work to be performed will be completed on or before the following dates:

    a. _____
    b. _____
    c. _____
    d. _____

    Contractor must have the entire work to be performed completed no later than _____ _____ (date).

4. Contractor hereby agrees to provide and pay for any and all materials, tools, and equipment that is needed for the completion of the work by the date listed above. Unless noted otherwise, materials must be good quality.

5. During the course of the work to be completed for the Owner, Contractor is required to have a sufficient number of skilled trade workers in his/her employ in order to perform the jobs required to complete the work.

6. Any changes and variations to the work listed above must be ordered by the Owner and be made in writing. The amount to be paid to the Contractor must also be ad-

justed, either more or less, by the Contractor. For increased amounts, the cost of the work must be submitted to the Owner in writing by the Contractor. Contractor must receive written approval from the Owner in order to proceed with the change order.

7. Owner and all of the Owner's representatives are allowed access to the work site at all times.

8. Contractor also agrees to re-do any work that does coincide with the plans and specifications that the Owner provided to the Contractor for the work to be completed. Contractor warrants the work being completed and agrees to reimburse Owner for any defects which result from the work completed — including faulty materials or workmanship — for up to one year after the work has been completed.

9. Owner hereby agrees to retain full coverage insurance on all work to be completed according to this Agreement during the time of the work being done. Said insurance should be in Owner's and Contractor's name.

10. If the work is delayed due to fire, flood, or other acts of God; materials delay; owner neglect; or labor strikes, then the time to complete the work will be extended the same amount of time as the delay has caused.

11. If, due to the Contractor's negligence, the work is delayed, the Contractor hereby agrees to pay the Owner $_____ for liquid damages until the time that the work has been finished.

12. Contractor hereby agrees to retain personal insurance to protect against bodily injury, property damage, or death due to the work being completed according to this Agreement.

13. Written consent is required for the Owner or Contractor to assign any rights or interest occurring under this Agreement. The Contractor may not assign any money due, or that will become due, to him/her as covered under this Agreement.

14. This Agreement is made under the State of _____ laws and statues.

15. The Defendant is required to pay any attorney's fees and court costs in the event that judgment must be, and is, obtained to enforce this agreement or any breach thereof.

    IN WITNESS WHEREOF, the Contractor and Owner hereby agree to all items listed in the Agreement under the State laws of _____.

_____

Contractor

_____

Owner

CHECKLIST FOR CONSTRUCTION LOAN DOCUMENTS

_____1.   Application form
_____2.   Consent form
_____3.   Signed disclosure
_____4.   Most recent pay stubs
_____5.   Other asset records
_____6.   Land contract or deed
_____7.   Survey
_____8.   Plans - 3 sets
_____9.   Specifications
_____10. Cost breakdown
_____11. Title Insurance
_____12. Construction Insurance
_____13. Architect information
_____14. Permits
_____15. 2 years' W-2s or last 2 years' tax returns (if self-employed)
_____16. Rental agreements, if you own rental properties
_____17. Three months of bank statements on all accounts
_____18. Retirement account statements
_____19. Loan documents (for land with loan)
_____20. Proof of regulatory compliance
_____21. Builder's contract

Extra Documents That Will Make You Stand Out from the Crowd:

_____1.   Copies of subcontractor and supplier bids
_____2.   Copy of your project timeline
_____3.   The bank's own lien release form, signed by subs (This is a form subcontractors sign saying they have been paid and will not put a lien on the property.)
_____4.   Resumes of contractor or major subs you are using

CHECKLIST FOR MONITORING THE SAFETY ON YOUR SITE

Sanitation

_____1.   Portable toilet and sanitation facilities on-site.
_____2.   Fresh drinking water and disposable cups available on-site at all times.

Safety Rules and Safety Awareness

_____3.   Safety Rules posted on-site in several places visible to all and communicated in writing and verbally to each trade contractor.
_____4.   First-aid kit(s) and first-aid training.
_____5.   Phone numbers for police, ambulance, and fire station posted in several locations. Emergency telephones available and all workers informed of their locations.

_____6. Post Warning and Danger signs as appropriate.

_____7. Keep a Material Safety Data Sheet on site for hazardous chemicals.

_____8. Conduct frequent, daily safety checks and clean-ups; these are most effective and will remind workers to be safety conscious.

Electricity

_____9. Ground the temporary electrical service and all electrical tools.

_____10. Check often to be sure electrical cords are kept away from water.

_____11. Use only equipment that is listed, labeled, or certified. Use in accordance with manufacturer's instructions.

_____12. Ensure that power tools are well-maintained and properly stored.

_____13. Insist that all workers maintain proper clearance from all power lines.

Protective Clothing

_____14. Enforce the wearing of hard hats and steel-toed boots as appropriate.

_____15. Cap protruding steel rebar, nails, and other protruding dangers.

_____16. Provide protective gear — goggles, gloves, and respirators.

_____17. Require protective goggles when eye injuries are possible.

_____18. Require wearing of personal protective equipment.

_____19. Set a good example.

Excavations

_____20. Ensure there is adequate slope and proper fencing on edges of all ditches and trenches over four feet deep.

_____21. Place excavated material at least two feet from edge of ditches and trenches.

_____22. Cover open holes in sub-floors.

Scaffolds and Heights

_____23. Safe access and correct use of all types of scaffolds.

_____24. Erection of scaffolds by trained personnel.

_____25. Guardrails installed on all open-sided floors or platforms.

_____26. Workers on roof only with proper equipment.

_____27. Stair rail system constructed on stairways of four or more risers.

Fire Safety

_____28. Remove excess and/or flammable scrap daily.

_____29. Store flammable or combustible liquids only in approved containers with labels.

_____30. Keep gas cans and other flammable liquids in secure area at all times.

_____31. Shut off welding tanks tightly when not in use — check and re-check.

_____32. Monitor area where soldering work is done — look for smoldering or burning wood.

_____33. Spread oily or paint rags outside to dry before disposal so they will not ignite.

JOB SITE SAFETY CHECKLIST

On-Site Hazards
___ Holes covered
___ Debris removed daily
___ Rebar capped
___ Protruding pipes eliminated
___ Lumber removed
___ Toxics eliminated

Equipment in Use
___ OSHA-grade scaffolding with stable towers, safety rails, wide platforms
___ Excavations supported
___ Ground fault interrupters on power cords
___ Heavy-duty ladders only
___ Toe boards and harnesses on roofs
___ Work boots — no sneakers
___ Kneepads in use
___ Ear protection and respirators a requirement
___ Hard hats
___ Safety glasses

Repairs
___ Blades sharpened
___ Worn out tools removed from use
___ No frayed cords

Training
___ No standing on top rungs of ladders
___ Training for apprentices on handling tools
___ Crew educated to handle any toxic materials on site

First Aid
___ First-aid kit on hand
___ CPR certification
___ Address and phone number of trauma center posted on-site

SUPPLIER CONTACT SHEET

Company Name	
Web Site	
Phone Number	
Fax	

Contact Name	
Contact Phone	
Contact E-mail	
Product Lines	
Minimum Order	
Payment Terms	
Warranties	
Return Policy	
Notes	

SUPPLIER REFERENCE SHEET

Company Name	
Supplier Name	
Reference Name	
Reference Phone number	
Reference Fax	
Reference E-mail	
Reference Comments About:	
Quality of Supplier's Products:	
Selection:	
Speed of Shipping:	
Handling of Returns:	
Other Comments:	

LIEN WAIVER SHORT FORM

Date:	Job Location:
Customer Name & Address:	Customer Phone #:

Contractor Name & Address:	Subcontractor Name & Address:	
Type of Work to be Completed:		
Work Completed (as of this date):		
Payments Received (to date): $ ___	Payments Received (this date): $ ___	Total Amount Paid: $ ___

By signing below the contractor and/or subcontractor:

- Hereby acknowledge payments stated above as received according to the contract signed between all parties. All work done has now been paid in full.
- Hereby releases and relinquishes and all rights to place a mechanic or material man lien against the aforementioned property for the worked detailed above. All parties agree that all payments have been made in full for all work performed and in compliance with the contract.
- Hereby release the customer from any liability for non-payment of material or services extended through this date.

We, the undersigned, have read and understand this agreement.

Contractor Signed: _____

Subcontractor Signed: _____

REQUEST FOR PROOF OF INSURANCE FROM CONTRACTOR/SUBCONTRACTOR

Date of Request:	Contractor/Subcontractor:
Address of Job Site:	

This is a request for the abovementioned Contractor/Subcontractor's Proof of Insurance. This proof is required to show you meet the insurance portion of the contractor agreement signed by both parties. Please provide your proof of insurance in one of the following ways:

1. Bring your insurance certificate to _____ (address of requestor), where a copy can be made and placed in the file along with your contract.
2. Fax a certified copy of your certificate to ___-___-___, ATTN _____.
3. Have your insurance provider mail an official copy to the following location _____.

The proof should be provided to the requestor no later than _____ or all work shall halt at aforementioned job site.

Thank you,

_____
(Requestor's Signature)

_____
(Requestor's Printed Name)

AFFIDAVIT OF ORIGINAL OR SUBCONTRACTOR

Date:	Property Address:
Contractor Name & Address:	Subcontractor Name & Address:

The abovementioned Subcontractor being duly sworn, certifies that he or she is the Subcontractor of the abovementioned original Contractor having a contract with _____ the _____ for _____ a _____ situated ❑ on/ ❑ around/ ❑ in front of the abovementioned property of which _____is the ❑ owner/ ❑ part owner/ ❑ lessee.

SUBCONTRACTOR:
The aforementioned Contractor also certifies that the names and addresses of every Subcontractor in the employ for this project is listed below. This list also includes any amount owed or which will become due for the work completed, or machinery, material, or fuel furnished to date hereof, under the terms of any Agreement with these Subcontractors.

NOTE: A similar sworn declaration signed by the Subcontractors listed here must be attached to this document.

Name of Subcontractor:	Address:
Specialty:	Amount Due/Owed: $_____
Name of Subcontractor:	Address:
Specialty:	Amount Due/Owed: $_____

MATERIAL MEN:
Contractor also certifies that this list provides the names and addresses of every person who will be providing machinery, material, or fuel for the abovementioned project. This list also provides any amount owed or which will become due for the work completed, or machinery, material, or fuel furnished to date hereof, under the terms of any Agreement with these persons.

NOTE: A Certificate of Material Man must be attached or, in place of this certification, material man may furnish a written waiver of lien, a written release, or receipt.

Name of Material Man:	Address:
Specialty:	Amount Due/Owed: $_____
Name of Material Man:	Address:
Specialty:	Amount Due/Owed: $_____

AGREEMENT BETWEEN CONTRACTOR AND SUBCONTRACTOR

Date: _____

Subcontractor: _____

Contractor: _____

Property: _____

Subcontractor, in consideration of the contracts enclosed in this agreement on the part of contractor, agrees with contractor as follows:

1. To supply all material and complete all work for _____ *[state work to be done and materials to be supplied, if possible by reference to numbers of drawings and pages of specifications]*.

2. To finish the work to be done on or prior to _____ *[date]*, and in failure to pay of completion of work to contractor _____ dollars ($_____) for each day that the work shall remain incomplete, as and for settlement of damages.

3. To provide contractor, directly on execution of this contract, with an agreeable guarantee company's bond in the sum of _____ dollars ($_____), promising all terms of this contract and conclusion of the contract within the time declared.

4. To obtain, at his [her] own expense, before entering implementation of this contract, payment insurance in a dependable insurance company, satisfactory to contractor, covering full legal responsibility for reimbursement to any of its employees for bodily injuries inadvertently sustained, whether resulting in death or otherwise, under the Workers' Compensation Act of the State of _____, and to uphold such compensation insurance in full force and effect at all times while this contract shall remain in force and not fully completed on his [her] part; to provide contractor a satisfactory indemnity accident policy defending owner and contractor in case of accident to workers employed on the building or themselves or their employees or the public, and that if any suits are entered against owner of the building or the contractor on explanation of acts committed, or lapses by subcontractor, his [her] agents or employees, to protect such suits and repay either or both owner

and contractor for any cost or charge that they may be put to, including court expenses and attorney fees.

5. At his [her] own charge and cost, to request for and acquire all required permits and conform firmly to the laws and regulations in force in the area where established.

6. To supply, both in the shops and in the building, adequate, secure, and appropriate facilities, at all times, for inspection of the work by owner, architect and contractor, or the official representative of any of them, and, on demand of contractor, to make all receipts showing the superiority of the material used.

7. Should appropriate, workmanlike and precise presentation of any work under this contract depend in any way on proper, workmanlike, or precise performance of any work by another contractor on the building, to use all means required to determine any imperfections in the contractor's work, and to report the defects, in text, to contractor before going on with his [her] work that is so dependent; and to permit to contractor a realistic time to remedy the defects.

8. To make no claim for extra work unless done in pursuance of a written instruction from contractor, and notice of all such requests shall be given to contractor in writing before the next following compensation or shall be considered as abandoned.

9. Before final compensation is made, to complete a written guarantee for his [her] work, agreeing to make good, without fee to owner or contractor, any and all faults due to imperfect workmanship or materials, which might appear during a realistic time, the length of such time to be determined by contractor.

10. To defend and cover contractor against any loss or damage experienced by anyone arising through the carelessness of subcontractor, or those working by him [her] or his [her] agent or servants; to bear any cost that contractor may have by cause of the negligence, or on account of being charged with negligence; and if there are any injuries to persons or property unsettled, when the work is completed, final payment between contractor and subcontractor shall be delayed until such claims are attuned or appropriate special protection satisfactory to contractor is granted by subcontractor.

11. To cover and hold owner and contractor risk-free from any and all loss or damage that owner and contractor, or either of them, may suffer on account of any claim, order, or suit made or brought against owner and/or contractor by or on behalf of any employee of subcontractor, or by or on behalf of any person injured by subcontractor, his [her] servants, agents, or employees.

12. To not allocate or move this contract or any part of this contract without written permission of contractor.

The contractor, in thoughtfulness of the contracts contained in this agreement on the part of subcontractor, agrees as follows:

13. To employ subcontractor to give the materials and to do the work agreement to terms and conditions contained in this contract.

14. If subcontractor shall realistically fulfill this contract to the approval of architect, and keep every contract on his [her] part contained in this agreement, to compensate the sub-contractor _____ dollars ($_____), for all of this work and material in place finished and accepted under this contract.

Expenses to be made on or about the _____ day of each month at the rate of _____ percent of the value of the work built in place during the previous month, as determined by contractor or architect and the remaining _____ percent within _____ days after conclusion and recognition of this work.

No compensation made under this contract shall function as an admittance, on the part of contractor, that this contract, or any part of this contract, has been abided by with, in case in fact it shall be otherwise, or so as to preclude any action for damages against subcontractor, should the work and material necessary not be performed and supplied in considerable and workmanlike manner, and of suitable quality, or should this contract not be realistically executed in every respect.

It is further agreed as follows:

15. No changes shall be made in the work or materials shown or explained by the draw-ings and specifications, apart from on written instruction of contractor, and when so made, the cost of work and materials added or omitted shall be calculated and determined by contractor, and the amount so determined shall be added to or subtracted from the contract price. [Provision may be added as to arbitration in case valuation is in dispute.]

16. Contractor shall supply all manual labor and materials not included in this contract in such manner as not to hold up the material progress of the work, and in the result of failure to do so, thereby causing loss to subcontractor, agrees to refund subcontractor for such loss; and subcontractor agrees that if he [she] shall delay the material progress of the work so as to work any damage for which contractor shall become legally responsible, then he [she] shall make good to contractor any such damage over and above any damage for general holdup otherwise granted for in this contract.

Contractor has the right, after _____ days' written notice to subcontractor, to supply labor or materials if subcontractor at any time refuses or fails to provide an adequacy of appropriately skilled workers or of materials of proper value and amount, and to subtract the price from any money due or to become due to subcontractor under this contract.

17. If subcontractor fails in any respect to take legal action promptly, or falls short in the performance of any contracts on his/her part contained in the terms of this agreement, contractor has the right, after _____ days' written notice to subcontractor, to end the employment of subcontractor for the work, and to enter on the grounds and take control of all materials and pieces of equipment of every kind whatsoever on the premises, and to employ any other person or persons to finish the work, and to provide materials for

the workers. In case of discontinuance of employment of subcontractor, he/she shall not receive any further compensation under this contract until the work shall be completely finished. At completion, if the outstanding balance of the amount to be compensated under this contract surpasses the operating costs incurred by contractor in completing the work, the excess shall be paid by contractor to subcontractor. If the expenses surpass the unpaid remainder, subcontractor shall pay the difference to contractor. The expense sustained by contractor as provided, either for supplying materials or for completing the work, and any damage incurred through such non-payment, shall be reviewed and certified by architect whose certificate shall be conclusive on the parties.

18. No oral command, opposition, claim, or notice of whichever party to the other shall be of consequence or binding, and no proof of such order, protest, claim, or notice shall ever be presented in any suit in law or fairness in which these parties are interested, both parties agreeing to carry out and provide in writing all communications from them by which the other party is to be charged, informed, or affected, and when they are given orally they shall be held as not material or binding, and none of requirements of this contract, plans, or specifications, shall be held to be surrendered, or interpreted, by reason of any act whatsoever, or in any manner, other than by an state waiver, or a absolutely agreed understanding in writing, and no evidence shall be presented of any other waiver or interpretation.

19. *[Section for extension of time in case subcontractor is postponed by acts of owner, architect or contractor, or by alterations required, or by damage occurring from fire, etc., may be included.]*

20. In case contractor and subcontractor neglect to agree in relation to any matters under this contract, these matters shall be referred to a board of adjudication, consisting of one person chosen by contractor and one person elected by subcontractor, these two to select a third person; the judgment of any two of this board shall be absolute and binding on the parties. The party cast in the decision shall pay the price of the arbitration, but, in the event that each party is permitted something on his [her] claims, they shall share the expenses equally between them.

Agreement made _____ *[date]*, between _____ of _____, called contractor, and _____ of _____, called subcontractor.

(Signature):_____
(Signature):_____

BOND OF CONTRACTOR

Date: _____
Contractor: _____
Address: _____
City: _____ State: _____ Zip: _____
Surety: _____

Address: _____
City: _____ State: _____ Zip: _____
Owner: _____
Address: _____
City: _____ State: _____ Zip: _____

This Agreement binds the Contractor and Surety listed above to the Owner listed above in the sum of $_____ that shall be paid to the Owner.

This serves as a formal announcement that we, _____ (Contractor) of Address:

_____,
City: _____ State: _____ Zip: _____,
known as the "Principal," for the purpose of this Agreement and_____ (Surety or Sureties) of Address:_____ City: _____
State: _____ Zip: _____, known as "Surety (or "Sureties") for the purpose of this Agreement, hereby firmly bind themselves, their heirs, executors, administrators, successors, and assigns, jointly and severally, to _____ [Owner] of Address: _____
City: _____ State: _____ Zip: _____, known as the "Owner" for the purposes of this Agreement, in the sum of _____ dollars ($_____), to be paid to Owner, or to his [her] executors, administrators or assigns, according to the conditions set forth below.

The Principal has, by a written agreement, dated _____ [date], entered into a Contract with the Owner for the building and construction of a _____ building, at a site located at _____
_____ City: _____ State: _____ Zip: _____, according to the plans and specifications prepared by _____, Architect. A copy of this Contract is attached to be considered a part of this Agreement.

The condition of this obligation is that if the Principal faithfully performs his or her obligations under this Contract to complete the building free and clear of all liens and/or claims for labor, encumbrances, material claims or otherwise, and satisfies all claims and demands incurred for the same, and fully indemnifies and saves harmless the Owner from all costs and damages of every kind that the Owner may suffer by reason of the Principal's failure to perform his or her obligations, and fully reimburses the Owner for all expenses, of every kind, which the Owner may incur in making good any such failure, and pays all persons for labor and/or material, then this obligation shall be null and void. Otherwise, it shall remain in full force and effect.

[Insert any provisions desired as to time limit for suing on bond conditions that shall or shall not release the obligors or the Surety, etc.]
Signature of Surety: _____
Date: _____
Signature of Contractor: _____

Date: _____
Signature of Owner: _____
Date: _____

BOND OF SUBCONTRACTOR

Date: _____
Subcontractor (Principal): _____
Address: _____
City: _____ State: _____ Zip: _____
Contractor: _____
Address: _____
City: _____ State: _____ Zip: _____
Surety: _____
Address: _____
City: _____ State: _____ Zip: _____

_____ (Principal), and _____ Surety Company, a cor-
poration organized and existing under the laws of the State of _____, as surety, are
held and firmly bound to _____ (Contractor), in the
sum of _____ U.S. dollars ($_____), to be paid to Contractor, his [her] attorney,
executors, administrators, successors, or assigns. The Principal and Surety bind themselves
and each of them, their and each of their heirs, executors, administrators, and successors,
jointly and severally, firmly to this payment by this Agreement.

_____

Signature of Principal

_____

Printed Name of Principal

_____

Authorized Signature of Security

_____

Printed Name of Agent of Security
Date: _____

Principal has entered into a written Contract, dated _____ [date],
with Contractor, for the performance of certain work and the furnishing of certain materials in connection with the building of a _____
_____ on a site located at:

_____
City: _____ State: _____ Zip: _____
for which a Contract, together with all of the terms, covenants, conditions, specifications,
and stipulations, is attached to and made a part of this bond. It is agreed that any deviations from, additions to, omissions in, or other changes to the Contract, specifications,
or plans of work required by the Contractor may be made from time to time during the
progress of the work, as often as required, without the consent or knowledge of the Surety
and without in any way releasing him [her] from liability under this present bond.

This obligation is under the condition that if the Principal truly and faithfully fulfills the conditions of the above-mentioned Contract, together with all of its terms, covenants, specifications, and stipulations to be observed by the Principal; and keeps harmless and protects the Contractor from all loss arising from nonperformance or nonfulfillment by the Principal of the terms, covenants, conditions, specifications, and stipulations to be observed by the Principal, contained in the contract; and also against actual loss arising from any and all delays, claims, defects, errors, obligations, liens, or encumbrances arising from nonperformance or nonfulfillment by Principal, then this obligation is to be null and void; otherwise, it is to remain in full-force and effect.

Signature of Surety: _____
Date: _____
Signature of Contractor: _____
Date: _____
Signature of Owner: _____
Date: _____

COMPLETION OF WORK BY OWNER IN THE CASE OF THE CONTRACTOR'S DEFAULT

Date: _____
Contractor: _____
Address: _____
City: _____ State: _____ Zip: _____
Owner: _____
Address: _____
City: _____ State: _____ Zip: _____

If, at any time, the Contractor:
a) refuses or neglects to supply a sufficiency of properly skilled workers
b) refuses or neglects to supply materials of proper quality
c) fails in any respect to conduct work with promptness and diligence
d) fails in the performance of any of the agreements contained in the Building Contract attached to this document

and such refusal, neglect, or failure is certified in a written statement signed by the architect(s) named in the Building Contract, Owner shall have the right, after serving _____ days' written notice to Contractor, to provide any such labor or materials, or to take over the performance of the agreement, and to deduct the cost from any money due then or in the future to Contractor under the attached Building Contract.

If architect(s) certifies in writing that such refusal, neglect, or failure of the Contractor is sufficient ground for such action, Owner may terminate the employment of Contractor for the work and enter on the grounds and take control, for purpose of completing the work included under this Contract, of all materials, tools, appliances, and equipment of any kind. Owner may employ any other person, or persons to finish the work, and may provide materials for the workers.

If the employment of the Contractor is discontinued, he/she shall not be entitled to receive any further payment under the attached Building Contract until the work is fully completed. At completion, if the outstanding balance of the amount to be paid under the Building Contract exceeds the expenses incurred by Owner in finishing the work, the excess shall be paid by Owner to Contractor. If the expenses exceed the unpaid balance, Contractor shall pay the difference to Owner. The expenses incurred by Owner for furnishing materials or for finishing the work, and any damages brought about through such default by the Contractor, shall be audited and certified by the architect(s) named in the attached Building Contract, whose certificate shall be conclusive on the parties.

Signature of Contractor:

_____

Date: _____

Signature of Owner:

_____

Date: _____

CONTRACTOR'S AFFIDAVIT OF COMPLETION, PAYMENT OF DEBTS AND CLAIMS, AND RELEASE OF LIENS

Project Name: _____
Location: _____
Contractor: _____
Address: _____
City: _____ State: _____ Zip: _____
Owner: _____
Address: _____
City: _____ State: _____ Zip: _____

I certify to the best of my knowledge and belief that all work has been completed and all requisite materials have been supplied in strict accordance with the terms and conditions of the attached Building Contract between Owner and Contractor for the project named above.

I further certify that all bills for materials, services, supplies, utilities, and for all other things furnished or caused to be furnished by the Contractor and used in the performance of the work as specified by the Building Contract, will be fully paid upon receipt of Final Payment from Owner. I certify that there are no unpaid obligations, liens, claims, security interests, fees, encumbrances, liabilities and/or demands of State Agencies, and no payments owing to subcontractors, material men, mechanics, laborers or any others resulting from or arising out of any work done, caused to be done or ordered to be done by the Contractor during the performance of the Building Contract

In consideration of the prior and final payments made and all payments made for authorized changes, the Contractor releases and forever discharges the Owner from any and all obligations, liens, claims, security interests, encumbrances and/or liabilities arising from performance of the Building Contract and from authorized changes to the Building Contract made between the parties, verbally or in writing. Owner is hereby released from any and all claims and demands of every kind and character whatsoever against the Owner arising out of or in any way related to the contract and authorized changes.

It is understood that, based on the truth of the statements contained in this affidavit, the Owner will make Final Payment under the terms of the Building Contract.

CONTRACTOR (Firm)

_____

(Signature)   (Title)
Subscribed and sworn to me this Day of _____
(Seal)
NOTARY_____
Notary Public for the State of _____
My Commission Expires: _____

CONTRACTOR'S WARRANTY

Date: _____
Contractor: _____
Owner: _____
The Contractor listed above hereby guarantees to the Owner that the construction being performed on or upon the building located at _____
(address) to be free from defects in material and workmanship for a time period of _____ from the date of completion of the construction.

This Standard Limited Warranty applies to and is limited upon the following conditions:

1. Applies to the property only for as long as it stays in control of the Owner named above.

2. Applies to all construction work that has not been subjected to any misuse, accidents, or abuse, as well as work that has not been misused, modified, altered, or had any repairs made or attempted by others.

3. The contractor should be notified right away in writing within _____ days of the first date of knowledge of defect by the Owner.

4. The contractor should be given the initial chance to make any repairs, replacements, or corrections to any defective construction at no cost to the owner within _____ time period.

5. Under no condition should the contractor be liable for damages to any person or property for any special, indirect, secondary, or substantial damages that have arisen due to the construction defect.

_____

Contractor Signed

_____

State License #

Address
_____

Phone #
_____

Owner
_____

Date
_____

Address
_____

Phone #

CONTRACTOR'S CONSENT AND AGREEMENT

Assignor: _____
Name: _____
Address: _____
Assignee: _____
Name: _____
Address: _____

This agreement is referenced to the Agreement between Owner and Contractor dated _____ (known as the "Agreement") which is one of the Construction and Operating Documents referred to in that Assignment of Contractor's Agreement dated _____ by the above named Assignor in order to assign benefits to the above named Assignee. The undersigned have received a copy of that "Assignment." Those parties signing below agree that the Agreement is in full force and effect. It is further agreed that none of those that sign below nor the Assignor are in default, nor do circumstances exist that would place any party in default.

Those parties signing below agree that, upon receipt of notice from Assignee, or its successors or assigns, that an Event of Default has occurred under the Assignment, that the Assignee shall perform all of its obligations, covenants, conditions, and agreements under the Agreement for the benefit of Assignee and its successors and assigns. This condition depends on the Assignee performing the duties and obligations of the Assignor under the Agreement from and after the date of such notice, and further that the Assignee shall remit to those parties below all amounts due and owing the parties as of the date of such Event of Default, which were not disbursed to Assignor by Assignee, provided such payment was to have been used for the purpose of paying such amounts to the parties below. The parties below agree that the Assignment shall not burden the Assignee with any liability or obligation. The parties below agree that Section 2.E of the Assignment empowers the Assignee the right to terminate the Agreement on the terms specified in such Section 2.E.

The parties below will not hold against Assignee, its successors or assigns, any set-off, defense counterclaims, or deductions that it had against Assignor, whether arose out of the Agreement or from somewhere else. The parties below will not withhold performance for

Assignee as a result of any breach of any agreement or any default caused by of Assignor. The parties below agree that the bankruptcy or insolvency of the Assignor is not automatically the cause of default if the parties continue to be paid pursuant to the terms of the Agreement. The parties understand that modifications in the Agreement or the plans and specifications in connection with the Agreement shall not be made without Assignee's consent. There will be no line item in the Project Budget that will be changed by more than two percent (2%) without Lender's prior written approval.

All notices, demands, or documents that are required or permitted to be given or served upon the parties set out below must be hand-delivered or, if mailed by United States registered or certified mail, postage prepaid, return receipt requested, addressed as follows:

_____.

The parties set out below agree that in a breach of contract by the Assignor, the parties shall give Assignee written notice, in the manner as set forth in the Assignment. The notice shall inform the Assignees the breach and the opportunity to remedy or cure such breach within sixty (60) days after the expiration of any cure period given to Assignor under the Agreement. The parties agree that no default shall be listed if the curing such default cannot by its nature be accomplished in such sixty (60) day period. It is the obligation of the Assignee to commence curing the same within such sixty (60) day period and will be expected to diligently and continuously prosecute the same to completion, (b) that the Assignee will obtain and maintain all insurance required to be carried by it under the Agreement, and shall name Assignee as an additional insured in the policies until one of the following occurs: (i) the Assignment has been released and Assignee has been paid in full, or (ii) Assignee can terminate the Agreement as set forth above, and (c) Any proceeds from the policies shall be payable to the Assignee, and in no event will Assignee be deemed a fiduciary with respect to such proceeds. This agreement shall not invalidate the parties from collecting under its liability insurance policies to the extent of its interest in the project.

The following are the parties that have a vested interest in the project set forth in the Agreement.

CONTRACTOR:
Date: _____
By: _____
Name: _____
Title: _____

COST-PLUS CONTRACT

Date: _____
Contractor: _____
Owner: _____

This Agreement is hereby made this date by and between the above-mentioned Contractor and Owner. The Parties agree to the following items:

1. Owner agrees under the following conditions and terms to employ the contractor in the construction of a building as outlined below.

2. Contractor agrees to provide complete plans and specifications, hire all labor and purchase all material and make contracts as necessary for departments that must be handled in that manner. Contractor also agrees to employ a qualified and competent superintendent to oversee all aspects of this project, which includes but is not limited to, inspection of material, paying all bills in connection with the work an insure and obtain a release of lien from all companies that provided materials, as well as all subcontractors.

3. Prior to entering in to this contract, the Contractor estimated the cost of the building to complete specifications not to exceed $_____. In the event that the final figures, compiled after making plans to proper specifications, exceed the above estimate, either party shall have the right to cancel this contract.

4. _____ percent will be added to actual cost to cover overhead expenses incurred by the contractor and _____ to cover overhead of services by the contractor. If the total cost exceeds the above estimate the remaining balance shall be paid by the contractor, and in the event that they are less then above estimate, the owner shall have the benefit. Guaranteed figured as listed above shall automatically be changed should any changes be made after this contract has been signed.

5. Owner will agree to pay any cost that may be necessary in the financing of the building and to compensate the contractor based on the following project milestones;

           _____ Percent when the foundation is poured and walls
           are complete.
           _____ Percent when the roof has been completed.
           _____ Percent when the plumbing and heating has been
           properly installed.
           _____ Percent when the interior finish is complete.

The remaining balance is due at the completion of the project.

_____   _____
Owner   Contractor

DEFAULT OF SUBCONTRACTOR

Subcontractor: _____
Contractor: _____

It is the responsibility of the abovementioned subcontractor to provide a sufficient number of skilled workers and quality materials, and to promptly and thoroughly execute work.

Should subcontractor fail to follow through with any of the abovementioned agreements, after _____ days' written notice to subcontractor, contractor shall have the right, with architects' approval, to provide required labor or materials and to deduct such costs from any moneys due or owed to subcontractor. Should subcontractor refuse, fail, or neglect to provide agreed-to services in the contract, contractor has the right to cease subcontractor's employment and to take ownership of all of subcontractor's tools, materials, and appliances on the premises in order to complete the work agreed to in the contract. Contractor also has the right to employ and provide materials for any necessary persons to complete the work.

Should subcontractor's employment discontinue for any reason, further payment shall not be issued to subcontractor until the work is completed, and should the unpaid balance at this time exceed the contractor's expenses incurred in completing the work, contractor shall pay excess moneys to subcontractor. However, subcontractor shall pay any differences to contractor should expenses exceed the unpaid balance. Subcontractor shall be responsible for any expenses the contractor incurs by finishing the work, supplying materials, or suffering any damage.

SUBCONTRACTOR DUTIES

Subcontractor: _____

Architects: _____ _____

Project: _____

City: _____

To complete _____, the abovementioned subcontractor shall, in full and in strict accordance with the plans' specifications and requirements, execute all required work, and furnish all labor and material as the plans and entire specifications require. Subcontractor shall additionally adhere to any and all changes, additions, alterations, details, and deductions to complete the abovementioned work, all of which shall be executed in a prompt and true manner sufficient to the acceptance of contractor, architect, and owners. "Work" in this contract shall refer to labor, actual work, and material.

The plans and specifications referred to above are the same as are provided by the abovementioned architects, and are on file with _____.

LABOR AFFIDAVIT

The following names and addresses of every unpaid laborer will be paid for labor done to date hereof in the employ of _____, contractor who is furnishing labor under said contract.

NOTE: Note that every laborer has been paid in full if such is the case. If not, each unpaid laborer's name and address and amount to become due should be noted.

NAME	ADDRESS	TRADE	HOURS	Amount Due or To Become Due for Labor

Additionally, for work performed or machinery, material, or fuel furnished to _____ *[Owner or Contractor]*, there is due or to become due to _____ *[Subcontractor]* in the sum of $_____ to date hereof under said contracts.

All amounts due or to become due to abovementioned subcontractors for work done or material, fuel, or machinery furnished to the date hereof to abovementioned Owner or Contractor are fully and correctly set forth opposite their names, respectively, in the aforesaid statements; amounts due or to become due are also evidenced by certificates of every person furnishing material, fuel, or machinery, hereto attached, and made a part hereof.

Affiant further states that the abovementioned Owner or Contractor has not employed or purchased or procured material, fuel, or machinery from, or subcontracted with any person, firm, or corporation, other than the abovementioned, and owes for no labor performed, or material, fuel, or machinery furnished, under said contracts, other than the abovementioned.

IN WITNESS THEREOF, at _____

This _____day of _____20_____.

_____

(NOTARY PUBLIC)

PAYMENT — CONTRACTORS OR SUBCONTRACTORS

I, _____, agree that _____ (lender) has the right to pay any fees invoiced by contractors, subcontractors, or material suppliers for such work performed in the construction of _____ or to pay any materials needed to build _____. These payments should be paid upon receipt of an invoice of services rendered or supplies purchased and that are approved by a building inspector. This inspector can be chosen by the lender and each invoice will contain any information deemed necessary by the lender. It is also agreed that the lender pay these invoices in such a way that it protects the lender's interests at all times.

The parties agree that the lender does not assume any liability arising from the owner, owner's contracts, any hired subcontractors, or material suppliers. The exception to this is in the case of misuse and misappropriation of said funds. The lender will work in good faith to pay invoices based upon receipt of those invoices and the inspector's certificate or release of lien. The lender will pay in good faith with the belief that such instruments are genuine and have been provided by appropriate parties. In addition, the owner will not hold the lender liable and will protect the lender from any claims based upon that are the result of damages, costs and expenses in which the application of these funds can occur with the stipulations stated above.

_____   _____
Signature of Lender   Date

_____   _____
Signature of Owner   Date

SUBCONTRACTOR PAYMENTS FOR LABOR & MATERIALS: RIGHT OF CONTRACTOR TO PAY UNPAID BILLS

Date: _____

Subcontractor: _____

Contractor: _____

The subcontractor is to turn over work to contractor free and clear from all liens, royalties, or claims. If the subcontractor fails to pay for materials and or labor resulting from this subcontract, the contractor may, without notice, pay for the materials and or labor and charge the unpaid amount to the subcontractor. In the event that a case is brought to place a lien on the property by anyone in relation to the subcontractor for any reason, the subcontractor must defend the suit and pay any such lien or claim. The subcontractor must defend any suit at his or her own cost, including but not limited to attorneys' fees.

The subcontractor is to furnish and make available to the contractor a detailed list of persons or companies providing labor and or materials for the subcontractor and how much, if any, is due to each.

The fee paid to the subcontractor are for the labor and materials of this job and is not to be used to satisfy any other obligations the subcontractor has on any other contract.

Signatures:

Subcontractor: _____   Contractor: _____

TERMINATION OF SUBCONTRACT AND COMPLETION OF WORK BY CONTRACTOR

Date: _____

Subcontractor: _____   Contractor: _____

The Subcontractor will complete his or her work quickly and effectively as to not delay the work of the Contractor or other subcontractors. If the Subcontractor fails to complete the job they were assigned to do, or it does not meet the standards of the contractor, then they will be notified in writing of the issues and, if not corrected within five days of the notice, the contractor may take over the work of the subcontractor. The contractor may exclude the subcontractor from any further participation in the project that is covered by this agreement. The contract may take over only a portion of the work if the contractor deems it to be in the best interest of the contractor and completing the project. In either case, the subcontractor agrees to any material, tools, and equipment on the site in the possession of the subcontractor if it is deemed beneficial to completion the project. Any costs incurred by the contractor in taking over or finishing the subcontractor's assignment will be taken from the monies due to the subcontractor. If the cost exceeds that owed to the Subcontract, the subcontractor and their sureties will be responsible to cover the contractor's difference.

_____

Signature of Contractor

_____

Signature of Subcontractor

CHAPTER 4

Forms for
Real Estate Professionals

This questionnaire lists questions that potential home buyers should consider when searching for a home. Answering these questions honestly will ensure that the home you purchase fits your lifestyle and will also help your real estate agent tailor your property search to fit your needs.

1. How many bedrooms do you want?
2. How many bathrooms do you want?
3. How many square feet would you like to have?
4. Do you like a garage or carport better?
5. Is it important to you to have either?
6. Do you like an attached garage?
7. What is your favorite room in any home?
8. Why?
9. Where will you spend most of your time in your new home?
10. Do you have a preference in school districts?
11. Where is your church?
12. Is it important to be near shopping areas?
13. What do you like to be close to at any given time?
14. Where do you shop?
15. Do you like a fenced yard?
16. Do you want a fireplace?
17. Do you want a hot tub or pool? On a scale of 1 to 10, with 10 being the highest, how important is this to you?
18. What kind of house payment do you want?

19. What price range do you think you should be in?
20. Do any neighborhoods or general areas stand out for you as a nice place to live?
21. Can you think of anything you would really like to have in a home?

HOMES VIEWED LOG

Dear Client,

When you begin shopping for a house, one thing you need to do is keep up with any pertinent information on the house so you can refer to it quickly when needed. The following worksheet is an example of what you may need to know on each house you are considering for purchase.

Property location: _____
Asking price: _____
Price the seller will accept: _____
Assumable mortgage? _____
Mortgage balance: _____
Total square feet: _____
Lot size: _____
Property taxes _____
Utilities per month: _____
City location or county location? _____
School district: _____
Age of House: _____
Age of roof: _____
Last termite inspection: _____
What I like most about the house: _____
What I like least about the house _____
Type of heating and air is in the house: _____
What stays with the house? (Include blinds, appliances, any ceiling fans, etc.) _____
_____

CANVASSING LETTER FOR THE REAL ESTATE AGENT

Date: _____
Dear _____,

Hello! I am _____ and I work with _____ Real Estate Agency. I am writing to you today to introduce myself to you and let you know I have added your name into my database so you can start receiving free newsletters about the current market conditions in our city.

As a lifelong member of the community, I know this area well, and I am particularly working to become more knowledgeable about your subdivision. This is, of course, excellent news for you as a member of the _____. I will keep you up-to-date on what is selling in the area, as well as market conditions and area homes for sale.

In short, when it comes to real estate news in your immediate vicinity, I am going to send you everything I know over the next 12 months.

This service is absolutely free and will cost you nothing. We provide this service to our customer because we enjoy our profession. I plan to become as knowledgeable about the area as possible in hopes you will remember me if you ever plan to sell your home.

_____, I stand on the belief that hard work pays off and I am willing to work hard to learn all I can about your area because your location is a great area. As you know, many buyers look for homes in your area, and, therefore, when it is time for you to consider selling your home, I hope you think of me. When you do, we will find a buyer for your property.

In the meantime, enjoy your first newsletter. It has some wonderful real estate articles for you to look over, and there is even a place for you to submit your questions to me by e-mail. Also, my Web site has an area where you can send me a referral or two and if you do, I will send you a special gift as my way of saying, "Thank you for thinking of me."

Let me know what your thoughts are on your market conditions, and put me to work for you when you need a real estate professional.

All the Best,

_____

Agent Signature
(Contact Information)

FINAL CANVASSING LETTER OUT OF ROTATION

Date: _____
Dear _____,

Thank you for allowing me to send you information on your community through market newsletters over the last year. I hope you have found the information pertinent and feel you have a better understanding of current market trends in your area. If you found questions left unanswered, please feel free to call me any time, as I would love to answer all of your real estate questions.

At this time, I would like to invite you to stay on my mailing list, free of charge of course, for the upcoming year. If you would like to remain on my mailing list, please fill out the response card and return it to me so we can continue to stay in touch over the next year. It has been my pleasure to bring you some of the most up-to-date information on your area. If you ever need any assistance in real estate, my hope is you will remember me. I would love to work with you in the future to help you realize your real estate dreams.

Kindest Regards,

_____

Agent Signature
(Contact Information)

LETTER FOR AUTO-RESPONDER

An author-responder letter allows the busy agent to reply to leads and referrals 24 hours a day, even when away from the computer. Keep in mind, some auto-responders have the ability to personalize the letter, but you should check the options on your software and ask your Web designer for further advice.

Dear _____,

Thank you for stopping by my Web site. I hope you enjoyed looking around the Web site. I am _____ and I have been with _____ Realty for _____ years. A lifelong resident of _____, I enjoy working with both buyers and sellers and am looking forward to talking with you soon.

If you are purchasing a home in the _____ area, please take a moment to send me a message with your new-home priorities. If you are thinking of listing your home for sale, submit the necessary information, and I will provide you with a comparative market analysis (CMA) within 24 hours.

My office hours are _____ through _____, _____ to _____, and I will contact you on my next business day so we can get to work on your real estate needs.

Again, thank you, _____, for dropping by the site, and I look forward to talking with you soon!

Kindest Regards,

_____

BASIC CANVASSING CYCLE TIMELINE

Month 1	Enter a group of 50-100 residential homes into the canvassing cycle and send out a letter of introduction.
Month 2	Send out your first newsletter.
Month 3	Call residents in the group to see whether they are thinking of selling or buying. Take anyone out of your canvassing cycle who asks you to put them into a "do not call" status.
Month 4	Send out your second newsletter.
Month 5	Send out your third newsletter.
Month 6	Send out a free market newsletter specific to the general area where you are canvassing. Be sure to include how many homes have recently sold in the area and current home listings in the area. Mention if you have buyers looking for a home in the area.
Month 7	Send out your fourth newsletter.

Month 8	Send out your fifth newsletter.
Month 9	Send out a personalized letter telling the resident about your desire to be their real estate agent, and include any investment properties for sale. Show a resident how to invest and make suggestions for great investment opportunities.
Month 10	Send out your sixth newsletter.
Month 11	Send out a letter not stating a "good-bye," but asking for the individual to keep you in mind whenever they have a real estate need.
Month 12	Send out your seventh newsletter, which includes a comment card with an option for the home owners to check if they are interested in staying on your mailing list.

BUYER'S MONTHLY EXPENSE WORKSHEET

This worksheet allows clients to analyze the cost of buying and owning a home. This should be completed before the agent begins showing the buyer homes in order to estimate whether buying a home is feasible.

Property
$___.__ Mortgage payment Taxes & Insurance
$___.__ Routine Maintenance
$___.__ Sub Total

Utilities
$___.__ Heating & Cooling
$___.__ Water
$___.__ Electricity
$___.__ Gas
$___.__ Phone
$___.__ Cable
$___.__ Internet
$___.__ Garbage Removal
$___.__ Laundry/Cleaning Service
$___.__ Automobile Expenses
$___.__ Sub Total

Personal Expenses
$___.__ Food
$___.__ Clothing
$___.__ Gifts/Donations
$___.__ Personal Allowances
$___.__ Pet Expenses
$___.__ Medical
$___.__ Prescriptions

$___.__ Vacation
$___.__ Educational Expenses
$___.__ Investment Contributions
$___.__ Total

Other
$___.__ Debts
$___.__ Fixed Financial Obligations
$___.__ Other
$___.__ Sub Total
$___.__ Grand Total

SELLER'S MOVING CHECKLIST

____1.   Contact your insurance agent; transfer property, fire, auto, and medical.
____2.   Obtain insurance as advised by your lender.
____3.   Get copies of your medical records or have them transferred.
____4.   Obtain a lockbox for your "impossible to replace," items or put them into a safety deposit box.
____5.   Designate items "will donate" or "sell," and dispose of them accordingly.
____6.   Make the arrangements for your move.
         a. Start early.
         b. Purchase necessary supplies.
         c. Give yourself extra time to get boxes.
____7.   Make your travel arrangements.
____8.   If you hire movers, plan to be present for loading and unloading.
____9.   Allow time for cleaning both properties (this includes freezer defrosting).
____10. Hire a babysitter.
____11. Arrange your change of address with the post office.
____12. Arrange to have the utilities transferred.
____13. Plan to begin packing early.
____14. Make arrangements to transfer your children to a new school.
____15. Plan meals and snacks for moving day.
____16. Pack your personal items, a first aid kit, and several changes of clothing.
____17. Have cash on moving day.
____18. Plan to pack some items at the last minute such as bedding.
____19. Other: _____.

AGENCY TO SELL LOTS IN A SUBDIVISION

Date: _____

Corporation: _____

Principal: _____

Realty Company: _____

Principal: _____

This contract, entered into on the above listed date between the corporation and principal aforementioned and the aforementioned realty company, witness:

- Principal is exclusive agent for the sale of lots in the subdivision known as _____ subdivision at _____; and
- Realty company is prepared to conduct a wide-ranging real estate and brokerage business and requirements to be appointed sole sales agent for a particular portion of the above-mentioned subdivision, all upon the terms and conditions set forth below.

As a result, in consideration of mutual agreements contained below, it is agreed between the parties as follows:

1. Principal allows to realty company complete right to sell any or all of the unsold lots in that part of _____ subdivision at _____, which is bounded by _____ Avenue, _____ Road, _____ Street, and _____ Avenue, such unsold lots being numbered as follows: _____.

2. Such privilege to sell is granted in agreement with provisions of the exclusive contract of principal to sell such lots and such sales are to be made by realty company on the following terms and conditions.

3. All lots sold by said realty company under the terms of this contract, shall be sold at prices not less than those shown on the plan or map, attached and made part of this contract, and on the terms as shown on the plan or map, a new plan or map with increased prices to be used after _____ *[date]*, to be prepared by principal.

4. If a _____% discount is permitted for cash, the commission to be paid to realty company is to be figured on the full sales price of such lot before the _____% discount is subtracted. All contracts for the sale of the above lots that may be sold by realty company shall be drawn up and prepared by principal upon its standard form of contract, and such contracts of sale are to be signed by principal.

5. On all sales of aforementioned lots made by realty company, it is to be given a commission in the amount of: _____%.

6. The term of this contract shall begin on _____*[date]* and shall run for _____ months with contract that in case realty company shall sell and turn in implemented contracts covering not less than _____ of lots above mentioned during such period of _____ months, then the term of this agreement shall be extended additionally for _____ days and for consecutive periods of _____ days each, so long as during each of such _____-day period realty company shall sell and deliver performed contracts covering the sale of not less than _____ of the aforementioned lots. In case realty company shall not sell these _____ lots during the first _____ months' phase or shall not sell at least _____ lots during each ensuing _____-day period, then at the end of such period wherein the realty company shall not put up for sale these lots as above provided for, this arrangement shall end and expire.

7. Realty company will not hire or impede with any of the sales people that are now or may in the future be associated with principal, and principal agrees not to hold up or hire any of the sales people associated with realty company.

(Signature):_____

(Signature):_____

AGREEMENT TO EXTEND THE PERIOD OF AN OPTION

Date: _____

Purchaser: _____

Seller: _____

In consideration of the additional payment of $_____.____ paid to the Seller by the Buyer (both listed above), the period of a specific option from the Seller to the Purchaser which was dated on _____ (month) _____ (day), _____ (year) is now hereby extended to _____ (month) _____ (day), _____ (year).

The extension will hereby apply to all the conditions and provisions of the option and will adjust to the Purchaser, his/her heirs, assigns, and other parties nominated by the Purchaser.

In Witness Whereof, the Purchaser and Seller have hereby agree to the terms set forth in this agreement and sign on this date listed above at the following location _____
_____.

Signed:	Printed:	Title:	Date:
Signed:	Printed:	Title:	Date:
Signed:	Printed:	Title:	Date:

AGREEMENT TO EXCLUSIVELY LIST A PROPERTY

Date: _____

Broker: _____

Address: _____

City: _____ State: _____ Zip: _____

Owner: _____

Address: _____

City: _____ State: _____ Zip: _____

This exclusive listing agreement is hereby effective as of the date listed on this Agreement by and between the above-listed Broker and Owner.

In contemplation of the services to be performed by the Broker, the Owner is hereby employing the Broker as an exclusive agent to sell the property located at _____ (street address), _____ (city), _____ (state), and _____ (zip) and described as _____, and is subject the below-listed terms and conditions.

1. Broker's Obligations

Broker hereby agrees to find a purchaser for the property in mention to the best of his/her ability. Broker must also list the property with any other listings the Broker is maintaining. The Broker is also required to put up signage on the property and to notify the Owner should any prospective buyers come forth. This notification should be made as soon as possible after occurrence. Additional requirements on behalf of the Broker include the following:

2. Broker's Commission

By signing this Agreement, both parties agree that the Broker is to receive a commission of _____% of the initial $_____ of the selling price and then _____% of the selling price after the initial amount if and only if the following guidelines regarding this commission are exclusive to this Agreement: _____

3. Listing Terms

1. On the date listed above, this Agreement will hereby be in effect until midnight of the following date _____ (date).
2. Within _____ days of the effective date of this Agreement, the listing may be concluded by written notice and signed by both parties.

4. Owner's Covenant to Sell

The Owner must provide a certificate of title or abstract from a reliable abstract company and provide a _____ deed that exhibits proper title to the property.

5. Governing Law

Both Parties hereby agree that this Agreement is governed and enforceable in accordance with the laws of the State of _____.

6. Entire Agreement

This Agreement is considered the entire agreement between both Parties and hereby supersedes any previous understanding or representation between these Parties.

7. Notifications

All notifications and information regarding this Agreement must be in writing and sent to both Parties at the above addresses by certified, registered, or a similar mail platform.

8. Receipt of this Agreement

In Witness Whereof, both Parties hereby agree to the items listed in this Agreement and have caused it to be executed at the following location _____ _____ on _____ (date).

Signed:	Date:
Signed:	Date:

AGREEMENT FOR SELLING LISTING EXCLUSIVITY

Date: _____
Broker: _____

Address: _____
City: _____ State: _____ Zip: _____

In consideration of the services to be done in the listing and undertaking to sell the property listed below, we hereby assign you the exclusive agent and the exclusive rights to sell the property located at _____ (street address), _____ (city), _____ (state), and _____ (zip), together with the improvements, appliances, and fittings described as _____
The minimum selling price should be $_____.
If the property is sold or traded by us or anyone else during the time frame provided in this listing, you will receive a commission for the sale in the amount of _____% of the purchase price. If the property is sold or traded within _____ days past the expiration date of this listing agreement to a buyer with whom you have been in negotiations with, then the commission for this sale shall be due and payable upon demand.

The expiration of this listing agreement shall be on the following date until the last hour of this date: _____ (month) _____ (date), _____ (year).

Signed:	Date:
Signed:	Date:

AGREEMENT FOR SELLING LISTING EXCLUSIVITY FOR LEASE OF A PROPERTY

Date: _____
Broker: _____
Address: _____
City: _____ State: _____ Zip: _____
Owner: _____
Address: _____
City: _____ State: _____ Zip: _____

This Agreement is effective as of the date listed above by and between the Broker and Owner listed above.

1. Employment of Broker
In consideration of the services to be performed by the Broker, the Owner is hereby employing the Broker as his/her exclusive agent. The Broker hereby agrees to obtain tenants for the rental property located at the following address: _____ (street address) _____ (city), _____ (state) _____ (zip) and described thoroughly as: _____
2. Broker's Commission
Broker's payment for his/her work being performed will be commission in the amount of _____% per month's rent for each tenant obtained.

3. Termination of Agreement

This Agreement may be terminated by either the Broker or owner with _____ days notice in writing.

4. Advertising

Broker is hereby authorized to advertise the rental properties in the manner they so desire and may also place signage on the property and remove any other signs located on said property.

5. Governing Law

Both Parties hereby agree that this Agreement is governed and enforceable in accordance with the laws of the State of _____.

6. Dispute Arbitration

Any and all disputes or questions concerning the rights and obligations of the Parties listed under the terms of this Agreement are hereby subject to arbitration. In order for said arbitration to occur, a demand in writing by either party must be provided to the other party within _____ days after said dispute occurs. The terms of the arbitration are as follows:

_____

(include date, location, etc).

In Witness Whereof, both the Broker and Owner have executed this Agreement on the date listed herein at the following location _____.

Signed:	Date:
Signed:	Date:

AGREEMENT TO PAY COMMISSION

Date: _____

To: _____ (Person receiving commission)

From: _____ (Owner/Seller)

This Agreement is made in conjunction with the Agreement for Purchase and Sale of Real Estate dated _____ by and between the Owner mentioned above and _____ (Buyer) concerning the property described as _____ (address), _____ (city), _____ (state), _____ (zip) and more specifically described as _____.

This Agreement is pursuant to the Buyer purchasing this property.

In consideration for your services provided in obtaining a Buyer for the property, the Owner signed below hereby agrees to compensate you with a commission in the amount of _____% of the sale contingent upon the final completion of the sale of the property to the Buyer.

This Agreement will guarantee and be binding upon the undersigned and his or her heirs, executors, successors, assigns, and any legal representatives.

Signed Property Owner:	Property Owner Printed:
Signed Witness:	Witness Printed:

AGREEMENT TO PURCHASE PROPERTY THROUGH A BROKER

Date: _____

Real Estate Agent: _____

Broker: _____

By signing this Agreement, I am hereby offering and agreeing to purchase through you, the Broker, the following property: _____ (street address), _____ (city), _____ (state), and _____ (zip). I am agreeing to purchase this property for the price of $_____.

Should this offer be accepted, I will place a cash deposit in the amount of _____% of the price I have offered for this property purchase. This amount will be non-interest bearing and will not be considered earnest money. This deposit will be made within _____ days of the acceptance of this offer.

If a good and merchantable title can be provided to me, I hereby agree to accept the title to this herein mentioned property and to pay the amount owed of the purchase price. This payment will be made at closing or within _____ days of the closing.

If I do not comply with the terms and conditions of this offer after this is accepted, I hereby require myself to pay the commission owed to you for this sale and any legal fees and costs you have incurred due to the enforcement of this collection.

This offer hereby remains binding and permanent until _____ (date).
I hereby accept the above offer and agree to pay you the commission of _____% on this herein mentioned sale.

Signed Owner:	Date:
Signed Witness:	Witness Printed:

AGREEMENT TO SHARE REFERRAL COMMISSIONS

Date: _____

Broker: _____

Sales Representative: _____

Both parties hereby agree to the following terms and conditions:

1. Broker hereby agrees to pay the Sales Representative a commission of _____% of the commission paid to the Broker for sales by the Sales Representative.

2. The Sales Representative hereby agrees to share all interested purchasers of this property to the Broker.

3. This Agreement is hereby made for a time period of _____ (days) and may be concluded within _____ (days) of written notice by either the Broker or Sales Representative.

In Witness Whereof, both the Broker and Owner have executed this Agreement on the date listed herein at the following location _____.

Signed:	Date:
Signed:	Date:

BROKER'S RECEIPT

Date: _____

Seller: _____

Husband (Purchaser):_____

Wife (Purchaser):_____

County: _____

State: _____

In regard to the Broker's Receipt made between abovementioned agent and purchasers, purchasers paid the seller the sum of $_____ in the form of cash, check, or note as deposit and part payment for the real property described above, located at (address): _____, which the seller has this day sold to purchasers, or their heirs and assigns, for the sum of $_____. Purchasers will pay the following balance on closing: _____.

Seller agrees to provide a purchaser's policy of title insurance in a timely manner and authorizes agent to apply immediately for such policy or report showing condition of title.

Title must be made insurable within _____ days from date of title report, or deposit shall be refunded, and all rights of purchaser terminated, unless purchaser elects to waive defects and proceed with the purchase as is. If the title is insurable, and purchaser neglects or refuses to complete purchase, the seller may opt to retain deposit as liquidated damages.

The property is to be conveyed by a _____ [e.g., warranty, or contract for] deed, free of encumbrance, [e.g., lien or mortgage]. Seller may remove encumbrances by making payments using the purchase money received at date of closing.

Taxes for the current year (_____), interest, mortgage reserves, insurance, rents, water, and all other utilities constituting liens shall be prorated as of the closing date.

Possession of property will be given upon _____ *[closing date]*.

Time is of the essence of this agreement.

By _____, Agent
_____, _____, Purchasers

The abovementioned purchasers accept and approve the above agreement, and will pay a commission of _____% on the total amount of this sale to the above agent for services rendered. Any deposit that is forfeited shall be apportioned equally to seller and agent provided that the amount to agent shall not exceed the agreed commission.

BUYER'S DEFAULT

Date: _____
Owner: _____
Broker: _____

The Broker's right to the commission of the sale of the property shall be given upon the execution of a sales contract to sell the property procured by the Broker. The Owner hereby understands and agrees that the execution of a sales contract is evidence that the Broker has indeed performed his or her obligations as stated within the Broker's Contract. The Broker's commission will paid out of the deposit provided from the Buyer for the property.

Signed:	Date:

BUYER-BROKER AGENCY AGREEMENT

Date: _____
Buyer: _____
Broker: _____
Length of Agreement (in months): _____
Ending Date of Agreement: _____

The broker shall be employed by the buyer to find and obtain specific property for the buyer. The broker shall be thorough and diligent in all attempts at locating satisfactory property for the buyer.

Both parties are in agreement in regard to the following:

The broker is a properly licensed real estate broker in the state of _____ and maintains an office capable of performing the agreed upon task.

The buyer wishes to acquire property located in
County:
State:

The desires for and intended uses of the property, are clearly explained in attached Exhibit A.

The buyer affirms availability of the necessary finances to purchase the property in accordance with the terms and conditions laid out in attached Exhibit B.

The broker is hereby given the right to find and buy property in accordance with the terms of this agreement and the attached exhibits.

The broker shall inspect any potential property and provide thorough information to the buyer prior to showing the property to the buyer.

The buyer shall purchase no property until a detailed, written account of such transaction has been supplied to the broker.

In the event that the broker's efforts lead to a purchase, either during or within _____ days of the termination of this agreement, the buyer shall pay the broker a commission of _____% of the property's purchase price upon closing. The broker is hereby granted the right to obtain commission from both the buyer and the seller of the property.

The buyer is free to enter into a purchase agreement independent of the broker, with no obligation to pay the broker commission. In such an event, the buyer shall reimburse the broker for any expenses incurred during the course of this contract on behalf of the buyer. The buyer also agrees to notify the broker within 24 hours of contact with such a prospective seller and to provide the broker with the property description and address, seller's name and contact information, and a detailed description of how the buyer located the property.
Either party may terminate this contract at any time by providing notice to the other party. Upon termination by the buyer, the buyer shall reimburse the broker for any expenses incurred during the course of the contract. In the event that a property that was presented to the buyer by the broker is purchased by the buyer at any time after cancellation of the contract, the buyer shall pay the broker the aforementioned commission.

Any monies paid by the buyer as a binder or deposit to the broker may be accepted and held by the broker or an authorized escrow agent according to the state laws of _____.
If a prospective seller forfeits, all such monies shall be returned to the buyer at once.

While this agreement is not a guarantee of the location or purchase or property, it does imply a guarantee that the broker's best efforts shall be put forth.

The buyer's name (may) (may not) be used in the broker's course of action in locating property on the buyer's behalf.

The finding of any portion of this agreement to be invalid shall in no way limit the validity of any remaining portions of the agreement.

This agreement is all-inclusive and can only be modified if both parties do so in writing. This agreement shall be unaffected by any previous oral or written agreements.

The laws of the state of _____ shall govern and enforce this agreement and all related transactions. Jury trial is hereby waived by both parties in favor of personal jurisdiction and venue and a subject matter jurisdiction court in _____ County, state of _____. In the case that this agreement results in such litigation, both parties agree that the losing party shall reimburse the prevailing party's reasonable expenses arising from said litigation. No action shall be pursued by the court if filed more than one year after the said violation took place.

This is a legally binding agreement for parties, as well as their assigns, heirs, legal representatives, and successors. Furthermore, this agreement shall not, in any way, be recorded in any public records.

_____   _____
Buyer   Witness

_____   _____
Seller   Witness

CONTRACT TO EMPLOY A REAL ESTATE BROKER FOR LEASE OF A PROPERTY

Date: _____
Owner: _____
Address: _____
City: _____ State: _____ Zip: _____
Broker: _____
Address: _____
City: _____ State: _____ Zip: _____

This Agreement is hereby made on this date by and between the above-listed Owner and Broker. The terms of this Agreement are as follows:

1. Property
The Owner owns the real estate located at _____ (street), _____ (city), _____ (state), _____ (zip).

2. Broker's Employment
The Owner hereby gives the Broker the sole right to rent the premises mentioned above to prospective tenants.

3. Broker's Commission

The Owner hereby agrees to pay a commission to the Broker in the amount of $_____ for his/her services in attaining tenants for the property and in the negotiations and closing of each lease for the property. The Owner retains the right to deny any lease and will not be held responsible for any commission for the property unless the Owner is in acceptance of the lease and receives payments for the lease. The commission of $_____ will be paid to the Broker for any lease renewals that were initially attained by the Broker. The commissions to the Broker are to be paid out of the rents received from those leases.

4. Sole Agency

The Owner hereby agrees to provide any and all inquiries from potential tenants or their agents to the Broker. The Broker hereby agrees to use all efforts and abilities to lease the property to these potential tenants.

5. Other Brokers

The Broker hereby agrees to seek the assistance of other Brokers as needed and to therefore pay out the same commission provided for herein. The Owner will in no way be liable for any additional commissions due to efforts on other Brokers' efforts.

6. Advertisements

The Broker (and any other Brokers as mentioned in E) are hereby entitled to advertise the rental property and take any steps needed to rent the property, including the use of signage to be approved by the Owner.

7. Terms

This Agreement will hereby remain in effect until the time that it is terminated or _____ (month) _____ (day), _____ (year).

8. Termination of this Agreement

The Broker or Owner may either terminate this contract with a written notification of _____ (days). This termination does not limit the right of the Broker to the commission that may result from any pending leases or negotiations. No commission will be paid to the Broker from rents paid after _____ (months/days) of the termination of this Agreement.

In Witness Whereof, both the Broker and Owner have executed this Agreement on the date listed herein at the following location _____.

Signed Broker:	Date:
Signed Owner:	Date:
Signed Witness 1:	Witness 1 Printed:
Signed Witness 2:	Witness 2 Printed:

BROKER DISCRETION AS TO PROPERTY SALES PRICE CONTRACT

Date: _____

Contract Ending Date: _____

Seller: _____

Seller's Company: _____

Broker: _____

Broker's Agency: _____

Property Address (including county and state):

_____

Effective immediately, the exclusive management and sale of the property, listed above and owned by the seller, is hereby transferred from seller to broker.

Following are the terms of the agreement:

The broker's inspection and resulting appraisal in the amount of _____ has been accepted by the seller.

The broker may sell the property for any price at their discretion, provided that it is not less than the aforementioned appraisal amount and that the amount and terms of payment have first been accepted by the seller.

The broker will invest due time and effort into the sale and management of the property. Broker also agrees to obtain the highest price possible for the company and to give a thorough, accurate account of all proceeds that may be derived therein. Broker shall make quarterly return of such sales and payment of any funds due to seller.

Broker shall put forth best effort to see that property sold is cultivated as quickly as possible by the buyer. In the event that the broker advances money for needed improvements to the property, broker may take any desired form of security and the money shall be returned to the broker with interest by the buyer before payment is made under the contract of sale.

Proceeds from sale of the property shall be applied first to the seller's receipt of $_____ per acre, combined with interest of _____% per annum from the contract date. Payment of all taxes accruing or due on the property from the contract date, including any _____ (year) taxes the company has paid, combined with interest of _____% per annum from payment date. Any remaining proceeds shall be divided equally between the broker and the seller.

Broker shall only retain profit after the full sum of $_____ per acre has been returned to the seller, with all applicable interest and taxes.

This legally binding contract can only be terminated in writing by both parties or upon the death of the broker. In the event of the broker's death during the term of the contract, the broker's assigns, administrators, or executives shall be entitled to interest in proceeds of property sold that would have been payable to the broker.

No interest in the property is herein conveyed from the seller to the broker.

The broker's only claim or right against the property or seller shall be the broker's half of the sales surplus, as described herein.

_____   _____
Broker   Witness

_____   _____
Seller   Witness

APPLICATION TO TRANSFER A BROKER OR AGENT

Adapted from the IOWA REAL ESTATE COMMISSION
(**www.state.ia.us/irec**). Please check with an attorney
for the correct format and procedure for your state.

_____ *[state]* REAL ESTATE COMMISSION APPLICATION TO TRANSFER

This form should be completed only if a licensee is transferring from one firm or broker to another firm or broker. When completed, this form must be mailed or hand-delivered together with the old license to the Real Estate Commission without delay within 72 hours. When the completed and correct transfer form and old license are received, a new license will be issued. The effective date of transfer will be the later of: 1). the effective date of the new affiliation, or 2) the date of release from the previous broker.

The three (3) steps to transfer MUST be completed in the order in which they appear on this form.

Step # 1 (To be completed by new affiliating broker)
Name of transferring licensee _____ *[Print or Type]*
Type of license _____ *[Salesperson or Broker Associate]*
License number _____
Effective date of new affiliation _____
Business name _____
Name of new broker _____ *[Print or Type]*
License number _____
Signature of New Broker_____

Step # 2 (To be completed by releasing broker)
Name of releasing broker _____ *[Print or Type]*
License number _____
Business name _____

The license of the transferring individual is attached to this form in compliance with the immediate return of a license to the Commission as required by _____ *[state]* Code section _____, (*Change of Employment.*)

Signature of Releasing Broker _____

Date of release: _____

Step # 3 (To be completed by transferring licensee)
I, _____ *[Print name of transferring licensee]*
hereby certify that the above information is true and correct. I further acknowledge that
providing false information on this transfer form would be in violation of _____
[state] Code section _____, (*Fraud in Procuring a License,*) which could result in
disciplinary action against my license.

Signature of transferring licensee _____
Date: _____

PROPERTY MANAGEMENT AGREEMENT

Adapted from **www.dpr.delaware.gov/boards/realestate/documents/
ManagementAgreement_Residential.doc**. Please check with an attorney for the correct
format and procedure for your state.

YOUR REAL ESTATE MANAGEMENT COMPANY
Address: _____
City: _____ State: _____ Zip: _____
Phone _____ Fax _____ Web site_____

In consideration of all of the covenants contained herein, _____
hereinafter "Owner," and Your Real Estate Management Company, a subsidiary of Any
Old Type Real Estate Company, a Delaware Corporation, or its assigns, hereinafter "Manager," agrees as follows:

The Owner agrees to exclusively employ Manager, and the Manager accepts Owner's exclusive employment to manage, lease, and operate the property known as   herein   after
"Property," upon the terms and conditions hereinafter set forth, for a period of One (1)
Year beginning _____, and continuing until the term of this Management Agreement, hereinafter "Agreement," shall expire as stated herein, unless sooner terminated by the
parties hereto. Upon the expiration of the agreed term of this Agreement, or termination
as contained herein, sole and absolute authority and responsibility for the Property shall be
returned to Owner, unless a Tenant (s) has been secured, in which case the terms of this
Agreement shall correspond and be identical to the term of any Lease Agreement (s) drawn
on the Property as a result of this employment.

1. The Manager agrees to:

a. Devote its reasonable best efforts consonant with first-class professional management to serving the Owner of the Property;

b. Make available to the Owner the full benefit of the judgment and experience of the
Manager's staff, and Agents, in renting, leasing, managing, servicing, and improving
the Property;

c. Not knowingly permit the use of the Property for any purpose that may be contrary to any municipal, county, state, or Federal ordinance, statute, law, or regulation, or which might void any policy of insurance held by the Owner, or which might render any loss insured under such a policy uncollectible;

d. Collect all rents and other payments due from any Tenant according to the terms and conditions of any and all lease agreements drawn on the Property by the Manager, or the Owner;

e. To make all repairs and perform all maintenance on or at the Property subject to the other terms and conditions of this Agreement.

2. The Manager further agrees to:

a. Collect a security deposit in an amount equal to one monthly rental, and to keep and to hold the said security deposit in its escrow account to be disbursed according to the terms of the lease agreement;

3. The Owner hereby grants the Manager the authority and responsibility to:

a. Advertise the Property for lease, and to sign, renew, and/or cancel lease agreements, said agreements not to exceed one (1) year in duration, and to collect and disburse security deposits according to the terms of the lease agreement, all on behalf of the Owner;

b. Use the Manager's, or its Agent's, lease agreements containing the terms and conditions as developed through the experience of the Manager and its Agents as property managers and leasing agents;

c. Sign tenant lease agreements as managing agent for the owner;

d. Collect rents and other assessments due, and to deposit the sums due, less any commissions or fees due Manager, in the place or places that the Owner may, from time to time, direct;

e. Sign & serve notices required under the lease agreements on behalf of the Owner;

f. Terminate tenancies, evict Tenants, and to recover possession of the Property, to institute legal proceedings including prosecution and suit, and to hire competent legal representation on behalf of the Owner, if and when required in order to protect the Owner and the Property;

g. When expedient, to settle, compromise, and release such actions or suits or reinstate such tenancies;

h. Pay any bills for any repairs or maintenance not to exceed $75 from the income received from the rental of the Property;

i. Call upon service Contractors or repairmen of Manager's choice, and on behalf of the Owner, in order to perform repairs or maintenance exceeding $100.00, as may from time to time be required so that the Property in no way shall depreciate, or in order to comply with the terms of the lease agreement, and to notify Owner promptly of said actions.

4. The Owner agrees to:

a. Pay to Manager a fee in the amount of one-half months rental, ten (10%) percent of each monthly rental received thereafter, in cash, and to be deducted from the rentals as received, in consideration of services rendered to the Owner;

b. Save the Manager harmless from any damage suits in connection with the management of the Property, and from liability from injury suffered by the Manager, its Agents or Employees, and from liability from injury suffered by any Tenant, or invitee, or Contractor, or whomever, and to carry public liability insurance adequate to cover the interests of the parties hereto, and such policy shall be so written as to protect the Manager in the same way as the Owner and which will name Manager as co-insured, and to deliver a copy of the said policy to Manager at Manager's request;

c. Save Manager harmless from liability for any error in judgment or for any mistake of fact of law, except for cases of willful misconduct or gross negligence;

d. Give to Manager the sole authority to determine necessary cleaning to render the Property marketable.

5. The Manager shall not be responsible for, nor obligated to:

a. Make repairs or perform maintenance at the Property out of Manager's funds or reserves;

b. Make, nor cause to be made, any payments of premiums of any policy of insurance, or any property taxes or special assessments;

c. File, nor cause to be filed, any income tax returns, or gross receipts tax returns;

d. Accept responsibility for any personal property that the Owner leaves in either secured or unsecured storage at the Property;

e. Legal representation in a case where judgment has been filed and case is turned over to bankrupt court.

This Agreement may be terminated for cause by either party hereto upon the deliverance of written notice by the terminating party to the other party of its intention to do so at least thirty (30) days in advance of any such termination.

The terms & conditions of this Agreement are the entire agreement & understanding between the parties hereto. This Agreement supersedes any oral understanding of the parties hereto. The Owner & the Manager have read carefully, understand, and approve of the provisions and covenants as stated herein. This Agreement may not be modified or altered under any circumstances. In the event a modification of the understanding of the parties shall be required, a new Agreement shall be prepared containing all of the provisions, including the modified provisions, representing the complete understanding of the parties hereto.

This Agreement shall be construed according to the laws of the State of Delaware.

This Agreement shall be binding upon the parties hereto, their heirs, assigns, and legal representatives.

IN WITNESS WHEREOF, the parties hereto have executed this Agreement as of the day and year first above written.

OWNER NAME: _____

By: _____

WITNESS NAME: _____

Signature: _____

MANAGER: YOUR REAL ESTATE PROPERTY MANAGEMENT COMPANY

By: _____

WITNESS NAME: _____

Signature: _____

REAL ESTATE MANAGEMENT CONTRACT

Seller: _____

Address: _____

City: _____ State: _____ Zip: _____

Buyer: _____

Address: _____

City: _____ State: _____ Zip: _____

EXHIBIT "A"
Property Descriptions

THIS MANAGEMENT Agreement was created on _____ day of _____, 20 ___, between the above named Owner and Manager.

The Manager agrees to supervise and manage on behalf of the Owner the real estate consisting of those properties described above in Exhibit "A," referred to in this Agreement as the "Property."

The Manager and the Owner agree to the following mutual covenants and agreements:

1. Retainer.

Owner will retain the manager to supervise and manage the property of the Owner under certain terms and conditions. This Agreement is created for the advancement, protection and preservation of the interests of the Owner in the Property.

2. Term.

This Agreement begins on the _____ day of _____, 20 _____ and remains in full force and effect until the termination date of _____ day of _____, 20 _____. Any extension, continuation, or renewal of this term can be agreed upon by the parties in writing.

3. Independent Contractor.

It is agreed that the manager is an independent contractor hired by the Owner to perform the above stated services. The Manager is not an employee of the Owner.

4. Manager's Duties and Responsibilities.

The Manager agrees to perform the following duties:

a.   Administrative:
   i.   Collect all rents and monies due to the Owner in relation to the Property.
   ii. If necessary, pursue legal action to collect delinquent rents due the owner. The Owner agrees to pay $40.00, plus all applicable court costs, for any legal action undertaken to collect unpaid or delinquent rent.
   iii. Maintain accurate records of the tenants and lease terms, and any other financial records of expenses or income relating to the Property.
   iv. Make any amendments to leases or other documents as needed and enforce the Rules, Regulations, and Policies of the Owner.
   v.   Receive and respond to requests from Tenants.
   vi. Attend all necessary meetings.

b.   Financial:
   i.   Deposit all payments for damages and rents collected in a timely manner, and maintain a bank account for owner's properties.
   ii. Take responsibility to make any payments approved by the Owner and to pay any invoices considered to be routine expenditures.
   iii. Maintain accurate financial records. All such records and books will be open for inspection by the Owner at any time during reasonable business hours. At the termination of this Agreement, all financial records shall be retained by the Owner.
   iv. Provide to Owner monthly financial statements containing a record of all receipts and disbursements for each month. A financial statement for each month will be given to Owner by the 15th of the following month.
   v.   Prepare upon request a tentative budget of expenses anticipated for the following year of operations. Upon Owner's approval, the Manager will administer the budget in its approved form.
   vi. Arrange for an annual audit of Owner's accounts if this is requested by Owner.
   vii. Get Owner's approval for any expenditure in excess of _____ dollars (_____) in regard to the Property.

c.   Maintenance and Supervision:
   i.   Employ and supervise the staff personnel needed to maintain and repair Property.

    ii. Purchase all materials, supplies, and equipment needed for repair and maintenance of Property.

    iii. Attempt to be efficient and use the most cost-effective methods possible to maintain Property. Review, approve, and authorize staff members to fulfill maintenance requests filed by tenants.

    iv. Contract with contractors and subcontractors to provide any necessary repair and maintenance services for Property.

    v. Inspect the grounds and buildings and suggest immediate and long-term projects necessary to maintain the property.

    vi. Manage the application and approval process for lease of the Property.

    vii. Inspect roof on the Property annually.

5. Owner's Duties and Responsibilities.

    a. The Owner will pay the Manager for all expenses incurred by the Manager in relation to the performance of Manager's duties.

    b. The Owner agrees to pay any amount owed to Manager for duties performed on the first day of the subsequent month.

    c. The Manager is held harmless from any and all claims, suits, debts, or demands arising in connection with the management of the Property and from any and all liability arising from injury to any person or property, except to the extent that said claims, suits, debts, or demands were caused by the Manager's negligence or failure to perform the duties set forth in this Agreement.

6. Termination.

This agreement may be terminated without cause, by either party at any time upon thirty (30) days written notice to the other party.

7. Modification.

Modifications, alterations, or amendments to this Agreement must be made in writing and signed by both parties.

8. Assignment.

This Agreement cannot be assigned by Manager to any other party.

9. Notices.

It is agreed that notices and communications are considered effective at the end of the fifth day after they have been sent by first-class U.S. mail with postage prepaid to the other party at the address above.

10. Governing Law.

This agreement is governed by the laws of the State of _____. The parties herein waive trial by jury and agree to submit to the personal jurisdiction and venue of a court of subject matter jurisdiction located in _____ County, State of _____.

If there is legal action that results from or arises out of this Agreement or the performance thereof, the parties will pay for the prevailing party's reasonable attorney's fees, court costs, and all other expenses.

Signed, sealed and delivered in the presence of:

"Owner"

Witness

Witness

"Manager"

Witness

Witness

REAL ESTATE SALESPERSON INDEPENDENT CONTRACTOR AGREEMENT

Date: _____

Broker: _____

Salesperson: _____

This Agreement is hereby made on the date above by and between the Broker and Salesperson listed above. Both parties hereby state the following:

1. The Broker is properly registered and licensed as a real estate broker with the State of _____. Broker's license expires on _____ (date).

2. The Salesperson is properly registered and licensed as a real estate salesperson with the State of _____. His/her license expires on _____ (date).

Both the Broker and Salesperson hereby agree to the following terms and conditions:

1. Employment
As of the date this Agreement is signed, the Broker hereby employs the Salesperson as a real estate salesperson.

2. Salesperson's Duties and Responsibilities
The Salesperson will perform all the normal duties of a real estate salesperson. These duties include, but are not limited to the following:

- Showing properties/land parcels of which the Broker has listings
- Selling of the aforementioned property/land according to the provisions of the listing
- Solicitation of new real estate property/land listings
- Other duties of which the Broker may require

Salesperson's duties are to be handled during his entire time working with Broker, and Salesperson understands he/she must work to get the duties done with best effort.

3. Sales Commissions
The Broker hereby agrees that the Salesperson will be paid a commission of _____% of the total commission that the Broker has earned on sales made by the Salesperson and of which were finished during the time of employment starting the date of this Agreement and ending on _____ (date). Also during this time frame, the Broker will

give Salesperson an advance in the amount of $_____ per month, which is to be paid against the commissions that the Salesperson will earn. This may occur only if the Salesperson has chosen to receive the monthly advance.

4. Time Frame of Agreement; Salesperson's Termination

The time frame for this Agreement to be in effect begins on the date this Agreement was signed and will be effective for _____ years with an end date of _____. Should either the Broker or Salesperson so choose to end this Agreement, the party must provide a minimum of 60 days notice to the other party in writing. Should the Salesperson have received any advances above the amount of commissions the Salesperson actually received, the Salesman must then immediately return to the Broker the excess amount.

5. Salesperson's Access to Listings and Other Important Information

The Broker hereby agrees to provide the Salesperson access to his/her confidential files relating to the property listings, sales prospects of the listings, and any other information of which the Salesperson should be apprised to. The Broker also agrees to provide the Salesperson with personal contacts of people interested in selling or buying a property and will help the Salesperson in any way possible in regards to the sales of the properties and the Salespersons duties so listed within this Agreement.

6. Salesperson's Loyalty to the Broker's Interests

During the length of time this Agreement is effective, the Salesperson may not be involved in any other business activities, whether or not it be for profit or any other financial gain, unless the Salesperson is investing his or her resources in a way so that it does not take up an excessive amount of time.

7. Nondisclosure Agreement

The Salesperson understands and hereby agrees that the information provided to him regarding any of the Broker's clients, property/land listings, investments, transactions, or any other areas that are confidential and which are considered the Broker's trade secrets. The Salesperson also may not disclose during any time of his/her employment or thereafter any of the information as described above to any person, business, or other entity for any reason or purpose whatsoever. To do so will constitute a violation of this agreement.

8. Entire Agreement

This written Agreement between the Broker and Salesperson hereby constitutes the entire contract and agreement between them, and both understand that no other agreements or unwritten agreements will be valid.

9. Binding

This Agreement between the Broker and the Salesperson will be binding upon signing by both parties and inure to the advantage of the respective legal heirs, successors, and assigns of Broker and Salesperson.

10. Governing Law

This Agreement will be governed, interpreted, and construed under the laws of the State of _____.

11. Legal Fees

Should either party desire to take legal action against the other in regards to this agreement, the prevailing party will be permitted to recover legal fees of reasonable nature.

12. Severability

Should any part of the Agreement be invalid or unenforceable, it will not affect the other items listed herein.

IN WITNESS WHEREOF, the Broker and the Salesperson hereby agree to and acknowledge their agreement hereof by the signing below of all parts of this Agreement on the date first mentioned above.

_____   _____
Broker   Witness

_____   _____
Salesperson   Witness

CANVASSING PHONE CALL SCRIPT

Agent: Hi! This is _____ with _____ Real Estate. May I speak with _____ please?

Homeowner: This is _____, what can I do for you?

Agent: _____, I sent you a newsletter and letter of introduction a few weeks back. Do you remember seeing it?

Homeowner: Sure I do. My wife liked some of the articles in the newsletter.

Agent: Great! _____, I just wanted to call you today to let you know I am working hard to become the recognized agent in your particular area and to ask you if you have just a moment to answer three quick questions.

Homeowner: OK, I guess I can do that.

Agent: Great! The first one is what information would be most beneficial to you as a home owner to see in my newsletters?

Homeowner: My wife said she would like to know more about how much the houses in our neighborhood are selling for.

Agent: I can do that! Second, let me ask you something, _____. Are you planning on selling in the next six months to a year?

Homeowner: No, we are not considering selling our home.

Agent: That is fine. Let me ask you a third question. Do you know anyone who will be selling or buying in the near future?

Homeowner: Sure do, my cousin is buying a home.

Agent: Well, _____, I would love to work with your cousin. Does he have a real estate agent?

Homeowner: No, he does not. If you will give me your number, I will have him give you a call.

Agent: That would be great; my number is ____-____-_____. What is his name and number?

Homeowner: _____ and his number is ____-____-_____.

Agent: Great! _____, I really appreciate this lead and more than anything, I am glad I had the opportunity to talk with you. Please let me know if I can do anything to help you in the future. Please feel free to call me with any questions you might have in the future.

CALLING "FOR SALE BY OWNER" PROPERTIES

Agent: Hello. My name is _____ and I am with _____ Real Estate. I saw your home listed in the paper and wanted to give you a call to see if I could set up an appointment with you to give you a free market analysis. Could I get your first name please?

Homeowner: Why? I am selling my home by myself. I am _____, by the way.

Agent: Yes, I understand. However, I would love the opportunity to work with you and show you how you can make your home more marketable to potential buyers as well as give you a free market analysis. _____, you are under no obligation to me, and we offer this service free of charge.

Homeowner: Why would you want to give this service to me for free?

Agent: I will be upfront with you. It is tough selling for sale by owner, but I really would like to help you by offering you some tools to use as you pursue selling for sale by owner. If you choose at a later date to list your property with an agent, I hope you will remember me, but if not, my service is still free because it is what I do best.

Homeowner: That sounds like a great deal. I will be around my home tomorrow if you want to stop by then. I will be here all day.

Agent: Would it be okay if I came at 4 p.m.?

Homeowner: That will be fine.

Agent: Great! I will see you then! And, _____, thanks so much for your time!

Note: It is important to remember that most homeowners are not going to be thrilled to give you the appointment, particularly if they have been bombarded with agent calls. Stay friendly and smile. It comes through over the phone.

COLD-CALLING

If you are going to cold-call, we recommend using one of your promotions to gain phone numbers and lead sheets; then, you can change the cold-calling script to meet your needs.

Agent: Hi! May speak to _____, please?

Homeowner: Sure, who is this?

Agent: This is _____ and I am calling with _____ Real Estate.

Homeowner: Yes, this is _____.

Agent: _____, as I said, I am with _____ Real Estate and I am working in your area this month and wanted to call you and see if you could answer a couple of quick questions for me?

Homeowner: Sure.

Agent: Great! _____, how long have you lived in the area?

Homeowner: _____ years.

Agent: How do you like the area?

Homeowner: It's great.

Agent: _____, did you know with home values increasing, you could possibly sell your home and make a nice profit while upgrading to another home?

Homeowner: Really, that is interesting. Drop something in the mail to me about it.

Agent: I would love to, and if you have a few extra minutes after I send over the information, I would really like to talk to you further.

Homeowner: Sure, I will look forward to it.

CALLING BUYER REFERRALS

Agent: Hello, may I please speak with _____?

Homeowner: This is _____.

Agent: Hi _____. My name is _____ and I am with _____ Real Estate. Your friends, _____,
gave me your name and number and suggested I call you.

Homeowner: Why?

Agent: They told me you are interested in buying real estate in the next few months, and I would like to have the honor of working with you. They have told me you are interested in lake property. Is this right?

Homeowner: Yes, but I am not looking to buy until next year.

Agent: I understand. I just wanted to call you and say hello and ask you for your mailing address so I can send you new information about lake properties as they come on the market. How does that sound?

Homeowner: Sure, that would be great! My address is _____.

Agent: Got it! I will drop some information to you from time to time and when you are ready to start home shopping, please keep me in mind.

Homeowner: Thanks for calling!

Agent: You are welcome.

CALLING SELLER REFERRALS

Agent: Hello, may I please speak to _____?

Homeowner: This is _____.

Agent: Hi _____. This is _____ and I am with _____ Real Estate. I am calling because _____ gave me your name and number and suggested I call you.

Homeowner: _____ told me you would be calling.

Agent: Great! I wanted to call and see if I could stop by your home some time in the next week or so and offer you a free market analysis on your home?

Homeowner: Why?

Agent: _____ told me you are interested in selling your home, and I would love to be your real estate agent. I know your area well and would like the opportunity to show you what is going on in your neighborhood. I can provide you with a market analysis to show you how much money you should be able to get out of your home, as well as what other have sold for in your area.

Homeowner: That would be fine. I will be working in my garden all day Friday. Just stop by any time.

Agent: Great! I will see you then!

CHAPTER 5

Commercial Real Estate Forms

AGREEMENT FOR SALE OF COMMERCIAL REAL ESTATE

Date: _____

Seller: _____

Address: _____

City: _____ State: _____ Zip: _____

Buyer: _____

Address: _____

City: _____ State: _____ Zip: _____

In consideration of the mutual promises, covenants, agreements, and conditions contained herein and for other good and valuable consideration, receipt of which is hereby acknowledged, the Buyer(s) and Seller(s) agree to the following:

1. Agreement.
The Sellers agree to sell to Buyers and Buyers agree to purchase the land and buildings located in _____ Township, _____ County, and _____ State as described in Deed to Sellers recorded in _____ County Record Book ____, on Page _____. The aforementioned property contains _____ acres, more or less.

2. Purchase Price and Deposit.
The agreed upon Purchase Price is $_____. The Sellers acknowledge that a Deposit in the amount of $_____ is due prior to the signing of this Agreement. Deposit will be held by _____ until closing has been completed, and will then be applied toward the Purchase Price.

3. Allocations.

Seller(s) and Buyer(s) agree that the allocations of the Purchase Price described below are fair and reasonable and are the result of negotiations between both parties for the terms and conditions of this sale:

Personal Property, Equipment, & Fixtures	$_____
Buildings	$_____
Land	$_____
Total Purchase Price	$_____

4. Damages.

Seller is responsible for all risk of any losses from fire, damages or other casualty until closing.

5. Condition of Property.

Seller(s) must remove all debris from Property before closing and must maintain the property and land in-like condition until closing.

6. Inspection.

Buyer(s) may inspect Property and land before closing provided they submit a forty-eight (48) hour written notice to the Seller's attorney.

7. Appliances.

The appliances listed below are to be conveyed with the property and must be in good working order at the time of closing. Seller(s) must complete any repairs prior to closing, or the cost of said repairs will be deducted at closing. List of Appliances: _____

_____.

8. Transfer Fees.

Each Party agrees to pay one-half of the _____ (State) and _____ (Local) Realty Transfer Taxes due. Each side's payment amount is expected to be $_____.
The real estate taxes for the dates __/__/20__ to __/__/20__ are to be prorated to the date of closing. Township and County taxes to be prorated on a calendar-year basis, and School tax is to be prorated on a fiscal-year basis. Buyer will take possession of Property at closing.

9. Septic System.

The Buyers are hereby notified that the premises described in this Agreement require an on-site septic system and are not serviced by a community sewage treatment facility. Buyers should contact the local government agency charged with wastewater disposal to learn the requirements prior to signing this Agreement.

10. Seller's Warranty.

As of the date of closing, Seller(s) represent and warrant that to the best of the Seller(s) knowledge and belief, no government agency, or employee or official of a government agency, has given any notice to the Seller that it considers the construction on the Property or the operation or use of the Property to be out of compliance with any law, ordinance, regulation, or order, or that any investigation has been or might be initiated respecting any possible non- compliance. There are no lawsuits involving the property and no unpaid expenses or outstanding invoices from any person, entity or authority, including, but not limited to, any tenant, lender, insurance carrier, or government authority, for the cost of repairs, restorations, or improvements to the Property.

11. Hazardous Substances.

To the best of the Seller(s') knowledge, understanding, and information, no person, firm, or entity has dumped any hazardous or toxic substance on the Property. Seller(s) also guarantee that the Deed conveying the property will contain a "hazardous waste clause."

12. Lead Disclosure.

Seller(s) and Buyer(s) both agree to comply with the Federal Lead Disclosure Act and the _____ (State, if one) Real Estate Sales Disclosure Act Laws and to execute all required disclosure statements.

13. Title.

Title to the Property will be transferred by General Warranty Deed. An attorney for the Buyer(s) will determine that the title to the Property is good and marketable based on a sixty-year (60) title examination and a good and sufficient General Warranty Deed. Any exceptions and reservations for oil, gas, and/or minerals in, on, and under the property existing in favor of another party in the chain of title will not be deemed a defect in title or detrimental to an otherwise good and marketable title to the Property.

14. Home Inspection.

The Buyer(s) may, at their own expense, choose to have licensed or otherwise qualified professionals inspect and/or certify the Property within _____ days of the execution of this Agreement. Any home inspection of the property, as defined in the _____ (State) Home Inspection Law, must be completed by a full member in good standing of a national home inspection association, or by a person supervised by a full member of a national home inspection association, in accordance with the ethical standards and code of conduct or practice of that association. If any written report of such an inspection reveals defects in the condition of the Property, Buyer may:

a. Accept Property as is with the information stated in the given inspection report(s); or

b. Terminate this Agreement within fifteen (15) days of the inspection by written notice to Seller(s). In this event, any deposits paid toward the Purchase Price will be immediately returned to the Buyer(s) and this Agreement will be null and void; or

c. Enter into a mutually acceptable written agreement with the Seller(s) providing for any repairs or improvements to the premises and/or any credit to the Buyer(s) for the cost of such repairs at closing. Should Buyer(s) and Seller(s) fail to arrive at a mutually acceptable agreement, the Buyer(s) must then either accept Property as is or terminate this Agreement within _____ days.

15. Default.

If Seller(s) fail to comply with the terms and conditions of this Agreement due to the failure of title or because a fire/casualty partially or completely destroys the premises, the Buyer(s), as their sole and exclusive remedy, may terminate this Agreement by delivering written notices to the Seller(s) at or prior to the closing. In such event, any deposit and all interest earned on the deposit will belong to the Buyer(s), this Agreement shall be dissolved and Seller(s) shall have no further obligation or liability to the Buyer(s) and the Buyer(s) shall have no further rights under this Agreement.

Signed this _____ day of _____ (Month) _____ (Year).

Witnesseth, both parties have executed this agreement at the day and year first above written.

_____   _____
Seller Printed   Seller Printed

_____   _____
Seller Signature   Seller Signature

_____   _____
Buyer Printed   Buyer Printed

_____   _____
Buyer Printed   Buyer Printed

COMMERCIAL LEASE AGREEMENT

Date: _____

Landlord: _____

Address: _____

City: _____ State: _____ Zip: _____

Tenant: _____

Address: _____

City: _____ State: _____ Zip: _____

This Commercial Lease Agreement (Lease) is entered into on the above date between Landlord and Tenant. Under this Agreement, Landlord leases the Leased Premises to Tenant, and Tenant leases the Leased Premises from Landlord for the entire term, at the rental rate described and under the terms and conditions set forth in this Agreement.

Landlord's Guarantee.

Landlord certifies that he/she is the owner of the parcel of land and the improvements on it, located at the legal address of: _____. Landlord makes available for lease the portion of the Building designated as _____ and described as _____ (Leased Premises).

1. Term.

The Term of the Lease shall begin on the _____ day of _____, 20__, and end on the _____ day of _____, 20__. Landlord shall make every effort to ensure that Leased Premises are available for Tenant's occupation on the first day of the Lease term. If Leased Premises are not available on the first day of the Lease term, the amount of $ _____ per day shall be subtracted from the rent for the period of the delay. Tenant shall make no other claim against Landlord for delays.

2. Renewal.

Tenant will be given the option to renew the Lease for one extended term of _____ by providing written notice to Landlord no less than ninety (90) days before the expiration of the Initial Term. The renewal term shall be at the rate set forth below and shall be under the same terms, covenants, conditions, and provisions as this Lease.

3. Rent.

Tenant shall pay to Landlord during the Initial Term rent of $ _____ (Dollars) per year, payable in monthly installments of $ _____. Each installment payment shall be due in advance on the first day of each calendar month during the lease term to Landlord at the following address:

_____

The amount of rent for any partial calendar months included in the lease term shall be prorated on a daily basis.

The rental rate for any renewal lease term, if created according to the terms of this Lease, shall be $ _____ (Dollars) per year payable in monthly installments of $ _____ (Dollars).

4. Security Deposit.

Tenant shall also pay to Landlord a Deposit of $_____ by _____ (Date). Landlord will hold the Security Deposit for the duration of the lease term as a guarantee that Tenant will perform all of its covenants and obligations under this Lease. Landlord will not be required to pay interest on deposit. It is expressly understood by both Landlord and Tenant that the Security Deposit will serve as an advance payment of rent or be applied to Landlord's damages in the event that Tenant defaults on its obligations under the terms of this Agreement. Unless law or regulation dictates otherwise, Landlord may commingle the Security Deposit with Landlord's other funds. Landlord may, from time to time, without forfeiting the right to any other remedy, use funds from the Security Deposit to pay overdue rent or to satisfy any other covenant or obligation of Tenant under the terms of this Agreement. In such case, Tenant shall, upon request, pay to Landlord an amount sufficient to restore the Security Deposit to its original amount. If Tenant is not in default at the termination of this Lease, Landlord agrees to return the balance of the Security Deposit remaining after any settlement of the obligations of the Tenant under this Lease.

5. Prohibited Uses.

Tenant agrees not to use the Leased Premises to store, manufacture, or sell any explosives, flammables, other inherently dangerous substance, chemical, hazardous or toxic substance, or any other dangerous thing or device, or for any other illegal activity.

6. Sublease and Assignment.

Tenant has the right, without Landlord's consent, to assign this Lease to a business with which Tenant may merge or consolidate, to any subsidiary of Tenant, to any corporation under common control with Tenant, or to a business that purchases substantially all of Tenant's assets. Tenant agrees not to sublease all or any part of the Leased Premises, or assign this Lease in whole or in part to any company or tenant that is not a direct business affiliate without Landlord's written consent. Landlord agrees to provide either consent or dissent within seven (7) days of any written request from Tenant for permission to sublease.

7. Property Taxes.

Landlord shall pay, in a timely manner, all real estate taxes and special assessments due before or during the Lease term on the Leased Premises, and all personal property taxes associated with any personal property located at the Leased Premises and belonging to the Landlord. Tenant shall be responsible for paying all personal property taxes associated with Tenant's personal property located at the Leased Premises.

8. Utilities.

Unless otherwise expressly agreed in writing by Landlord, Tenant shall pay all charges for water, sewer, gas, electricity, telephone, and other services and utilities used by Tenant on the Leased Premises during the term of this Lease. For any utility or service provided to the

Leased Premises that is not separately metered, Landlord shall pay the total amount due and separately invoice Tenant for Tenant's fair share of the charges. Tenant shall pay such all such utility charges on or before their due dates. Tenant acknowledges that the Leased Premises have been electrically wired for standard office use and standard office lighting, and agrees not to use any equipment or devices that require excessive electrical energy or which may, in Landlord's reasonable opinion, overload the wiring or otherwise interfere with electrical services to other tenants.

9. Insurance.

Landlord agrees to maintain fire and extended coverage insurance on the Building and the Leased Premises in an amount deemed appropriate by the Landlord. Tenant shall be responsible for maintaining fire and extended coverage insurance on all of Tenant's personal property located in the Leased Premises, including removable trade fixtures, at Tenant's expense.

Tenant and Landlord shall each maintain a policy or policies of comprehensive general liability insurance that pertain to the particular activities of each in the Building. The signing of this Agreement serves as affirmation that both parties have paid in full the premiums for these policies on or before due date. These insurance policies shall be issued by and binding upon an insurance company approved by Landlord, and shall afford minimum protection of not less than $1,000,000 combined, single-limit coverage of bodily injury, property damage, or combination thereof. Tenant shall provide Landlord with current Certificates of Insurance documenting Tenant's compliance with this Paragraph.

10. Repairs.

During the term of this Lease, Tenant shall be responsible to make, at Tenant's expense, all necessary routine repairs of floors, walls, ceilings, and other parts of the Leased Premises damaged or worn through normal occupancy, and other similar items. Repairs of major mechanical systems or the roof are subject to obligations of the parties otherwise set forth in this Lease.

11. Alterations and Improvements.

Tenant has the right, as Tenant may deem desirable, and upon obtaining Landlord's written consent, to remodel, redecorate, and make additions, improvements, and replacements of and to all or any part of the Leased Premises from time to time, at the expense of the Tenant. Tenant agrees that such improvements and modifications should be carried out in a workmanlike manner and utilize quality materials. Tenant may place and install personal property, trade fixtures, equipment and other temporary installations in and upon the Leased Premises, and physically affix such installations to the premises. All personal property, equipment, machinery, trade fixtures, and temporary installations, whether installed by Tenant at the commencement of the Lease term or after the lease has begun, shall remain Tenant's property free and clear of any claim by Landlord. Tenant may remove such personal property, equipment, trade fixtures, and installations at any time during the term of this Lease and must repair, at Tenant's own expense, all damages to the Leased Premises caused by their removal.

12. Signage.

With Landlord's written consent, Tenant shall have the right to place on the Leased Premises, at locations selected by Tenant, signage that is in compliance with local zoning ordinances and private restrictions. Regardless of whether or not they are permitted by local zoning ordinances, Landlord retains the right to refuse consent to any proposed signs that are, in Landlord's opinion, too large, deceptive, unattractive, or otherwise inconsistent with or inappropriate to the Leased Premises or may have a negative effect on the business of any other tenant, Landlord shall collaborate with Tenant to obtain any necessary permission from governmental authorities or adjoining owners and occupants for Tenant to place or construct signs. At end of lease term, Tenant is responsible to repair all damage to the Leased Premises resulting from the removal of signs installed by Tenant.

13. Access to Premises by Landlord.

Landlord or Landlord's agent shall have the right to enter Leased Premises during reasonable hours to conduct inspections, provided Landlord does not thereby unreasonably interfere with Tenant's business on the Leased Premises.

14. Parking.

For the duration of this Lease, Tenant is entitled to non-exclusive use in common with Landlord, other tenants of the Building, and their guests and invitees, of the non-reserved common parking areas, driveways, and footways on the Property. Tenant must follow the rules and regulations for their use set forth by Landlord. Landlord reserves the right to assign designated parking areas for Tenant and Tenant's agents and employees. Tenant shall provide Landlord with a list of all license numbers of the cars owned by Tenant, its agents, and employees.

15. Building Rules.

Tenant will comply and will cause all of its agents, employees, invitees, and visitors to comply with the rules of the Building. Building Rules may be altered and new rules may be adopted by Landlord from time to time; Landlord will provide written notice to Tenant of all changes. The initial rules for the Building are attached to this Agreement as Exhibit "A" and considered a part of this Agreement.

16. Damage and Destruction.

If the Leased Premises or any part thereof is damaged by fire, casualty, or structural defects that are not the result of any act of negligence by Tenant or by any of Tenant's agents, employees, or invitees, to the point that the Leased Premises cannot be used for Tenant's purposes, then Tenant shall have the right within ninety (90) days following the occurrence of the damage to notify the Landlord in writing that Tenant wishes to terminate this Lease as of the date of such damage. In the event of minor damage to any part of the Leased Premises that does not render the Leased Premises unusable for Tenant's purposes, Landlord shall promptly repair such damage at Landlord's expense. In making these repairs, Landlord will not be liable for any delays resulting from matters that are beyond the Landlord's reasonable control such as strikes, governmental restrictions, unavailability of necessary materials or labor, or other delays. Rent and other charges will be waived during any portion of the Lease term that the Leased Premises are inoperable or unfit for occupancy or cannot be used, in whole or in part, for Tenant's purposes. Rentals and other monies paid in advance for any such periods shall be credited to the next ensuing payments, if any. If no further payments are due because Tenant has terminated the lease or the term of the lease has expired, then any such advance payments shall be refunded to Tenant. The provisions of this paragraph extend to any occurrence that is beyond Tenant's reasonable control and which renders the Leased Premises, or any appurtenance to the Leased Property, inoperable or unfit for occupancy or use, in whole or in part, for Tenant's purposes. Rent shall not be waived or decreased during periods when Leased Premises is under repair because the Leased Premises or any other part of the Building have been damaged by fire or other casualty resulting from any act of negligence by Tenant or by any of Tenant's agents, employees, or invitees. Tenant shall be responsible for the costs of repair not covered by insurance.

17. Condemnation.

If any legally constituted authority condemns the Building or takes other action that renders the Leased Premises unsuitable for leasing, this Lease shall cease on the day that public authority takes possession, and Landlord and Tenant shall account for rental as of that date. Such termination shall not affect the rights of either party to recover compensation from the condemning authority for any loss or damage caused by the condemnation. Neither party shall have rights in or to any award made to the other by the condemning authority.

18. Default.

In the event that Tenant defaults in the payment of rent when due to Landlord, Landlord will submit written notice giving Tenant fifteen (15) days after receipt to resolve the default. In the event that Tenant defaults in performing any of the other covenants or conditions of this Agreement, Tenant shall be given thirty (30) days after receiving written notice to resolve the default. If the Tenant fails to resolve any default within the time allotted in this paragraph, Landlord may at his/her discretion give Tenant written notice that the Lease is terminated. If Tenant does not surrender possession of the Leased Premises upon receiving such a notice, Landlord may re-enter Leased Premises, using any right or remedy available in law or in equity to Landlord on account of any Tenant default. Landlord may use reasonable efforts to mitigate its damages.

19. Quiet Possession.

Landlord guarantees that if Tenant performs its obligations under this Agreement, Landlord will maintain Tenant in exclusive, quiet, peaceable, undisturbed, and uninterrupted possession of the Leased Premises during the term of this Lease.

20. Subordination.

Tenant understands that this Lease is subject and subordinate to any mortgage, deed of trust or other lien presently existing or arising during the term of the Lease upon the Leased Premises, or upon the Building and to any renewals, refinancing and extensions of such liens, but Tenant agrees that any mortgagee shall have the right at any time to subordinate such mortgage, deed of trust, or other lien to this Lease under terms and conditions deemed appropriate by the mortgagee. Landlord is given irrevocable authority to subordinate this Lease to any mortgage, deed of trust, or other lien now existing or hereafter placed upon the Leased Premises of the Building. Tenant agrees that it will, upon request by Landlord, execute and deliver a statement to any person the Landlord designates certifying that this Lease is in full force and effect, giving the dates to which rent and other charges payable under this Lease have been paid, and stating that Landlord is not in default under this Lease and any other matters as Landlord shall reasonably require. If there have been modifications, Tenant will state that the modified Lease is in full force and effect.

21. Notice.

All notices and communications required by this Agreement shall be made in writing and shall be delivered to each party's address as listed on this Lease. The mailing of a notice by registered or certified United States mail, certified or return receipt requested, postage prepaid, shall constitute delivery. A notice or demand shall be deemed constructively made at the time it is personally delivered. If a communication is given by mail, it shall be conclusively deemed given five days after its deposit in the United States mail addressed to the party at the address given below:

Landlord: _____

Tenant: _____

Landlord and Tenant may change the address to which notices should be sent by notifying the other party in writing.

22. Waiver.

Failure to take action over any default on the part of either party under this Agreement shall not be construed as a waiver if the default persists or is repeated. No express waiver shall apply to any default other than the default specified in the express waiver, and shall apply only for the time and in the manner therein stated. A one-time waiver by Landlord or Tenant shall not be construed as a waiver of a subsequent breach of the same covenant, term, or condition.

23. Memorandum of Lease.

The parties hereby agree that this Lease shall not be part of any public record. If either party requests it, Landlord and Tenant shall execute a Memorandum of Lease, giving notice of the appropriate provisions of this Lease, to be submitted in compliance with any governmental filing requirements.

24. Paragraph Headings.

The headings used in this Lease are for convenience of the parties only and shall not be considered as part of any provision of this Lease.

25. Successors and Assigns.

The provisions of this Lease shall extend to and be binding upon Landlord and Tenant and their respective legal representatives, successors, and assigns.

26. Consent.

Landlord shall not unreasonably withhold or delay its consent on any matter for which Landlord's consent is required, requested, or desirable under this Lease.

27. Performance.

If Landlord defaults on any of its covenants, warranties, or representations under this Lease, and if this default continues more than fifteen (15) days after Tenant has given written notice to Landlord specifying the default, Tenant may, at its discretion and without forfeiting any other remedy available under the terms of this Agreement, correct the default and deduct the cost of doing so from the next installment or installments of rent payable to Landlord until Tenant has been fully reimbursed for the total amount, plus interest on that amount at a rate equal to the lesser of _____ percent per annum or the highest lawful rate. If Tenant has not been fully reimbursed when this Lease terminates, Landlord agrees to pay the un-reimbursed balance plus accrued interest to Tenant on demand.

28. Compliance with Law.

Tenant and Landlord each agree to comply with all laws, orders, ordinances, and other public requirements now or hereafter affecting the Leased Premises.

29. Final Agreement.

This Agreement is considered the entire agreement between Landlord and Tenant and hereby supersedes any previous understanding or representation, oral or written, between these parties. Changes to this Agreement must be made in writing and signed by both parties.

IN WITNESS WHEREOF, the parties have executed this Lease as of the day and year written at the beginning of this Agreement.

Landlord:_____Date: _____
Tenant:_____Date:_____

COMMERCIAL LEASE FORM

Date: _____
Landlord: _____
Address: _____
City: _____ State: _____ Zip: _____
Tenant: _____
Address: _____
City: _____ State: _____ Zip: _____

This Lease is made by and between Landlord and Tenant. In consideration of the mutual promises, covenants, agreements, and conditions contained herein and for other good and valuable consideration, receipt of which is hereby acknowledged, the Landlord and Tenant agree to the following:

1. Premises.

The Landlord is hereby leasing to the Tenant the premises located at _____ _____, and the Tenant is now renting said property from the Landlord. The premises are described as: _____.

2. Term.

The Lease term, beginning _____ (date), and ending _____ (date), is for _____ number of months.

3. Rent.

Tenant agrees to pay Landlord rent in the amount of $_____ per year, payable in equal monthly installments of $ _____.

4. Use.

Tenant may use and inhabit said premises only as a _____ (Tenant Rental Status) and is at all times subject to approval of the Landlord.

5. Utilities.

The Landlord, at his own expense, will provide following utilities or amenities for the Tenant's use and benefit: _____.

6. Tenant's Responsibilities.

The Tenant, at his own expense, agrees to provide the following:

_____

7. Insurance.

The Tenant is required to purchase, at his own expense, public liability insurance in the amount of $ _____, as well purchase fire and hazard insurance in the amount of $ _____ for the property and must provide Landlord satisfactory evidence of purchase of said insurances and must keep insurance policies in force and effect during entire life of Lease.

8. Waste.

The Tenant is prohibited from permitting or committing waste on said premises.

9. Alterations and Improvements.

The Tenant is prohibited from making any alterations, additions, or improvements to said property without first receiving written consent from the Landlord.

10. Legal Compliance.

The Tenant will abide by and comply with all rules, regulations, ordinances codes, and laws of all governmental authorities who have jurisdiction over the property.

11. Liability and Nuisance.

The Tenant is prohibited from being involved in, or allowing, any activity that will impose an insurance increase for the building and/or property in which the premises is contained. Tenant is also prohibited from committing or permitting any nuisance to said building or property.

12. Assignment.

The Tenant shall not sublet or assign the premises nor allow any other person or business to use or occupy the premises without the prior written consent of the Landlord, and that consent may not be unreasonably withheld.

13. Maintenance.

At the end of Lease, Tenant must surrender and relinquish said property in the same condition (subject to any additions, maintenance, alterations, or improvements, if any) as property presently exists in (excluding reasonable wear and tear).

14. Default.

If Tenant defaults on any term or condition provided in this Lease, the Landlord is permitted the right to undertake any or all other remedies as permitted by Law.

15. Subordination.

This Lease is subject to all mortgages, whether present or future, affecting property described above.

16. Heirs and Assigns.

This Lease is hereby binding, and inure to the benefit of the parties as well as their heirs, successors, and assigns.

Signed this _____ day of _____ (Month) _____ (Year).

_____   _____

Tenant Printed   Tenant Signature

_____   _____

Landlord Printed   Landlord Signature

TRIPLE NET COMMERCIAL LEASE

Article of Agreement made on _____ (date) between _____ _____ (name and address of landlord), hereafter referred to as "Landlord," and _____ (name and address of tenant), hereafter referred to as "Tenant."

It should be know that the Landlord is the owner of the property located at _____ in the township of _____ in the county of _____. Hereafter, this property will be referred to as the "Leasehold Premises."

It should be known that the Tenant wishes to rent and lease the Leasehold Premises, and that the Landlord and the Tenant have reached an agreement based upon the following terms and conditions.

This agreement is legally binding; the Tenant shall pay all rents herein discussed, and the Landlord shall lease the property to the Tenant, while adhering to the following guidelines:

1. Term:

This Lease shall be in effect for _____ years and _____ months and shall begin on _____ (date) and shall end on _____ (date).

2. Rent:

The Tenant shall pay the Landlord _____ (amount in dollars and cents) on _____ (rental due date) each and every month that the Tenant occupies the Leasehold Premises.

3. Security Deposit:

In addition, the Tenant shall also pay the Landlord a security deposit in the amount of _____ before the Tenant uses or occupies the Leasehold Premises. This deposit will be held as security for any damages, costs, or expenses incurred to the Leasehold Premises while the Tenant is occupying the Leasehold Premises. Unless the Landlord intends to withhold the deposit, the amount shall be returned, whether in part or in whole, to the Tenant within 30 days after termination of this lease.

4. Utilities:

During the term of this lease, the Tenant shall pay all utility bills for the Leasehold Premises, including the gas, electric, telephone, cable, water, sewer, and garbage collection, as well as any service charges pertaining to these utilities.

5. Clean and Sanitary Condition:

While occupying the Leasehold Premises, it is the Tenant's duty to keep and maintain the Leasehold Premises and the surrounding area in a clean and sanitary condition. This includes keeping the area free of garbage and debris, which shall be deposited in the proper garbage collection containers, for which the Tenant is responsible for placing curbside for pickup and moving once pickup has occurred. The Tenant is responsible for any fines incurred due to not keeping the Leasehold Premises in a clean and sanitary condition.

6. Maintenance:

It is the Tenant's responsibility to keep and maintain the Leasehold Premises in good condition at all times. The Tenant shall abide by the rules and regulations set forth by the health officer, fire marshal, building inspector, and any other property officials. All costs pertaining to the keeping and maintaining of the Leasehold Premises are the responsibility of the Tenant, even if the Tenant neglects doing so. In such a case, the Landlord may make the repairs and charge the costs to the Tenant. When the lease expires, the Tenant must surrender the Leasehold Premises in good condition, with reasonable amounts of wear and tear.

7. Liability Insurance:

The tenant shall have a policy of public liability and property damage insurance for the Leasehold Premises. These amounts shall not be less than _____ for injury or death to one person in an accident, _____ for injury or death for an occurrence, and _____ for property damage for an occurrence. The insurance policy shall list the Landlord and Tenant as the insured and shall also include a clause stating that the insurer will not make any changes to the policy without first notifying the Landlord in writing 30 days prior to doing so. The insurance company must be approved by the Landlord and the Landlord shall be given a copy of the policy.

8. Personal Property Insurance:

The Tenant agrees to carry insurance for all fixtures, furnishings, equipment, and any other personal property located on or in the Leasehold Premises. This insurance shall be no less than 100 percent of the replacement cost of the property. The Tenant must provide the Landlord with a copy of this policy.

9. Off-Set Statement:

The Tenant agrees to provide the Landlord with a written statement confirming a) that this lease is in effect, b) that the commencement date stated above is correct, c) that the rent has been paid in advance, and d) if the lease has been modified, and identifying any changes. The Landlord must verify that these statements are valid.

10. Attornment:

If the Leasehold Premises are brought for foreclosure, the Tenant shall attorn to and agrees to recognize the successor as the new Landlord under this lease.

11. Subordination:

The Tenant agrees that this lease is secondary to any mortgages or deeds of trust that may be placed on the Leasehold Premises. Any advances, interest, renewals, replacements, and extensions will be recognized by the Tenant if there is a foreclosure, if the Tenant is not in default.

12. Assignment and Subletting:

The Tenant cannot assign or transfer the Lease without the written consent of the Landlord. The Tenant cannot sublet the Leasehold Properties or any part of the property without written consent from the Landlord. If the Tenant chooses to assign or sublet the Leasehold Premises, the Landlord will not lose any rights as assigned in this lease. Additionally, the Tenant will in no way be released from the provisions in this lease if the Tenant does choose to assign or sublet the Leasehold Premises.

13. Waste or Nuisance:

The Tenant is prohibited from leaving waste on the Leasehold Premises and from placing any load on the floor that is greater than the floor load per square foot area. The Tenant also will not use or permit the use of anything that may be a nuisance.

14. Reconstruction of Damaged Premises:

If the Leasehold Premises are damaged by fire, whether in part or in whole, and the property is no longer inhabitable, the damages will be immediately repaid. However, the Landlord may choose not to rebuild; as such, the minimum rental and other charges, as they are in proportion to the damaged property, will cease. The Landlord will not be required to repair or replace the Tenant's fixtures, furnishings, or personal property. If more than 25 percent of the Leasehold Premises is damaged, the Landlord may choose to end the lease but must give the Tenant written notice of this decision within 90 days of the damage.

15. Total Condemnation of Leased Premises:

If the Leasehold Premises is acquired by any public authority, the lease will cease on the day the public authority takes possession of the property. The Tenant is responsible for paying the rent up to that day, and the Landlord must present the Tenant with a refund for any rent that was paid in advance.

16. Partial Condemnation:

If the whole property is not acquired by a public authority but more than 25 percent is taken, the Landlord has the right to end the lease or to restore part of the Leasehold Premises to the complete unit. If the Landlord chooses to do the latter, the lease and all terms herein established will remain in effect; however, the rent must be reduced in proportion to the amount of the Leasehold Premises seized.

17. Landlord's and Tenant's Damages:

Any damages awarded in part or in whole to the Leasehold Premises when it is seized by a public authority are the property of the Landlord in whatever form the award is in. The Tenant does not have any claim to these awards.

18. Default:

All rights of the Landlord discussed here are cumulative and do not exclude any other rights given by law. The tenant agrees that:

    a.   If the Tenant does not pay any portion of the rent at any time or for any reason and remains in default for ten days;

    b.   If the Tenant leaves the property or fails to keep the Leasehold Premises open for business each day or fails to uphold any parts of the lease for a period of ten days or more; if the Tenant is found to be in default the Landlord has the right to enter the property, whether the Tenant or a third party is occupying it; if the Landlord must go to court to collect the due fees, the Tenant must compensate the Landlord for any fees pertaining to collection, including attorney's fees up to 10 percent or $500, whichever is greater.

19. Right of Entry:

The Landlord has the right to enter the Leasehold Premises at any reasonable times to inspect and make repairs, alterations, improvements, or additions as necessary or as desired. While the repairs are being done, the Tenant is not responsible for paying rent if the Tenant is unable to occupy the Leasehold Premises while said repairs are being completed.

20. Loss and Damage to Tenant's Property:

The Landlord is not responsible for any loss or damage to the Leasehold Premises due to any loss or damages caused by the adjoining tenants. This includes the bursting or leaking of any water, gas, sewer, or steam pipes.

21. Notice by Tenant:

The Tenant must notify the Landlord immediately if there is a fire in the building or if an accident has occurred in the building or on the premises as a result of any defects, fixtures, or equipment belonging to the Leasehold Premises.

22. Holding Over:

Any holding over after the lease expires will be on a month-by-month basis at a minimum rental amount of _____

23. Successors:

All rights given to the Tenant and the Landlord, as outlined in this lease, extends to the heirs, executors, administrators, successors, and assigns of the Tenant and the Landlord. If there is more than one Tenant, they are both bound by the terms of this lease.

24. Landlord's Covenant:

If the Tenant pays the rent and observes the terms outlined in this line, the Tenant will be able to peacefully and quietly hold and enjoy the Leasehold Premises for the entire rental term without being hindered or interrupted by the Landlord or any party acting on the part of the Landlord.

25. Option to Purchase:

The Buyer, _____ (name) has the option to purchase the Leasehold Premises from the Seller, _____ (name). The Seller will pay the Buyer _____ (amount) for this option. The receipt of this sale must be recognized by the Buyer and the Buyer's heirs, successors, assigns, or representatives. The receipt of this sale gives the Buyer the right to the property located at _____ _____ (street address), with the following terms and conditions:

    a.   Option Period: This option begins on _____ (date and time).

    b.   Exercise: The Buyer may exercise this option at any time during the Option Period by providing the Seller with a written notice that the Buyer wishes to exercise the option.

    c.   Contract Upon Exercise: When this option is exercised, the Buyer must complete a standard agreement to purchase real estate.

    d.   Application of Option Money: In the event that this option is exercised, the option money __will __ will not go toward the purchase price at closing.

26. Waiver:

If the Landlord chooses to waive any part of this lease, this does not mean any subsequent breaches will be waived. The Tenant must obtain permission from the Landlord prior to committing a similar act. Only waivers signed by the Landlord will be accepted.

27. Notices:

Any notice, demand, or request surrounding this lease must be sent by United States certified mail with a return receipt requested, postage prepaid, and addressed to the Landlord or the Tenant at their specified addresses.

28. Recording:

The Tenant may not record this lease without the Landlord's written consent. If the Landlord grants this request, a short form of this lease may be made for recordation. The short form must include descriptions of the parties involved, the Leasehold Premises, the lease terms, and any special provisions.

29. Transfer of Landlord's Interest:

If the Landlord transfers his or her interest in the Leasehold Premises, the party to whom the interest was transferred is relieved from any obligations beginning with the date of transfer. This includes the security deposit.

30. Accord and Satisfaction:

If the Tenant pays the Landlord a lesser amount than the agreed upon rent, this money will be viewed as a payment toward the rent.

31. Entire Agreement:

This lease and its contents contain all the agreements made between the Tenant and the Landlord concerning the Leasehold Premises. The Tenant and the Landlord have not made any other agreements, be they verbal or written, concerning this property. No changes may be made to this lease unless the Tenant and the Landlord sign and approve it.

32. New Taxes:

The Tenant will be responsible for any taxes levied by the government in any form.

33. Heirs and Successors:

The terms of this lease are binding and passes to the parties' heirs, successors, representatives, and assigns.

34. Counterparts:

The Tenant and the Landlord may sign this lease in one or more counterparts, and each counterpart will be combined into one agreement. This lease is valid if the signatures are executed by facsimile.

_____   _____
WITNESS   LANDLORD

_____   _____
WITNESS   TENANT

COMMERCIAL REAL ESTATE SALES AGREEMENT

Date: _____

Buyer: _____

Address: _____

City: _____ State: _____ Zip: _____

Seller: _____

Address: _____

City: _____ State: _____ Zip: _____

This Agreement is made between Seller(s) and Buyer(s). The parties listed above hereby agree to the following terms:

1. Real Estate.

The Sellers agree to sell to Buyers and Buyers agree to purchase from the Sellers the land and building(s) located in _____ (City), _____ (County), _____ (State), described in the Deed recorded in _____ (record book), Page _____, with a total area of approximately _____ acres.

2. Price.

The purchase price will be $_____. Buyer shall make a Deposit of $_____ prior to the signing of this Agreement. The Deposit will be held by _____ until the time of closing and will then be applied to the final purchase price.

3. Appliances.

The following appliances are to be conveyed with the real estate and must be in good working order at closing:

a. _____   _____
b. _____   _____
c. _____   _____
d. _____   _____
e. _____   _____

4. Contingency.

This Agreement is contingent upon the Buyers selling the parcel located at _____ in _____ (City), _____ (County), _____ (State) prior to closing. If the Buyers are unable to sell the abovementioned property by _____ (Date), then this Agreement shall be null and void and the Deposit will be returned to the Buyers. An extension of up to _____ days from the date of _____ shall be granted at the Buyer's request if recorded in a written agreement signed by both the Buyers and Sellers.

5. Removal of Debris.

Once Sellers have been given final notice of closing, any and all personal property and debris must be removed from the property within a minimum of _____ days after the closing date.

6. Allocations.

The Buyers and Sellers hereby agree that they have negotiated the terms and conditions of the sale and that the allocations provided below are fair and reasonable. The Purchase Price will be allocated as follows:

   i.   Land: $_____
   ii.   Personal Property, Equipment, and Fixtures: $_____
   iii. Buildings: $_____
   iv.   Total: $_____

7. Taxes.

The Buyers and Sellers agree that each shall pay one-half of the _____ taxes due. The projected amount is $_____ each.

8. Proration of Taxes.

The _____ (year) real estate taxes shall be pro-rated based on the date of closing, with the _____ and _____ (county) taxes to be pro-rated on a calendar-year basis. School taxes will be pro-rated on a fiscal year basis.

9. Transfer of Possession.

Possession of the land and buildings will be transferred at closing.

10. Risk.

The Seller will bear the risk of loss due to fire, flood, or other casualty until closing.

11. Condition of Property.

The Sellers will maintain the property and land in its current condition until closing. The Buyers may inspect the property before closing, after giving _____ hours' written notice to the Sellers' attorney.

12. Notices: Requests.

No government agency, or employee or official of a government agency, has given any notice to the Seller that it considers the construction on the Property or the operation or use of the Property to be out of compliance with any law, ordinance, regulation or order, or that any investigation has been or might be initiated respecting any possible non-compliance. There are no unpaid expenses or outstanding invoices from any person, entity or authority, including, but not limited to, any tenant, lender, insurance carrier or government authority, for the cost of repairs, restorations or improvements to the Property. The Property is not affected by any lawsuits.

13. Hazardous Materials.

The Sellers hereby certify that to the best of their knowledge, no hazardous material has been discarded or placed on the premises by any company, person, or entity, and that a "Hazardous Waste Clause" will be part of the Deed to convey the Property.

14. Lead Disclosure.

The Buyers and Sellers agree to comply with the Federal Lead Disclosure Act and any and all state laws concerning Lead Disclosure and to provide the necessary disclosure statements.

15. Brokerage Commissions.

All brokerage commissions will be paid by the Sellers to _____.

16. Transfer of Title.

The Title to the property will be transferred by _____. The Title shall be good and marketable in the opinion of the attorney for the Buyers, based on a _____ (year) title examination and a good and sufficient General Warranty Deed. Any exception and reservation existing in favor of another party in the chain of title for oil, gas, and minerals in, on, and under the premises will not be considered a defect in title or detrimental to a good and marketable title to the real estate. The Buyers may have the property surveyed within _____ year(s) from the date of the closing. The Buyers shall escrow $_____ from the Purchase Price to pay for the actual cost and expense of the survey. If a survey is not performed within _____ year(s) or if the survey costs less than $ _____, then the Buyers must immediately return the balance of the escrowed amount to the Sellers.

17. Inspection.

The Buyer(s) may, at their own expense, choose to have licensed or otherwise qualified professionals complete inspections and/or certifications for said premises within _____ days of the execution of this Agreement. Any home inspection of the property, as defined in the _____ (State) Home Inspection Law, must be completed by a full member in good standing of a national home inspection association, or by a person supervised by a full member of a national home inspection association, in accordance with the ethical standards and code of conduct or practice of that association. If any written report of such an inspection reveals defects in the condition of the Property, Buyer may:

    a.   Accept Property as is with the information stated in the given inspection report(s); or

    b.   Terminate this Agreement within fifteen (15) days of the inspection by written notice to Seller(s). In this event, any deposits paid toward the Purchase Price will be immediately returned to the Buyer(s) and this Agreement will be VOID; or

    c.   Enter into a mutually acceptable written agreement with the Seller(s) providing for any repairs or improvements to the premises and/or any credit to the Buyer(s) for the cost of such repairs at closing. Should Buyer(s) and Seller(s) fail to arrive at a mutually acceptable agreement, the Buyer(s) must then either accept Property as is or terminate this Agreement within _____ days.

18. Seller's Default.

If the Seller(s) fail to comply with the terms and conditions of this Agreement due to the failure of the title or the instance of a fire or other catastrophe that in part or fully destroys the property, the Buyers, at their discretion, may:

a.   terminate this Agreement by written notice to be provided to the Sellers at or before the closing, in which case the Deposit and any interest accrued will belong to the Buyers. Seller will have no other obligation or liability to the Buyers, and the Buyer will have no other rights hereunder.

b.   enter into a mutually acceptable written agreement with the Sellers providing for any repairs, improvements to the property and/or any credits to be given to the Buyers at settlement. If discussions to come to a mutually acceptable agreement fail, the Buyers must decide to either accept the Property as is, or to terminate this Agreement within the time frame provided in this Agreement.

IN WITNESS WHEREOF, the parties have hereby caused this Agreement to be duly executed the aforementioned day and year.

_____

Seller

_____

Seller

_____

Buyer

_____

Buyer

UNDERLYING LEASE OF SHOPPING CENTER

Date: _____

Lessor: _____

Address: _____

City: _____ State: _____ Zip: _____

Tenant: _____

Address: _____

City: _____ State: _____ Zip: _____

By virtue of this document, Lessor leases to Tenant, and Tenant leases from Landlord, for the rent specified in this Lease agreement and subject to the provisions of this Lease agreement, the premises situated in the county of _____ and state of _____ and described in Appendix "A" attached to and made a part of this Lease agreement; together with all rights, privileges, easements, and appurtenances belonging to or in any way pertaining to the leased premises.

Lessor represents and warrants to Tenant that it has a simple title to the leased premises and the power and authority to execute and deliver this lease, and to carry out and perform all covenants required under the terms of this lease.

1. Term.

The term of this lease shall commence on the date specified at the beginning of this document and shall continue for a period concluding 99 years from the day and year specified.

2. Nature of Occupancy.

The Tenant agrees to use the leased premises only in accordance with all applicable laws, ordinances, and regulations for the following and no other purposes, namely:

Construction, operation, and rental of a shopping center and such structures as are incidental to that purpose.

3. Rental.

The Tenant agrees to pay, and the Lessor agrees to accept as the monthly rental for these premises, commencing at a time when not less than _____% of the shopping center is open for business, but no later than January 1, _____ (year), the sum of $_____. This rent shall be paid in equal monthly installments in advance on the first day of every month during the term of this lease.

For the period prior to the commencement of the annual rental, pending construction of the shopping center, Tenant agrees to pay and Lessor agrees to accept a monthly rental of $_____.

In addition to the rentals specified above, Tenant agrees to pay to Lessor a sum equal to the percentage amount, _____%, by which the rentals on subleases exceed the minimum rental on the said subleases.

Within 30 days after the end of each calendar year of this lease, after the commencement of the period in which the annual rental of $_____ is due, Tenant shall deliver to Lessor a complete statement signed by a duly authorized officer of Tenant, showing accurately and in reasonable detail the full amount of all rents collected by Tenant from subLessees. If the amount of rental due under the percentage established above exceeds the amount of rental already paid for the same lease year, Tenant shall pay the balance at the time that such statement is submitted.

Tenant agrees that the Lessor or Lessor's agents may inspect the tenant's books and records during normal business hours in order to verify Tenant's statement of rent collections.

In ascertaining Lessor's share of subLessee rent under the percentage arrangement set forth above, it is understood that all sums collected by Tenant from its subLessees for the sub-Lessees' share of taxes, insurance, common area maintenance, and repairs shall not be deemed to be rentals collected by the Tenant.

This lease shall, excluding the exceptions set forth in this lease agreement, yield net to Lessor the rent as described above, to be paid in each year during the term of this lease. All costs, expenses, and obligations of every kind relating to the leased premises, or any improvements on the premises that may arise or come due during the term of this lease, shall be paid by the Tenant. The Lessor shall be indemnified and held harmless by the tenant from and against such costs.

All rental payments shall be paid in United States dollars to the Lessor at its office located at _____, or at such other place as may be designated in writing from time to time by the Lessor.

4. Taxes and Assessments.

The Tenant agrees to pay when due all taxes, installments of special assessments, fees, or other charges of any nature levied, assessed, or imposed on the leased premises. This includes any improvements located on the premises that are due and payable during the term of this lease, beginning with any that are due and payable on or after the day and year named above and concluding with those due and payable in the calendar year in which the term of this lease expires.

Tenant shall not be considered to be in default under this lease in respect to the payment of any taxes, special assessments, fees, or other charges if, at least 15 days before they are due, the Tenant notifies the Lessor in writing of its intention to contest them and thereafter in good faith contests such payment. Tenant may file all such protests or other contests in the name of Lessor, and at the request of Lessor will furnish reasonably satisfactory assurance that the Tenant will compensate the Lessor for any loss or liability arising from such contest.

5. Tenant's Right To Build and Alter.

At any time, during the term of this lease, in accordance with any restrictions on the nature of occupancy set forth in this lease agreement, and in accord with applicable laws, ordinances, and regulations, Tenant shall have the right, at its own cost and expense:

a. To construct a building or buildings upon the leased premises, and any other improvements that the Tenant may deem desirable.

b. To alter, enlarge, remodel, or improve any building or buildings or other improvements upon the leased premises.

The Tenant covenants and agrees that it will do its utmost to complete the construction of a shopping center on the leased premises at the earliest possible date, and further agrees that in all events, the construction of a shopping center on the leased premises will be substantially completed no later than January 1, _____ (year).

Tenant agrees to submit the preliminary drawings to Lessor for approval before commencing construction. Approval shall not be unreasonably withheld by Lessor. When preliminary drawings are submitted as required, they shall be considered approved unless the Lessor indicates its disapproval and gives an explanation within 10 days after submission.

6. Ordinances and Regulations.

During the term of this lease, the Tenant agrees, at its own expense, to comply with all valid applicable laws, ordinances, and regulations of duly constituted public authorities now or in the future in any manner affecting the leased premises, its use, and any improvements made on it. The Tenant agrees to indemnify and hold the Lessor harmless from the consequences of any violation of any such law, ordinance or regulation.

7. Tenant to Have Title to Improvements.

During the term of this lease, Tenant shall at all times have title to the buildings and improvements that Tenant makes or installs in, on or under the leased premises. Upon the expiration, termination, or forfeiture of this lease for any reason whatever, title to the buildings and other improvements, to the extent that they are located upon the leased premises, shall be automatically vested in the Lessor, its successors, and assigns. During the term of this lease, if any building, buildings, or other improvements are damaged or destroyed by fire or other casualty of any kind, the Tenant shall be entitled to the entire proceeds of all insurance that are payable by reason of such damage or destruction.

8. Liens.

The Tenant shall keep the Premises free from any mechanic's, laborer's, or material man's liens arising out of any work performed on the leased premises or on the adjoining premises, materials furnished, or obligations incurred by Tenant. Tenant shall have the right to contest the validity or amount of any such liens if the Tenant, at Lessor's request, gives reasonable security (no less than one and one-half times the amount of the lien claim) to the Lessor to insure payment and to prevent any forfeiture of the leased premises. Upon final determination of such lien action, the tenant shall immediately pay any judgment rendered.

9. Surety Bond.

If at any time during the term of this lease the Tenant desires to erect a building, buildings, or other improvements that in the Tenant's architect estimate will cost $_____ or more, either wholly or partially upon the leased premises, the Tenant agrees to furnish to the Lessor, prior to commencing construction, a performance bond in a sum at least equal to the estimated cost of such building, buildings, or other improvements. This bond shall be executed by Tenant and its prime contractor, if any, as principals and by a responsible surety company authorized in the state of _____ as surety. The bond shall provide that no judgment entered against the leased premises or any part of the premises because of any lien or claim shall constitute a breach of the conditions of the bond until such a judgment is made final, either by the Tenant's or prime contractor's failure to appeal, or by a judgment from the highest court to which judgment may be appealed.

10. Indemnification of Lessor.

The Tenant agrees to hold the Lessor harmless from any and all claims for damage or injury arising out of or as a result of the Tenant's use of the leased premises. Without limiting the Tenant's liability under the terms of this lease, the Tenant agrees to maintain comprehensive general liability insurance insuring the Lessor (as an additional insured) and the Tenant against any liability arising out of the ownership, use, occupancy, or maintenance of the leased premises and all associated areas, in reasonable amounts but not less than $_____ for injury or death to any person, $_____ for injuries or deaths arising out of any one accident, and $_____ for any property damage claims arising out of any one accident. The insurance companies must be approved by Lessor. Tenant will deliver to the Lessor a certificate of such insurance providing for the Lessor to receive 15 days' written notice prior to any cancellation. Tenant may carry this insurance as part of its comprehensive general liability insurance coverage, provided that a Landlord's protective liability endorsement is attached to it. In the event that the Tenant fails to procure and maintain such insurance, the Landlord, may, but is not obligated to, procure and maintain it at the expense of Tenant.

11. Eminent Domain.

In the event that 10% or more of the total area of the leased premises is taken under the power of eminent domain, then the Tenant shall have the option of terminating this lease as of the date of such taking, and the Lessor agrees to return to the Tenant any unearned rent paid in advance. If the Tenant does not terminate this lease by giving written notice to the Lessor within 60 days from the date of such taking, the Tenant's right to terminate shall be waived. If the partial taking does not result in a termination of this lease, the rent for the period or periods after the date of such will be reduced in the proportion that the taken area on which the Tenant had constructed buildings or improvements bears to the entire area of the leased premises.

12. Assignment, Subletting, and Mortgaging.

The Lessor agrees that the Tenant has the right at any time and from time to time during the term of this lease to assign this lease and to sublet the leased premises in whole or in part, and to mortgage, pledge, and hypothecate this lease. Any assignment or subletting will not release Tenant from its obligations under this lease. It is anticipated by the Lessor and the Tenant that the Tenant or its successors or assigns will be constructing improvements on the leased premises and will be placing a mortgage or mortgages on the leased premises or on portions of the leased premises to finance such improvements. Lessor agrees to cooperate in the execution of any such mortgage or mortgages by pledging its interest in the leased premises to the lien of such mortgage or mortgages, without assuming any obligation for the payment or performance thereof. Such mortgages shall be with reputable lending institutions, and the Lessor shall not be personally liable for the payment or performance thereof.

13. Lessor To Join in Leases.

Lessor hereby agrees at Tenant's request to join in the execution of leases for space in the building or buildings to be constructed on the leased premises; provided, however, that Lessor shall have no personal liability under such leases except after the effective date of the termination of this lease. Lessor hereby further agrees to cooperate in the execution of assignments of Lessor's interest in lease or assignments of rent or other security documents relating to leases of such space in such building or buildings pertaining to the leased premises which may be required by the mortgage or mortgages referred to in article XII.

14. Quiet Enjoyment.

As long as the Tenant pays the rent required by the terms of this lease, and observes and performs all of the covenants, conditions, and provisions set forth in this lease, the Tenant shall have quiet possession of the leased premises for the entire term of this lease, subject to all of the provisions of this lease.

15. Notice to Mortgagee Upon Request.

If the interest of the Tenant in the leased premises is conveyed by mortgage by the Tenant, and if the mortgagee notifies the Lessor in writing of the existence of such a mortgage, together with the name and address of the mortgagee, a duplicate copy of all notices and demands given by the Lessor to the Tenant shall be served on the mortgagee. Notwithstanding the provisions of article 18, no notice shall be deemed to have been served upon the Tenant unless a duplicate copy of the notice is served on the mortgagee at or prior to the time such notice. Such notice shall be considered to have been served on the mortgagee on the date that it deposited in the United States mail, registered or certified, postage prepaid, addressed to the mortgagee at the address furnished to the Lessor.

16. Default.

If the Tenant shall default (a) in the payment of any installment of rent, or (b) in the payment of any mortgage installment or other obligation under any mortgage joined in by Lessor as provided above, or (c) in the observance or performance of any of the Tenant's other covenants, agreements or obligations under this lease, and if the Lessor gives written notice of such default to the Tenant, and Tenant fails to pay such rent or rectify such other default within 90 days after receiving such notice; or if such other default is of a character that requires more than 90 days to be rectified and the Tenant fails to exercise reasonable diligence in rectifying that default, then:

(1) Lessor may, at its option, rectify any default included in (b) or (c) above on behalf of and at the cost and expense of the Tenant, and all sums so expended by the Lessor shall be considered to be additional rent, payable upon demand by the Tenant on the day on which the next rental payment hereunder shall become due and payable.

(2) The Lessor, at its option, may declare a forfeiture of this lease and may thereupon re-enter into possession of the leased premises and remove all persons from the leased premises and collect all rents owing but unpaid for all periods to and including the last day of the month during which the Lessor obtains possession of the leased premises, together with any costs, expenses, or damages incurred or suffered as a result of such default, which sums will immediately become due and payable.

If the Tenant defaults in the observance or performance of any of the Tenant's covenants, agreements, or obligations under the terms of the lease, and a duplicate copy of a default notice or demand is served on the mortgagee under the provisions of article 15, then — notwithstanding the provisions of this article 16 — the mortgagee has the right to rectify the fault within the same time and in the same manner as the Tenant before Lessor may declare a forfeiture of this lease and reenter into possession of the leased premises.

17. Remedies are not Exclusive.

No right or remedy conferred upon the Lessor by this lease is intended to be exclusive of any other right or remedy, and each right and remedy shall be cumulative and in addition to any other right or remedy given under the terms of this lease, or existing now or in the future under law or in equity.

18. One-time Waivers.

No waiver by the Lessor of any breach by the Tenant under this lease shall be construed as a waiver of any subsequent breach, nor shall any forbearance by the Lessor to seek a remedy for such breach by the Tenant be construed as a waiver by the Lessor of its right and remedy with respect to such breach.

19. Attorney's Fees.

Reasonable attorneys' fees and other expenses incurred by the Lessor by reason of any default of the Tenant in complying with any requirement of this lease shall constitute an additional rental, payable upon demand with interest on it at the rate of _____% per annum until paid.

20. Force Majeure.

In the event that Lessor or Tenant is delayed, hindered in, or prevented from the performance of any act required under the terms of this lease because of strikes, lockouts, labor troubles, inability to procure materials, power failure, restrictions imposed by governmental laws or regulations, riots, insurrection, war, or other reason beyond their control, or by the act, failure to act, or default of the other party, then performance of such act can be postponed during the period of the delay. The time period specified for the performance of any such act shall be extended for a period equivalent to the time that the delay was in effect.

21. Notices.
Wherever this lease requires or permits the service of notice or demand by Lessor or Tenant, such notice or demand shall not be considered duly given or served unless it is in writing and forwarded by registered or certified United States mail, postage prepaid, addressed to Lessor or Tenant at the addresses given at the beginning of this document. Either party may change their address from time to time by written notice.

22. Successors and Assigns.
Except for any limitations and conditions set forth elsewhere in this lease, the terms of this Lease shall apply to the respective heirs, legal representatives, successors, and permitted assigns and/or subLessees of the Lessor and the Tenant.

23. Short-Form Lease.
The parties agree that at the request of either party, a short-form lease shall be prepared in form and substance reasonably satisfactory to each of the parties to this agreement, and shall be executed by each of the parties in duplicate, to be filed for record in the office of the Register of Deeds or in the office of the Registrar of Titles, as the case may be, in and for _____ county, _____.

LESSOR: _____

WITNESS: _____

TENANT: _____

WITNESS: _____

STATE OF _____, COUNTY OF _____

The foregoing instrument was acknowledged before me, this

_____ day of _____, 20 _____.

_____ Notary Public

State of _____

My Commission Expires: _____

SHORT-FORM OFFICE LEASE

Date: _____

Lessor: _____

Lessee: _____

This Lease is made on this date by and between the Lessor and Lessee mentioned above. Witnesseth:

The Lessor hereby leases and demises to the Lessee the property described as

_____

to have and hold from the date of _____ for the period of

_____, the Lessee will pay to the Lessor the monthly rent amount of
$_____ due on the _____ of every month.

The Lessor and Lessee hereby agree to the following:

1. Default on Payments.

The Lessee agrees to pay the monthly rent due at the time mentioned above and will pay for all utilities on the premises; including, but not limited to the water, gas, and electricity. If the rent or utilities go unpaid for a period of _____ days after the due date, the Lessor at his/her option may directly re-enter the property and the entire rent for the rental period and the next rental period will become due at once and payable immediately by distress or otherwise.

2. Security Deposit.

Lessee agrees to pay a Security Deposit of $_____ to secure the Lessee's full pledge of compliance with the terms outlined herein this Lease. Security Deposit may not be applied to any rent payment. Security Deposit will be refunded to the Lessee at the time of the end of the tenancy, less any charges for damages found during the move-out inspection.

3. Use of Property.

The Lessee is not permitted to use the property for any illegal or improper purposes. The Lessee will not be permitted to create disturbances, noise, or annoyance that may be detrimental to the property or to the comfort of other tenants of the property or its neighbors.

4. Assignment of Lease.

The Lessee is not permitted to sublet or assign this lease nor any part of it thereof without the written consent of the Lessor.

5. Maintenance.

The Lessee agrees to keep the property, interior and exterior, all windows, walls, doors, fixtures, pipes, and all other trappings and trimmings, in good and considerable repair and in good condition (damage from fire or storm excepted). Lessee agrees to implement all reasonable care in the use of stairs, bathrooms, closets, hallways, and any other part of the premises used in common with other tenants in the building that is required for the continuation of the property and the comfort of the other tenants. Lessee agrees to permit entrance into the premises by the Lessor or the Lessor's agents or employees, at all reasonable times to inspect the condition of the property as mentioned above as well as to make necessary repairs. Lessee agrees to give up possession of the premises in-like condition without any demand at the end of the Agreement.

6. Damage to Property.

The Lessor and Lessee covenant with each other the performance of the maintenance hereby set forth to be continued throughout the Lessee's tenancy, and all exterior parts of the premises will remain in good repair. In the instance that the building and/or premises are unfit for occupancy due to damage of fire or storm or for other reason why the property was destroyed, the Lessor will have the option to terminate this Lease or to repair/rebuild the premises and refund any rents, or a fair and just portion of said rents, according to the damage sustained, until the premises and property are repaired and fit for occupants and use.

7. Quiet Enjoyment.

At all times during the term of this Lease, provided Tenant is not in default under this Lease, the Landlord or any person claiming to represent the Landlord will not disturb or interfere with Tenant's quiet and peaceable enjoyment of the premises.

8. Unpaid Rent.

The Lessee hereby agrees that the Lessor shall retain all control and security of furniture, fixtures, goods, and belongings for payment in the event the rent goes unpaid. The Lessee understands that said lien of Lessee's property may be enforced by distress, foreclosure, or other reason at the election of the Lessor. Lessee hereby waives all rights of homestead or exemption in aforementioned belongings to which the Lessee may be entitled under State law. In the case of the Lessee's failure to pay rent, the Lessee hereby also agrees to pay any legal fees and costs associated with the Lessor's attempt to get payment for the costs owed.

9. Heirs and Assigns.

This Lease hereby binds the Lessor and Lessee, their respective heirs, assigns, administrators, legal representatives, and executors.

10. Governing Law.

This Lease shall be governed by, construed, and enforced in accordance with the laws of the State of _____. Lessor and Lessee agree that should legal action be enforced, they will waive a trial by jury and submit to the personal jurisdictions of a court of subject matter jurisdiction located in _____ (County), _____ (State). No action may be initiated after more than one year has passed from the reason for the action. Lessee hereby waives any and all right to assert an affirmative defense if any eviction action is initiated by the Lessor with the exception of a defense that all payments were made to the Lessor and therefore no legal action was necessary.

IN WITNESS WHEREOF, the said parties have hereunto set their hands and seals this day of _____ (month), _____ (year).

Signed, sealed, and delivered.

_____

Lessor

_____

Lessor's Witness

_____

Lessee

_____

Lessee's Witness

STATE OF _____, COUNTY OF _____
The foregoing instrument was acknowledged before me, this
_____ day of _____, 20 _____.

_____ Notary Public

State of _____
My Commission Expires: _____

COMPREHENSIVE LEASE ADAPTABLE FOR BUSINESS OR RESIDENTIAL PURPOSES

On _____ [date], _____ [name of Lessor], hereby known as the Lessor, agrees to lease the property located at _____ [address of property] to _____ [name of Lessee], hereby known as the Lessee. Upon signing this lease, the Lessor and Lessee agree to the requirements listed under sections A and B of this lease agreement. This lease begins on _____ [date] and ends on _____ [date] and is for a total term of _____ year(s), unless this lease agreement is terminated under the requirements provided in sections A and B.

A. Agreements by the Lessee

The Lessee, in signing this lease, agrees to the following:

1. The Lessee agrees to pay the total amount of $_____/month as rental of the premises listed above. This amount is due on the _____ day of the month and will be due each month for the complete term of the lease. The total amount should be paid at the following location _____.

2. The Lessee agrees to pay for all utility charges that are provided to or on any part of the property listed above, including but not limited to, electricity, fuel, and water.

3. The Lessee agrees to pay any and all taxes or fees for the year(s) of _____ that are assessed to the property listed above.

4. The Lessee agrees to pay any and all costs and expenses, such as attorneys' fees, that are incurred by the Lessor in order to reinforce this lease agreement.

5. The Lessee agrees to occupy the property listed above for the purposes of _____ [business/residential] only. In order to occupy the property for any other reason, the Lessee must get written agreement from the Lessor. The Lessee will not use the premises for unlawful or hazardous purposes.

6. The Lessee agrees to maintain the property in the same condition that it was in when this lease agreement was signed. This condition of the property will be expected at the end of the lease term. Reasonable wear and tear resulting from daily use and any damages by natural elements is acceptable.

7. The Lessee agrees to keep all buildings and structure on the property insured at all times for an amount no less than $_____. Said insurance should be made payable to the Lessor as owner of the property, and the property will be insured under a responsible and licensed insurance agent/company.

8. The Lessee will allow the Lessor or any of the Lessor's agents to enter the property listed above in order to make necessary repairs or to examine the property provided that the Les-

sor visits the property at a reasonable time of the day. The Lessor is also allowed to place any "For Sale" or "For Rent" signs on the property.

9. The Lessee will deliver a surety bond to the Lessor at the address listed above within _____ days of signing this lease agreement in the amount of $_____ in order to ensure that the Lessee will comply with the terms and conditions listed in this lease agreement.

10. The Lessee will not sublet the property listed above or any part of that property without prior written consent by the Lessor.

11. The Lessee will not conduct or contract another agent to conduct any construction to any part of the property. The Lessee will not enter into any contract that requires a mechanic's or material men's lien in dealing with the property listed above during any time of the lease term. If for some reason contract hire is obtained by the Lessee, any and all persons conducting work or providing materials are bound by this provision as well. Notice is given that any lien made by the Lessee against the property listed above will not affect the title for the land or any improvements on the land. If the Lessee enters into a contract for improvement or repairs to the above listed property, the Lessee will ensure that within that contract, the hired contractor or subcontractor agrees to waive all rights to any liens against the property. Contracts made by the Lessee with a contractor or subcontractor will be recorded in _____county of _____ state. The Lessee will also provide the Lessor with a copy of the contract.

12. The Lessee, prior to signing this lease, has examined the property listed above and, by signing this lease, has agreed to accept this property in this condition.

13. The Lessee agrees for the Lessor to have a lien on all property owned by the Lessee located on the property listed above during the term of the lease, in order to ensure that payment of rent is made. If at any time the Lessee fails to make payment of rent, the Lessor is allowed to take possession of any liened property in the amount of back rent due to the Lessor.

14. The Lessor has the right to sell the property listed above at any time. The Lessee will be given written notice of the intent to sell at least _____ days prior to the date that the Lessee must vacate the property. The Lessee must also have the option to buy the property listed above at the sale price. If the Lessee does not take the option to purchase the property and the Lessor sells the property, the Lessee must vacate the property within _____ days of notice of sale.

15. If the Lessee, at any time during the term of this lease agreement, abandons or vacates the property listed above, the Lessor has the right to lease the property to another tenant. The Lessee will be required to pay any rent that is due to the Lessor.

16. The Lessee will return the property to the Lessor after the term of this lease as expired in the same condition it was in when the Lessee signed the lease. Reasonable wear and tear resulting from daily use and any damages by natural elements is acceptable.

17. The Lessor has the right to terminate this lease upon breach of any of the agreements listed within the lease.

18. If the Lessee is deemed by any court to be bankrupt the Lessor has the right to terminate this lease.

19. The Lessee is required to comply with any county, state, or federal laws that are in effect during the time of tenancy that have jurisdiction on the property at the address listed above.

20. Any amount of money that the Lessor pays or is required to pay due the Lessee's failure to comply with the agreements listed in this lease will be added the next rent due. The Lessee agrees to pay this additional amount along with the amount that is next due in the same manner in which the routine monthly rent is payable. The Lessor may make necessary repairs to the property providing that the Lessee does or will not and the amount of such repairs will be added to rent that is due the first month after the repairs have been made. The Lessee will pay this additional rent along with any routine rent currently due.

21. The Lessee shall be required to comply with the agreements listed within this lease despite the Lessor's insistence of strict compliance of such agreements.

22. If for any reason damage to any person or property occurs on the premises of the property listed above during the term of this lease agreement, the Lessor will not be liable.

23. _____ [add in any other provisions agreed upon by the Lessee and Lessor]

B. Agreements by the Lessor

The Lessor, in signing this lease, agrees to the following:

1. The Lessor agrees to keep the property listed above in good condition and to complete any necessary repairs requested by the Lessee within a reasonable timeframe.

2. The Lessor agrees that, provided the Lessor has given written consent prior to the start of alterations, the Lessee may conduct said alterations.

3. The Lessor agrees that the Lessee may lease of sublet the property listed above, or any part of the property listed above. This is subject to the following limitations: _____ _____.

4. The Lessor agrees to give an extension to the lease for a term of _____ years. The lease will be for the same rental rate and payable in the same manner as listed in the above agreements within this lease. The Lessee will give written notice to the Lessor within _____ days of expiration of current lease of intent to renew lease. If the Lessee is not in compliance with the agreements of the current lease, the option to renew lease will not be given. If current lease is terminated prior to the expiration of lease term, the option to renew will not be given.

5. If at any time, the Lessor fails to _____ [state condition], the Lessee has the right to terminate the lease on the property listed above. The Lessee must give the Lessor notice of intent to terminate _____ days prior to termination.

6. If during the term of the lease, the Lessee attaches any fixtures to the property, the Lessee may remove the fixtures from the property at the end of the lease term as long as the Lessee is in compliance with the agreements of the current lease. The Lessee shall have this right as long as the removal of said fixtures does not harm the property and that removal is made before the end of the lease term.

7. The Lessor agrees that at the termination of or at any time during the current lease, the Lessee has the option to purchase the property listed above from the Lessor for the amount of $_____. The Lessor will immediately, upon receiving this amount, give the Lessee a legal deed of the property.

8. If at any time during the term of this lease agreement the Lessor gives an outside tenant a more favorable lease arrangement, in reference to the termination of the lease or the amount of monthly rental dues per square foot, these arrangements will also be made a part of this lease agreement as well.

9. During the term of this lease agreement, the Lessor will not take part in any _____ [competition] business, a rival of the Lessee's business, in any way, directly or indirectly. This arrangement is binding in the city of _____, _____.

10. During the term of this lease agreement, the Lessor will not rent any part of the property listed above to a business that is in competition with the business of the Lessee's. The industry in which the Lessee's business is categorized is _____.

C. Agreements Made by Both the Lessor and Lessee

1. At the time of the signing of this lease, the Lessee will pay $_____ as a security deposit to the Lessor. By paying this security deposit, the Lessee agrees to comply with all agreements within this lease. This security deposit will also ensure that the Lessor not be held financially responsible for any damages or other expenses should the Lessee not comply with this lease agreement. The Lessor will pay the Lessee interest on said security deposit of $_____ at the rate of _____ % per annum. The Lessor will repay the Lessee the full amount of the security deposit by crediting the Lessee's rental payment during the last _____ months of the current lease term. If the Lessee does not comply with the agreements within this lease agreement, the security deposit will not be refunded to the Lessee.

2. If the property listed above becomes, at any time during the term of this lease agreement, destroyed permanently by fire or the elements this lease will be terminated and become null and void. At the time of said damage, the Lessee will surrender the property to the Lessor. The Lessee will only pay the amount of rent due to the precise time of the damage. If the Lessor is able to complete repairs to the property within a reasonable amount of time, the Lessor has the right to repair the property. The Lessee will be given a fair discount on the rent payment to make up for the time that the Lessee is unable to use the property.

3. This lease will be renewed for a term of _____ after the end of the current lease term unless the Lessee or Lessor makes their intent to not extend the current lease known in written form with _____ months prior to end of the current lease term. The rental payment and terms and conditions of lease will be the same as outlined within the text of this lease.

4. If at any time during the term of this lease agreement, payment of the rent is not made in a timely manner or the agreements of this lease are broken, the Lessor shall have the right to seize the above listed property without prior notice to the Lessee and declare this lease terminated. Noncompliance of the agreements to this lease by the Lessee will automatically terminate the lease. The Lessor has the right to enter the property with or without first processing the case with law enforcement, and to remove the Lessee or any other persons or property occupying the property. The Lessor has the right to use the property for any purpose. The Lessor is not required to give the Lessee notice of said seizure of property and all notices required by the state of _____ are, with the signing of this lease agreement, waived by the Lessee.

5. Unless written notification is given by wither the Lessor or Lessee, this lease will be automatically renewed for a term of _____. Notice of intent to terminate must be given within _____ days of the end of this lease agreement.

6. Notices sent by Lessor or Lessee must be sent through registered mail with prepaid postage addresses to the recipient at _____[address of Lessor] or _____ [address of Lessee]. The Lessee and Lessor must notify the opposite in writing if a new address is available.

7. All agreements listed within this lease agreement are also binding against all representatives or heirs of the Lessor or Lessee as if it were their name signed on this lease.

8. The words "Lessor" and "Lessee" shall be interchangeable with "Lessors" and "Lessees" within the text of this lease agreement if there is more than one Lessor or Lessee to make this lease agreement grammatically correct.

By signing below, the parties agree to the conditions and agreements listed within this lease agreement.

In witness whereof, the parties have set their hands [and seals] the day and year first above written.

_____
Lessor   Date

_____
Witness   Date

_____
Lessee   Date

_____
Witness   Date

RESTAURANT LEASE

Date:_____

Landlord: _____

Address: _____

City: _____ State: _____ Zip: _____

Tenant: _____

Permanent Address: _____

City: _____ State: _____ Zip: _____

By signing this Lease agreement, Landlord leases to Tenant and Tenant hires from Landlord, for the term and according to the covenants and conditions contained in this Lease agreement, all the land together with the improvements and buildings on it, located at:

_____

Address: _____

City: _____

County: _____

State: _____ Zip:_____

This property is described in detail in Exhibit "A," which is attached to and made a part of this Lease. The property includes the appurtenances and easements that are shown on the Survey, attached to and made a part of this Lease as Exhibit "B" (inclusively referred to in this Agreement as the "Premises).

1. Assignment of Leases.

If applicable, Landlord assigns to Tenant all of Landlord's right, title, and interest in and to all of the leases (or subleases) now associated with the Premises for the term of this Lease. Tenant shall be granted all the rights of a landlord in regard to any of those leases, including the right to receive rent, the right to terminate a lease (or sublease), and the right to extend any such lease for a term not exceeding the term or any extension of the term of this Lease. Tenant assumes any duty or liability to any of its franchisees, licenses, tenants, or subtenants created under the terms of any such lease, and agrees to hold Landlord harmless against any claim, loss, or liability that may arise out of any such lease.

2. Term.

The term of this Lease shall be _____ (_____) years, beginning on
_____ (date) and ending on _____(date).

3. Renewal of Lease.

If the Tenant is not in default under the terms of this Lease, the Tenant shall have one (1),
_____ (_____) year option under the same terms and conditions as specified in this Lease, except that the rent for the option period shall be _____
_____ Dollars ($_____) per year. In order to exercise the option to renew this Lease, Tenant must exercise this option by notifying the Landlord of its intention in writing at least six (6) months before Lease, or any extension of this Lease, expires.

The Tenant shall have an additional _____ (____) year option upon the same terms and conditions as this Lease, except that the rent-for-sale option period shall be in the amount of _____ Dollars ($ _____) per year.

4. Security Deposit.

Tenant will, when this Lease is signed, give the Landlord a deposit of _____ Dollars ($ _____), equal to two (2) months' minimum base rental, as a guarantee that Tenant will fully and faithfully carry out every provision of this Lease, including but not limited to the payment of rent, additional rent, percentage rent, property taxes, and insurance or any other sums due under this Lease, and any other actions required of Tenant under this lease. The Landlord may apply all or any part of this security deposit to any unpaid rents, additional rents or other sums in default, or to pay any costs to the Landlord arising from Tenant's default. If Landlord is obliged to use any portion of the security deposit in this manner, within five (5) days after receiving a written demand from the Landlord, Tenant must deposit enough cash with the Landlord to restore the security deposit to its original amount. Failure to do so shall constitute a material breach of this Lease by the Tenant. The Landlord may commingle the security deposit with its general funds, and Tenant will not receive any interest on the security deposit.

Any time that the monthly minimum base rental is increased, Tenant must deposit with Landlord an amount equal to twice the increase, subject to the same terms and conditions as the original deposit.

1. Rent.

a. **Minimum Annual Base Rent.** The minimum Annual Base Rent shall be _____ Dollars ($), payable to Landlord on the first day of each calendar month during the full term of this Lease in twelve (12) equal installments of _____ Dollars ($ _____).

b. **Percentage Rental.** In addition to the minimum monthly rent, Tenant will pay an additional rent, equal to_____ percent (_____%) of the amount of Tenant's Gross Sales realized in, upon or from the buildings on the Premises during each calendar year of the term of this Lease, minus the aggregate amount of the minimum monthly rent already paid by the Tenant for the same calendar year. The Percentage Rental shall be paid quarterly on the 15th day of the month immediately following each quarterly period in which the Gross Sales are made and shall be calculated using the amount of Tenant's Gross Sales for the previous quarterly period. If the sum of the quarterly payments of Percentage Rental during a calendar year does not equal the Percentage Rental as calculated on an annual basis, then an adjustment shall be made within twenty (20) days after the end of each year of the term of this Lease, and the party owing money shall promptly pay the amount owed to the other party. Upon the expiration, or early termination of this Lease, the Tenant shall pay Landlord the Percentage Rental on the 15th day of the month immediately following the end of the Lease for the last quarterly period or fraction of a quarterly period of the term of this Lease. If either of the first and last quarterly periods of the term of this Lease are less than a full calendar quarter, the Percentage Rental for that fractional period shall be calculated by deducting the pro-rated minimum rental for that period from the percentage of sales realized during that period.

i. **Gross Sales.** For purposes of this Lease, the term "gross sales" is defined as the selling price of, or rental charges for, all merchandise sold or delivered to customers in, at, on, or from any part of the leased Premises; and the charges for services of any sort sold or performed in, at, on or from any part of the leased Premises. "Gross sales" includes sales and charges for cash or credit, regardless of whether the amount sold for credit has been collected, but excludes returns and refunds made by the Tenant during the quarterly period, and the amount of any city, county, state or federal sales, luxury, or excise tax on such sales paid to the taxing authority by Tenant, whether tax is added to the selling price or absorbed in the selling price. A sale shall be considered to be realized in the leased Premises if the sales order is secured or received in the leased Premises, regardless of whether the order is filled in the leased Premises or elsewhere.

ii. **Statements.** At the time the quarterly Percentage Rental is paid, the Tenant shall furnish Landlord with a written statement of the total Gross Sales realized in, upon, through, or from the leased Premises for the same period. If requested by the Landlord, the Tenant will also provide two true and complete copies of Tenant's quarterly state retail sales tax returns at the time they are furnished to the state. The Landlord agrees that all gross sales figures, and other information obtained from Tenant's records, will be kept confidential.

iii. **Audits.** At any time, the Landlord may, at its own expense, audit the gross receipts and financial procedures of Tenant. If the gross sales reported for the Percentage Rental are found to be less than actual gross sales during any period, and if the Landlord determines that the erroneous report has been deliberate, it shall be deemed a material breach of this Lease. Whenever there is a difference between actual and reported gross sales, and it is determined that the amount of Percentage Rental paid to the Landlord was incorrect, the Landlord or Tenant shall promptly pay the excess or deficient amount owed to Tenant or Landlord. If the Tenant is found to have paid less than the Percentage Rental due, the Tenant shall also pay to Landlord the costs associated with performing the audit.

iv. **Accounting.** The Tenant shall keep full, complete, and proper books, records, and accounts of its daily gross cash and credit sales, for every separate department and concession operated at any time in the leased Premises. The Landlord and his agents and employees may, after providing reasonable notice and during regular business hours, examine and inspect all of the Tenant's books and records, including any sales tax reports, pertaining to the business of the Tenant conducted in, upon, or from the said Premises. The Tenant agrees to produce these records at the request of the Landlord or Landlord's agents for the purpose of investigating and verifying the accuracy of any statement of gross sales.

c. **Proration.** If the first day of this Lease is not the first date of any calendar month, the rent for the balance of that first month shall be prorated and paid by Tenant on a daily rate based upon a thirty (30) day month.

2. Use of Premises.

The Tenant shall occupy and use the Premises for the purpose of conducting a restaurant business, for incidental activities related to the restaurant business, or for any other legally permissible business or commercial venture. The Tenant will not use the Premises in any manner that violates any applicable law, rule, ordinance, or regulation of any governmental body, or in violation of the certificate of occupancy issued for the leased Premises. If any use of the leased Premises is declared by any governmental authority having jurisdiction, or by the Landlord, to be in violation of law or said certificate of occupancy, or if any use imposes any additional obligations upon Tenant or Landlord with respect to the leased Premises or with respect to the use or occupation of the leased Premises, Tenant will discontinue such use upon receipt of five days' written notice from the Landlord.

3. The Business.

During the entire term of this Lease, including any extension, Tenant agrees to continuously conduct and carry on Tenant's restaurant business in the demised Premises, and keep the Premises open for business and conduct Tenant's business each and every business day during the customary business hours for businesses of a similar type in the county in which the leased Premises are located. This provision shall be waived in the event that the demised Premises are closed and the business of Tenant temporarily discontinued because of strikes, lockouts, damage to the building or equipment, or other circumstances beyond the reasonable control of Tenant. This provision will also be waived if the business is closed for not more than three (3) days out of respect for the memory of any deceased officer or employee of Tenant or the relative of any such officer or employee.

a. **Zoning, Disclaimer of Warranties, and Condition of Premises.** The Tenant accepts all real and personal property, if any, under the terms of this Lease, "AS IS," in its present condition without any warranty from the Landlord, express or implied, in fact or by law. The Landlord makes no guarantees of any kind concerning the condition of the leased Premises, its fitness for the use intended by Tenant, or its zoning, and hereby disclaims any personal knowledge of these matters. This acceptance "AS IS" applies to the Premises, whether or not it has been inspected, fixtures that are readily visible to inspection, fixtures within the Premises that are not visible to inspection, including, but not limited to, the plumbing, electrical, heating, and air conditioning systems; and personal property, if any.

4. Triple-Net Lease.

It is expressly agreed that this is a triple-net lease.

5. Taxes and Assessments.

Tenant shall pay all property taxes, assessments, and governmental charges, on both real and personal property, as due, during the entire term of this Lease, including any taxes that accrue during the term of this Lease and are billed after the Lease expires. Tenant shall pay all taxes, assessments, and governmental charges to Landlord in equal monthly installments along with the rent payment, beginning on the first day of this Lease and continuing on the first day of each month for the balance of the term of this Lease. The amount of these taxes and assessments shall be based on the previous year's assessments, subject to adjustment for the actual amount due for the current year. After such an adjustment has been made, any additional sums owed by Tenant to Landlord shall be due with the next succeeding month's minimum monthly base rental payment.

For the purposes of this section, "Property Taxes" is defined as real property taxes, personal property taxes, occupancy taxes, assessments upon the property, the improvements that are imposed by any governmental authority or agency, and any tax on or measured by the rentals and imposed wholly or partly in place of real property taxes, but does not include net income, franchise, capital stock, estate, or inheritance taxes, except as specifically stated in this Lease.

If, at any time during the term of this Lease, the method of taxation in effect on the date this Lease becomes effective is changed so that all or any part of the current ad valorem real property taxes are replaced, in whole or in part, by one or more replacement taxes measured, calculated according to, or based, in whole or in part, upon the land, the improvements or the rents derived from the Premises, and imposed upon Landlord, then the Tenant shall be responsible to reimburse Landlord for these taxes. Tenant maintains the right to contest in good faith any such taxes, assessments, or charges. In the event that the Tenant contests such charges, Tenant shall indemnify and hold the Landlord harmless from any cost, expense, or penalties associated with such contest.

7. Utilities.

Tenant shall be responsible to pay directly the cost of all utilities consumed on the Premises, including but not limited to power, electricity, gas, water, garbage disposal, sewer services, and telephone.

8. Insurance.

Tenant agrees to obtain and keep in full force, at its own expense, throughout the term of this Lease, at a minimum, the following types and amounts of insurance:

Public Liability:
-Personal Injury in the amount of $500,000 per person, and $1,000,000 per occurrence;
-Property Damage in the amount of $50,000 per occurrence.

Casualty: Fire and Extended Coverage for 100% of replacement cost of buildings, leasehold improvements and furnishings, and fixtures and equipment, excluding foundation and excavation costs.

Business Interruption Insurance: In order to assure that Tenant will be able to maintain payment of the rent and taxes under the terms of this Lease, the Tenant shall obtain business interruption insurance coverage, with the Landlord named as a coinsured, that will include an increment sufficient to cover the rent and taxes payable under this Lease for at least sixteen (16) weeks. Tenant will obtain a business interruption policy that assigns the proceeds of any proof of loss to Landlord, to the extent of the rent and taxes payable under this Lease for the period of the loss, together with any other sums due Landlord from Tenant. If leased Premises are damaged or destroyed in any manner, rent, taxes, and any other sums payable under the Lease will continue to be due to Landlord, even while the leased Premises are closed for restoration.

The business interruption insurance must be procured from an insurer authorized to do business in the state in which the leased Premises are located and approved in writing by the Landlord. The insurance policy will provide primary and not excess coverage; name the Landlord as an additional insured; waive subrogation rights, if any, which the insurer may have against Landlord. It must require that Landlord receive at least sixty (60) days prior written notice before any such insurance may be canceled or changed with respect to the parties, coverage, limits of liability, or costs of insurance.

The Tenant may, at its discretion, include the business interruption insurance obligations within the coverage of any so-called blanket policy or policies of insurance which it may already carry, or purchase in the future, by adding an appropriate amendment, rider, or endorsement, provided, however, that the interest of Landlord shall be as fully protected by such coverage as it would be if this option to Tenant to use blanket policies were not permitted.

Tenant shall, before the term of this Lease begins, provide Landlord with a copy of such insurance policy or policies, or a certificate of insurance in the case of blanket coverage, together with satisfactory evidence that the policy is in full force on the beginning day of this Lease.

If Tenant fails to maintain any of the above required insurance coverage, the Landlord may, after giving ten (10) days notice to Tenant, act as Tenant's agent to procure any or all of stipulated insurance coverage, and pay the premium. Upon receiving notice from the Landlord that these premiums have been paid, Tenant shall be liable to reimburse the Landlord immediately. Failure to do so shall be treated in the same manner as a breach of the Tenant's covenant to pay rent under this Lease.

9. Alterations and Improvements.

Written consent from the Landlord is required before making any alterations or improvements to the leased Premises. Upon receiving written approval from the Landlord, the Tenant may, at its own expense, make improvements to the Premises or may install or replace equipment, lighting, partitioning, or furnishings within the premises as may be required by the business conducted on the Premises. Such alterations or installments may not diminish the value of the Premises. These installations shall remain the property of Tenant who may remove them from the Premises at any time during the term or at the termination of Tenant's occupancy of the Premises, provided that the Tenant repairs any damage caused by the removal. Any improvements and installations not removed by the Tenant shall become the property of Landlord when Tenant gives up possession of the premises. Tenant agrees that any and all alterations or additions must be in compliance with the building codes and ordinances, and laws and regulations applicable to the premises. The Landlord agrees to execute all documents required to obtain any building or other permit, including dedication documents, needed by Tenant to accomplish these improvements.

10. Work Done on Leased Premises.

The Tenant agrees to provide written notice to the Landlord fifteen (15) days in advance of performing any work on the leased Premises that might give rise to any mechanic's lien, containing the names and addresses of the contractor(s) who will perform the work. The Tenant will also post and record a notice of non-responsibility. When the work has been completed, the Tenant will record a notice of completion in accordance with the laws of this state and provide Landlord with a copy of the notice within 5 days.

11. Maintenance.

For the entire term of this lease, Tenant agrees to keep the interior and exterior of the buildings and appurtenances, including the parking areas, the roof; and all building systems, including, but not limited to, plumbing, electrical, heating and cooling systems, which are a part of the Premises, in good working order, repair, and condition at Tenant's own cost and expense.

Tenant will, at its own expense, perform all necessary repairs and maintenance required under the terms of this Lease. Tenant will repair any damages caused by the use or misuse of the leased Premises by Tenant or its agents, employees, or representatives, or by any other persons while in or about the leased Premises. All such work and the materials used shall be at least equal in quality to the original work.

At any time during the term of this Lease, if any governmental agency requires that certain repairs or improvements be made, or fixtures or equipment be furnished or replaced as a condition to doing business on the leased Premises, Tenant shall bear the full cost of carrying out such repairs or improvements according to plans and specifications prescribed by such agency, with no reimbursement from Landlord.

12. Assignment.

Tenant may not assign this lease in whole or in part, or sublet the Premises, without the prior written consent of Landlord. Landlord shall not withhold such consent unreasonably. The Landlord will be entitled to withhold its approval based on the credit, character, and business or professional standing of any proposed assignee or subLessee; whether the proposed assignee's or subLessee's occupation is consistent with the terms and conditions of this Lease; and whether the proposed assignee or subLessee agrees to be bound and directly responsible for all of the Tenant's past, present, and future obligations under this Lease. Landlord's consent to any such assignment or subletting shall not release Tenant from its past, present, and future liabilities and obligations under this Lease.

13. Condemnation.

If any part of the Premises is condemned or claimed by governmental authorities for a public or quasi-public use, and a part of the Premises remains that is reasonably suitable for the Tenant to continue to use for its business, the rent payable under this Lease shall be adjusted so that, for the remainder of the term of this Lease, the Tenant will be required to pay only a portion of the previous rent, equivalent to the portion of the value of the entire Premises at the date of condemnation represented by the remaining part of the Premises. If all of the premises are appropriated or condemned to the extent that, in the reasonable judgment of Tenant, the Tenant's use of the Premises is substantially impaired, Tenant may elect to terminate this Lease. If the Lease is terminated, no further rent shall accrue from the date that Tenant notifies the Landlord in writing of such termination, and any prepaid rent shall be refunded to Tenant.

Any dispute arising between Landlord and Tenant under this clause shall be submitted to arbitration in accordance with the rules of the American Arbitration Association.

The Landlord shall be exclusively entitled to any and all compensation, damage, income, rent, awards, and any other amounts that may be paid in connection with the condemnation or appropriation, and the Tenant shall have no claim whatsoever against Landlord for the value of the unexpired term of the Lease. The Tenant shall be entitled to any award made expressly for, and only for, the unamortized portion of any and all improvements paid for by the Tenant.

14. Transfer of Interest in Corporation.

If the Tenant is a corporation, then, when either the person in the position of responsible operational officer of the Tenant is replaced by another person; or there is a cumulative transfer of more than fifty (50%) percent of equity interest in the Tenant to another entity within any two (2) year period, then such a transfer or change of control shall be treated an assignment as set out in Section 12 of this Lease.

If the Tenant is a corporation, the Tenant shall submit to the Landlord the names, addresses, and titles of the officers, directors, and resident agent of the corporation in the state in which the Premises are located, a list of the names and addresses of the shareholders and the number of shares issued to each, and the address of the principal office of the corporation. Tenant shall inform the Landlord whenever this information is updated or changed.

15. Indemnification of Landlord.

It is understood and agreed that Tenant releases Landlord from, and indemnifies Landlord against, all claims, demands, charges, liens, and causes of action, as well as proceedings, of every kind and nature associated with the person or property of Tenant, and arising directly from the use of the leased Premises or any public sidewalk, by anyone other than an agent or representative of the Landlord.

16. Defaults.

Any of the following events shall constitute a default and material breach of this Lease:

a. Abandonment of the leased Premises by Tenant. Abandonment is defined as, but is not limited to, any absence by Tenant from the leased Premises for five (5) days or longer.

b. A failure by Tenant to pay the rent, including Percentage Rental or additional rent; or to make any other payment required under this Lease on the date the payment is due and owing.

c. The making by Tenant of any general assignment for the benefit of creditors; the filing of a petition for reorganization or arrangement under any law relating to bankruptcy, except for a petition filed against Tenant that is dismissed within sixty (60) days; the appointment of a trustee or receiver to take possession of substantially all of Tenant's assets located at the leased Premises or of Tenant's interest in this Lease, if possession is not restored to Tenant within thirty (30) days; or the attachment, execution, or other judicial seizure of substantially all of Tenant's assets located at the leased Premises or of Tenant's interest in this lease, if not discharged within thirty (30) days.

d. The closing of the business of Tenant on the leased Premises for a period of five (5) or more consecutive days without the written consent of the Landlord.

e. A failure of Tenant to comply with any of the terms, covenants, or conditions set forth in this Lease.

17. Remedies.

If Tenant does not make a payment of money within five days after Landlord has given written notice to Tenant that payment is overdue, or if a default of any other kind is not resolved within 15 days after the Landlord has given written notice to the Tenant, Landlord may, at any time, at the Landlord's option, exercise any and all rights or remedies available to the Landlord under law or in equity, and with or without notice or demand, may:

a. Take possession of the leased Premises and of all equipment and fixtures of Tenant on the Premises, with or without process of law, and expel or remove Tenant and all other parties occupying the leased Premises, using reasonably necessary force to do so, without being liable to any prosecution for such re-entry or for the use of such force, and without terminating this Lease, at any time, relet the leased Premises or any part of the Premises on behalf of the Tenant, for the term, under the conditions and at the rental that the Landlord considers to be proper. The Landlord may apply the rent from such reletting to any amounts due from Tenant under the terms of this Lease, including, without limitation, expenses incurred by the Landlord in recovering possession of the leased Premises, cleaning the Premises, altering or repairing the Premises for reletting, and all other expenses, commission, and charges, including attorney's fees, which Landlord may have paid or incurred in connection with such repossession and reletting. The Landlord, at his discretion, may execute any such sublease in the Landlord's name or in the name of the Tenant. The Tenant will have no responsibility in the application of any rent collected by the Landlord to outstanding amounts owed by the Tenant, and the Tenant will not have any right to collect any rent.

Whether or not the leased Premises are relet, Tenant shall pay Landlord all amounts required under the terms of this Lease up to the date of Landlord's re-entry. After the Landlord's re-entry, the Tenant shall pay Landlord the amount of all rent and other charges due until the end of the term of this Lease, minus the proceeds of any reletting as set forth above. Payments by Tenant shall be due at the times stipulated in this Lease. Landlord is not required to wait until the termination of this Lease to recover these payments by legal action or otherwise. The re-entry of the Premises, or any other act, by the Landlord does not constitute termination of this Lease or termination of the Tenant's liability for the total rent under this Lease, unless the Landlord gives Tenant written notice that the Landlord has elected to terminate this Lease.

b. Give written notice to Tenant that Landlord has elected to terminate this Lease, take possession of the leased Premises and of all equipment and fixtures of Tenant on the Premises, with or without process of law, and expel or remove Tenant and all other parties occupying the leased Premises, using reasonably necessary force to do so, without being liable to any prosecution for such re-entry or for the use of such force. If the Landlord elects to terminate the Lease, the Landlord may recover from Tenant:

i. any unpaid rent at the time of the award that had been earned at the time the Lease was terminated; plus

ii. the value, at the time of award, of the amount by which the unpaid rent would have been earned between termination until the time of award exceeds the amount of rental loss that the Tenant proves could have been reasonably avoided; plus

iii. the value, at the time of award, of the amount by which the unpaid rent for the balance of the term after the time of award, exceeds the amount of such rental loss that Tenant proves could be reasonably avoided; plus

iv. compensation for any and all harm caused to Landlord by Tenant's failure to fulfill its obligations under this Lease, or that, in the ordinary course of things, would be likely to arise from the Tenant's failure to fulfill its obligations under this Lease. For the purposes of Subsection i and ii above, the "value at the time of award" is calculated using an interest rate of ten percent (10%) per annum. For Subsection iii above, the "value at the time of award" is computed by discounting that amount at the discount rate of the Federal Reserve Bank of _____ at the time of award, plus one percent (1%).

18. Transfer of Title by Landlord.

If title of Landlord in or to the demised Premises, or any part of the Premises, is changed or transferred, voluntarily or involuntarily, or by the act of Landlord or by operation of law, Tenant shall not be required to pay rents accruing after such a change or transfer until notified in writing and given satisfactory proof by Landlord of such change in title. The withholding of rents in this case shall not in any sense constitute a default upon the part of Tenant.

19. Damage to Building.

If fire or other casualty damages or renders the building on Premises unfit for occupation, the Tenant will use any insurance proceeds available to promptly repair or replace the damaged building so that Tenant may again occupy it. Rent due to the Landlord shall not be abated as a result of any such damage.

It is further agreed if damage or destruction of 50% or more of the insurable value of the building occurs during the last five (5) years of the original term of this Lease, or during any extension of the Lease, Tenant will have the option to terminate this Lease from the date of the damage or destruction rather than replacing the building. In such case Tenant must notify the Landlord of its intentions in writing within thirty (30) days after the occurrence of such damage or destruction. The Landlord shall then be entitled to receive the proceeds of any insurance representing the insured value of the building, minus any amount specifically attributable to the personal property of Tenant.

20. Liability for Damages.

Tenant waives all claims against the Landlord for damage to goods, wares, and merchandise, in, on, or about the Premises, and for injuries to persons in or about the Premises from any cause arising at any time.

21. Covenants Against Liens.

The Tenant shall keep the Premises or any part of the Premises free from any liens arising out of any work performed, materials furnished, taxes owed, obligations incurred, by act or omission, on the part of the Tenant, its agents, or employees. Should the leased Premises be subjected to any such lien at any time during the term of this Lease, then Tenant shall, within fifteen (15) days after receiving written notice to Tenant of the existence of the lien, discharge the lien, secure a bond, or issue a statement declaring the Landlord harmless. Notice of this restriction must be posted in a place visible to everyone within and about the leased Premises.

If required by any of Landlord's mortgages or financing entities, the Tenant shall provide to Landlord, at Tenant's sole cost and expense, a lien and completion bond for an amount equal to _____ times the estimated costs of any planned improvements, additions, or alterations in the Premises, so that Landlord will be protected against any liability for mechanics' and material men's liens, and to ensure completion of the work where the amount contracted for exceeds U.S. $ _____.

23. Contest of Liens and Encumbrances by Tenant.

Tenant may engage in appropriate legal proceedings to contest the validity or amount of any mechanics', laborers', material men's lien, or other claimed lien or encumbrance in connection with work undertaken by Tenant on the Premises, and will indemnify and hold Landlord harmless from any cost and expense in connection with such proceedings.

24. Inspections.

Landlord, or Landlord's agents, shall have the right to enter the demised Premises at any reasonable time to conduct inspections of the property, show the Premises to prospective purchasers or tenants, and for any other reason that the Landlord deems necessary, or desirable. The Landlord shall have the right to enter the Premises in order to post or keep posted, notices of non-responsibility or any form of notice reasonably necessary to protect Landlord or the Premises against mechanics' or material men's liens, or charges, or other liens or charges that might arise out of the use of the Premises by Tenant, or the construction of improvements or the making of alterations or repairs to the Premises.

25. Fixtures and Personal Property.

All restaurant and other equipment and fixtures that are currently the property of Landlord, located on the leased Premises, and described in detail in Exhibit "C," attached to this document, shall remain the property of Landlord and shall be kept at all times on the leased Premises. All furniture, fixtures, and equipment installed by Tenant in the Premises shall at all times remain Tenant's personal property, regardless of the method used to install it in the premises, and may be removed by Tenant at the expiration or termination of this Lease, provided Tenant, at its own expense, repairs any damage to the building caused by such removal.

26. Signs.

The Tenant may affix, erect, and maintain on the Premises, at its own expense, any signs or advertisements that the Tenant considers reasonably necessary to the conduct of its business. At the expiration of this Lease, Tenant has the option to remove all such signs.

27. Quiet Enjoyment.

As long as the Tenant pays the rent required by the terms of this lease, and observes and performs all of the covenants, conditions, and provisions set forth in this lease, the Tenant shall have quiet possession of the leased premises for the entire term of this lease, subject to all of the provisions of this lease.

28. Surrender.

When the term or any extension of the term of this Lease expires, the Tenant agrees to surrender possession of the Premises to Landlord in as good condition as at when the Tenant first occupied the Premises, except for reasonable wear and tear, damage by acts of God and the elements, and damage covered by a standard form Fire Insurance Policy with an extended coverage endorsement or any other insurance policy.

29. Holding Over.

Any occupation of the Premises by the Tenant remains beyond the expiration of the Lease or any extension of the Lease will be treated as a tenancy from month to month, under all the conditions of this Lease and at the rental rate effective as of the last month of the expired term. Such month-to-month tenancy can be terminated either by the Tenant or the Landlord by giving the other party thirty (30) days' written notice of its intention to terminate. The Landlord's right of re-entry and all other rights of Landlord under this lease or as otherwise provided by law are not affected by the provisions in this paragraph.

30. Rights of Parties.

Nothing in this contract will be construed as a waiver or abridgement by either the Landlord or the Tenant of any rights or remedies that might be available to under law or in equity. Any one-time consent, waiver, compromise, or indulgence by one party of a breach by the other of any of the provisions of this Lease will not constitute a waiver of the former party's right to enforce performance of the conditions and terms of the Lease at all other times.

31. Subordination.

Landlord has authority to subordinate this Lease to any mortgage, deed of trust or other lien that is now existing or is hereafter placed upon the Leased Premises of the Building. Tenant agrees that it will, upon request by Landlord, execute and deliver a statement certifying that this Lease is in full force and effect to any person the Landlord designates. If there have been modifications, Tenant will state that the modified Lease is in full force and effect. Tenant shall not be required to provide consents involving any interest in the Premises unless the mortgagee, beneficiary, or creditor named in the mortgage or deed of trust first agrees in writing that this Lease and the Tenant's rights under this Lease will not be terminated or modified by any provision of the mortgage, deed of trust or consent, or by any sale of the Premises upon foreclosure, or other legal proceedings by the mortgagee, beneficiary, or creditor, as long as the Tenant is not in default of any of the terms or conditions of this Lease.

32. Affidavit and Memorandum of Lease.

It is expressly agreed that this Agreement will not be recorded in the public records of any county. At the Landlord's discretion, simultaneously with the execution of this Lease, the parties shall execute an Affidavit and Memorandum of Lease for recording purposes, containing a statement that it is not intended to alter the terms and conditions of this Lease in any way. The Affidavit and Memorandum of Lease will not contain information on the rental or other charges payable by the Tenant under this Lease. If the Landlord or Tenant terminate and cancel this Lease for any cause other than Landlord's breach of the terms of the Lease, the Tenant shall prepare, execute, and provide to the Landlord a recordable release and cancellation of this Lease.

33. Time is of the Essence.

Time is of the essence of this Lease and all covenants, agreements, conditions, and obligations contained in it.

34. Notices.

Any communication or written notice required under the terms of this Lease shall be considered served when it is either hand-delivered to the Landlord at the above address and or to the Tenant at Tenant's office and principal place of business, or sent by U.S. mail, certified or registered, return receipt requested, properly addressed with postage prepaid. The address to which communications should be delivered to either party may be changed by giving notice in writing to the other party.

35. Heirs and Assigns.

Each and all of the terms and agreements contained in this Lease agreement shall be binding upon and inure to the benefit of the Landlord and Tenant, their heirs, personal and legal representatives, successors, and assigns.

36. Use of Singular, Plural, and Gender.

If required by the context, wherever the singular number is used in this contract the plural is also included, and any gender used likewise includes any other gender.

37. Paragraph and Section Headings.

The Paragraph and Section headings are used in this document only for convenience and shall in no way limit or restrict the interpretation of any word or phrase in the paragraphs under each heading.

38. No Oral Modification.

This Lease document contains the entire agreement made between the parties. No previous oral agreement or contract between the parties is valid unless it is incorporated in this Lease agreement. Any changes or modifications to this Lease agreement must be made in writing and signed by both parties, or by their respective successors in interest.

39. Broker's Fees.

The Landlord and Tenant each guarantee that it has not entered into any agreement with any person, firm, or corporation, directly or indirectly, or taken any other action that could result in any claim against the other party for the payment of any commission, brokerage, or finder's fee in connection with the execution of this Lease.

40. Attorney's Fees.

Should the Landlord initiate legal proceedings in connection with this Lease, including but not limited to obtaining possession of the leased Premises or recovering any payment due under this Lease, the Tenant will pay to Landlord all costs and expenses, including reasonable attorney's fees incurred by Landlord, whether or not a suit is filed. If the Tenant's occupancy of the Premises under the terms of this Lease results in the bringing of any suit against Tenant or Landlord in which Landlord is named as a defendant, Tenant shall pay costs and expenses incurred by the Landlord in defense of such suit, including reasonable attorney's fees.

41. Interest.

If the Landlord for any reason makes payments on behalf of the Tenant, or if the Tenant fails to pay the rent, additional rent, or other sums due under this Lease, interest at the rate of twelve (12%) percent per annum or the maximum rate of interest permitted under the laws of this state, if less than twelve (12%) percent per annum, will be charged on those amounts, beginning with the date the money was advanced or the rent was due.

42. Counterparts.

This Lease may be executed in counterparts or by two or more complements, each of which shall be considered an original and all of which together shall comprise one and the same instrument. If executed by faxed signatures, this Contract will be effective as of the date of the last signature.

43. Lease not Binding Until Signed.

This Lease shall not be binding on either party or become effective until it is completed and signed by both Tenant and Landlord.

44. Governing Law.

This Agreement, and all transactions carried out in connection with it, shall be governed by, construed, and enforced in accordance with the laws of the State of _____.
Should litigation result from this Agreement, Owner and Agent agree to reimburse the prevailing party for reasonable attorney's fees, court costs, and all other expenses, whether or not taxable by the Court as costs, associated with the litigation, in addition to any other remedy to which the prevailing party may be entitled. No action shall be entertained by said Court or any Court of competent jurisdiction if filed more than one year from the date that the cause(s) of action actually accrued, regardless of whether damages could be accurately calculated at that time.

45. Waiver by Tenant.

Tenant waives any and all right to make defenses or counterclaims in any eviction action instituted by Landlord, except for an affirmative defense based upon payment of all amounts claimed by Landlord not to have been paid by Tenant. Any other matters may only be pursued by filing a separate suit instituted by Tenant.

46. Notice on Radon Gas.

Radon is a naturally occurring radioactive gas that, when it has accumulated in a building in sufficient quantities, may present health risks to persons who are exposed to it over time. Levels of radon that exceed federal and state guidelines have been found in buildings in this state. Additional information regarding radon and radon testing may be obtained from your county public health unit.

47. Reliance on Statement.

At the time of signing this Lease, the Tenant shall furnish its financial statement prepared by an accountant. The Tenant, both as a corporation, if applicable, and individually, represents and warrants that all the information contained in the financial statement is complete and accurate. The Tenant understands that in making this Lease agreement, the Landlord is relying upon the accuracy of the information contained in this financial statement. If the financial statement is found to misrepresent the Tenant's financial standing, or if the Tenant's financial circumstances materially change, the Landlord may demand additional security in an amount equal to an additional two (2) months' rent. This additional security shall be subject to all terms and conditions of this Lease, and require a fully executed guaranty by a third party acceptable to Landlord. If the financial statement is discovered to contain inaccuracies that misrepresent the Tenant's financial standing, Landlord may elect to terminate this Lease, or hold Tenant personally and individually liable.

IN WITNESS WHEREOF, the parties have duly executed this Lease on the day and year listed at the beginning of this agreement. Individuals signing on behalf of a principal warrant that they have the authority to bind their principals.

Signed, sealed, and delivered in the presence of:

LANDLORD: _____

WITNESS: _____

TENANT: _____

WITNESS: _____

STATE OF _____, COUNTY OF _____

The foregoing instrument was acknowledged before me, this

_____ day of _____, 20 _____.

_____ Notary Public

(SEAL) State of _____

My Commission Expires: _____

EXHIBIT "A"
LEGAL DESCRIPTION

The following described real property, together with all improvements thereon:

_____

_____,

which has a street address as follows:

_____

City: _____ State: _____ Zip: _____

EXHIBIT "B" (Attach copy of survey)

EXHIBIT "C"
Equipment and Personal Property

CONDEMNATION

Adapted from **www.dnr.wa.gov/Publications/psl_og_sample_lease_oct06.pdf**, pg. 25.
Please check with an attorney for the correct format and procedure for your state.

If all of the Property is taken by any lawful authority under the power of eminent domain for a period, which will end on or extend beyond the expiration of the Term of this Agreement, this Agreement terminates as of the date the condemner takes possession. If part of the Property is taken by any lawful authority under the power of eminent domain for a period that will end on or extend beyond the expiration of the Term of this Agreement, the State or Lessee may choose to terminate this Agreement as of the date the condemner takes possession. If either the State or Lessee elects to terminate this Agreement, the rents or other charges to be paid by Lessee will be apportioned by the State and paid by the Lessee to the date of taking. If neither the State nor Lessee elects to terminate this Agreement, the rent will be reduced in the same proportion that the value of the portions of the site to be taken bears to the value of the entire site as of the date condemner takes possession. If the taking is for a period that will end on or extend beyond the expiration of the Term of this Agreement, Lessee will have no claim or interest in or to any award of damages for the whole or partial taking of the site, except that the Lessee will be entitled to an amount equal to the fair market value of any improvements as of the date of taking (except trade fixtures) considered by this Agreement to be owned by the Lessee taken by the condemner. If temporary use of all or part of the site is taken by any lawful authority under the power of eminent domain for a period ending before the expiration of the Term, this Agreement will continue in full force and Lessee will be entitled to receive any award from the condemner for the use of all or part of the Property. The State and Lessee will give to the other immediate written notice of any proceedings with respect to a condemnation and of any intentions of any authority to exercise the power of eminent domain.

CONTRACT FOR SALE OF INTEREST IN HOTEL

By signing this agreement, the seller agrees to sell a _____ [percentage or fraction amount] interest in _____ [name of hotel], including any and all effects used or in connection with said hotel, to _____ [buyer], together with a _____ [percentage or fraction amount] interest in lease. The seller agrees to sell this interest for a total amount of $_____. The buyer will pay $_____ in cash at the time of signing this agreement, and $_____ in equal monthly payments in the amount of $_____. These monthly payments are due on _____, _____, and _____, 20__ and should be paid at _____ [seller's location].

To have and to hold the abovementioned hotel and all effects used or in connection with said hotel to buyer or any parties of the buyer, for the buyer's personal uses for the term of the lease agreement.

Seller agrees to be the lawful owner of _____ [percentage or fraction amount] of the abovementioned hotel and all effects used or in connection with said hotel and that it is free and clear of all encumbrances. The seller has the right to sell the abovementioned hotel and any or all effects used or in connection with said hotel and will defend the said hotel against any claims.

The buyer agrees to give a lien to seller on all personal property to ensure the full above mentioned payment for the purchase of the above mentioned hotel.

CHAPTER 6

Lease Agreements

LEASE ASSIGNMENT

Date: _____

Assignor: _____

Address: _____

City: _____ State: _____ Zip: _____

Assignee: _____

Address: _____

City: _____ State: _____ Zip: _____

_____, Assignor,

in consideration of the sum of $ _____ ,

paid by _____, Assignee,

assigns to the Assignee the Lease, a copy of which is attached to this document as Exhibit "A," made by

_____ (Landlord) and

_____ (Tenant),

and dated _____, covering that portion of the property de-scribed in the Lease as follows:

_____

together with the premises described in the Lease, the buildings on the property, and all appurtenances associated with those premises and buildings, to be held by the Assignee from _____ (Date) for the remainder of the term of the attached Lease, subject to the rents, covenants, conditions, and provisions of that Lease.

1. Obligations of Assignee.

Under this Agreement, the Assignee takes on all the obligations, terms, covenants, and conditions of the Lease assigned by the Assignor to the Assignee, and will perform them with full force and effect as if the Assignee had signed the Lease originally as Tenant. The Assignee will pay the rent specified by the Lease beginning with the next rent day and every month afterward until the termination of the Lease.

2. Hold Harmless.

The Assignee agrees to indemnify and save harmless the Assignor from any and all suits, actions, damages, charges, and expenses, including attorneys' fees and costs that might arise from the Assignee's failure to pay the rent as stated in the attached Lease, or from the Assignee's breach of any of the terms, covenants, and conditions of the attached Lease.

3. Relationship Between Assignor and Landlord.

The Assignor's interest in the premises is as Lessee under a Lease made by
_____ (Landlord) and
_____ (Tenant),
and dated _____, a copy of which is attached to and included this Agreement as Exhibit "A." Except for any provisions stated in this Agreement, this assignment is expressly made subject to all the terms and conditions of the underlying Lease. The Assignee agrees to use the premises in accordance with the terms of the underlying Lease, and not to perform any action or omission that will breach any of the terms of that Lease. If the underlying Lease is terminated for any reason, this assignment shall terminate together with it. Provided that such termination is not the result of a breach by Assignee of the terms of the Lease, any unearned rent paid in advance shall be returned to the Assignee after such a termination of the Lease. The Assignee hereby agrees to assume the obligation for performance of all the Assignor's obligations under the attached Lease.

4. Relationship with Landlord and Assignor.

The Assignee understands that the obligations assumed by the Assignee in this Agreement shall inure jointly and severally to the Landlord named in the attached Lease and to the Assignor.

5. Governing Law.

This Lease, and all transactions carried out in connection with it, shall be governed by, construed, and enforced in accordance with the laws of the State of _____. The parties to this Agreement waive trial by jury and agree to submit to the personal jurisdiction and venue of a court of subject matter jurisdiction located in _____ County, State of _____. Should litigation result from this Agreement, Owner, and Agent agree to reimburse the prevailing party for reasonable attorney's fees, court costs, and all other expenses, whether or not taxable by the Court as costs, associated with the litigation, in addition to any other remedy to which the prevailing party may be entitled. No action shall be entertained by said Court or any Court of competent jurisdiction if filed more than one year from the date that the cause(s) of action actually accrued, regardless of whether damages could be accurately calculated at that time.

6. Contractual Procedures.

Should litigation arise out of this Agreement, process will be considered served if delivered through certified mail, return receipt requested; the parties to this Agreement waive any and all rights they may have to object to the method by which process was served.

ASSIGNOR: _____

WITNESS: _____

ASSIGNEE: _____

WITNESS: _____

The foregoing instrument was acknowledged before me, this

_____ day of _____, 20 _____.

_____ Notary Public

(SEAL) State of _____

My Commission Expires: _____

EXHIBIT "A"
PRIMARY LEASE AGREEMENT

CONSENT OF LANDLORD IN PRIMARY LEASE

The Landlord consents to this Lease Assignment from Assignor to Assignee. If any outstanding debts or obligations remain unsatisfied after the breach or termination of the Lease, Landlord agrees to look principally to Assignee and only subsequently to Assignor for their fulfillment.

IN WITNESS WHEREOF, this Assignment has been duly executed by the Landlord on _____ (Date).

Signed, sealed and delivered in the presence of:

_____   _____

Signature of Landlord   Date

_____   _____

Witness   Date

BANK NOTE

Account Number: _____

Date: _____(Date of execution and delivery)

Amount: $_____

Lender: _____

Address: _____

City: _____ State: _____ Zip: _____

Borrower: _____

Address: _____

City: _____ State: _____ Zip: _____

Borrower(s) state here that this loan is being obtained for the following primary purpose:

[ ] Personal family or household
[ ] Farming operations
[ ] Business

For money loaned, the undersigned Borrower(s) named above (hereafter collectively termed "Debtor"), jointly and severally (if more than one Debtor), promise(s) to pay to _____ (Bank) (hereafter termed "Lender") at its office in the city above, the sum of $_____ that includesinterest for the term of this loan at the agreed contract rate of _____ % (percent) per year, and with interest at the contract rate after maturity, until paid.

[ ] If checked here, repayment terms are stated on attached Appendix "B," incorporated as part of this document. Otherwise, the amount is payable after _____ (date), or payable in ___ consecutive monthly installments, commencing on _____(date), in _____ equal payments of $_____ plus an irregular payment of $_____ due on _____ (date) *(Delete payment terms that do not apply.)* The Debtor agrees to pay a delinquency charge of _____ % (percent) of each installment in default for _____ or more days. In the event that, upon Debtor's default (as defined below), the Lender finds it necessary to enforce collection of any unpaid balance due under this note, Debtor agrees to pay all collection and legal expenses and the reasonable attorneys' fees incurred by Lender. Debtor agrees that _____ % (percent) of the sum of the unpaid principal and all interest due on principal at the time action is instituted by Lender, shall be deemed reasonable attorneys' fees.

Each of the undersigned, whether Debtor makers, sureties, endorsers, or guarantors, and all others who may become liable for all or any part of the obligations associated with this loan, jointly and severally waive presentment, demand, protest, notice of protest and/or dishonor, and also notice of acceleration of maturity on default or otherwise. It is agreed that the Lender may, without notice to or consent of any of the undersigned and without affecting the liability of the undersigned, as deemed appropriate, extend or renew this note for any period and grant any releases, compromises, or indulgences with respect to the note or any extension or renewal of or any security for, or to any party liable under this note. The undersigned waive notice of acceptance of their guarantee and expressly agree to pay all amounts under this note, upon demand, without requiring any action or proceeding against the principal Debtor maker(s).

This promissory note is subject to the additional provisions, terms, undertakings, and rights set forth on the reverse side, which are considered to be a part of this contract.

Additional Disclosures to Borrowers Required by Federal Law:
Balloon payment, if any, is $_____.
If the payment is not paid when due, it may not be refinanced.
If the loan contract is prepaid in full by cash, by a new loan, by refinancing, or otherwise before the final installment date, borrowers shall receive a rebate of precomputed interest, computed under _____ % (percent) of the rule of 78's.
The only security for the loan is Lender's right of set-off, as provided by law.

Insurance Disclosures:
Credit life and/or disability insurance are not required as a condition of obtaining this loan. The purchase of credit life and/or disability insurance through the Lender is voluntary. No

credit insurance is provided unless the borrower to be insured under the credit insurance policy signs the appropriate statement below:

  (a) The premium (cost) for credit life insurance will be $_____, for the term of the credit.

  (b) The premium (cost) for credit life and disability insurance will be $_____, for the term of the credit.

I desire credit life and disability insurance.

_____
(Date)

_____
(Signature of customer to be insured)

I desire life insurance only.

_____
(Date)

_____
(Signature of customer to be insured)

Basic Terms of Loan Agreement:
1. Loan Proceeds $ _____
2. Other Charges (Total) $ _____
      a. Premium, Credit Life $ _____

      b. Premium, Disability Ins. $ _____

      c. Other $ _____
3. Less: Prepaid Finance Charge $ _____
      Required Deposit Balance $ _____
4. Total Prepaid Finance Charge and Required Deposit Balance $ _____
5. Amount Financed $ _____ (Nos. 1 + 2 minus No. 4)
6. Finance Charge $ _____
7. Total of Payments $ _____
8. Annual Percentage Rate _____ % (percent)

Acknowledgment of Receipt of Disclosures:
The undersigned borrowers acknowledge that they have received and understood the disclosures contained in this agreement and in the negotiable promissory note, and that by the time they received a copy of this statement and of the negotiable promissory note, these forms were complete and filled-in, and that all blanks in such were filled in prior to their executing them.

Date: _____ *(month, day, year)*

Signature of Borrower: _____
Witness: _____
Signature of Borrower: _____

Witness: _____

Signature of Borrower: _____

Witness: _____

[Reverse side]

ADDITIONAL PROVISIONS

Debtor further warrants, covenants, and agrees, as follows:

1. Security and Right of Set-Off

Debtor agrees that if any installment due and payable under this note is in default for _____ or more days, or if the payment and maturity of the entire unpaid outstanding balance under this note shall be accelerated and matured by any of the "events of default," as described below, Lender has the express authority to exercise its right of set-off or bank lien against any monies deposited in demand, checking, time, savings, or other accounts of any nature maintained in and with the Lender by any of the undersigned, without advance notice. The right of set-off shall also apply to any amount owed by the Lender to any signer of this note, such as a certificate of deposit, bond, note, or other debt instrument. As further security for the payment of this note, the Lender is granted a lien and security interest in and to any funds now or at any future time loaned to or deposited with it by any of the signers of this note.

2. Events of Default

Any of the following events, circumstances, or conditions constitute a default of the Debtor under this agreement:

(1) Default in the timely payment of any of the installments or performance of any other obligations of any covenant, warranty, or liability contained or referred to in this note; or

(2) The proof that any warranty, representation, or statement made or furnished by or on behalf of Debtor, to induce Lender to make a loan to Debtor and enter into this agreement, was false in any material respect when it was made;

(3) Death, dissolution, termination of existence, insolvency, business failure, or the commencement of any bankruptcy proceeding by or against Debtor or any endorser, guarantor, or surety for the Debtor;

(4) Failure of a corporate Debtor or endorser, guarantor, or surety for the Debtor to maintain itself in good standing;

(5) Any monetary judgment or the assessment and/or filing of any tax lien against Debtor, or the issuance of any writ of garnishment or attachment against any property of, debts due or rights of Debtor, specifically the commencement of any action or proceeding to seize monies that the Debtor has on deposit in any bank account with Lender;

(6) The belief, in good faith, of the Lender that the debt is unsafe or insecure, or that the prospect of payment or other performance is impaired.

Upon the occurrence of any of these events, circumstances, or conditions of default, all of the obligations evidenced in this agreement and secured by this means shall, without notice, immediately become due and payable.

(See other side for signatures and seals.)

Guarantee of Third Persons

We, the undersigned, jointly and severally, guarantee the payment, when due, to any holder of this note, of all amounts owing under it, and in the event of a default, the payment, upon demand, of the entire amount owing on the agreement stated above. The undersigned waive(s) notice of acceptance of this guarantee, accept that they are fully bound by all provisions of this.

_____

Signature of Guarantor

_____

Witness

_____

Signature of Guarantor

_____

Witness

_____

Signature of Guarantor

_____

Witness

ACCEPTANCE OF ASSIGNMENT BY ASSIGNEE, INDORSED ON LEASE

Date: _____

Lessor: _____

Lessee: _____

By signing this document, the Lessor gives written consent to assign the attached Lease to the Lessee.

By signing this document, the Lessee agrees to make all payments, and to honor all the conditions and agreements set out in the attached Lease. The Lessor and Lessee agree that the attached Lease is, for all intents and purposes, considered part of this acceptance of assignment.

The Lessor and Lessee agree that no further assignment or subletting of the premises described in the attached Lease, or of any part of those premises, will be made without the prior written consent of the Lessor.

It is agreed that in the event that the Lessor seeks any remedy, such as a legal judgment, against the Lessee or the Lessee's guarantor in regard to a violation of the terms of the attached Lease, that remedy can be exercised simultaneously against the Lessee or guarantor, Lessee's or guarantor's heirs, executors, administrators, successors, or assigns. If any such remedy is sought, the Lessor will be limited to only one satisfaction of any obligations or debts accrued under the attached Lease and any assignment, renewal, or extension of the attached Lease, or accrued after the Lease has been terminated because of any holdover caused by the Lessee's failure to honor any covenant, promise, or agreement in the attached Lease.

If the assignee defaults on payment of the rent as required by the attached Lease and by this acceptance of assignment, or on payment of any holdover or any installment after the Lease has been terminated, the assignee irrevocably authorizes any attorney of any court of record in this state, attorney for assignee and in assignee's name to appear in any court of record of this state in term time or vacation to waive the issuance and service of process and trial by jury and to accept judgment in favor of the Lessor, Lessor's heirs, executors, administrators, or assigns, and against the assignee of Lessee, assignee's heirs, executors, administrators, or assigns for the amount of rent that is due and in default. In addition, the assignee will be responsible for the legal costs of such a proceeding, including a reasonable sum, no less than $_____ for the fees charged by the plaintiff's attorney for the entry of this judgment, and for filing the assignee's cognovit waiving and releasing all errors that may interfere with the proceeding, all right of appeal and right to writ of error, and consenting to immediate execution of the judgment. By signing this document, the assignee confirms that the plaintiff's attorney may lawfully do all the things listed above. If more than one assignee is signing this document, the warrant of attorney contained in this acceptance is given jointly and severally, and shall authorize the entry of a waiver of issuance of process and trial by jury, and a confession of judgment, against any one or more of such assignees; and shall also authorize the performance of every other act mentioned in this acceptance on behalf of any one or more of such assignees.

Signature of Lessor: _____

Date: _____

Signature of Assignee: _____

Date: _____

AGREEMENT TO EXTEND LEASE I

Date: _____

Landlord: _____

Tenant: _____

Premises: _____

This Agreement is hereby made regarding the Premises above on this date between the Landlord and the Tenant listed above. The Premises are leased to the Tenant by way of the Lease Agreement between the Tenant and Landlord, which was signed on _____ (date) and of which the agreement is set to expire on _____ (date).

The Landlord and Tenant hereby agree to the following:

1.   The aforementioned Lease Agreement is extended for a period of _____ (days/months/years). This extension hereby begins on _____ (date) and will end on _____ (date).

2.   The terms and conditions of the previously mentioned Lease Agreement are to remain intact and be in full force during the period set forth above for the

extension of said Lease. Any exceptions are noted here: _____
_____.

3.   Upon signing of this Lease Extension, the monthly rent due will be $_____ payable on the _____ of every month to the Landlord.

IN WITNESS WHEREOF, the Landlord and Tenant hereby agree to this Extension of the Lease Agreement on this date _____.

_____
Landlord Signature

_____
Tenant Signature

AGREEMENT TO EXTEND LEASE II

Date: _____
Owner: _____
Renter: _____
Property: _____

This Agreement is hereby made regarding the Property above on this date between the Owner and the Renter listed above. The Property are leased to the Renter by way of the Lease Agreement between the Renter and Owner, which was signed on _____ (date) and of which the agreement is set to expire on _____ (date).

The Owner and Renter hereby agree to the following:

1.   The aforementioned Lease Agreement is extended starting on _____ (date) and will end on _____ (date).

2.   The terms and conditions of the previously mentioned Lease Agreement are to remain intact and be in full force during the period stated in #1 for the extension of said Lease.

3.   Upon signing of this Lease Extension, the monthly rent due will be $_____ payable on the _____ of every month to the Owner or Owner's Assigns.

4.   In every other aspect, the Lease Agreement will remain unchanged.

IN WITNESS WHEREOF, the Owner and Renter hereby agree to this Extension of the Lease Agreement on this date _____.

_____
Landlord Signature

_____
Tenant Signature

Signed, Sealed, and Delivered in the Presence of:

_____   _____
Witness 1 Signature   Witness 2 Signature

_____   _____
Witness 1 Printed Name   Witness 2 Printed Name

AGREEMENT GIVING PERMISSION TO SUBLET

Date: _____

Landlord: _____

Landlord Address: _____

Renter: _____

Renter Address: _____

This Agreement is hereby made on this date by and between the Landlord and Renter listed above. This Agreement is in regards to the Property located at _____ _____, which is currently leased to the Renter under the Lease Agreement signed on _____ (date). This Lease is not subject to expiration until _____ (date).

Therefore, both Landlord and Renter hereby agree to the following terms:

1. Landlord grants to the Renter the permission to sublease the aforementioned property from _____ (date) until _____ (date).

2. Renter hereby understands that any tenants subleasing the property are required to follow all rules, covenants, and obligations of the Renter all of which were outlined in the Lease Agreement signed by the Renter. All provisions of the Lease Agreement are to remain in full force and effect for the full term of the sublease.

3. All adult renters of the sublease are required to provide the Landlord with a completed rental application and must meet any requirements for tenancy put forth by the Landlord, including but not limited to employment, credit, rental history, and character.

4. In such event that legal recourse is necessary for the Landlord to enforce any part of this Agreement or the original Lease Agreement, then the prevailing party will have the right to recover reasonable legal fees and costs associated with said legal action.

5. The permission granted in this Agreement in no way releases the Renter from his/her obligations and responsibilities as Renter as were provided for in the aforementioned Lease Agreement.

IN WITNESS WHEREOF, both the Landlord and Renter agree to and have carried out this Agreement on the date listed above.

_____

Landlord Signature

_____

Tenant Signature

AMERICANS WITH DISABILITIES ACT — ADDENDUM

Notwithstanding anything else in this lease to the contrary, this paragraph shall apply to all issues related to compliance with both the Americans with Disabilities Act ("ADA") and the _____ [state statute]. In the event of any conflict between the rest of the lease and this Paragraph, this Paragraph shall control.

(a). Any remodeling, construction, reconstruction, installation of improvements, or other work done to the common areas or other portions of the property of which the Premises are a part (the "Property") shall be performed by Landlord, at Landlord's expense, in compliance with the requirements of the ADA and the _____ [state statute] and regulations promulgated pursuant to them.

(b). Any remodeling, construction, reconstruction, installation of improvements, or other work done to the Premises shall be done in compliance with ADA and _____ [state statute] requirements, at the expense of the party who is performing the work.

(c). In the event that a regulatory agency, private party, organization or any other person or entity makes a claim under either the ADA or the _____ [state statute] against either (or both) parties, the party whose breach (or alleged breach) of responsibility under this lease gave rise to the claim shall promptly retain attorneys and other appropriate persons to advise the parties regarding the same, and shall in good faith and at that party's sole cost and expense take whatever actions are necessary to bring the Premises or the Property, as the case may be, into compliance with ADA or _____ [state statute] requirements. That party shall defend, save, and hold harmless the other party from any and all expenses incurred in responding to such a claim, including without limitation the fees of attorneys and other advisors, court costs, and costs incurred for bringing the Property and/or the Premises into compliance. If the claim relates to an aspect of the Premises or the Property as it existed at the time of the execution of the lease, as opposed to work performed by either party after the execution of the lease, then Landlord shall be deemed to be the party whose breach of responsibility gave rise to the claim. [Alternatives: if a claim is made, Tenant has the option of terminating the lease; the parties split the cost in an agreed-upon proportion (e.g., 50/50, 60/40, etc.); Tenant bears the cost if the claim pertains only or primarily to the Premises, while Landlord bears the cost if the claim relates only or primarily to the Property; etc.]

(d). Common area maintenance charges shall not include any costs or expenses incurred by Landlord in bringing the Premises or the Property into compliance with ADA or _____ [state statute] requirements, either voluntarily or in response to a claim of non-compliance. [Alternatives: only a certain dollar amount or percentage may be included; all of the cost for such items may be included; those pertaining to the Premises could be passed on in CAM charges, but not those pertaining to common areas; etc.]

(e). Tenant shall not change its use of the Premises without the prior written consent of Landlord. If the proposed change in use would, in the good faith written opinion of Landlord's advisors, trigger expenditures to comply with ADA or _____ [state statute] requirements not applicable to the then-current use of the Premises by Tenant, Landlord may refuse the proposed change in use on that ground or condition approval of the change in use on Tenant's agreement to bear the expense of compliance with ADA and _____ [state statute] requirements triggered by Tenant's proposed change in use. This subparagraph shall also apply to proposed assignments or subleases which would change the use of the Premises. [Alternatives: An outright prohibition on change of use; Landlord's options limited to approval or disapproval; Tenant bears the first $_____ of expenses; etc.]

(f). Notwithstanding the above, neither party shall be responsible for any costs or expenses relating to practices of the other that are deemed to be discriminatory under the ADA or _____ [state statute] and that relate solely to the conduct of such party (as opposed to physical barriers), and each party shall indemnify the other against costs or expenses relating to the other party's conduct.

(g). Notwithstanding the above, Tenant shall be solely responsible for expenses necessary to comply with ADA and _____ [state statute] requirements triggered solely by a disability of one or more of Tenant's employees. [Alternative: If the expense to be incurred would be for an item which would become a fixture to the real estate, the cost might be shared in some proportion.]

(h). Both parties covenant with one another to cooperate reasonably to comply with ADA and _____ [state statute] requirements in the least expensive reasonable manner, and to create as little disruption as possible to the business operations of Landlord, Tenant, and the other tenants of the Property.

(i). Any rules and regulations that would prohibit either party from complying with ADA or _____ [state statute] requirements are deemed by this subparagraph to be modified to the extent necessary to allow compliance.

(j). Non-compliance with the provisions of this Paragraph, after written notice to the non-complying party and an opportunity to cure within a reasonable period, shall be an event of default under the lease. A reasonable period to cure shall mean cure or commencement of efforts to cure within ten days, which efforts are diligently pursued to completion.

REAL ESTATE AGENT COMMISSION AGREEMENT FOR POTENTIAL TENANT

Date: _____

Real Estate Agent Name: _____

Address: _____

Potential Tenant Information Sheet:

Name: _____

Current Address: _____

Business: _____

Home Phone: _____

Business Phone: _____

E-mail: _____

Wants a ❑ furnished ❑ unfurnished rental

# of family members/tenants to be occupying property: _____

Pets: ❑ Yes ❑ No If Yes, type: _____

Date needed: _____

Potential Rental Properties:

Address	Date Available	# of Rooms	# of Baths	Monthly Rent $	Key Located

I hereby acknowledge that I have received the information above from _____ (company). In the event that I rent, lease, or purchase any of the properties listed in the Potential Rental Properties list, I promise to do so through the office of the aforementioned company and to make due payment of their regular commission as provided by the _____ (state) Real Estate Board.

_____
Company

_____
Agent/Salesman Printed

_____
Agent/Salesman Signature

AGREEMENT TO EXECUTE LEASE

Date: _____

This agreement is made this day by and between _____ ("Landlord") and _____ ("Lessee").

The amount of _____ dollars ($_____) has been paid by the Lessee to the Landlord and will be credited toward the first month's rent under the lease of the premises described below, and receipt of this payment is hereby acknowledged.

The parties mutually agree that the lease agreement for the following subject property described as: _____
shall be made, signed, executed, and delivered by both the Landlord and Lessee.
  1.   The execution and delivery of said Lease shall take place on _____ (month/day/year) at the location described as:
_____

_____   _____
Landlord   Date

_____   _____
Tenant   Date

AGREEMENT TO TERMINATE LEASE

Date	Lessor

Property Address	Lessee

For Good Consideration, the abovementioned Lessor and Lessee as of this date do hereby mutually agree to terminate and cancel the Lease Agreement dated _____ (Date) on premises described above. Both Lessor and Lessee do hereby concur that this termination agreement cancels all rights and obligations under aforementioned lease excepting only for any unpaid rental obligations accruing under the lease prior to the set forth date for termination.

Lessee agrees to immediately surrender the property by said termination date and to return the premises to Lessor in the same condition received to the extent reasonably possible, free of Lessee's possessions.

This agreement shall be binding upon the Lessor and Lessee, their successors, assigns, personal agents, and representatives.

_____
Lessor

_____
Witness for Lessor

_____
Lessee

_____
Witness for Lessee

AGREEMENT TO CANCEL LEASE

Date: _____ (month, day, year)

Landlord (as listed on the Lease Agreement): _____

Retailer (the successor in interest to Tenant under the Lease Agreement):

_____

The Retailer has stopped operating a business on the premises and wishes to cancel all of its obligations under the Lease Agreement; and the Landlord is willing to cancel the lease providing the following terms and conditions are met.

The Landlord and the Retailer agree to the following conditions:

1. The Landlord will sign and deliver at closing to Retailer:
    (1)   a Surrender of Lease form (attached to this document as Exhibit "A").
    (2)   an Assignment of Lease and Assumption Agreements form attached to this agreement.

2. The Retailer agrees at closing to:
    (1)   provide to the Landlord a check for $_____.
    (2)   sign and deliver to the Landlord a "Bargain and Sale Deed with Covenant Against Grantor's Acts" form, appended to this agreement, for the property located at:

Street address: _____

City: _____ State: _____ Zip:_____

As of the date of closing, title to the property must be legal and insurable according to the requirements of _____ Title Insurance Company, at regular rates, free of all liens, encumbrances and conditions, except those that might be detailed in an appendix to this document.

(3)   sign and deliver to the Landlord a form, appended to this document, assigning to Landlord all of the Retailer's right, title, and interest as Lessee in the Lease dated _____,

between _____ (Lessor) and

_____, (Lessee),

for property located at:

Street address: _____

City: _____ State: _____ Zip:_____

as described in the Lease, a copy of which is already held by the Landlord.

(4)   sign and deliver to the Landlord an assignment of all of Retailer's right, title and interest as Landlord in the Lease dated _____(year), between Retailer as Landlord, and _____as Tenant, for property located at:

Street address: _____

City: _____ State: _____ Zip:_____

as described in the Lease, a copy of which is already held by the Landlord, together with the sum of $_____ representing the deposit paid by Tenant to the Retailer (as Landlord) on the making of the Lease.

3. Any adjustments, including adjustments for real estate taxes, fuel, and rents, shall be made as of the closing date.

4. The closing shall be held at _____(time) _____(date) _____(year) at the office of: _____
Street address: _____
City: _____ State: _____ Zip: _____

5. If the Landlord, after receiving from the Retailer of all of the items required in Paragraph 2 above, fails to sign and deliver a Surrender of Lease as set forth in Paragraph 1 above, the Retailer shall nevertheless be released from all of its obligations under the Lease Agreement as of the closing date given in Paragraph 4.

6. If Retailer fails to supply all of the items required of it in Paragraph 2 above, the Landlord may (1) sue for the Retailer to provide specific legal documents and payments, or (2) cancel this Agreement, in which case the Landlord and Retailer named in this Agreement will no longer be party to this Agreement.

7. The Landlord agrees to accept, in its present condition as of the date of this Agreement, the property located at:

Street address: _____
City: _____ State: _____ Zip: _____

8. This Cancellation Agreement is subject to the approval of the Bank of _____. None of the rights or obligations set forth in this Agreement are valid until the Bank has given approval. If approval from the bank is not obtained within ten (10) days from the date of this Agreement, the Retailer may terminate this Cancellation Agreement, after giving fifteen (15) days' notice. This Cancellation Agreement will be null and void from and after the date specified in such a termination notice.

9. This Cancellation Agreement is complete concerning the matters referred to in this document. Changes, modifications, and amendments must be requested in writing and signed by both parties.

10. This Cancellation Agreement is binding upon the parties listed in this document and their respective successors, assignees, and agents.

11. Any communications or notices required by this document shall be in writing and shall be considered delivered if sent by registered or certified U.S. mail, return receipt requested, postage prepaid, either to the Landlord at the address given above, or to any other address that the Landlord may give in writing to the Retailer; or to the Retailer as two copies sent separately to the attention of the President of Retailer, and to the attention of the Vice-President in charge of real estate, at the address of Retailer given above, or at any other address that the Retailer may give in writing to the Landlord. In the case of a postal strike or other interference with the mails, personal delivery of documents and notices will take the place of registered or certified mail.

Date: _____ *(month, day, year)*

Signature of Landlord:

_____

Signature of Retailer:

_____

Witnessed by:

_____

SALE OF LEASEHOLD AGREEMENT

Date: _____
Landlord: _____
Address: _____
City: _____ State: _____ Zip: _____
Tenant: _____
Address: _____
City: _____ State: _____ Zip: _____
Prime Lessee: _____

Address: _____

City: _____ State: _____ Zip: _____

THIS AGREEMENT is made between and among _____ (Tenant), and _____ (Prime Lessee), and, _____ (Landlord).

Tenant and Landlord desire to terminate the Lease Agreement entered into on _____ _____ (Date of original Lease), a copy of which is attached to this Agreement as Exhibit "A."

Prime Lessee and Landlord desire to enter into a new lease agreement, the "Prime Lease," a copy of which is attached to this Agreement as Exhibit "B," beginning on the date that Prime Lessee takes possession of the leased Premises from Tenant.

Effective from the date of delivery of possession, the Prime Lessee and Tenant desire to enter into a "Sublease," a copy of which is attached to this Agreement as Exhibit "C." All the right, title, and interest of Tenant in the leasehold improvements and the premises leased under the Lease Agreement ("Leased Premises") will be transferred to the Prime Lessee.

The parties agree as follows:

1. Lease and Sublease.

Tenant and Landlord agree that all rights and obligations of Tenant and Landlord under the Lease Agreement shall terminate when Tenant delivers possession of the Leased Premises to Prime Lessee, subject to the terms of the Sublease. The Tenant consents to the execution by Prime Lessee and Landlord of the Prime Lease Agreement; and the Landlord consents to the execution by Tenant and Prime Lessee of the Sublease. Tenant and Landlord individually covenant, represent, and warrant that the Lease Agreement will remain in full force and effect, unmodified, and with no defaults, from the date of this Agreement and until the time the Sublease comes into effect.

2. Rent Payments.

The Tenant shall continue to pay to the Landlord rent and all payments required under the Lease Agreement for periods up to the date that Prime Lessee takes possession of the Leased Premises including, but not limited to, the full rental and leasehold amortization payments due and payable on _____ (date of transfer). Prime Lessee agrees to give Tenant a credit under the Sublease for any amounts Tenant has paid relating to any portion of the Leased Premises for periods following the delivery of possession of the premises to Prime Lessee.

3. Possession Date.

Tenant agrees to give possession of the Leased Premises, subject to the provisions of the Sublease, to Prime Lessee no later than _____(date). The Tenant may give possession to Prime Lessee earlier than this date. Prime Lessee shall become the lessee under the Prime Lease Agreement on the date of such possession.

4. Transfer of Leasehold Improvements.

On delivery of possession of the Leased Premises to Prime Lessee, Tenant transfers and assigns to Prime Lessee all right, title, and interest of Tenant in all leasehold improvements installed in the Leased Premises, listed as Exhibit "D" with detailed costs and depreciation and amortization schedules and attached to this document. The Landlord consents to this transfer and assignment. Tenant will prepare and deliver to Prime Lessee any and all documents necessary for Tenant and Prime Lessee to accomplish this transfer and assignment.

5. Title Information to be Supplied to Prime Lessee.

The Landlord shall promptly provide Prime Lessee with a set of the working drawings of the Leased Premises, and a copy of the survey of the Leased Premises described in the Lease Agreement. Landlord will give Prime Lessee copies of all title insurance policies or title guarantees relating to the Leased Premises, and to the extent that these policies or guarantees are assignable, they shall promptly be assigned to Prime Lessee.

6. Commission to Broker.

_____is the only real estate broker who has represented any party to this transaction. The Commission of said real estate broker shall be calculated and payable as follows:

a. **Tenant Payment.** Tenant will pay to _____ the sum of _____ dollars ($_____), on the date that possession of the Leased Premises is given to Prime Lessee.

b. **Assignee Payment.** Prime Lessee will pay to _____ the sum of _____ dollars ($___), with _____ dollars ($___) payable when Prime Lessee takes possession of the Leased Premises, and _____ dollars ($____) payable one year afterward.

c. **Landlord Payment.** Concurrently with the execution of this Agreement, Landlord will pay to Prime Lessee the sum of _____ dollars ($_____), in full consideration of any and all liability of Landlord with respect to any Commission due to broker on the date that possession of the Leased Premises is given by Tenant to Prime Lessee.

d. **Repayment.** If Prime Lessee exercises the right to cancel according to the terms and conditions of paragraph _____ of the Prime Lease Agreement, along with the delivery of written notice of cancellation, the Prime Lessee shall repay to Landlord the sum of _____ dollars ($___).

7. Commencement Date.

When Tenant has delivered possession of the Leased Premises to Prime Lessee pursuant to Paragraph 3 above, Prime Lessee and Landlord agree to amend Paragraph _____ of the Prime Lease Agreement by inserting the date of delivery of possession as the date of commencement of the term of the Prime Lease Agreement. The delivery of possession shall be documented by a letter signed by Prime Lessee and Tenant on the date of delivery.

8. Heirs and Assigns.

Each and all of the terms and agreements contained in this Lease agreement shall be binding upon and inure to the benefit of the Landlord and Tenant, their heirs, personal and legal representatives, successors, and assigns.

9. Entire Agreement.

This Lease Agreement contains the entire agreement between the Owner and the Agent. No prior agreements, verbal statements, or understandings pertaining to any of the matters in this Agreement shall be effective for any purpose.

10. Governing Law.

All matters pertaining to this Lease (including its interpretation, application, validity, performance and breach), shall be governed by, construed, and enforced in accordance with the laws of the State of _____. Landlord and Tenant agree to waive trial by jury and to submit to the personal jurisdiction and venue of a court of subject matter jurisdiction located in _____ County, State of _____. If litigation arises out of this Agreement or the performance thereof, the parties agree to reimburse the prevailing party's reasonable attorney's fees, court costs, and all other expenses, whether or not taxable by the court as costs, in addition to any other relief to which the prevailing party may be entitled. In such event, no action shall be entertained by said court or any court of competent jurisdiction if filed more than one year subsequent to the date the cause(s) of action actually accrued regardless of whether damages were otherwise as of said time calculable.

11. Extraordinary Remedies.

In the event that this Agreement, including the attached Prime Lease and Sublease agreements, is breached, in addition to any and all other remedies available under the terms of the Agreement, any of the parties may obtain injunctive relief to the extent available under local, state, and federal law, regardless of whether the injured party can demonstrate that no adequate remedy exists at law.

LANDLORD: _____

WITNESS: _____

TENANT: _____

WITNESS: _____

PRIME LESSEE: _____

WITNESS: _____

EXHIBIT "A"
LEASE AGREEMENT BETWEEN TENANT AND LANDLORD

EXHIBIT "B"
PRIME LEASE AGREEMENT BETWEEN PRIME LESSEE AND LANDLORD

EXHIBIT "C"
SUBLEASE BETWEEN TENANT AND PRIME LESSEE

EXHIBIT "D"
LIST OF LEASEHOLD IMPROVEMENTS

AMENDMENT TO LEASE LETTER

AMENDMENT TO LEASE

_____ (Landlord) and _____ (Tenant) hereby modify and amend the lease, dated _____, regarding the property at _____in the following details: _____, _____, _____.

(Describe the details)

Landlord and Tenant agree that all other terms and conditions of the Lease remain in effect throughout the term of the Lease.

Date: _____

_____
Landlord's Signature

_____
Landlord's Printed Name

CONTRACT TO LEASE WITH OPTION TO PURCHASE

Date: _____
Purchaser: _____
Address: _____
City: _____ State: _____ Zip: _____
Seller: _____
Address: _____
City: _____ State: _____ Zip: _____

In respect of the expenses, agreement, contracts, and circumstances contained in this contract, the above parties hereby agree to lease with an option to purchase the following property: _____ (address).
Official Description of property:

_____

Personal Estate included_____
Personal Estate will be transferred at closing by an unencumbered bill of sale.

1. Open Loans.

At time of closing, Purchaser may elect to take title and assume the open loans to_____ in the amount of $_____ bearing interest rate of _____% owed _____ (P & I).

If Purchase does not elect to take on the open loan, the loan will be paid off by the seller.

Loan Number_____
Date last payment made_____
Other Liens, back taxes, etc._____
Term of lease and option: _____months commencing _____
Monthly Fee will be $_____due on the _____day of each month commencing_____ 20_____
Monthly credit toward acquisition price when rent is paid on time $_____
Acquisition Price $_____, added options consideration _____to apply toward acquisition price.

2. Conditions.

Seller agrees that if the Purchaser elects not to assume open loans, Seller will assist in funding by taking as part of the Acquisition price a note in the amount of $_____ with payments of $_____ beginning _____.

3. Maintenance.

All repairs costing less than $_____ per month will be done at Purchaser's expense. Seller will be responsible to pay for repairs costing $_____ or more. Should the Seller fail to make necessary repairs to maintain the house in good order, Purchaser may have said repairs made and receive a credit equal to 200% of the cost of the repairs toward the acquisition price and a full credit toward the next payment due.

3. Seller Will Not Further Burden.

Sellers agree that they will not refinance the property, nor alter any existing loans, nor move any interest in the property during the term of this agreement.

4. Payments of Open Loans, Taxes, and Insurance.

During the term of this contract, Seller shall be responsible for paying the taxes and loan payments and for keeping the property insured for its full substitute value. In the event Seller fails to make timely payments of taxes, insurance, or loan payments, buyer may elect to make these payments and receive a credit of 200% of their amount credited toward the Acquisition price and full credit toward the next payment due the Seller.

5. Prorations.

Taxes and indemnity and loan interest shall be prorated as of the date of closing of the Acquisition.

6. Documents.

Buyer and Seller agree to fully perform and place all documents necessary to express title in escrow with _____. Seller shall deposit an implemented service contract deed, copies of existing mortgages, notes, title insurance policies, and surveys. Buyer shall deposit an implemented quitclaim deed that will be transported to the Seller if the Buyer defaults under this agreement. All agree to sign an escrow contract authorizing the escrow agent to close the deal if all terms of the agreement are met, and that will hold the escrow agent harmless.

7. Conveyance of Title.

If Buyer chooses to exercise their option to Acquisition, they will notify the Seller during the term of this agreement. Within 15 days of receipt of such notice, Sellers will convey good and marketable title free from all encumbrances except those that buyer wishes to take title subject to. Sellers further agree to furnish an owner's title binder within __ days after receiving notice, showing no exceptions other than as listed above, and furnish a policy of title insurance at closing.

8. Default.

If Seller fails to transfer title, Buyer will be permitted to recover all money paid on this contract, and may have recourse to all other available legal remedies. Seller will be responsible for all costs incurred by such a failure including a reasonable attorney's fee. In the event Buyer fails to exercise the option to buy, all option consideration and rents paid will be forfeited as fully-liquidated damages.

9. Recordation.

All parties agree that this contract, or in its place a communication including those parts of their contract acceptable to the Buyer, may be recorded.

10. Successors, Heirs, and Assigns.

The conditions and circumstances of this agreement shall be binding on the successors, heirs, administrators, executors, and assigns of Buyer and Seller, and those subletting.

11. Access and Advertising.

Sellers agree that the Buyer may promote the property and shall have direct access during reasonable hours to show the property to others.

12. Time is of the Essence.

Time is of the essence in all matters pertaining to this agreement.

13. Other Terms.

_____

The undersigned agree to buy and sell on the above terms, and assert that they have read, fully understand, and verify the information contained herein as being correct. All parties recognize that this is a lawfully binding agreement and are advised to seek the counsel of an attorney.

_____   _____
Seller   Date

_____   _____
Purchaser   Date

State of _____   County of _____

STATE OF _____, COUNTY OF _____
The foregoing instrument was acknowledged before me, this
_____ day of _____, 20 _____.

_____ Notary Public
State of _____
My Commission Expires: _____

SELLER OPTION TO PURCHASE REAL ESTATE

(MUST BE USED IN COMBINATION WITH A SEPARATE LEASE AGREEMENT!)

THIS AGREEMENT is between the Optionor _____
and the Optionee_____.

1. Optioned Property:

Optionor hereby grants the Optionee the right and option to purchase the property located at _____. Entering into this agreement will end the Rental Agreement between _____(Landlord) and _____ (Tenant). This Agreement binds the property listed above including all improvements and fixtures with the exception of the following: _____
_____.

2 Term:

The term of this Agreement shall be _____ months beginning on the first day of _____ and ending on the last day of _____, 20___.

3. Option Fee:

Optionee agrees to pay a non-refundable fee of $_____, as consideration for the Optionor to grant the Option to Optionee to purchase the above property. Concurrently with the execution of this Option Agreement, the Optionee shall deposit the sum of $_____ with Optionor and agrees to pay $_____ on _____, 20___ or installments of $_____ at intervals of _____until the total option fee has been paid in full. If the Optionee maintains the premises in accordance with the rental agreement and pays the monthly rent on or before the first day of each month, he will receive a $_____ discount, to be applied to the non-refundable option fee.

4. Option Price:

The Option price for this property is derived from a combination of the base price and the change in the Consumer Price Index. The base price shall be $_____. The base price shall be increased by the same percentage as the change in the Consumer Price Index (CPI-U) of the U.S. Department of Labor from the beginning of the term of this option. The purchase price shall be the base price plus the percentage derived from the CPI-U. When the Optionee purchases the property, the Option Fee required in paragraph 3 of this agreement shall be applied as a down payment toward the full purchase price of said property.

5. Repairs and Maintenance:

Optionee agrees to maintain the building in good to excellent condition. This includes but is not limited to maintaining the lawn, snow removal, repairs and any other preventative maintenance throughout the term of this agreement. Repairs that cost a total of $500 or less shall be the responsibility of the Optionee. Optionor is fully responsible for any roof leak if notified immediately by the Optionee. If Optionee fails to notify Optionor immediately of the roof leak, the Optionee shall pay for fixing the roof and all resulting damage to the building, regardless of cost. Repairs that cost a total of more than $500 are to be shared equally by the Optionor and Optionee, provided that the Optionor has approved the repairs in writing before any work is performed or materials are ordered. If repairs are made necessary as a result of negligence by Optionee or his or her guests, entire cost of such repairs shall be paid in full by the Optionee.

6. Improvements and Modifications:

Optionee must receive written approval from Optionor before making any improvements or modifications to the property. Any unapproved modifications must be removed, at Optionee's expense within 7 days of receipt of written notice from Optionor.

7. Terms of the Option:

Provided that the Optionee has paid all sums due and fulfilled all covenants under the Rental Agreement and has paid the Option price outlined in Paragraph 2, the Optionee my exercise the option to purchase the said property after one year. Optionee must provide the Optionor sixty (60) days' written notice of intent to exercise option. Upon exercising the option to purchase, Optionee agrees to cooperate with the Optionor in affecting an Internal Revenue Code Section 1031 exchange, at no cost to the Optionee. Optionee will arrange his own financing and pay all closing costs associated with the transfer of the property and obtaining the loan, in order to complete the sale or exchange within sixty

(60) days of the exercise of the option. Optionor agrees to deliver a good and sufficient General Warranty Deed conveying a marketable title to Property to the Optionee.

8. Disclosures:

Optionee acknowledges receipt of the "Residential Property Disclosure" statement, the EPA "Disclosure of Information on Lead-Based Paint and Lead-Based Paint Hazards" statement, and the EPA "Protect Your Family From Lead In Your Home" booklet and understands their contents.

9. Title:

Optionee verifies that he has reviewed the title to the Property and has found no errors in the title and accepts all encumbrances upon the property.

10. Heirs and Assigns:

This Option and the agreements contained in this Agreement shall be binding upon and inure to the benefit of heirs, executors, administrators, successors, and assigns of the respective parties.

11. Governing Law:

This agreement, and all transactions carried out in connection with it, shall be governed by, construed, and enforced in accordance with the laws of the State of _____.

IN WITNESS WHEREOF, Optionor and Optionee have executed this agreement on the _____ day of _____, 20_____.

OPTIONOR _____

OPTIONEE _____

OPTION TO PURCHASE REAL ESTATE

Date: _____

Optionor: _____

Optionee: _____

1. Option.

This option granting Optionee the exclusive right to purchase real estate described as_____ for $_____ from Optioner shall originate on _____ and expire on _____, according to the following terms of sale:_____.

2. Prorations.

At closing, the following items shall be prorated: _____.

3. Personal Property.

All personal property, appliances, attachments, and fixtures shall be included in the sale except:_____.

4. Conveyance of Title.

Optioner will convey title by a good warranty deed and furnish a policy of insurance from a reputable title insurance agency. Optionee shall have the right to extend abovementioned option under the same terms and conditions, upon payment of $_____, by _____ year(s), with or without notice to Optioner.

5. Documents.

To secure this agreement, Optioner shall execute a deed of trust or mortgage in favor of Optionee, and a warranty deed and bill of sale, and all other documents necessary for title transfer, shall be executed and held in escrow with an escrow agent of Optionee's choosing.

6. Insurance.

Optionor shall maintain hazard insurance on the property and name the Optionee as insured, to protect Optionee's interest. In the event that all or part of the property is destroyed, Optionee shall also have the option to either proceed with the closing or to declare this agreement null and void, in which case both parties would be released from any future obligations after Optionee pays Optionor any insurance monies previously received.

7. Encumbrances.

Optioner shall detail the following current encumbrances on the property: _____ and guarantee to place no further encumbrances on the abovementioned property without the express permission of Optionee. Should Optionor default on any security payments, the right to satisfy said payments will fall to Optionee, along with 10 percent interest on actual expenses incurred, though the Optionee shall not be permitted the right of assignment.

8. Heirs and Assigns.

This Agreement shall be binding upon the abovementioned parties and their respective heirs, administrators, successors, and assigns.

9. Governing Law.

This Agreement shall be governed by, interpreted, and enforced in accordance with the laws of the State of: _____. In the event that litigation results from this Agreement or the actions thereof, the parties agree to reimburse the prevailing party's reasonable attorney's fees, court costs, and all other expenses, in addition to any other reimbursement that the prevailing party may be entitled.

IN WITNESS THEREOF, the abovementioned parties have hereunto reached agreement on the day and year first above written.

Optionor: _____

Optionee: _____

STATE OF _____, COUNTY OF _____
The foregoing instrument was acknowledged before me, this
_____ day of _____, 20 _____.

_____ Notary Public
State of _____
My Commission Expires: _____

AGREED-UPON LEASE TERMINATION I

This mutual agreement is made on this day_____ of _____ (month) and year _____ between the Landlord_____ and Tenant_____.

Previously, the Landlord and Tenant entered into a lease dated _____ and now both parties desire to terminate the lease. It is agreed upon by both parties to the following terms:

1. The lease shall end on _____ date.

2. Except in circumstances that arose prior to cancellation of the lease on the date_____, both parties agree to release each other of all liability under the lease.

3. If the agreement has any other conditions that are not contained in this document or the lease agreement, then these conditions shall stay in full force and effect.

In Witness of the parties have agreed on this agreement on the day, month, and year listed above.

Signatures: _____

_____

Landlord: _____
Tenant: _____
Date: _____

AGREED-UPON LEASE TERMINATION II

_____ (Date)
_____ (State)
_____ (County)
_____ (Lessor)
_____ (Lessee)

Lessor and Lessee both wish to end Lease of certain real property located at _____ (Address), dated _____ and free each other from all liability under the Lease.

Therefore, in consideration of the mutual covenants and obligations stated herein, Lessor and Lessee agree as follows:

1. The Lease is ended as of the date of this Agreement.

2. Lessor hereby frees Lessee from all obligation and liability to Lessor of any nature whatsoever coming out of or pursuant to the Lease.

3. Lessee hereby frees Lessor from all obligation and liability to Lessee of any nature whatsoever coming out of or pursuant to the Lease.

In Witness whereof, the parties have executed this Agreement on the date stated above.

Lessor: _____
Lessee: _____
Witness: _____

CERTIFICATE OF ACKNOWLEDGMENT BY TENANT

Date: _____

To: _____

This acknowledgment is in regards to the lease agreement dated _____ between the Landlord (name) _____ and the Tenant(s) _____ regarding the property _____ known as the Leased Property.

The undersigned tenant or tenants at the Leased Property accept the following conditions:

1. The occupancy is in accordance with the lease agreement beginning on _____ and ending on the following date_____.

2. The rent is payable under the agreement to be $_____ per month. It is payable to _____ on the first of each month.

3. The tenant _____ has prepaid rent in the sum of $_____ as part of the lease agreement.

4. The lease agreement provides no options or clauses to renew the agreement nor does it provide any option to purchase the property leased by the tenant.

5. The tenant has no right to counter claim against the landlord.

Date of Agreement: _____

Signature of Tenant(s): _____

Signature of Landlord: _____

Witness: _____

ALTERNATE LEASE AGREEMENT

Date _____

Property Owner _____

Tenant _____

Property Address _____

The property owner assigns all rights, title, and interest in lease agreement to the tenant. The lease agreement is dated on _____. The property located at _____ _____ particularly described in Exhibit A attached and described in detail.

The assignment of all transactions shall be governed and enforced by the laws of the State of _____. The parties waive trial by jury and agree to submit to the personal jurisdiction of the court located in County_____ and State of_____.

In the event that litigation arises from this lease the parties agree to reimburse the prevailing party reasonable attorney fees. This includes court costs and all other expenses.

This lease has been executed by the landlord on the day of _____

It has been signed, sealed and delivered in the presence of:

Witness _____

County and State _____

Notary Public Seal _____

Date _____

Landlord _____

Tenants _____

RESIDENTIAL APARTMENT LEASE

Date: _____

Landlord: _____

Address: _____

City: _____ State: _____ Zip: _____

Renter: _____

Address: _____

City: _____ State: _____ Zip: _____

This lease is made on the date above by and between the Renter and Landlord listed above.

1. Lease Conditions:

The landlord leases to the Renter apartment number _____ in the building located at _____ for a period of _____ beginning on _____ (date) and ending on _____ (date). Occupancy shall be determined by the current Renter vacating the premises.

2. Rent Conditions:

The Renter shall pay the landlord rent in the sum of _____ for the amount of per month on the first day of the month and every month beginning on _____ (date). The rent will be paid to landlord's office or the locations where landlord may determine. The Renter shall also pay a further sum of $_____ representing pro-rated rent for period of _____ to _____ dates.

3. Rental Deposit Conditions:

The Renter will pay the landlord with the signing of the lease. The sum of $_____ is the agreed upon as prepaid rent that will be applied to the very last month. The landlord will pay interest on the deposit as the rate by law deems fair and reasonable.

4. Utilities Conditions:

The Renter will pay the cost of all utilities used on the premises. This includes water, electricity, gas, telephone, and cable TV. The Renter will also pay any deposits required by these utilities.

5. Parking Conditions:

The Renters can park one car or truck outside the building in the parking lot for residents.

6. Use and Occupancy of Premises:

The Renter agrees to use the premises for residential purposes only and will not allow anyone to occupy or live in the property except the Renter or Renters.

7. Overdue Rent and Returned Checks:

The Renter will pay the landlord interest on overdue Rent payments at the rate of _____% per compounded monthly. The Renter also agrees to pay the landlord $_____ service fee for all checks returned due to insufficient funds.

8. Subletting:

The Renter cannot sublet this property with written consent of the landlord. The landlord will be entitled to be reimbursed for any damages caused or that occur due to such an arrangement.

9. Care of Property:

The landlord agrees to maintain the property and keep it clean and in good repair. The landlord agrees to fix any appliances or utilities that break due to his willful neglect of the items. The Renters agrees not to make any repairs or alterations without the written consent of the landlord.

10. Property Tax:

All real estate taxes will be paid by the landlord on the property or apartment leased.

11. Entry of Premises by Landlord:

The landlord can enter the premises to look at repairs needed and for emergency purposes. The entry shall meet the standards of applicable law governing this agreement.

12. Rules and Regulations:

The Renter agrees to follow the Rules and Regulations in Schedule 1 attached. With the variations or changes that may be made by the landlord from time to time.

13. Other Legal Obligations of the Renter:

a.   On termination of the lease the Renter will return all keys to the landlord for the property rented.

b.   The car shall be kept in the parking lot at the risk of the Renter. The parking space will not be used to repair or wash cars. The landlord can change the locations of parking at any time he chooses during the time of the Renter's occupancy. The Renter cannot rent or sublet his parking space to anyone without written permission of the landlord.

c.   No awnings, flower containers, or other obstructions shall be erected over outside windows without permission of the landlord. The Renters will keep the balconies clean and free of clutter and debris.

d.   The Renter will refrain from any activity deemed a fire hazard. Any bicycles owned by the Renter will be stored in areas approved by the landlord. Bicycles are not allowed in the hallways and elevators. The removal of any furnishings will be with the approval of the landlord. Written consent will be needed before any appliances can be brought into the premises. No pets are allowed to live on the premises and can be deemed a cause for termination of the agreement.

14. Delivery Services:

The landlord can restrict the use of delivery services when the service is not in the best interest of the other Renters.

15. Electrical or Mechanical Breakdowns:

In the event of any electrical, plumbing, or heating breakdown the landlord will be responsible for the necessary repairs in a timely manner. He will not be responsible for any illnesses that result to Renters due to breakdown of the equipment.

16. Pool, Sauna Rules:

Renters will maintain pool area and saunas using only for purposes deemed by lease. They will follow the rules of safety and cleanliness when using area. No towels, beach gear, or clothing will be left behind, or it will be thrown out.

17. Locks:

The Renter will consent to any changes made in the premises locks or the buildings locking system made by the landlord during their time living on the premises.

18. Notice of Termination:

a. If the landlord or Renter wish to terminate the agreement at the end of the term, they shall give each other 30 days written notice of the expiration or termination. It will be in accordance with the laws governing the agreement.

b. After delivery of such a notice the landlord will be able to show the property to the prospective new Renters at all reasonable hours during the day. If no notice is given about termination at the end of the agreement the Renter becomes a monthly Renter subject to terms and conditions of the monthly payment schedule. The landlord can increase the rent at any time but must give the Renter proper notice.

19. Termination:

Any agreement can be terminated by giving at least 60 days notice to landlord. This is in event the termination is not hurtful to the landlord and he can show the premises. The terminations will be effective on the last day of the month. If the Renter fails to vacate the premises by a certain date that new occupant moves in, he will be liable for all damages against the landlord.

20. Breach of Agreement and Remedies:

a. If either party breaches the contract, they will have to give the other at least 30 days written notice about the breach. They must allow the defaulting party reasonable time to find a solution to the breach. When each party fails to notify the other no remedy to the breach will occur. When the party that made the breach finds a solution or acts to solve the problem, then they will be relieved of any liability for the breach.

b. If the premises have been vacated and rent is due, then the landlord can take possession of the property and assume the Renter has abandoned the contract. If the Renter breaches the contract, the landlord has the right to change the locks and evict the Renter.

21. Liability:

The landlord will not be responsible for damage to personal property of the Renter, like furniture and automobiles, owned by Renters and the family. Furthermore, he will be relieved of liability for any damage caused by gas, steam, water, and other items like drainage pipes, which often break and malfunction. The landlord shall not be liable for any injury or death of the Renters or visitors while on the property. The Renter will be liable for leaving running water on that ends up damaging the property.

22. Miscellaneous:

This lease and all the conditions will bind and ensure the parties to it. The consent of the Landlord must be obtained to assign or sublease by the Renters. If there is more than one landlord or Renter the provisions of this lease shall be read with all needed grammatical changes. All agreements in this leases entered into by more than one tenant shall be considered joint and new terms will be written.

Signatures:

Renter _____

Landlord _____

Owner _____

Date _____

SCHEDULE 1
RULES AND REGULATIONS

Moving Furniture
Household furniture will be moved in a manner that will not damage the property. Renters will not drag heavy furniture over the floors or stairs causing serious damage and marks.

Floors
The floors will be kept clean and polished by Renter. Rugs will be laid properly for safety and to lessen noise to other Renters

Walls
The Renter will not paint, paper, or decorate any wall on the property without permission of the landlord.

Window Doors and Locks
Locks and glass on the windows and doors will be treated with safety. Any damage caused by Renters on doors and windows will be repaired by the Renter with the approval of the landlord. No locks shall be placed or altered without the consent of the landlord on the property.

Ventilators and Radiators
Renters will not damage or tamper with air vents on radiators. If any damage is found, the janitor should be notified to make the needed repairs. The Renters should not damage or force the grills on the ventilators. Any problems, notify the janitor or landlord for repairs. The Renter will be liable for any damage caused by reckless behavior.

Water and Water Closets
Water for the laundry room or in water closets should not be left running unless for specific reasons. It is important to keep laundry facilities and water closets clean and free from debris like ashes, dirt, garbage, and rags.

Electrical Installations
The landlord will tell the electrician how to connect telephone wires. No Renter will connect wires or do electrical work under any circumstances. If a Renter wants to install or change electrical components, he must contact the landlord to get a qualified person to do

the work. The Renter must get written permission from the landlord to do any electrical or plumbing work.

Aerials
The Renter will not install any telephone, radio, or television aerials to the building by the Renter.

Laundry Appliances
No washing machines or dryers can be installed or brought into the building without written permission of the landlord.

Balconies and Windows
Awnings are not allowed to be placed on windows or balconies. Balconies will not be used for barbecuing or hanging clothes. No utensils bedding or rugs can be shaken from the balcony or window. Only summer furniture can be placed on the balcony. It is not to be used for storage.

Excessive Noise
Noise of any kind that is disruptive to neighbors will not be allowed. Very loud radios and TV levels will not be allowed. Renters are expected to keep the noise at a moderate level. Someone playing an instrument will not be allowed to do so after 10 p.m. Loud music must be turned down or off if a complaint arises from other Renters.

Animals
No animals or birds are allowed on the premise unless the Renter has written permission of the landlord.

Fire and Health Safety
The Renters will follow the regulations of fire safety while living in the building. They will not obstruct a fire exit or bring in equipment or supplies that constitute a fire hazard. They will follow safety and health rules when living on the premises.

Garbage
Renters will not leave refuse or debris in any common area of the building. They will wrap refuse in paper, tie it, and place it in the incinerator. Any other garbage delivery or pickup will be instructed by the janitor.

Entrance and Exits
Renters shall use the entrances and exits for the purpose they were meant. They will not obstruct or place any items in the area like umbrellas, boots, or toys. Safety in these areas must be practiced by all Renters.

Notices
Signs, advertisements, and posters may not be hung or put up on the outside or inside of the building without the permission of the landlord.

Parking and Landscaping

The Renter will not park his car in an authorized area or he may have to pay for it being towed away. Renters and guest shall not damage, destroy, or ruin any landscaping around the building.

The Renter has read and understands the following rules by signing below:

Signature

Renters_____

Landlord_____

Date _____

RETAIL AND OFFICE LEASE AGREEMENT

Date: _____

Landlord: _____

Address: _____

City: _____ State: _____ Zip: _____

Tenant: _____

Address: _____

City: _____ State: _____ Zip: _____

1. Premises:

Landlord leases to Tenant, and Tenant leases from Landlord, for the rent specified in this Lease and subject to the terms and conditions of this Lease, the specific parcel of vacant land ("Premises") described in Appendix "A" attached to and made a part of this Lease agreement; and/or shown on a Site Plan, marked Appendix "B" and attached to and made a part of this Lease agreement. Landlord and Tenant agree that a Building will be constructed on the Premises according to the terms of the Development Agreement attached to this document as Appendix "C." The Building and related improvements shall be constructed on the Premises according to the plans and specifications approved by Landlord and Tenant and set forth in Appendix "C" attached to this document. If, after the Building and any related improvements outlined in the following agreement have been completed, the actual square footage of the building is more or less than planned, this Lease and its provisions shall be amended and prorated to reflect the true square footage of the Building, and, if applicable, to reflect the contributions made by the Landlord to the Tenant's Improvements while carrying out the provisions in Appendix "C."

2. Term:

a. The term of this Lease shall be _____ years, beginning on the Commencement Date as defined in this document, and ending at noon on _____("Expiration Date"), unless the Lease is terminated sooner by the Landlord according to the provisions in this document. After the Expiration Date the Tenant shall be given (_____) Option Periods to extend the lease (_____) years per Option Period, according to terms and conditions mutually acceptable to Landlord and Tenant.

b. If on the Commencement Date any of the following "Rental Abatement Conditions" have occurred and are still occurring, rent under this Lease Agreement will be abated accordingly. Rental Abatement Conditions are strictly defined as any event or item which either a) prevents the Landlord from delivering to Tenant a legally defensible leasehold interest in the premises; or b) is the result of delays of any review and response required by Landlord that exceeds the deadlines set out in the Development Agreement (Appendix "C"). Neither the Landlord nor the Landlord's agents will be liable for any claim, loss, liability, damage resulting from such a delay, or expenses associated with any failure to complete construction by the deadline or tender possession. This Lease shall be void or voidable only at the express option of the Landlord.

c. The Commencement Date of this Lease shall be whichever date occurs first: (a) the 45th day immediately following (i) the date on which the architect supervising construction certifies in writing to the Landlord and to the Tenant that the Building and all of its facilities are complete and ready for use, except for any personal property to be installed or supplied by the Tenant, or (ii) the date on which the appropriate governmental authority issues a temporary certificate of occupancy for the entire Building, whichever is later; or (b) the date on which the Tenant commences business at the Building. After the determination of the Commencement Date, if requested by either the Landlord or the Tenant, both Landlord and Tenant will sign and record a written declaration stating the specific commencement and termination dates of the initial term of this lease.

3. Rent:

a. Annual Base Rent:

In accordance with any adjustments to the Base Rent as set forth in this Lease Agreement, the Tenant will pay to Landlord a base annual rental ("Base Rent") for the first lease year of _____ U.S. dollars, payable in monthly installments of _____ U.S. dollars on the first day of each calendar month of the first lease year. The tenant will remit Base Rent to Landlord in U.S. Dollars, without imposition of any notice, demand, deduction, offset, or abatement, to the place or person designated by the Landlord, or to any other person or place that the Landlord may designate in a written notice.

b. Annual Rent Escalation:

The Base Rent agreed to in Article 3.01 shall increase each year during the Term of the Lease on the anniversary of the Commencement Date ("Escalation Date"). The amount of this increase in the Base Rent shall be whichever is greater: (i) _____ percent (%) of the Base Rent charged for the previous year, or (ii) an amount calculated as follows: The calendar month ending immediately prior to _____ months before each Escalation Date during the Term of the Lease shall be selected as the "Comparative Month." The increase in the Consumer Price Index (meaning the Consumer Price Index for all Urban Consumers, All Cities Average, all items (1967 = 100), not seasonally adjusted, published, and issued by the Bureau of Labor Statistics of the United States Department of Labor (the "Bureau of Labor Statistics")) for the _____ month period immediately preceding the Comparative Month, shall be calculated as a percentage (Percentage Increase). The amount of the annual rent escalation shall be determined by multiplying the Base Rent charged for the previous year by this Percentage Increase. (If the Consumer Price Index ceases to use the 1967 average of One Hundred (100) as its basis of calculation, or if a change is made in the terms of particular items contained in the Consumer Price Index, the Landlord may adjust the Consumer Price Index at the Landlord's discretion, to the figure that would have been arrived at if the changes had not been made to the method of computing the Consumer Price Index that was in effect at the Commencement Date of the Lease Term. The Landlord may elect to use a reliable governmental or other non-partisan publication, evaluating the purchase power of money, if a Consumer Price Index, or substituted Consumer Price Index, is not available.

The increase in the Base Rent shall be paid in _____ monthly installments. Each installment shall be paid in advance on the first day of each calendar month, beginning on the Escalation Date and continuing until the next Escalation Date. The Landlord must provide the Tenant with written notice of the increase in Base Rent as soon as reasonably possible after the increase has been determined. If this written notice is not delivered to the tenant until after the Escalation Date, any increased amounts that were due but not paid since the Escalation Date shall be payable within ____ days after receipt of such notice.

c. Initial Term Rental:

The Landlord and the Tenant agree that the property is leased for a total amount equal to the number of years of the initial term multiplied by the adjusted Annual Base Rental, for the Term of this Lease. This amount is payable at the time of the signing of this Lease, and the provisions contained in this Lease for the payment of rent in monthly installments are only for the convenience of the Tenant. If the Tenant defaults in the payment of the rent as specified in this lease, or defaults on any of the terms of this Lease, the entire rent, as adjusted on the date of default, remaining unpaid for the full term of the Lease will immediately become due and payable without any notice or demand from the Landlord.

4. Security Deposit/Escrow Deposit:

The Tenant has deposited a "Security Deposit" or "Escrow Deposit" of U.S. $ _____ with the Landlord. After the Commencement Date of the Lease, this amount will be treated as a Security Deposit and as an Escrow Deposit. If the Tenant fails to comply with any provisions of this Lease, the Landlord may apply all or any part of the Security Deposit to the default, without obligation and without consideration of any other deposit or account held by the Landlord on the Tenant's behalf. If all or part of the Security Deposit has been used to pay off a default, the Tenant shall, upon demand, deposit enough additional cash with Landlord to restore the original amount of the Security Deposit. The Tenant's failure to do so will be considered a material breach of this Lease.

The Landlord may commingle the Security Deposit with other funds. The Tenant will not receive interest on the Security Deposit. The Security Deposit or any balance of it will be returned to Tenant within ____ days after the Expiration Date of the Lease, if the Tenant is not in default. The Tenant does not have the right to use the Security Deposit to offset or satisfy any payments due to Landlord under this Lease.

The amount paid by the Tenant to the Landlord as an Escrow Deposit, referred to in this section, will be held by Landlord as security to ensure that the Tenant meets all the conditions of the Development Agreement, (Appendix "C"), prior to the Commencement Date of this Lease. If the Tenant fails to fulfill the terms of the Development Agreement, the Landlord may retain, as liquidated damages for the breach of this Lease, all or an agreed amount of the Escrow Deposit,. Upon the Commencement Date of the Lease, this Escrow Deposit shall automatically become a Security Deposit as described above.

5. Net Lease:

The Landlord and Tenant agree that the payments due to Landlord under the terms of this Lease shall be made in full to the Landlord, and that the Tenant rather than the Landlord will be responsible for the Premises Expenses as defined below in this Lease.

6. Sales Tax on Rents:

The Tenant will include Sales Tax and/or any other applicable tax on all rentals paid under this Lease, including, without limitation, Base Rent, all increases to Base Rent and Additional Rent, as part of the Additional Rent paid to the Landlord.

7. Leasehold and Personal Property Taxes:

The Tenant will pay any and all taxes assessed and payable during the Term of this Lease on all of the Tenant's equipment, furniture, fixtures, and personal property located in the Premises, in a timely manner.

8. Real Estate Taxes:

The Tenant will be responsible for paying all real estate taxes levied, assessed or imposed on the Premises during the term of this Lease as soon as they become due.

9. Tenant's Premises Expenses:

(a) For each calendar year, or portion of a calendar year, of the Term, Tenant shall pay the following Additional rent to the Landlord: (i) all Common Area Costs as set forth in Section 4.04 of this Lease; (ii) all real estate and other ad valorem taxes and assessments relating to the Premises; and (iii) all insurance premiums, charges and/or assessments paid or owed by Landlord for insurance on the Premises, and the personal property used in the maintenance of the Premises (collectively referred to as the "Premises Expenses").

The Landlord will deliver a written estimate of Tenant's Premises Expenses, before the Commencement Date, and regularly during the term of the Lease. Installments equal to _____ of this estimated amount will be paid in advance on the first day of each calendar month, along with the Base Rent. The first of these installments will be due on the Commencement Date.

(b) After the end of each calendar year or portion of a calendar year, during the Term of this Lease, the Landlord will deliver to the Tenant within (__) days a certified statement of the actual Premises Expenses for the previous calendar year. At the time of delivery of this statement to the Tenant, the Landlord will refund any excess amount paid by the Tenant for that period. If the actual Premises Expenses for the previous calendar year are greater than the total amount paid by the Tenant during that year, the Tenant shall pay the difference within _____ days after receipt of Landlord's statement.

If Premises Expenses change or increase at any time during the term of the Lease, the Landlord has the authority to increase the Tenant's Premises Expenses by providing written notice of the amount of this increase to the Tenant. The Tenant, who retains the right to audit Premises Expenses, agrees to begin payment of this increase in the next due monthly installment. Tenant, at its own cost and expense, has the right to conduct an annual examination or audit of the Landlord's records of these Premises Expenses, within _____ days after the Landlord provides the statement of actual Premises Expenses to the Tenant.

10. Common Area:

For the purposes of this Agreement, "Common Area" is defined as all areas, facilities and improvements provided by Landlord and/or the adjoining shopping center for the convenience and use of the Tenant of the Premises, and for the Tenant's subtenants, agents, concessionaires, employees, customers, invitees, and licensees. The Common Area includes, without limitation, all parking areas, sidewalks, service corridors, truckways, loading docks, delivery areas, ramps, landscaped areas, public bathrooms, access and interior roads, retaining walls, and lighting facilities. The Tenant agrees that a reasonable determination of the nature and extent of the Common Areas, whether within or adjacent to the Premises, may be made at any time by the Landlord and a master maintenance association (as described below). The Landlord and the master maintenance association shall have the right to make any changes, rearrangements, additions, or reductions to these areas that are deemed to be desirable from time to time by their reasonable judgment, or that are required by law.

11. Master Maintenance Association:

The Landlord and the Tenant agree that a master maintenance association (the "Association") will be responsible to oversee the property upon which the Premises are located and will administer Tenant's pro rata share of association expenses. The Association will provide consistent management of the Common Areas on the leased Premises and within the adjoining shopping center. The Tenant may be required to be a member of such an association to the same extent that the Landlord is required to be a member. A portion of the Common Area Costs, as defined in 4.03 above, shall be included within Premises Expenses.

12. Utilities:

The Tenant is solely responsible to apply and pay all charges for water, heat, electricity, sewer, telephone, and any other utility used on, or provided to, the Premises. Tenant must pay these charges in a timely manner and hold Landlord harmless from any charge or liability for these utilities. The Landlord is not held responsible for any interruptions in utility services and shall not be in breach or default under this Lease if, after receiving written notice of any failure or defect that impedes the provision of utility services, the Landlord acts diligently to restore such a failure or defect.

13. Use of Premises:

The Tenant agrees to use the Premises solely for the purposes and activities specified in the attached Appendix "D," including the activities and programs associated with the operation of the premises that the Tenant carries out in other similar facilities operated by the Tenant. Approval must be obtained from the Landlord in writing before the Premises can be used for any other purpose. The Tenant shall not allow Premises to be used for any improper, immoral, unlawful, or objectionable purpose. The Tenant shall not cause or allow any public or private nuisance in, on, or about the Premises, including but not limited to, objectionable or harmful noises and odors. The Tenant shall not damage or permit damage to be done to the Premises, except for reasonable wear and tear. The Tenant agrees not to permit any activity that conflicts in any way with any private restrictive covenant, law, statute, ordinance; any rule or regulation of the Landlord; or any governmental or quasi-governmental authority that is now in force or may be enacted or promulgated in the future, to be done in the Premises. The Landlord must demonstrate to the Tenant that applicable zoning laws and present covenants of record do not restrict the use of Premises as specified in this Lease. The Landlord certifies that it will not give consent to any private restrictive covenant or enact any rule or regulation during the term of this Lease and any extension of it that would impair the ability of Tenant to use the Premises as specified in this Lease.

14. Alterations and Additions:

Beginning on the Commencement Date, the Tenant must obtain prior written consent of Landlord before making any alterations, installations, additions, or improvements in or to the Premises. Any improvements, including the Building, and any alterations, installations, additions, or improvements in or to the Premises, except movable furniture and movable trade fixtures, made beginning with the date of execution of this Lease, will become a part of the Premises and belong to Landlord. Building and any such improvements and alterations will be surrendered with the Premises at the expiration or termination of this Lease. Tenant may be required, at Tenant's own expense, to remove any alterations, installations, additions, or improvements made by the Tenant. Tenant shall remove all Tenant's property and all of the property designated by the Landlord for removal from the Premises prior to the expiration or termination of this Lease. The Tenant must repair any damage caused by the removal of this property, or reimburse the Landlord for the costs of such repairs.

15. Maintenance:

By taking possession of the Premises, the Tenant acknowledges that the Premises are in good, sanitary order, condition, and repair. The Tenant, at its own cost and expense, will maintain in good order and repair the Premises and any associated property, wherever it is located, including without limitation the interior portion of all doors, door checks, windows and window frames, plate glass, store front, all plumbing facilities within the Premises, signs, fixtures, and electrical systems (located in the Premises or outside), sprinkler systems, walls, floors, and ceilings. Whenever necessary, Tenant will replace parts and equipment at tenant's expense.

The tenant shall maintain the heating and air conditioning systems associated with the Premise in good order and repair, replacing parts and equipment if necessary. Before occupying the Premises, the Tenant must commit to a maintenance contract in a form and with a subcontractor approved by Landlord, to properly maintain the heating and air conditioning systems. Landlord will be named as an additional loss payee or co-beneficiary. As a condition of taking possession of Premises, a copy of this maintenance contract must be provided to Landlord, together with documentation showing that the premiums of other fees necessary to activate the maintenance contract have been paid. Annually on each anniversary date of this Lease, Tenant shall provide Landlord with evidence that this maintenance contract has been renewed or replaced. The obligation to provide a maintenance contract does not limit the Tenant's duty to maintain the heating and air conditioning systems, but is in addition to that duty.

The Tenant shall carry out regular maintenance and repair schedule, including painting or refinishing of all interior areas of the Premises to keep it in an attractive condition and to prevent, as much as possible, deterioration caused by ordinary wear and tear. At the expiration of this Lease, Tenant shall surrender the Premises in good condition, except for reasonable wear and tear or loss by fire or other casualty.

The Tenant is responsible for keeping the foundation, exterior walls and roof of the premises, as well as the structural elements including the doors, door frames, door checks, windows, and window frames located in exterior building walls of the Premises in good repair.

Landlord must give written approval before Tenant undertakes any repairs or maintenance that will affect the exterior appearance of the Premises.

If the Tenant fails to adequately perform the maintenance and repairs specified in Section 6.02 for a period of _____ business days after the Landlord has delivered a written demand, the Landlord or its authorized representatives may, but are not obligated to, perform necessary maintenance and repairs and will not be liable to Tenant for loss or damage to Tenant's stock or business resulting from this work. Tenant shall reimburse Landlord for all the costs and expenses for these repairs, plus interest on these costs at the rate specified in Section 9.04, calculated from the date that the costs and expenses are incurred until the date of reimbursement. Landlord's performance of Tenant's responsibilities under this Article does not constitute a waiver of the Tenant's default under this Lease. Tenant's failure of the to reimburse the Landlord for such costs upon demand shall be considered a breach of this lease, and the Landlord will have the right to be use all of the remedies specified in Article IX of this Lease.

16. Compliance with Ordinances:
The Tenant agrees to comply with all laws, regulations, and ordinances affecting the premises, including without limitation, all laws, regulations, and ordinances applicable to banking facilities. The Premises must be maintained in a clean, sanitary and safe condition according to the standards established by state and federal laws, and in compliance with all directions, rules, and regulations of health officers, fire marshals, building inspectors, or regulatory jurisdiction over the Premises. The Tenant will install and maintain appropriate and adequate fire extinguishers and other fire protection devices, and comply with all the requirements of any insurance policies and the insurance underwriters insuring the Premises.

17. Defects:
If the Premises has defects, Landlord agrees that Tenant may accept possession subject to a punch list. The presence of defects and existence of a punch list will not affect the Tenant's obligation to pay rent as required in this Lease. Landlord agrees to repair or replace any items that are defective in materials or workmanship when Tenant takes possession within one year after the Commencement Date. Landlord will assign to Tenant all extended warranties provided by suppliers, contractors, subcontractors, and material men.

18. Landlord Repairs:
Except as set forth in the preceding paragraph, Landlord has no duty to repair or maintain the Premises or any part of the Premises after Tenant takes possession. No fence or barrier that segregates or separates the Premises from the Common Area, will be erected by either the Landlord or the Tenant.

18. Tenant's Insurance:
The Tenant is responsible, at Tenant's sole expense, to obtain and keep in force during the term and any extension or renewal of this Lease, the following insurance policies:

    (i)   fire and extended coverage insurance with vandalism and malicious mischief endorsements and a sprinkler leakage endorsement (where applicable), on the Premises, insuring the building for 100% of its replacement cost;

    (ii)   comprehensive general liability insurance, including contractual liability coverage (according to the terms in Section 7.03 below), with a company approved by the Landlord, protecting the Landlord (as an additional insured) and the Tenant from any liability arising out of the ownership, use, occupancy or maintenance of the Premises and all associated areas. The insurance shall provide for a minimum of $ _____ for loss of or damage to property from any one accident, and $_____ for death of or injury to any one person from any one accident;

(iii) if not included in the insurance in (i) above, insurance to provide full replacement of contents and personal property in case of loss or damage. The limits of this insurance do not limit the liability of the Tenant. Tenant may carry this insurance under a blanket policy, provided that a Landlord's protective liability endorsement is attached to it. The Landlord, and any mortgagee for which the Tenant has received written notice as mortgagee, shall be named as insured parties under the fire and extended coverage insurance on the building. In the event that the Tenant fails to procure and maintain such insurance, the Landlord, may, but is not obligated to, procure and maintain it at the expense of Tenant.

Before occupying the Premises, the Tenant shall deliver to the Landlord copies of the policies of liability insurance required in Article 7.01, or certificates documenting the existence and amounts of such insurance. Loss payable clauses must be satisfactory to Landlord. No insurance policy shall be cancelled or subject to reduction of coverage without written notice having been delivered to Landlord not less than _____ days in advance.

19. Waiver and Subrogation:

If either Landlord or Tenant suffers any loss, costs, damage, or expense because of fire, explosion, or any other casualty or occurrence in connection with the Premises, for which that party is covered, or is required to have coverage under this Lease, in whole or in part by insurance, the insured party will release the other party from any liability for the portion of that loss, damage, or that is recovered from insurance. The insured party waives any right of subrogation that might otherwise exist, provided that such waiver of the right to subrogation will not invalidate the insurance coverage or increase its cost. In the event that insurance costs will be increased by the waiver of subrogation rights, the other party shall have the right to pay such increased costs within ( ) days after receiving written notice, in order to keep the release and waiver in effect. Landlord and Tenant shall make every possible effort to obtain such a release and waiver of subrogation from their respective insurance carriers, and shall obtain any special endorsements required by their insurer, to document compliance with the waiver and release of subrogation rights.

20. Liability:

The Landlord and Landlord's agents and employees will not be liable for the injury or death of any persons, or damage to property in or about the Premises, caused by Tenant, or Tenant's employees, servants, agents, subtenants, licensees, concessionaires, or invitees; arising out of the Tenant's use of the Premises; or arising out of the Tenant's failure to fulfill its obligations under this Lease. The Tenant indemnifies and holds Landlord harmless from any loss, expense (including reasonable attorney's fees), or claims arising out of any injury, death, damage, use or default. The Landlord and Landlord's agent and employees shall not be liable to Tenant for the injury or death of any persons, or damage to Tenant's property, or to any person making a claim through the Tenant, resulting from any accident or occurrence in or about the Premises. The Landlord shall not be liable to the Tenant for any loss or damage caused by or through the acts or omissions of any persons except the Landlord, its agents, and employees.

21. Casualty or Damage:

When damage to the Premises, or any portion of the Premises, caused by fire or another casualty covered by the insurance carried by Tenant, and the cost of repairing the damage is less than _____ percent (%) of the cost of fully replacing the Premises or damaged portion of the Premises, as determined by the Landlord, the Tenant shall repair the Premises then, subject to the following provisions of this Article.

When damage to the Premises, or any portion of the Premises, caused by fire or another casualty, is not covered by the Tenant's insurance under the terms of this Lease, or the cost of repairing the damage is greater than _____ percent (%) of the cost of fully replacing the Premises, the Landlord will may elect either to have the Tenant repair or reconstruct the Premises to substantially the same condition it was in immediately before the fire or other casualty, or to terminate this Lease by giving written notice to the Tenant within _____ days after the date of the fire or other casualty. If the Landlord elects to terminate the Lease, termination will be effective as of the date of such fire or other casualty. If Landlord elects or is required to repair or reconstruct the Premises, the Tenant will earnestly cooperate with efforts to complete the repair or reconstruction, provided all the proceeds of the insurance are assigned to and made available to the Landlord and are adequate for the purpose.

22. Business Interruption Insurance:

The Rent required to be paid under the terms of this Lease shall continue to be in effect and shall not be abated while repairs of the Premises are being carried out. To cover such an eventuality, the Tenant shall carry, at Tenant's sole cost and expense, appropriate Business Interruption Insurance. The Landlord shall not be liable for any damages, compensation, or claims related to Tenant's inability to use the Premises or any part of the Premises or to use Tenant's personal property, or any inconvenience, loss of business, or annoyance arising from any such repair and reconstruction. The Landlord shall not be required to repair or replace any furniture, furnishings or other personal property, equipment, inventory, fixtures, or goods that are the property of the Tenant.

23. End of Term Casualty:

In spite of anything to the contrary in this Article, when the damage resulting from any casualty covered under this Article occurs during the last _____ months of the Term of this Lease or any extension of it, the Landlord shall not be under any obligation whatsoever to repair, reconstruct or restore the Premises if the cost of doing so amounts to more than _____ percent (%) of the cost of fully repairing the building on the Premises and the repairs cannot be completed within _____ days.

24. Condemnation:

If more than _____ percent (%) of the Premises is appropriated, purchased, or leased by any public or quasi-public authority under the power of eminent domain, either party to the Lease shall have the option to terminate this Lease on the date when public authority takes title or possession. If the Lease is terminated by either party, Tenant shall be refunded all Rent paid for any period beyond the date of termination. The Landlord shall be entitled to any award and all income, and rent which may be paid in connection with such public or quasipublic use of the Premises. The Tenant shall have no claim against Landlord for the value of any unexpired Term of this Lease. The Tenant shall be entitled, as provided under the general law, to receive compensation for the value of its leasehold improvements, business interruption and moving expenses. If _____percent (%) or less of the Premises is taken, or more than _____ (%) percent of the Premises is taken and neither party elects to terminate this Lease, the amount of the rental will be reduced accordingly to reflect the percentage of the original Premises still occupied by the Tenant. The Landlord will be obligated to repair, reconstruct, or restore the Premises to fulfill the original terms of the Lease, provided the cost of such reconstruction or restoration is not greater than the proceeds received by Landlord for the condemnation of the Premises.

25. Default:

Any one or more of the following events shall constitute a default under this Lease by Tenant:

(a) The Tenant's failure to pay the Rent or any other payment required to be made by Tenant according to the terms of this Lease, for a period of _____ days after the date when the payment is due.

(b) The material breach by the Tenant of any condition in the Lease, or the Tenant's failure to fulfill or perform, in whole or in part, any of its obligations under this Lease, other than the payment of any monetary obligations, in the event that such a failure continues for a period of _____ days after the Landlord delivers written notice to the Tenant. If a period of more than _____ days is reasonably required for the remediation of Tenant's default, the Tenant shall not be deemed to be in default if the Tenant begins remediation within the _____ day period, and thereafter diligently completes the obligation.

(c) Tenant's failure to remove any lien filed as a consequence of the Tenant's actions against this leasehold estate, or the Premises within _____ days after the Tenant has received written notice of the filing of the lien.

(d) The initiation of bankruptcy proceedings by the Tenant, or the making of any general assignment by the Tenant for the benefit of creditors; or the initiation of bankruptcy proceedings against the Tenant unless those proceedings are dismissed within _____ days; or the appointment of a trustee or receiver to take possession of substantially all of the Tenant's assets located at the Premises, or of Tenant's interest in this Lease where possession is not restored to Tenant within _____ days; or the judicial seizure of substantially all of Tenant's assets located at the Premises, or of Tenant's interest in this Lease, where such seizure is not discharged in _____ days.

(e) The transfer, mortgage, assignment, or other encumbrance by Tenant of the Premises, except as set forth below.

(f) Tenant's failure to occupy the Premises on or before the Commencement Date given in this Lease agreement.

(g) Abandonment by Tenant as defined in Paragraph 10.04 below.

26. Rights Upon Default:

If a default occurs and Tenant fails to take the actions required by the terms of this Lease, the Landlord may at any time, with or without giving further notice or demand, take all actions that are permitted under this Lease, at law, or in equity, including, without limitation, terminating this Lease or terminating the Tenant's right to possession of the Premises without terminating the Lease. If the Tenant defaults, the Landlord may, without additional notice and without court proceedings, take possession of the Premises and remove all persons and property from the Premises. In the event of default, the Tenant agrees to surrender possession of the Premises and to waive any claim arising from surrender of the Premises or from the issuance of any distress warrant or writ of sequestration, and agrees to hold Landlord harmless from any such claims.

If the Landlord elects to terminate this Lease, it may treat the default as a complete breach of this Lease, and the Tenant shall immediately become liable to Landlord for damages equal to:

(i)   the costs of recovering the Premises, putting the Premises into good order, and finding and renting to a new tenant, including the costs of lease commissions attributable to the unexpired portion of the Term of this Lease.

(ii)   all unpaid Base Rent and other amounts earned or due through the date of the termination.

(iii)   any amount by which the present value of the Base Rent and other amounts scheduled to be paid by Tenant under this Lease for the remainder of the full Term, exceeds the amount that can be realized from the Premises at their present fair market value for the remainder of the full Term. Present fair market values are to be computed as of the date of termination and based on a _____ percent (%) per year discount rate.

If the Landlord elects to terminate Tenant's right to possession of the Premises without terminating the Lease, Landlord may, but is not be obligated to, sublet the Premises or any part of the Premises on behalf of the Tenant to any person or persons under terms and conditions established by the Landlord and for an amount that the Landlord deems appropriate. The Landlord shall receive all proceeds from such subletting of the Premises. If the outstanding Rent for the unexpired balance of the Term of this Lease exceeds the net amount, if any, received by Landlord from such re-letting, after deduction of Landlord's expenditures for repossession, re-letting, remodeling, and other expenses associated with re-letting the Premises, the Tenant shall be liable to pay this amount to the Landlord in monthly installments on the first day of each month of the Term. In the event of default by the Tenant, the Landlord shall make a reasonable effort to re-let the Premises. The Landlord will not be held responsible for failure to re-let the premises or to collect the rent due under such re-letting. The Tenant shall not be entitled to any excess rents received by the Landlord. All rights and remedies of the Landlord can be used singularly and severally and are not exclusive.

27. Costs:

The Tenant shall pay, on demand, all costs reasonably incurred by the Landlord in connection with a default including, but not limited to, reasonable attorney's fees, court costs and related costs. Interest will be due on these costs starting from the date such costs are paid by Landlord until the date that the Tenant reimburses Landlord, at the rate specified in Section 9.04 below.

28. Interest:

Landlord will charge interest on any late payments of Rent, costs, or other amounts due from Tenant under the terms of this Lease beginning on the date they come due, until they are paid, at the maximum legal rate of interest at which Tenant may legally contract.

29. Landlord's Lien:

In order to secure all sums due by Tenant under this lease, the Landlord is hereby granted a first and superior lien and security interest (in addition to and not in replacement of the statutory Landlord's lien) on all leasehold improvements, fixtures, equipment, and personal property (tangible and intangible) placed by Tenant in or on the Premises now or later. Landlord may enforce this lien and security interest in any legal manner, including without limitation, acceptable under the Uniform Commercial Code. The provisions contained in this Section shall serve as a security agreement under the Uniform Commercial Code. At the Landlord's request, the Tenant shall file, all documents necessary to grant this security interest in accordance with the Uniform Commercial Code.

At the request of the Tenant, the Landlord shall subordinate its lien and security interest as described in this Lease (as well as any statutory Landlord's lien), to any lien that secures bona fide financing for Tenant to purchase movable personal property placed in the Premises.

30. Non-Waiver:

A failure by the Landlord to insist upon the strict performance of, or to seek remedy for any violation of the terms of this Lease, shall not prevent a subsequent violation of this Lease from being treated as an original violation. The Landlord's acceptance of Rent payments, whether or not Landlord knows that the Tenant has breached any provision of this Lease, shall not be regarded as a waiver of Tenant's breach. If this Lease or the Tenant's right of possession of the Premises has been terminated by Landlord, payment of rent shall not reinstate the Lease and shall not have any effect on any notice, election, action, or suit by Landlord.

Any surrender of the Premises by the Tenant, and any agreement by Landlord to accept such surrender must be made in writing and signed by the Landlord and Tenant.

31. Assignment and Subletting:

The Tenant will not, knowingly, by operation of law or by other means, assign, transfer, mortgage, pledge, hypothecate, or encumber this Lease, and shall not sublet the said Premises or any part thereof, or any right or privilege associated with the Premises, or allow any other person except the employees, agents, servants, and invitees of the Tenant to occupy or use the Premises, or any portion of the Premises, without the prior written consent of Landlord.

Any such assignment, transfer, mortgage, pledge, hypothecation, encumbrance, sublet, or permission to use will be collectively referred to as a "Transfer" for the purposes of this document. A consent to one Transfer shall not constitute a consent to any future Transfers. Any Transfer made without the signed consent of the Landlord shall be considered void and a default under this Lease; however, the Landlord may collect Rent from the assignee or sublessee without releasing Tenant from this Lease or waiving any provision of the Lease. A Transfer by Tenant which has been approved by Landlord does not relieve Tenant of its direct and primary liability under the terms of this Lease for the full Term of this Lease. The Landlord may enforce the provisions of this Lease against the Tenant or any assignee or sublessee without making any demand or proceeding in any way against any other person or entity.

32. Consent Factors:

In determining whether or not to give or deny consent to a sublet of the Premises or an assignment of this Lease, the Landlord may consider any reasonable factor, including:

(a) Financial strength: The creditworthiness of the proposed subtenant/assignee must be equal to or greater than the creditworthiness of the Tenant on the Commencement Date of this Lease. The proposed subtenant/assignee must be able to provide Landlord with reasonably acceptable evidence of its capacity to carry out the financial obligations of the Tenant under the Lease.

(b) Business reputation: The proposed subtenant/assignee must meet generally acceptable commercial standards.

(c) Not in violation of laws or covenants: The nature and activities of the proposed subtenant/assignee must not violate or create any potential violation of any laws, or be in conflict with any covenants or other agreements affecting the Premises or other leases in the adjoining shopping center development.

(d) Tenant not in default: The Tenant shall not be in default under this Lease.

(e) Term of sublease: The term of the sublease is shorter than the remaining Lease Term and/or at a rental rate less than the then-current market rate for comparable premises.

33. Proceeds of Sublease or Assignment:

After Landlord has given consent, any sublet or assignment must be submitted in writing in a form acceptable to Landlord. In the event that the Landlord consents to a sublet or an assignment, the Tenant will to pay the Landlord _____ percent (%) of any lump sum received by the Tenant for such sublet or assignment, plus _____ percent (%) of all rental payments made by any subtenant or assignee that are in excess of the rent payable by Tenant under the terms of this Lease. Any payments made by an assignee or sublessee to the Tenant for personal property, goodwill, or the value of the business as a going concern are not be included in the amounts to be paid to Landlord under this Section. All reasonable attorney's fees and any other direct costs incurred by the Landlord and arising out of such sublet or assignment shall be reimbursed by the Tenant.

34. Abandonment:

Abandonment is defined as the Tenant's absence from the Premises or cessation of operation of the Premises for its intended purpose for a period of _____ or more days after the Commencement Date. Following the _____ day period the Landlord will have the right to terminate this Lease after giving _____ days' notice. The termination notice will contain a statement that if the Tenant does not recommence operations within the _____ day period the Lease shall be automatically terminated without further notice at the end of the _____ days. The Tenant shall then vacate the Premises immediately and surrender the Premises to Landlord on the same terms set forth in this Lease for the expiration of the Lease term. If the Landlord does not provide such written notice, the Tenant may keep possession of the Premises and not operate it for its intended purpose provided the Tenant continues to pay the Rent required under the terms and conditions of this Lease and to fulfill all other obligations under the Lease.

36. Access to Premises:

Entry by Landlord: The Landlord and Landlord's agents, employees, and representatives shall have the right to enter the Premises at all reasonable times, provided prior notice is given to Tenant, to inspect the Premises; supply any service to be provided by Landlord to Tenant under the terms of this Lease; show the Premises to prospective purchasers, mortgagees, or tenants; post notices of nonresponsibility; conduct alterations or repairs to the Premises, or for any other purpose that Landlord may reasonably consider necessary or desirable. At the Tenant's request, when visiting the Premises the Landlord shall display identification provided by the Tenant and/or consent to being accompanied by an escort.

The Tenant waives any claim for damages, or for any injury or inconvenience to or interference with Tenant's business, any loss of occupancy or quiet enjoyment of the Premises, and any other loss arising from such activities on the part of the Landlord, except for damages caused by the Landlord's gross negligence or willful misconduct.

In an emergency, the Landlord may use any means that the Landlord considers proper to obtain entry to the Premises, and will not be liable to Tenant except for any failure to exercise due care for Tenant's property.

37. Subordination and Non-disturbance:

This Lease and all rights of the Tenant under this Lease are subject and subordinate any mortgage, deed of trust, or other lien that is now existing or is hereafter placed upon the Leased Premises, and to any and all increases, renewals, modifications, consolidations, and extensions of any such leases, mortgages, and/or security instruments, provided that the Landlord under any of these agreements does not disturb the Tenant's rights under this Lease if the Tenant attorns to such a Landlord under such mortgage. The Tenant will execute a Subordination, Non-disturbance, and Attornment Agreement within _____ days after written request from Landlord, containing a non-disturbance agreement customarily used in the industry. Such Agreement will be sufficient to document such subordination.

38. Attornment:

If any mortgage is terminated or foreclosed, the Tenant shall, upon request, transfer its obligations under this Lease to the mortgagee or purchaser of the Premises at such foreclosure or sale, as the case may be, and sign documents confirming the transfer. If this Lease is approved and accepted in writing by such mortgagee, the Tenant's transfer of obligations shall be conditional upon the agreement by the mortgagee not to disturb the Tenant's possession under this Lease during the Term as long as Tenant performs its obligations under this Lease. If a termination or foreclosure occurs and the Tenant transfers its obligations as described above, the Tenant will automatically become the Tenant of the mortgagee without any change in the terms or provisions of this Lease.

39. Landlord's Liability:

Landlord is liable to the Tenant for any default under the terms of this Lease only to the extent of the interest of Landlord in the Premises. It is expressly understood and agreed that the Landlord shall not be personally liable for any judgment or deficiency beyond the equity of Landlord's interest in the Premises.

40. Transfer and Assignment by Landlord:

If the Landlord transfers or assigns the Premises, or the Landlord's interest in this Lease, in whole or in part, to another party, the Landlord will no longer be subject to any liability under any of its covenants and obligations under this Lease or derived from it, arising out of any act, occurrence, or omission taking place after the transfer of assignment has been completed. The transferee or assignee, or any subsequent transferee or assignee, shall be considered, without any further formal agreement between the parties or their successors in interest, or between the parties and any such transferee or assignee, to have agreed to carry out any and all of the covenants and obligations of the Landlord under this Lease.

41. Quiet Enjoyment:

As long as the Tenant pays the rent required by the terms of this Lease, and observes and performs all of the covenants, conditions, and provisions set forth in this Lease, the Tenant shall have quiet possession of the Premises for the entire Term of this Lease, subject to all of the provisions of this Lease.

42. Holding Over:

Tenant must vacate the Premises at the termination or expiration of this Lease. If the Tenant remains in possession of the Premises after the termination or expiration of this Lease, and a new lease or an extension of this Lease have not been executed, the Tenant shall be continue to be subject to all of the covenants and obligations of this Lease, and will pay a per diem Base Rent, effective immediately after the Lease has expired or been terminated. In addition, the Tenant agrees to pay Landlord the costs of any and all claims and/or damages (consequential or otherwise) resulting from such holding over by the Tenant. It is expressly understood and agreed that the Tenant's holding over does not constitute an extension or renewal of the Term of this Lease.

43. Estoppel Certificate:

The Tenant shall, at any time upon not fewer than _____ days prior written notice from Landlord, execute, acknowledge, and deliver to Landlord an estoppel certificate in the form attached hereto as Appendix "F," or in such form as may be reasonably required by Landlord. Such a certificate will be made for the benefit of the Landlord, any prospective purchaser or transferee of Landlord's interest under this Lease or of the Landlord's property, or any current or prospective mortgagee of all or any portion of the real property of which the Premises are a part.

44. Rules and Regulations:

The Tenant agrees to observe and comply with the rules and regulations promulgated from time to time by the Landlord, including but not limited to, those set forth in Appendix "E" attached to and included in this Lease. The Landlord may from time to time make reasonable additions, modifications, and deletions to these rules and regulations. These additions, modifications, and deletions will become binding on the Tenant as soon as the tenant receives a copy of the document setting them forth. The Landlord shall not be responsible to the Tenant if any other Tenant or person fails to follow any of said rules and regulations.

45. Parking:

The Tenant shall have the nonexclusive right to use the parking facilities of the Premises, subject to the rules and regulations established by the Landlord. The Landlord has the right to make reasonable alterations to these regulations at any time.

46. Tenant's Financial Condition:

(a) As a material condition for the acceptance of this Lease, the Tenant guarantees to Landlord that (i) the Tenant has the financial capability to discharge its obligations under this Lease, and (ii) the Tenant has never been declared bankrupt, taken advantage of any bankruptcy law or regulation to reorganize, made an assignment for the benefit of creditors, or been insolvent, nor is currently insolvent or involved in any proceeding or action.

(b) Upon request, the Tenant shall provide copies of its most recent audited financial statements, distributed to the shareholders or filed with the Securities and Exchange Commission, to the Landlord.

(c) The Tenant understands that Landlord is entering into this Lease based on the representations made and obligations undertaken in this Section 12.06, and that any misrepresentation or failure to provide the required documentation will constitute a default under this Lease.

47. No Liens:

The Tenant shall keep the Premises or any part of the Premises free from any liens arising out of any work performed, materials furnished, taxes owed, obligations incurred by, or act or omission on the part of the Tenant, its agents or employees. If required by any of Landlord's mortgages or financing entities, the Tenant shall provide to Landlord, at Tenant's sole expense, a lien and completion bond for an amount equal to _____ times the estimated costs of any improvements, additions, or alterations in the Premises, to protect Landlord against any liability for mechanics' and material men's liens, and to insure completion of the work where the amount contracted for exceeds U.S. $ _____. The Landlord shall not be subject to liens for improvements made by the Tenant. The Tenant is responsible for notifying any and all contractors, subcontractors, and/or material men and posting notices of non-responsiblity in a place on the Premises visible to all.

48. Brokers:

The Landlord and the Tenant each guarantee to the other that they have had no dealings with any real estate broker or agents in connection with the negotiation of this Lease, and that to their knowledge no real estate broker or agent is entitled to any commission in connection with it. They each hereby indemnify and hold the other harmless from and against all claims of any broker(s) or similar parties claiming a commission in connection with this Lease, and of any costs of defending against and investigating such claims.

49. Notices and Communications:

Except as otherwise indicated in this Lease agreement, any statement, notice, or other communication which Landlord or Tenant may desire or be required to give to the other shall be in writing. It will be considered delivered if it has been hand delivered, or if it has been sent by registered or certified mail, to the address(es) given at the beginning of this Lease document or to any other address(es) that the other party may designate from time to time by prior written notice, delivered and effective before the communication is sent. Until further notice, written communications will be sent to the following addresses:

Landlord: _____

Address: _____

City: _____ State: _____ Zip: _____

Tenant: _____

Permanent Address: _____

City: _____ State: _____ Zip: _____

50. Joint Obligation:

If there is more than one Tenant, the obligations imposed upon Tenants under the terms of this Lease shall apply equally to all Tenants.

51. Paragraph Headings:

The captions and paragraph headings in this Lease are used only for convenience and for reference, and shall have no effect upon the construction or interpretation of any provision in this Lease.

52. Time is of the Essence:

Time is of the essence of this Lease, particularly for those of its provisions in which performance is a factor.

53. Heirs and Assigns:

Except for restrictions and conditions set forth in this Lease, the terms of this Lease shall apply to the respective heirs, legal representatives, successors and permitted assigns and/

or sublessees of the Landlord and the Tenant. The term "Landlord," as used in this Lease, refers only to the owner of the Premises at the time in question. On the date that title to the Premises is transferred to another owner, the party making the transfer is relieved of all liability and obligations of the Landlord under this Lease.

54. Recordation:

Either Landlord or Tenant may record a short form memorandum of this Agreement without the prior written consent of the other party, as shown on Appendix "F," attached to and considered a part of this Lease.

55. Prior Agreements and Amendments:

This Lease contains the entire agreement between the Landlord and the Tenant. No prior agreements or understandings, verbal or written, pertaining to any of the matters in this Lease shall be effective for any purpose. Any changes made after the signing of this Lease must be made in writing and signed by both parties.

56. Inability to Perform:

If either the Landlord or the Tenant is unable to perform any of its obligations under the terms of this Lease, or is delayed in doing so because of circumstances beyond its reasonable control, including strike, riot, labor disputes, acts of God, war, or shortages of labor or materials, this inability or delay will not be considered a breach or default under this Lease. Under such circumstances, this Lease and the obligations of both the Tenant and the Landlord under it will not be affected or impaired, and neither party shall be liable to the other.

57. Use of Name:

The Tenant shall not have the right to use the words, "_____ _____," as any portion of the name of its business located on the Premises without the consent of the Landlord and the Association.

58. Severability:

If any provision in this Agreement is found to be unenforceable under the law, the remaining provisions shall continue to be valid and subject to enforcement in the courts without exception.

59. Cumulative Remedies:

Any remedy or election under the terms of this Lease will not be exclusive of all other remedies or elections, but cumulative with all other remedies at law and in equity.

60. Governing Law:

This Agreement, and all transactions set forth in this Lease, shall be governed by, construed, and enforced in accordance with the laws of the State of _____.

The Landlord and the Tenant waive trial by jury and agree to submit to the personal jurisdiction and venue of a Court of subject matter jurisdiction located in _____ County, State of _____. Should litigation result from this Lease or from performance of the obligations set forth in this Lease, the Landlord and Tenant agree to reimburse the prevailing party for reasonable attorneys fees, court costs, and all other expenses, whether or not taxable by the Court as costs, associated with the litigation, in addition to any other remedy to which the prevailing party may be entitled. No action shall be entertained by said Court or any Court of competent jurisdiction if filed more than one year after the date of the cause(s) of action actually accrued, regardless of whether damages could be accurately calculated at that time.

61. Tenant's Waiver:

The Tenant waives any and all right to fight any eviction action instituted by Landlord, with the exception of an affirmative defense based upon payment of all amounts that the

Landlord claims the Tenant has not paid. Other matters must be dealt with in a separate suit instituted by Tenant.

62. Prorations:

Any monthly payment due to Landlord under the terms of this Lease, which is for a period of less than _____ month(s), shall be prorated based upon a _____ day month.

63. Appendices:

The appendices attached to this Lease are hereby incorporated herein and considered a part of this Lease for all purposes.

64. Reliance on Financial Statement:

At the time of the execution of this lease, the Tenant shall furnish a financial statement of Tenant prepared by an accountant. The Tenant, both in corporate capacity, if applicable, and individually, represents and warrants that all the information contained in this financial statement is complete, true, and correct. The Tenant understands that the Landlord is entering into this Agreement based upon the accuracy of the information contained in this financial statement. If the financial statement is found to misrepresent Tenant's financial standing, or if the Tenant's financial circumstances materially change, the Landlord may demand, as additional security, an amount equal to an additional two (2) months' rent. This additional security shall be subject to all terms and conditions of this Lease. If the financial statement is found to be inaccurate, the Landlord may elect to terminate this Lease, or hold Tenant personally and individually liable hereunder.

65. Notice on Radon Gas:

Radon is a naturally occurring radioactive gas that may present health risks to persons who are exposed to it over time when it has accumulated in a building in sufficient quantities. Levels of radon that exceed federal and state guidelines have been found in buildings in this state. Additional information regarding radon and radon testing may be obtained from your county public health unit.

66. Authority of Tenant's Signatory:

If the Tenant is a corporation or a limited partnership and a representative of the Tenant is singing this Lease, the corporation or limited partnership guarantees that the person signing this Lease on behalf of Tenant is authorized to execute and deliver this Lease according to a duly adopted resolution of the Board of Directors of this corporation, or according to the by-laws of said corporation, or as part of the limited partnership agreement. The corporation or limited partnership agrees that this Lease is binding upon it in accordance with its terms. The Landlord may request any reasonable documentation from the Tenant showing that he or she has authority to execute this Lease.

EXECUTED on the date at the beginning of this document.

LANDLORD: _____

WITNESS: _____

TENANT: _____

WITNESS: _____

APPENDIX "A:" LEGAL DESCRIPTION

APPENDIX "B:" SITE PLAN

APPENDIX "C:" DEVELOPMENT AGREEMENT

APPENDIX "D:" USE OF PREMISES

APPENDIX "E:"
RULES AND REGULATIONS

1. Tenant must obtain written consent from Landlord before any sign, placard, picture, symbol, mark, advertisement, name, or notice may be inscribed, displayed, printed, placed, or affixed on or to any part of the outside or inside of the Premises. Landlord has the right to remove any such unapproved sign, placard, picture, symbol, mark, advertisement, name, or notice without notice to and at Tenant's expense. Tenant agrees not to place anything, or allow anything to be placed, near the glass of any window, door, partition, or wall that is visible from outside the Premises. Tenant must obtain the prior written consent of Landlord before covering or otherwise sunscreening any window.

2. The sidewalks, walks, corridors, passages, exits, entrances, stairways, and ramps of the Premises must be used only for ingress and egress to and from the Premises, and shall not be obstructed or used by Tenant, or the employees, agents, servants, visitors, or licensees of Tenant for any other purpose.

3. Landlord must approve all workmen who perform repairs, installations, alterations, painting, material moving, and other similar work done in or on the Premises. Non-structural alterations and installations may be carried out by Tenant's employees or persons under their supervision.

4. The toilet rooms, urinals, wash bowls, and other apparatus shall not be used for any purpose other than that for which they are constructed, and no foreign substance of any kind whatsoever shall be thrown therein. The Tenant will be responsible for any expense caused by the breakage, stoppage, or damage resulting from the violation of this rule by Tenant, or its employees or invitees.

5. Tenant shall not overload the floor of the Premises or in any way deface the Premises. Maximum floor loading shall be _____ pounds per square foot.

6. Tenant shall not permit or suffer the Premises to be occupied or used in a manner offensive or objectionable to Landlord because of light, radiation, magnetism, noise, odors, and/or vibrations. Neither Tenant, nor the employees, agents, servants, visitors, or licensees of Tenant shall place, leave, or discard any rubbish, paper, articles, or objects of any kind whatsoever outside the doors of the Premises. No animals or birds may be brought into or kept in or about the Premises.

7. Tenant may not use or keep in the Premises any poisonous, corrosive, caustic, explosive, inflammable or combustible gas, fluid or substance, or use any method of heating or cooling that is not approved by Landlord.

8. Landlord will determine where and how electricians can introduce telephone and telegraph wires. Prior consent must be obtained from Landlord before boring or cutting holes for wires. Landlord must approve the location of telephones, call boxes, and other office equipment affixed to the Premises.

9. Tenant shall not use any of the common areas of the Premises for the care or maintenance of vehicles.

10. Landlord reserves the right to exclude or expel from the Premises any person who, in the judgment of Landlord, is intoxicated or under the influence of liquor or drugs, or who shall in any manner violate any of the rules and regulations of the Premises.

11. Landlord may prohibit any advertising by Tenant that the Landlord judges to impair the reputation of the Premises, and upon written notice from Landlord, Tenant will refrain from or discontinue such advertising.

12. Canvassing, soliciting, peddling, and similar activities are prohibited in the Premises without the prior approval of Landlord. Tenant agrees to cooperate to prevent same.

13. Tenant shall not place any additional locks or bolts of any kind on any door in the Premises or alter or change any lock on any door in the Premises. Landlord shall furnish ( ) keys for each lock on exterior doors to the Premises. Duplicate keys shall be obtained from the Landlord at Tenant's expense. Upon the expiration or termination of this Lease, all keys shall be returned to Landlord and Tenant shall give to Landlord instructions and combinations for all safes, vaults, and combination locks remaining with the Premises. Landlord may at all times keep a pass key to the Premises. All exterior doors to the Premises shall be kept closed at all times and left locked when the Premises are not in use.

14. Tenant shall immediately notify Landlord of any occurrence of any theft, unauthorized solicitation or accident in the Premises, or of defects in the Premises or in any fixtures or equipment, or of any known emergency in the Premises.

15. Tenant shall not use the Premises or permit the Premises to be used for photographic, multilith, or multigraph reproductions, except in connection with its own business and not as a service for others, without Landlord's prior permission.

16. Tenant shall not advertise for laborers giving the Premises as an address, nor pay such laborers at a location in the Premises.

17. Tenant shall is responsible to keep the Premises neat and orderly at all times.

_____   _____
Landlord   Tenant

EXHIBIT "F:" MEMORANDUM OF LEASE

THIS MEMORANDUM OF LEASE, dated _____ (date)

by and between _____ ("Landlord"),

with its principal place of business located at:

_____

City: _____ State: _____ Zip: _____

and _____ ("Tenant"),

with its principal place of business located at:

_____

City: _____ State: _____ Zip: _____

WITNESSETH

1. That according to the Lease ("Lease") dated _____

between Tenant and Landlord, Landlord has leased to Tenant, and Tenant has leased from Landlord, the premises described on Exhibit "A" attached hereto ("Leased Premises") for a term beginning on the day of _____("Commencement Date"), and ending on the last day of the month during which the _____ anniversary of the Commencement Date occurs.

2. The Landlord shall not be subject to any liens or claims asserted against the Leased Premises in connection with Tenant's improvements on the Leased Premises or Tenant's use of the Leased Premises, and Tenant shall provide notice of such limitation to all contractors, subcontractors, and material men as required under Section 12.09 of this Lease.

3. This Memorandum of Lease is executed according to Article 13.06 of the Lease and is not intended to make any change to the terms and conditions of the Lease.

IN WITNESS WHEREOF, the parties have caused this instrument to be duly executed and sealed as of the date above.

LANDLORD: _____

WITNESS: _____

TENANT: _____

WITNESS: _____

LEASE CANCELLATION

Date: _____

Address: _____

As of today, _____ (Landlord) and _____ (Tenant) agree to cancel its lease. The lease will be officially terminated and canceled effective _____ (Date). At this chosen date, the Tenant has agreed to vacate the leased premises.

Besides those rights and obligations accruing prior to the chosen date that have not been exercised, performed, or discharged, all rights and obligations of the parties involved in this lease shall be canceled and discharged.

This Agreement shall be binding upon, and inure to the benefit of, the parties involved, and also both of their heirs, successors, and assigns.

Dated: _____

_____
Landlord Sign

_____
Landlord Print

_____
Tenant Sign

_____
Tenant Print

COMBINATION ASSIGNMENT OF LEASE, CONSENT OF LESSOR, AND ACCEPTANCE BY ASSIGNEE

This agreement made and executed in triplicate parts:

Date: _____
By and between
Lessee: _____, of _____, state of _____
Assignee: _____, of _____, state of _____
AND
Lessor: _____, of _____, state of _____

Lessor witnesses that A Lease agreement made and executed in_____[year], leased to Lessee for and during the period of _____ years beginning on the first day of _____[year], and terminating on the 31st day of _____[year]. The piece or lot of real estate, located in the city of _____, county of _____ and state of _____, described as follows: _____

According to paragraph ___ (or Article ___) of that Lease agreement, at any time during the Term when Lessees are not in default under The Lease, Lessees may assign all of their interest to any financially responsible person of good character provided Lessees shall provide written notice to Lessor at least 20 days before making such an assignment, stating name, business, and business or residence address of proposed Assignee.

The Assignee shall, at the time when the assignment is made, bind Assignee, Assignee's heirs, legal representatives, and assigns, by a legal document, properly executed and acknowledged, and then recorded in office of _____ of _____ county, _____, to perform, release, and fulfill all Lessees' engagements and actions under lease.

Lessee, has informed Lessor of Lessee's intention to assign all of Lessee's interest in the Lease to Assignee, and Lessor has accepted such notice in full compliance with paragraph ___ (or Article ___) of that Lease, and is willing to consent to such assignment on conditions provided by Lease.

It is therefore agreed by and between the parties that:

1. Lessee, for and in consideration of one dollar and other important considerations to Lessee paid by Assignee, hereby assigns all rights, titles, and interests in and to Lease for the balance of the Term of the Lease to Assignee, Assignee's heirs, legal representatives, and assigns.

2. Assignee, in consideration of assignment and of consent to assignment by Lessor, hereby agrees that Assignee, Assignee's heirs, legal representatives, and assigns, will faithfully perform, discharge, and fulfill all of Lessees' obligations and undertakings under Lease and will pay to Lessor, Lessor's heirs, legal representatives, or assigns, all rent reserved under Lease, as rent may become due and payable, in the manner and form set forth in the Lease.

3. Lessor, in consideration of assignment and agreement of Assignee to perform, release, and fulfill all Lessees' obligations and actions under Lease, hereby agrees to such assignment and to the substitution of Assignee in place of Lessee, in respect to Lessee's liability as Lessee created by Lease, from further liability under Lease.

The above is understood by each party and will become official on _____.

DATE:
Lessee   _____
Assignee   _____
Lessor   _____

APPLICATION FOR LEASE RENEWAL

Date: _____

This application is in regards to renewing the lease agreement executed on _____ (date). The premises are broadly described as _____ for a term of _____ (months/years) and ending on _____ (date). Paid in advance, the rent will be $_____ each month.

The initial security deposit will now be transferred over as the security deposit on the renewed lease.

It is also understood that if this application for lease renewal is not accepted, the mentioned deposit will be refunded to the applicant.

Please fill out the following:

APPLICANT

Name: _____

Present Residence: _____

How long have you been at your current residence? _____

Previous Residence: _____

How long were you at your previous residence? _____

Married: _____

Spouse's Name: _____

Children? _____

If yes, list his/her (or each one's) name(s) and respective age(s): _____

Pets? _____

If yes, list the kind(s): _____

YOUR EMPLOYMENT

Employer: _____

Employer's Address: _____

Title: _____

Supervisor's Name: _____

Business Phone #: _____

How long have you been at your present job? _____

Annual Income: _____

SPOUSE'S EMPLOYMENT

Employer: _____

Employer's Address: _____

Title: _____

Supervisor's Name: _____

Business Phone #: _____

How long has he or she been at its present job? _____

Annual Income: _____

REFERENCES

Bank: _____ Phone: _____

Personal Reference: _____ Phone: _____

Credit Reference: _____ Phone: _____

The Landlord is allowed to use the information provided herein to conduct any and all investigations as deemed sensible by the Landlord.

The terms of the initial lease agreement referred above are reaffirmed as of the date below, except as modified by the terms herein.

LANDLORD _____

TENANT _____

LEASEHOLD PROPERTY ADDENDUM

Date: _____

Buyer: _____

Seller: _____

Property: _____

The Buyer and Seller agree that:

Any names, numbers, or dates that were not completed in this Addendum were not yet available at the time the Agreement was prepared. The Buyer should confirm all names, rent amounts, numbers, and dates by referring to the Lease. If there is a conflict regarding the information in this Addendum and in the Lease, the Lease will take precedence.

1. The Property is Leasehold

The Buyer:

Understands that the Property is leasehold and not fee simple. The leasehold estate was created by a Lease, containing the terms, provisions, covenants, and agreements between the Lessor and the Lessee. The Lease controls the rights and obligations of the parties.

Understands that the Property is subject to all of the terms, conditions, provisions, covenants, obligations, and agreements contained in the Lease.

Is purchasing the balance of the Term of the Lease.

The Seller:

Is the owner of the Lessee's interest in the Lease, or is the Purchaser under an Agreement of Sale regarding such interest.

Will transfer its interest in the Lease to the Buyer by an Assignment of Lease.

The Lessor:

Name: _____ and Lease No. (if any): _____ .

If permission of the Lessor is necessary to allow the transfer, this sale will be dependent upon obtaining such permission.

The Seller and the Realtors in this transaction have no power over the Lessor's permission procedures and timing.

2. Basic Lease Terms

The Lease rent varies over time.

The following Lease rents are provided for the Buyer's reference, but should be independently confirmed by referring to the Lease:

$_____ per _____until _____, 20 _____

$_____ per _____until _____, 20 _____

Renegotiation:

The Lease rent will be renegotiated on _____ according to terms contained in the Lease. This means that the Lease rent after the Renegotiation Date is not fixed or already agreed upon.

3. Expiration

The Lease expires on _____ . The Buyer's right to own the Property will end on the Expiration Date unless the Lease is extended, the buyer purchases the Lessor's fee simple interest, or other arrangements are made.

The Realtors in this transaction have no authority to give advice about this matter and cannot represent that the Lease may be extended, that the Lessor's interest may be purchased, or that other arrangements may be made.

The Lease contains a "Reversionary Clause" or "Surrender Clause," which describes what will happen on the Expiration Date, including the disposition of any improvements on the Property. The Buyer should make certain to thoroughly comprehend these clauses, and also all of the other terms, conditions, provisions, covenants, obligations, and agreements of the Lease.

4. Possibility of Purchase

A. Current Fee Simple Offering

If the fee simple title is presently being offered, the parties should address the issue as a Special Term in paragraph 8 of the Agreement.

B. Possible Fee Simple Conversion

The Buyer is advised to check the status of the possibility of conversion of the Property to fee simple now or in the future, and to check with the owner's association (if any) to see if there is an ongoing or planned lease/fee conversion action.

The Realtors in this transaction are not representing that the Lessor will offer the fee simple title for sale now or in the future and have no authority or responsibility other than to keep the Buyer informed.

5. Lease Document

This paragraph includes the Buyer's receipt of the Lease.
The term "Lease" encompasses any and all amendments to the Lease.

Choose either A, B, or C, as applicable, by putting a check on the appropriate line, and cross out the paragraphs which are not selected. One box must be checked.

_____ A. The Lease has been received, reviewed, approved, and accepted by the Buyer.

The Buyer acknowledges that it has received and reviewed a copy of the Lease and approves of and accepts all of its terms, conditions, provisions, covenants, obligations, and agreements, including but not limited to the Lease rents, Renegotiation Date, Expiration Date, and "Reversionary Clause" or "Surrender Clause" (as applicable).

_____ B. The Lease will be provided to the Buyer for its review, approval, and acceptance.

Within (__) calendar days of acceptance of this Agreement, the Seller agrees, at the Seller's sole cost and expense, to provide the Buyer with a copy of the Lease. This offer is reliant upon the Buyer's review, approval, and acceptance of the Lease within (__) calendar days after it has been provided by the Seller; such approval will be deemed to be automatically given unless written notice of disapproval is given within the specified period. If written notice of disapproval is given within the specified period, this contract shall become non-existent and all deposits shall be immediately returned to Buyer, minus any escrow expenses or fees chargeable to the Buyer. Afterward, neither the Buyer, the Seller, nor any Realtors shall have any further rights, obligations, or liabilities under this Agreement.

If the Buyer approves of and accepts the Lease, the Buyer agrees to accept all of its terms, conditions, provisions, covenants, obligations, and agreements, including but not limited to the Lease rents, Renegotiation Date, Expiration Date, and "Reversionary Clause" or "Surrender Clause" (as applicable).

_____ C. Other arrangements which have been made with respect to the Lease (continue as a Special Term as necessary).

6. Recommendation of Legal Advice

The Buyer should seek advice from an attorney about any legal questions regarding this Addendum and the Lease, especially the Lease re-negotiation and "Reversionary Clause" or "Surrender Clause" terms.

By signing this Addendum, the Buyer agrees and acknowledges that the Buyer is not relying on the Realtors in this transaction for any legal advice about the Lease, and also that the Buyer has been advised to contact an attorney.

7. The Term "Lease"

As used in this Addendum, the term "Lease" refers to and includes the Lease and any amendments to the Lease, and the terms "Sublease," "Apartment Lease," "Condominium Conveyance Document," "Proprietary Lease," and other leasehold terms, as pertinent.

The undersigned acknowledge receipt of a completed copy of this Leasehold Property Addendum, and agree to all of its terms and conditions.

DATE: _____

BUYER: _____

SELLER: _____

MONTH-TO-MONTH LEASE AGREEMENT

Date: _____

Landlord: _____

Address: _____

City: _____ State: _____ Zip: _____

Resident: _____

Address: _____

City: _____ State: _____ Zip: _____

Rent: $_____ for the first month's rent of the premises owned by Management

Located at:_____

Month-to-Month Rental: $ _____, payable in advance on the___ day of each subsequent calendar month.

Resident agrees that:

1. Appearance of Premises.

Premises must be kept in a clean, orderly, and law abiding manner. The premise's surroundings must be free of weeds, debris, and/or material that may become unsightly or detrimental to the appearance of premises. Management shall have the right to enter and inspect Premises at any and all reasonable times.

2. Alterations.

No alterations or redecorating of any kind is to be done without prior written permission of Management.

3. Utilities.

Resident is responsible to pay for all utility services furnished to the property.

4. Damage to Premises.

Resident will pay the cost of all repairs for any damage done to premises and any clean-up necessitated by any activity of the Resident or Resident's invitees or employees.

5. Pets.

No birds, animals, or other pets shall be kept on the premises without the knowledge and written permission from Management. Permission to keep such a bird, animal, or other pet may be withdrawn, if, in the opinion of Management, it is a nuisance, initiates complaint from neighbors, or negatively affects the normal maintenance of the property.

6. Subletting.

Resident may not let or sublet the whole or any part of the premises to anyone for any reason whatsoever without prior written consent from Management. The number of persons occupying premises shall not exceed (___) without written consent from Management.

7. Notice Before Vacating Premises.

Resident must give 30 days' written notice by registered mail to Management before vacating the premises. After giving notice to the Management, resident must allow prospective tenants a reasonable opportunity to inspect the property.

8. Clean-up.

Resident must clean up premises and restore them to the same condition as they were in when the Resident took possession of the premises, except for reasonable wear and tear and damage by the elements.

9. Violations.

Nonpayment of rent or a violation of any part of this agreement shall be ample cause for eviction from Premises, after receipt by registered mail or personal delivery of three (3) days' written notice from Landlord. If suit is brought to collect rent or damages, to cause eviction from said the premises, or to collect the costs of repair or cleaning of the premises, the Resident agrees to pay all costs of such action, including reasonable attorney fees as established by the Court.

10. One-time Waiver.

No one-time waiver by Management at any time of any of the terms of this agreement shall be construed as a permanent waiver or as a release from any of the obligations of the Resident under the terms of this Agreement.

11. Rent.

All rent payments shall be made at the office of_____, or any other place selected by Management.

Each party shall receive a copy of this agreement.
Management Resident   _____
Resident   _____

LEASE AGREEMENT FOR MULTIPLE TENANTS

Apartment #: _____

Commencement Date: _____

Termination Date: _____

Monthly rent: $ _____

Security Deposit: $ _____

# of Occupants: _____

Name(s) of Resident(s): _____

Address: _____

Owner/Community: _____

Address: _____

COVENANTS AND AGREEMENTS

1. Rent.

Resident will pay in advance on the first day of each month the rent mentioned above to Owner or Owner's Agent at the address mentioned above or at any other address the Owner may designate in writing. If not received by the first day of each month, a rental payment will be considered delinquent and will incur a late charge of $___ if received after the fifth day of the month. Late charges shall be protected by the security deposit provided in this Rental Agreement and by the Owner's lien for rent.

2. Term.

The term of this Rental Agreement will start on_____(date) and end on_____(date). If the first month of occupancy does not begin on the first day of a calendar month, rent from the start date through the last day of that calendar month shall be prorated at a rate of $_____ per day and paid together with the first full month's rent in advance on _____ (date).

3. Security Deposit.

Resident has deposited with Owner the Security Deposit mentioned as a guarantee of performance of each and every covenant and agreement of the Rental Agreement.

Owner shall have the right but not the obligation to apply the Security Deposit in whole or in part to any unpaid rent or other amounts due because of an unperformed covenant or agreement by Resident. Resident's liability is not limited to the amount of the Security Deposit. At the termination or expiry of this Rental Agreement, after full payment of all amounts due and performance of all of Resident's covenants and agreements (including the surrender of the Apartment in accordance with this Rental Agreement), the Security Deposit or any part of it remaining unapplied shall be returned to Resident.

Before any apartment is vacated by Resident, it must be inspected by the Owner and Resident. The Resident's failure to do so shall be just grounds for Owner to retain the entire Security Deposit after properly notifying Resident as required by law.

4. False Application.

The application for the Rental Agreement and all the information it contains are part of this Rental Agreement. Resident represents, warrants, and agrees that the information in the application is true and material. If any information is false or if there is any misrepresentation, Owner may at Owner's discretion end this Rental Agreement.

5. Condition of Apartment: Maintenance.

Resident has examined the Apartment and confirms that the Apartment is in the physical shape and condition as outlined in the "Statement of Apartment Condition," attached to and made a part of this Rental Agreement.

By signing this Agreement, Resident acknowledges receipt of the Apartment in good order and repair as set forth in the "Statement of Apartment Condition." If possession is deferred or delayed beyond the execution of this Rental Agreement, occupation of the Apartment by Resident shall be regarded as evidence of his/her acceptance of the Apartment in the physical shape and condition mentioned in the "Statement of Apartment Condition."

Unless otherwise specified in the "Statement of Apartment Condition," Resident agrees that Owner or his/her agent has made no representation as to condition or repair, and that no promise to decorate, modify, repair, or improve either before or at the execution of this Agreement that is not contained in the "Statement of Apartment Condition" has been made by the Owner or his agent.

Resident will, on demand (written or oral), reimburse Owner for the costs of any repair or replacement necessitated by the negligence or willful act of the Resident or Resident's invitees.

Resident shall comply with applicable Municipal Code and other regulations. Resident shall not damage or leave waste in the Apartment or the Building and shall keep the Apartment clean and in good order and repair at his or her own expense. Resident shall at all times comply with Statute.

At the termination of this Rental Agreement, Resident shall return the Apartment to Owner in similar condition, except for reasonable wear and tear. If Resident fails to keep the Apartment in such condition and repair or comply with Statute, Owner or Owner's agent may enter and put the Apartment in good condition and repair and/or compliance. Resident shall, on demand (written or oral) pay Owner the cost of such work.

6. Use of Apartment.

Resident and those other persons listed in the application for this Rental Agreement, and any children born or legally adopted by Resident during the Term. shall occupy the Apartment solely as a residence. None of the persons residing in the Apartment shall perform or permit any practice that may damage the reputation of or otherwise be detrimental to the Building or the neighborhood, or disturb other Residents or increase the insurance rate on the Building. Household pets may be kept in the Apartment in accordance with the "Pet Agreement," which is part of this Rental Agreement.

7. Assignment and Subletting.

Resident shall neither sublet the Apartment or any part of it, nor assign his/her Rental Agreement, nor allow any transfer of Resident's interest by operation of law, nor offer the Apartment nor any part thereof for lease or sublease without, in each case, the prior written permission of Owner. If Owner approves such transfer, Resident shall continue to be responsible for all of obligations under this lease, unless expressly released from such obligations in writing by Owner.

8. Abandonment, Reletting, and Termination.

In addition to any rights and remedies which Owner may have at law, this Rental Agreement shall end immediately if Resident vacates or abandons the Apartment or breaches any covenant or agreement in this Rental Agreement, or transfers his/her interest, voluntarily or involuntarily, or by operation of law such as Resident's bankruptcy or insolvency, in the Rental Agreement without Owner's permission. Owner may relet the Apartment for such rent and upon such terms and such period as Owner may elect without releasing Resident from any liability under this Rental Agreement.

Owner may reasonably decline any prospective new tenant offered by Resident or by others. Owner may let other vacancies in the Building first before reletting or attempting to relet the Apartment.

Resident's right to possession of the Apartment shall immediately end when the Rental Agreement is terminated, and the Apartment shall be immediately surrendered to Owner or the Owner's agent. Resident shall, on demand, pay the difference between the rent specified on the Lease and the rent charged for reletting if it is not enough to satisfy the Rent recommended by the local Board of Realtors, or Real Estate Board.

If this Rental Agreement is terminated before the expiration date, then in addition to any other rights and remedies available to Owner, Owner shall be entitled to adjust and retain Security Deposit after providing written notification to Resident. Resident agrees to such retention as liquidated damages under this Rental Agreement.

9. Alterations, Additions, Fixtures, and Appliances.

Resident shall make no alterations to Apartment nor install nor maintain in the Apartment or any part of the Building interior or exterior appliances, or devices of any kind without first obtaining the written consent of Owner, and according to the terms and conditions specified in such written consent. All alterations, add-ons, and fixtures (including locks and bolts) shall remain as part of the Apartment unless Owner dictates otherwise.

10. Access.

Owner, Owner's agents, and any other person authorized by the Owner shall at any time have the right of free access during the Term to inspect, repair, change, or exhibit the Building or the Apartment for sale. At any time within 90 days before the end of the Term, Owner and Owner's agents shall have the right to exhibit the Apartment for rent and affix "For Rent" signs in such places as Owner or Owner's agent shall determine, without hindrance of any kind and regardless of permission by Resident or others.

12. Water, Heating, and Cooling.

Owner shall supply water for the use of Resident in fixtures provided for such purpose. Owner shall provide and properly service equipment to heat water and to provide heating and cooling in the Apartment.

13. Fire and Casualty.

If fire, explosion, or other casualty makes the Apartment un-tenantable, Owner may elect to end this Rental Agreement or to repair the Apartment within 120 days. If Owner does not repair the Apartment within this time, or if the Building is entirely destroyed, the Term of this Lease shall end. If Owner elects to repair the Apartment, the rent shall be abated and prorated from the date of the fire, explosion, or other casualty to the date of re-occupancy, provided that during repairs, Resident has left the Apartment and removed Resident's possessions if required by Owner. The date of re-occupancy shall be the day that Owner delivers notice to Resident that the Apartment is ready for occupancy.

14. Eminent Domain.

If the entire or any part of the Building or the Apartment is taken or condemned by any competent authority for any public use or purpose, the Term of this Rental Agreement shall terminate on, and not before, the date when possession is required for such use or purpose. Resident will not share in any award made to the Owner in compensation for the taking of the property. Resident shall have no right to appear and defend in any suit brought by such competent authority, and Resident shall have no right in any award. Current rent shall be shared as of the date of such termination.

15. Surrender of Apartment.

At the expiration of the Term of this Rental Agreement, Resident shall defer immediate possession to Owner and deliver all keys to Owner or Owner's agent at the place where rent is payable.

16. Holding Over.

If Resident retains possession of the Apartment after the Term of the Lease has expired, such tenancy shall be on a month-to-month basis, with rent due in advance on the first day of each calendar month. Resident agrees to give Owner 30 days' notice before vacating the premises. If Tenant fails to give 30 days' notice, whether at the expiration of the Term or otherwise, Tenant must pay the Owner rent for one additional month.

17. Legal Expenses.

Resident agrees to pay all Owner's costs, expenses, and attorney's fees arising from the implementation of covenants and agreements of this Rental Agreement or the implementation of any rights and remedies afforded to Owner by statute.

18. Rules and Regulations.

The Rules and Regulations and Pet Agreement attached to this Rental Agreement are an integral part of this Rental Agreement. Resident agrees to keep and observe these rules and regulations. Resident also agrees to keep any additional reasonable rules and regulations that Owner or Owner's agent establish for the necessary, proper, and orderly care of the Property.

19. Furnishings.

The furnishings and appliances supplied to Resident by Owner and described in the "Statement of Apartment Condition" shall be available for Resident's use in a normal manner and shall be left at expiration of this Lease in good condition, except for ordinary wear and tear.

Owner makes no specific representations and warranties as to the general condition of these furnishings and appliances.

20. Miscellaneous.

Owner and Tenant agree that all provisions, covenants, and agreements of this Rental Agreement to be performed by Resident are "material provisions" of the Rental Agreement.

Owner and Tenant agree that any action brought by either party against the other for the implementation of the covenants and agreements of this Rental Agreement, other than an action for possession of the Apartment shall take place in the court of proper jurisdiction, unless waived or changed by mutual agreement.

21. Severability.

If any provision in this Agreement is found to be unenforceable under the law, the remaining provisions shall continue to be valid and subject to enforcement in the courts without exception.

22. Responsibility to Pay Rent.

Resident's responsibility to pay rent during the term or any extension of this Lease or during any extended residency shall not be waived, released, or ended by:

- demand for possession
- the service of any notice
- notice of termination of residency
- institution of any action
- enforceable detainer
- eviction
- any judgment for possession or any other act or acts resulting in termination of Resident's right of possession

Except as provided by statute, the payment or receipt of rent shall not surrender or affect any such notice, demand, suit, or judgment or in any manner waive, affect, change, or modify, or alter Owner's rights or remedies. Acceptance of rent or liquidated damages pursuant to paragraph 10, or any other act by the Owner that appears to affirm residency, shall not be construed as an extension of this Lease or operate as a waiver of the right to end this Rental Agreement. The provisions of paragraph 10 do not affect Owner's right to elect to treat Resident as a holdover tenant under the terms of this Rental Agreement.

23. One-time Waiver.

A one-time waiver by Owner of any of the provisions of this Rental Agreement or Owner's knowledge of any breach of this Rental Agreement by Resident does not constitute a permanent waiver. The giving of any notice or making of any demand or any other act or waiver by Owner other than a specific written waiver or election shall not be construed as a waiver of any rights of Owner under this Rental Agreement or as an election not to proceed under the provisions of this Rental Agreement.

24. Cumulative Remedies.

Owner's rights and remedies under this Rental Agreement are cumulative, and the exercise of one or more rights or remedies does not exclude or waive any other right or remedy.

25. Subordination.

Resident's rights under this Rental Agreement and any extensions of this Agreement shall be subordinated at all times to any present or future mortgages on the real estate (or any part of it) on which the Building is situated and to all advances upon the security of such mortgages. Resident shall execute any documents required by Owner to effect such subordination and hereby permanently appoints Owner (and, if more than one person's name appears as Owner, any one of them) as attorney-in-fact to execute and deliver such documents in Resident's name.

26. Governing Law.

The interpretation, application, validity, performance, and breach of this Agreement shall be governed by, construed, and enforced in accordance with the laws of the State of _____. Should litigation result from this Agreement, Owner and Agent agree to reimburse the prevailing party for reasonable attorney's fees, court costs, and all other expenses, whether or not taxable by the Court as costs, associated with the litigation, in addition to any other remedy to which the prevailing party may be entitled. No action shall be entertained by said Court or any Court of competent jurisdiction if filed more than one year from the date that the cause(s) of action actually accrued, regardless of whether damages could be accurately calculated at that time.

27. Tenant's Waiver.

Tenant hereby surrenders any and all right to assert affirmative defenses or counterclaims in any eviction action instituted by Landlord with the exception of an affirmative defense based upon payment of all amounts claimed by Landlord not to have been paid by Tenant.

Any other matters may only be advanced by a separate suit instituted by Tenant.

28. Notices.

Any notice required to be given under this Rental Agreement or by statute shall be considered served when delivered to the Apartment, except where by statute an alternative means is required. Any notice required by this Rental Agreement or by statute to be given to the Owner shall be considered served when the written notice is delivered in person to Owner or Owner's agent at the above address.

29. Hold Harmless.

Resident shall indemnify and hold harmless Owner and Owner's agent from any loss, damage, injury, claim, demand, costs, and expenses (including legal expenses) arising out of or associated with the Resident's use, operation, or maintenance of the Apartment, or any personal property or equipment Resident now or later has placed, stored, or located therein. Resident also covenants and agrees that he/she is legally responsible to any invitee, licensee, or trespasser of the Apartment for any injury, claim, damage, loss, demand, costs, and expenses arising out of that person's use and operation of the Apartment, or the use of any Resident's personality, fixtures, or equipment located in the Apartment.

30. Personal Property.

It is specifically covenanted and agreed between the Owner and Resident that all personal property and equipment of Resident now or in the future placed, stored, or located in the Apartment shall be the sole responsibility and risk of Resident and any damage, loss, theft, or destruction of personal property and equipment shall be borne solely by the Resident and shall be his/her sole responsibility. Except only as otherwise specifically provided by statute, neither Owner nor Owner's agent shall be liable for damages to Resident or to any persons claiming through Resident (nor shall rent be abated) for damage to or loss of property wherever located from any cause whatever.

31. Heirs and Assigns.

All covenants and agreements in this Rental Agreement shall be binding upon and inure to the benefit of the heirs, executors, administrators, successors, and assigns of Owner and Resident, subject to the restrictions in paragraph 7.

32. Additional Agreements and Covenants.

IN WITNESS WHEREOF, the parties hereto have executed this lease on the day of ,
20___.

Owner's Agent: _____

Resident: _____

PRE-PAYMENT RENT DISCOUNT

To take advantage of the Pre-payment Rental Discount, the rent must be paid before the first of the month. The rent must be received by _____ prior to the first of the month. If payment is received later due to poor mail service, holidays, or any other reason, this will not be acknowledged as valid grounds for late payment, and you will be charged the contract amount.

If rent is received by _____ days prior to the first of the month, you may subtract the amount of the pre-payment discount listed below from the normal rent amount. Rent paid on the first to the fourth of the month is the standard monthly amount. A late fee of _____ dollars per day ($_____) will be charged beginning with the fifth day of the month, and until all late rent charges plus all late fees are fully paid. These charges will continue to accrue even after an eviction notice has been served and action has been taken. All late and present charges must be paid in full to prevent the additional late payment charges.

Regular monthly rent if paid on the first to the fourth of the month: $_____

Pre-payment Discount:

Standard monthly rental amount:	$_____
Pre-payment Discount if paid before the 1st of the month:	$_____
Rental amount due with discount:	$_____

Monthly rent if paid after the fourth of the month:

Standard monthly rental amount:	$ _____
$____ per day late fee if paid after the 4th day of the month: Number of days _____ X $____ =	$ _____
Rental amount due with late fee	$ _____

I have read the above and I am in full agreement with it.

Date: _____

Resident

(Name)_____

(Signature)_____

Resident

(Name)_____

(Signature)_____

Manager

(Name)_____

(Signature)_____

LEASE AGREEMENT

This Agreement is made on _____ (date) between _____
of _____ (Landlord) and _____ of
_____ (Tenants).

The landlord is the owner of the premises located at _____, County of
_____ in _____State also referred to as premises.

The tenants desire to lease the premises from the landlord and the landlord has agreed to the same upon these following conditions.

The parties both legally bound by agreement do agree to the following:

1.   The landlord agrees to lease the premise to the tenant for an agreed upon time period and price. The tenants agree to lease the premise from the landlord.

2.   The lease shall extend from _____ (date) to _____ (date) during that time the tenants leasing the premise will be entitle to use of the premise.

3.   The rent determined by landlord will be $_____. The tenant agrees to pay the landlord for use and occupancy of the premise payable on the first of the month during the term of this agreement.

4.   The tenant shall pay landlord prior to occupancy of the premise a deposit of $_____. The receipt is acknowledge by being deposited with the land-lord in conjunction with the lease on _____ (date) to be held as security should any damages to premise or failure of tenants to surrender the premises under conditions listed in Paragraph 9. Unless withheld by the landlord due to damages the security deposit will be returned to the tenants within 30 days after termination of the lease. This is that tenant have given landlord a for-warding address in writing prior to surrender of the premise.

5.   During the lease, the landlord will pay the water bill and garbage collection. The tenants will be responsible for all utilities including gas, electric, tele-phone, cable, and any requiring service of these utilities.

6.   The landlord provides garbage containers for tenants. A recycling container is also provided for tenants for plastic, glass, and aluminum cans. It will be the respon-sibility of tenants to place garbage and recycling containers at the curb on the evening before pick up. They are to return the garbage and recycling container no later than the evening after pick up. Tenants agree to maintain the parking lot and premises at all times keeping it fee of debris and garbage. They will comply with municipal regulations imposed by the city/county ordinances regarding collection of trash.

7.   During the term of the lease the landlord will make necessary repair to the prem-ises. The tenants shall not provide or arrange any repairs because the landlord will

not be responsible for such actions. The tenants will notify the landlord of any repairs or maintenance need on premise.

8.   The tenants agree to use premises for residential purposes only. There will be no pets allowed on the premise.

9.   Tenants agree to keep the leasehold premises in good repair and condition until terminations of lease.

10.   No loud music will be played at any time and tenants will conduct themselves properly at all times. They agree to observe all the rules and regulations imposed by the land lord. The landlord will provide parking space for one motor vehicle truck or van. All rules will be strictly enforced by the landlord.

11.   The lease may not be transferred or sublet by the tenant without written consent of the landlord.

12.   The tenants may waive the usual notice to terminate the lease at the end to term and without any notice whatsoever.

13.   This agreement contains all information and supersedes all prior agreements. It cannot be modified, canceled, or annulled unless in writing by both parties.

14.   This agreement shall be binding to both parties. It may be signed in one or more parts and will form one agreement. The lease may be executed by facsimile signatures. The obligations of tenants shall be joint if more than one.

Date_____

Witness_____

Landlord_____

Tenants_____

LEASE AGREEMENT FOR FURNISHED HOUSE

Date: _____

Landlord: _____ Landlord Address: _____

Tenant: _____ Tenant Address: _____

This agreement is made on the above date by and between the Landlord and Tenant listed above. The Landlord hereby agrees to rent to the Tenant the property located at _____ _____ and described as: _____ _____.

1.   Landlord leases to tenant or tenants the furnished property described above for a term of _____ (years), at a monthly rate of $_____.

2.   The property is leased with furnishing to include a list of furnishing that is part of the lease. It is part of lease signed by both parties and dated.

3.   Tenants agree to pay the rent provided subject to terms and conditions of the agreement.

4.   Rent is payable each month in installments of the first day of the month to the address of the Landlord or where he may from time to time request.

5.   Tenants will pay all utilities including gas, water, electric, and oil during lease and any extensions made.

6.   Landlord says that to the best of his knowledge the property is in good condition and violated no housing code, law, or regulations.

7.   Tenant agrees to comply with all sanitary and reasonable housing codes to keep the place clean and well organized while on property.

8.   The tenant will use the property for private residence of no more than _____ people unless otherwise specified and shall make no alterations to the house without written consent of the landlord.

9.   Tenants shall keep the premises in good order and should notify the landlord when repairs are needed or expected to cost _____ or more.

10. Tenants agree to take care of the furnishing, carpeting, draperies, appliances, and all household good of the landlord on the property.

11. Tenant shall replace or repair at own expense any loss or damage caused to furniture, carpets, draperies, or appliances when damage was caused by misuse, waste, or neglect.

12. Tenants shall make all repairs to air conditioning, heating, electric, gas, or fixture at their own expense when loss or damage is caused by misuse waste or neglect.

13. Tenants shall not keep any items on premise that are dangerous, explosive, highly flammable, or considered hazardous by reputable insurance companies.

14. The tenant shall give prompt notice to the landlord of any defective, emergency condition on the premise in a suitable manner. The landlord will be responsible for repair or correct the problem.

15. The landlord will set forth the following rules for the tenant to enjoy the property and follow as guidelines.

16. Tenant agrees not to damage the property or act in a way that is intrusive or offensive to his neighbors. He agrees not to allow anyone on the premise to engage in conduct that will damage or interfere with the comfort to residents and neighbors.

17. Tenants agrees to place a security deposit with neighbors of $_____ used by the landlord at the termination of the lease to pay for cost of replacing or repair damage to the house's furnishings, grounds, and personal effects from negligent acts.

18. The landlord agrees to return security deposit after 10 days of termination under the following conditions listed.

19. Tenants shall give access to the landlord and his agent for reasonable and lawful circumstances. Except in an emergency landlords must give tenants 24 hour notice of needing to enter the property.

20. In the event the tenant defaults on the rent they will be responsible for all rent due during the term of the lease. Landlords will have the option to rent the premises to another tenant for the remainder of the term and will apply the money towards reducing the tenant's financial obligations.

21. Tenant shall permit the landlord or his agents to show property at reasonable hours to persons desiring to rent or purchase within 30 days of agreement expiration date. They will permit a sign to be placed on the property For Sale or For Rent.

22. In the event the tenant breaches the agreement, the landlord will give him _____ days' written notice to correct the problem. If within _____ days he has not made any attempt to correct the problem, the landlord can terminate his lease. The terminations shall be voided if the tenant corrects the problem. After termination proceeding may be made to remove the tenant by law if he has not vacated the premises.

23. The landlord agrees to deliver the possession of agreed property at the beginning of term to the tenant. If he fails to have property ready for occupancy when stated the tenant has the right to rescind the lease and have any money paid returned to him.

24. Any notice required will be give in writing mailed U.S.-certified mail with a return receipt requested and one copy mailed via U.S.-first class mail. Notice will be sent to tenants at lease property and notice to landlord or agent at its correct address.

25. This lease represents the entire agreement between both Parties and hereby supersedes any previous understanding or representation, oral or written, between these Parties. No changes will be made except in writing by each party and dated.

26. In the event that legal action is required to enforce any provision of this agreement the prevailing party shall be entitled to recovery of reasonable attorney fees.

27. Landlord and tenant agree that this lease when filled out and signed is a binding legal agreement.

Date _____

Landlord _____

Tenant or Tenants _____

CONDO UNIT RIDER

1. Lease and Rider:

The Lease and Rider is attached to and part of a lease dated _____ between the undersigned _____ and _____ leasing a Condo at the following address: _____.

In the event of any conflicts concerning the rider or the lease the terms of the Rider shall overwrite or control. Unless the agreement clearly states otherwise the rider refers to the lease and vice versa. Defined terms in the lease such as landlord, tenant, apartment, or condo will be modified to correspond to the agreement made or that has been defined in the rider.

2. Condo Status:

Tenants agrees the unit being rented is a condo unit. It is subject to the Declaration of Condominium Ownership that was recorded in the Office of the Recorder of Deeds _____ (location) _____ (state). Leased to the tenant as part of the unit is the right to use any limited common elements and use these elements along with other condominium owners and occupants. Tenants will abide by any rules and regulations written by the Condominium's association rules.

Upon written request, the landlord will make a copy of the Declaration of Condominium Ownership or association rules. Tenants agree to abide by all rules and restrictions imposed on owners and occupants of the premises. Any violations of rules by tenants will be considered a breach of the lease. Tenant agrees to let the association proceed with determining the consequences of the breach. The condo association is a third-party beneficiary of this provision.

3. Indemnification:
Tenant releases the landlord from any legal responsibility, loss, cost, damages, or expenses incurred by tenant as result of breach of Paragraph 2 above.

4. Tenant Maintenance:
It is the responsibility of the tenant to replace light bulbs, filters, and common replaceable elements in fixtures when necessary. They will be responsible for damage of overflow of drains or plumbing if they or guests purposely misused the fixture.

5. Right to Refuse:
Tenant agrees that this agreement is_____ or is not_____ subject to the right of refusal to the condominium associations or board of manager. If such an option is exercised than the lease will terminate and the landlord will have no obligation to the tenant except to refund any money paid.

6. Notices:
Tenant will forward to the landlord any notice from the condo association or board relating to meetings or complaints about the tenants actions or breach of rules.

7. Exculpation:
The tenant acknowledges that the Condo association and not the landlord are responsible for provisions, repairs, and maintenance of the facilities and services. Landlords shall have no responsibility to maintain the facilities and services controlled by the association provided that through written request of the tenant the landlord will contract the association to request the necessary repairs needed for the unit.

Signature _____
Landlord
Signature_____
Condo Association Rep
Signature_____
Tenant
Date _____

REAL ESTATE SUBLEASE

Date: _____
Landlord: _____ Landlord Address: _____
Tenant: _____ Tenant Address: _____

This sublease is entered on this date by and between the Landlord and Tenant listed above.

The landlord agrees to sublease to the tenant the following premises to be used for a
_____ for the term beginning _____ and ending
_____ at the monthly rent as provided in paragraph 19.

1.   Payment of rent tenant shall be paid at the following address:
_____.

2.   The tenant will keep the property in good condition. The landlord will repair the roof, exterior and other problems unless caused by negligence on the tenant's part.

3.   The tenant shall comply with all regulations and ordinances of federal, state, and county. The tenant will not be required to make any changes or repairs to the exterior of the building.

4.   The tenant during the last three months of the lease will permit the landlord to show the property to other people and to put a sign up advertising the vacancy. The landlord and agent may enter the premise for the purpose of checking the condition of the property and making repairs.

5.   The tenant will not make or permit changes or additions to property with written consent of the landlord. If the landlord agrees, the tenant shall make changes to the property. If required, the tenant must obtain written permission of the owner too.

6.   The tenant will not leave the premise unoccupied thus causing an increase in insurance or cancellation of the policy. In event of an increase caused by the tenant, they agree to pay the increase or supply another insurance policy to the satisfaction of the landlord.

7.   The tenant will not put any awnings or signs on the premises without written consent. They will keep sidewalks clear of ice, snow, and all obstructions.

8.   The tenant will make arrangements for all utilities and be responsible for payment of electric, phone, water, and heating.

9.   The tenant will not be responsible for any defect or damage to premises unless caused by acts of negligence or purposeful destruction of the property by the tenants or occupants.

10.   Fire Clause. If the property is damaged by fire or other casualty occurrences, the lease will terminate and the unpaid rent will be returned to the tenant.

11.   If the tenant fails to observe the following conditions the landlord may terminate or cancel the lease notifying the tenant in writing of such termination or cancellation. The tenant will be responsible for all damages occurred. The tenant will have ten day to correct the problem before further action is taken. If the problem is corrected, the lease will be still in effect. If no action is taken, the landlord will be able to remove the tenant through proper legal action.

12.   Any notices will be sent to each party through registered mail and addressed to the proper address where the tenant or landlord resides.

13.   This is a sublease to the tenant on the premises made by _____ on the date _____. A copy is attached here and made part of Exhibit A.

The sublease contains all terms and condition of the lease and does not omit anything that will breach the lease agreement. If the lease is terminated, the sublease will terminate and tenant will be reimbursed for any unearned rent paid in advance. The landlord and tenant waive all rights against each other for damages are sustained on the premises caused by fire, flood, hurricane and other perils covered by insurance.

14. Rent payments. Beginning on _____(date) and ending on _____(date) the monthly rental shall be $_____ . During the term of this sublease, no term of the underlying lease shall be effective to increase or decrease the monthly rental. Rent will be payable in advance on first day of each month during the term of this sublease to the landlord or tenant owning the lease.

15. The tenant agrees to pay a security deposit of $_____ to the landlord for compliance with the terms of the agreement. The security deposit cannot be applied to delinquent rent. Landlord's costs for repairing unreported damages will be deducted with the security deposit.

16. In the event that litigation results from sublease and this agreement, agreement and all transactions shall be enforced in accordance with law of the State of _____. The parties waive trial by jury and agree to submit to the personal venue of the court of subject matter located in _____ County, State of _____.

17. This agreement is binding between the owner, landlord, and tenant when signed, and all terms will be complied with.

Signed
Landlord_____
Tenant_____
Building Owner_____
Date_____

Consent of Building Owner in Primary Lease
The owner consents to the sublease of the property located at

_____

Dated_____
Owner_____

CHAPTER 7

Residential Lease/ Purchase Agreements

RESIDENTIAL LEASE

Date: _____

Landlord: _____

Address: _____

City: _____ State: _____ Zip: _____

Tenant: _____

Address: _____

City: _____ State: _____ Zip: _____

1. Parties and Premises:

This Lease agreement is made on _____, 20__, between _____,
(Landlord) and _____ (Tenant). Landlord rents to Tenant
and Tenant rents from Landlord for use as a residence, an unfurnished apartment, located at _____ in the City of _____, County of
_____, State of _____.

NOW, THEREFORE, for and in consideration of the covenants and obligations contained herein and other good and valuable consideration, the receipt and sufficiency of
which is hereby acknowledged, the parties hereto hereby agree as follows:

2. Term:

Landlord leases to Tenant and Tenant leases from Landlord the above described Premises
together with any and all appurtenances thereto, for a term of _____
[specify number of months or years]. The initial term of this lease begins on____ , 20__ ,
and ends on_____ , 20____, under the following terms and conditions:

3. Rent:

Tenant agrees to pay in advance on the first day of each month, a total of _____Dollars ($_____) rent for the premises, payable by check or money order, at the Landlord's address. If not received by Landlord before the 6th of the month, rent will be considered late unless an alternative payment plan has been established by written agreement. Late payments will affect future tenant credit references.

4. Security Deposit:

On execution of this agreement, Tenant will deposit with Landlord a Security Deposit of _____Dollars ($_____), receipt of which is acknowledged by Landlord, as guarantee for the full and faithful performance by Tenant of this agreement. Deposit shall be refundable within 14 days after the date that the premises are surrendered. Landlord may retain all or a portion of the security deposit as compensation for the following: nonpayment of rent; damages to property; nonpayment of utilities for which Tenant is responsible; cleaning or maintenance fees outside of normal wear and tear; expenses for removal or disposal of articles abandoned by Tenant.

5. Utilities:

The responsibility for payment to entities providing utilities, and other services to the premises during the term of the Lease shall be as follows:

Heat:			
Electricity:			
Water/Sewer:			
Trash:			
Other (Specify):			

6. Household Members:

Tenant agrees that the demised premises shall be occupied solely by the following house-hold members:

Any person not named above may not live in the unit without the written permission of Landlord. Tenant shall not assign this Agreement, or sublet or grant any license to use the Premises or any part thereof without the prior written consent of Landlord.

7. Peaceful Enjoyment:

Tenant shall conduct himself or herself and require other persons on the premises to conduct themselves in a manner that will not disturb other tenants' or neighbors' peace-ful enjoyment of the premises. Tenant will not use the building for immoral or illegal purposes. Tenant will comply with the terms of any local noise ordinances which may apply. Receipt of two (2) notices of violation of such ordinance will constitute grounds for termination of this lease.

8. Property Access:

Landlord may enter the apartment with the Tenant's consent, which shall not be un-reasonably withheld. Landlord may also enter the apartment for the following purposes between the hours of 9 AM and 9 PM after giving at least 48 hours' notice: to inspect the premises, to make repairs, alterations, or improvements, or to show the unit to prospective purchasers, mortgagees, tenants, contractors, and/or workers. Landlord may also enter the dwelling without notice if there is a reasonable belief that any person or property is in imminent danger.

9. Default:

Failure to comply with any of the provisions of this Agreement or of any present or future rules and regulations prescribed by Landlord, will result in Termination of the Lease. Notice will be delivered in writing by Landlord specifying the non-compliance and indicating the intention of Landlord to terminate the Lease by reason thereof and within seven (7) days after delivery of written notice Landlord may terminate this Agreement. If Tenant fails to pay rent when due and the default continues for seven (7) days thereafter, Landlord may declare the entire balance of rent payable immediately and may exercise any and all rights and remedies available, or may immediately terminate this Agreement.

10. Late Charge:

If payment by Tenant is not made within five (5) days of when due, Tenant shall pay to Landlord, in addition to such payment or other charges due hereunder, a "late fee" in the amount of _____ dollars ($_____).

11. Eviction:

Failure by the Tenant to pay rent or other charges promptly shall constitute a default of this agreement and permit Landlord at its discretion to terminate this lease after giving 14 days' written notice to Tenant. Failure to comply with any other term or condition of this agreement shall also constitute a default and Landlord may terminate this tenancy after giving 30 days' written notice to Tenant. Upon such termination(s), Tenant agrees to forfeit all leasehold rights of and surrender possession.

12. Housekeeping:

Tenants will keep and maintain the premises in a clean and sanitary condition at all times. At the expiration or termination of this lease, tenant will surrender the premises to Landlord in as good condition as when received, ordinary wear and tear and damage by the elements excepted. Tenant will not deliberately destroy, damage, or remove any part of the premises or its fixtures, appliances, mechanical systems or furnishings or permit any person to do so. Tenant will not remove any tree, shrubbery, vine, or plant from the premises. Personal possessions cannot be stored in the common area or basement without prior written consent from Landlord.

(a) To keep the premises as clean and sanitary as the condition permits.

(b) To remove from the dwelling unit all garbage and other waste in a clean and sanitary manner.

(c) To properly use and operate all electrical, cooking, and plumbing fixtures and to keep them as clean and sanitary as their condition permits.

13. Repairs and Alterations:

Landlord is responsible for repairs to the interior and exterior of the premises, unless caused by the negligence of the Tenant. Tenant is responsible to notify Landlord promptly of any damage or malfunction of which the Tenant is aware. Tenant will be responsible for any repairs caused by his/her negligence. Tenant will immediately reimburse Landlord for all expenses for repairs made by Owner/Landlord/contracting party due to Tenant's negligence. Tenant agrees to occupy the premises as a residential dwelling, and to use the areas of the premises for living, sleeping, cooking, or dining purposes as they were intended to be used.

Prior written consent of Landlord must be obtained before making any alterations, additions, or improvements on the premises. Landlord's consent to a particular alteration, addition, or improvement does not constitute consent to future alterations, additions, or improvements.

14. Fire or Other Casualty:

If the premises are destroyed or damaged by fire or other casualty to the extent that the Landlord decides that repair is not warranted economically, then this lease shall terminate and rent will not be owed for the period that premises are not habitable. If the premises become partially uninhabitable because of fire or other casualty, then a proportionate part of the rent will be abated until the premises are restored to their former condition. If heat or other utilities cease to function for any cause beyond the control of the Landlord, the obligation of Tenant under the terms of this lease shall not be affected, and tenant shall not make any claim be made against the Landlord by Tenant.

15. Month-To-Month Holdover:

Should Tenant remain in possession of the premises with the consent of Landlord after the lease expires, a new month-to-month agreement shall be created between Landlord and Tenant that shall be subject to all the terms and conditions of this lease.

16. More Than One Tenant:

In the event that two or more Tenants are named in this lease, delivery of any notice by Landlord to any one of the Tenants shall be construed as effective service of notice to all Tenants residing on the premises. Each Tenant signing this lease shall be jointly and severally liable to Landlord for all obligations arising under this lease.

17. Attorneys' Fees:

If suit is brought by Landlord for possession of the premises for the recovery of any rent due under the provision of this agreement, or for breach of any obligation by Tenant arising under this agreement or by law, Tenant agrees to pay Landlord all costs including reasonable attorneys' fees.

18. Tenant's Possession:

Tenant agrees to buy Renter's Insurance in order to protect his or her belongings.

19. Parking:

The apartment is provided to Tenant without off-street parking.

20. All Conditions of Lease Agreement:

This lease constitutes the entire agreement between the parties. The breach of any condition of this lease is to be considered substantial. This lease is executed in two copies, each copy to be considered an original for all purposes.

This lease shall be governed by the Laws of the State of _____.

In witness whereof, the parties have executed this agreement on the date given at the beginning of this document.

_____

[Landlord's Name]

_____

[Landlord's Address]

_____

[Tenant's Name]

_____

_____

[Tenant's Address]

ADDENDUM TO RESIDENTIAL LEASE AGREEMENT FOR RENTAL ITEMS

Date: _____

Landlord: _____

Tenant: _____

Property Address: _____

In regard to the Residential Lease Agreement made between the abovementioned Landlord and Tenant and the property listed above, the Parties hereby make agreement that the following will be rented to the Tenant at the extra charge listed below. During time of rental of said items, any maintenance and repairs should be made by Tenant unless otherwise stated below. The additional charge may be in the form of a one-time deposit due at the signing of this addendum or in a monthly charge to be added to the monthly rent due. If payment is not made on time, Landlord has the right to repossess the item/appliance.

Name of Rental Item/Appliance	Additional Charge for Rental	Maintenance/Repair Responsibility
Refrigerator		
Stove/Range		
Washer		
Dryer		
Microwave		
Dishwasher		
Furniture: _____		
Furniture: _____		
Electronic: _____		
Electronic: _____		
Grill (Gas/Propane)		
Lawn Mower		
Weed Eater		

Other:		
Other:		

Both parties by signing below hereby agree to this addendum and in this make it a part of the abovementioned Residential Lease Agreement. Any changes to this addendum must be made in writing and signed by both the Landlord and Tenant.

_____

Tenant Signed

_____

Landlord Signed

CHAPTER 8

Rental Agreements, Applications, and Forms

RENTAL APPLICATION 1

Date: _____

Application is hereby made to rent premises described as _____ for a term of _____ and ending the ___ day of _____, 20__, for which monthly rental shall be _____, payable in advance, and for which a security deposit of $ _____ shall be due before occupancy of the above-described premises.

A deposit of _____ is made herewith for the first month's rent, with the understanding that it will be forfeited as liquidated damages if this application is accepted and the applicant fails to execute a lease before the beginning date specified above, or if the applicant fails to pay the balance due as first month's rent. It is also understood that if this application is not accepted, or if the premises are not ready for occupancy by the applicant on the date specified above, the deposit will be refunded to the applicant at the applicant's request.

APPLICANT/SPOUSE INFORMATION

Name: _____ SS #: _____
Driver's License #: _____ State: _____
Spouse's Name: _____ SS#: _____
Driver's License #_____ State: _____
Number of children: _____
Number of dogs: _____
Number of cats: _____
Other pets, please state what kind and how many of each:

_____

ADDRESS INFORMATION:

Current Address: _____

How long have you been at your current address? _____

If less than 5 years, please give your previous address: _____

How long were you living at the previous address? _____

EMPLOYMENT INFORMATION:

Applicant:

Current Employer: _____

Employer Address: _____

Name of person to contact at your employment: _____

Contact Phone number: _____

Number of years employed? _____

Annual Income: _____

If you have been employed with this company less than 5 years, where was your former employment? _____

Name of person to contact at your former employment: _____

Contact Phone Number of Former Employment: _____

Spouse:

Current Employer: _____

Employer Address: _____

Name of person to contact at your employment: _____

Contact Phone number: _____

Number of years employed? _____

Annual Income: _____

If you have been employed with this company less than 5 years, where was your former employment? _____

Name of person to contact at your former employment: _____

Contact Phone Number of Former Employment: _____

REFERENCES:

Employer Reference: _____ Phone: _____

Personal Reference: _____ Phone: _____

Credit Reference: _____ Phone: _____

The information provided here may be used by the landlord or his agent to determine whether to accept this application. On written request within _____ days, the landlord or his agent will disclose to applicant in writing what kind of investigation landlord has requested, if any. If this application is refused, applicant will receive a written statement of the reason for the refusal.

Accepted _____ Denied_____

RENTAL APPLICATION II

An application should be filled out for each adult applying for tenancy.

Applicant: Be sure to fill out application in its entirety. No blanks should remain. The result of your credit history and reference check will be our main decision-maker on whether or not we will rent to you. Only those applicants who are responsible should apply.

Where did you hear about us?
❑ Newspaper   ❑ Signage   ❑ A Friend   ❑ Other: _____

1. PERSONAL INFORMATION:

Full Name: _____

Phone: _____

Work Phone: _____

Social Security Number _____-_____-_____

Current Driver's License #_____ State_____

Current Address _____

City _____ State_____ Zip_____

How Long? _____

If you currently rent, list your apartment name/location: _____

Landlord Name: _____

Phone: _____

Alternative Phone: _____

Current Rent Amount $_____

Why are you leaving your current residence?

_____

Previous Address _____

City _____ State_____ Zip_____

How long? _____

If you rented, list the name/location: _____

Landlord Name: _____

Phone: _____

Alternative Phone: _____

Rent Amount $_____

Why did you leave your previous residence?

_____

Current Employer: _____

Position/ Title: _____

How long have you been with your current employer? _____

Address: _____

Phone: _____

Gross Monthly Income *before deductions*: $_____

Other Income Amount: $_____ Source of other income: _____

Former Employer: _____

Position/Title: _____ How long with this employer? _____

Address: _____

Phone: _____

Why did you leave your previous employer?

_____

Are you a smoker? ❑ Yes   ❑ No

2. CREDIT REFERENCES:
This section may include bank accounts, credit cards, store credit accounts, etc.

1.   Bank Name: _____
       Address: _____City _____
       State _____ Zip _____
       Account Number(s): _____
       This account is a: ❑ Checking Account   ❑ Savings Account
                       ❑ Loan Account(s)
       Approx. Balance $_____ How long? _____

2.   Other Active Credit Account: _____
       Type of Account: _____
       Account Number(s): _____
       Expiration Date: _____
       Credit Limit: $_____
       Length of Account: _____
       All Payments Made on Time? ❑ Yes ❑ No

3.   Other Active Credit Account: _____
       Type of Account: _____
       Account Number(s): _____
       Expiration Date: _____
       Credit Limit: $_____
       Length of Account: _____
       All Payments Made on Time? ❑ Yes ❑ No

Have you ever been evicted from any residence? ❑ Yes ❑ No
Have you ever had a foreclosure/repossession (home, vehicle, etc)?
❑ Yes ❑ No
Date of occurrence: _____
If yes, please explain: _____

Have you ever filed for bankruptcy?
❑ Yes [❑ Chapter 7 or ❑ Chapter 13]   ❑ No
If yes, please explain: _____

Have you ever been convicted of a crime? ❑ Yes ❑ No
If yes, please explain: _____

3. PERSONAL REFERENCES:
(Please provide us with three (3) people (non-relatives that we may contact to verify your character.)

1.   Name: _____
       Relationship: _____
       Address: _____
       Phone Number: _____
2.   Name: _____
       Relationship: _____
       Address: _____

Phone Number: _____
3.   Name: _____
Relationship: _____
Address: _____
Phone Number: _____

4. EMERGENCY:

Please list two relatives we may contact in case of an emergency.
Name: _____
Relationship: _____
Address: _____
Phone Number: _____

Name: _____
Relationship: _____
Address: _____
Phone Number: _____

5. OTHER INFORMATION:

Please list other persons who will be living in the residence, including any children.
Name: _____
Child or Adult: _____
Name: _____
Child or Adult: _____

6. PETS:

Name: _____
Type: _____
Weight: _____
Name: _____
Type: _____
Weight: _____

NOTE: Management MUST approve of any pets on the premises. A fee of $____ will be required before any approved pet may be brought onto the premises. NO exceptions will be made.

7. AUTOMOBILES:

Please list all automobiles you plan to keep on the premises.

MAKE	COLOR	MODEL	YEAR	LICENSE PLATE#	STATE	MONTHLY PAYMENT

Desired Move-in Date: _____
Anticipated Length of Tenancy: _____

In order to process your application, a non-refundable $_____ application fee is required. This fee is due at the time you put in your application for processing and may not be waived for any reason. By signing below, you hereby agree that if you are approved for tenancy after review of your application, you will rent this residence. You also agree that if you are accepted for residency and you decide not to move in, any and all fees or rents paid will not be returned. The money retained will not be returned in order to cover costs associated with your decision not to rent this property as other potential tenants may have been refused tenancy. Landlord will need to pay for costs associated with re-advertising the property and reviewing other applications.

Your application will be processed in a timely manner and the results of our review will be delivered in one of three ways: telephone, fax, or via mail. Once your application has been approved, you agree to pay the remainder of funds due and complete all paperwork within _____ hours. If you do not do so, management will assume that you have elected to forfeit your reservation and deposit management will re-advertise the unit. If your application is denied, all money paid with this application will be reimbursed, minus the application fee.

Please attach a copy of the following required documents when submitting your application:
- Driver's License/Photo I.D.
- Social Security Card
- Most Recent Pay Check Stub(s)
- Most Recent W-2 Form OR Last Year's Tax Return

I declare that the application is complete, true, and correct and I herewith give my permission for anyone contacted to release the credit or personal information of the undersigned applicant to Management or their authorized agents, at any time, for the purposes of entering into and continuing to offer or collect on any agreement and/or credit extended. I further authorize Management or their Authorized Agents to verify the application information including but not limited to obtaining criminal records, contacting creditors, present or former landlords, employers, and personal references, whether listed or not, at the time of the application and at any time in the future, with regard to any agreement entered into with Management. Any false information will constitute ground for rejection of the application, or Management may at any time immediately terminate any agreement entered into in reliance upon misinformation given on this application.

_____   _____
Applicant's Signature   Date of Application

RENTAL APPLICATION III

This application is subject to the Landlord/Owner's approval. We require a separate application to be filled out for every resident over the age of 18.

THIS SECTION TO BE COMPLETED BY LANDLORD/OWNER

Property Address: _____
UNIT _____
Rental Term: ____ Lease (From _____ to _____)
____ Month-to-Month
Amount Due Before Tenancy: $_____ (1st Month) $_____ (Last Month)
$_____ (Security)

THIS SECTION TO BE COMPLETED BY APPLICANT

Full Name: _____
Date of Birth: _____
Social Security Number: _____
Home Phone Number: _____
Work Phone Number: _____
Vehicle Information: _____ (Make)
_____ (Model) _____ (Year)
License Plate Number: _____ State: _____
Driver's License Number: _____ State: _____

Lessor's Disclosure of Information on Lead-Based Paint and/or Lead-Based Paint Hazards

Lead Warning Statement

Housing built before 1978 may contain lead-based paint. Lead from paint, paint chips, and dust can pose health hazards if not managed properly. Lead exposure is especially harmful to young children and pregnant women. Before renting pre-1978 housing, lessors must disclose the presence of known lead based paint and/or lead-based paint hazards in the dwelling. Lessees must also receive a federally approved pamphlet on lead poisoning prevention.

Lessor's Disclosure

(a) Presence of lead-based paint and/or lead-based paint hazards (check (i) or (ii) below):

    (i)   _____ Known lead-based paint and/or lead-based paint hazards are present in the housing (explain).

        _____

    (ii)   _____ Lessor has no knowledge of lead-based paint and/or lead-based paint hazards in the housing.

(b) Records and reports available to the lessor (check (i) or (ii) below):

    (i)   _____ Lessor has provided the lessee with all available records and reports pertaining to lead-based paint and/or lead-based paint hazards in the housing (list documents below).

        _____

    (ii)   _____ Lessor has no reports or records pertaining to lead-based paint and/or lead-based paint hazards in the housing.

Lessee's Acknowledgment (initial)

(c) _____ Lessee has received copies of all information listed above.

(d) _____ Lessee has received the pamphlet *Protect Your Family from Lead in Your Home.*

Agent's Acknowledgment (initial)

(e) _____ Agent has informed the lessor of the lessor's obligations under 42 U.S.C. 4852d and is aware of his/her responsibility to ensure compliance.

Certification of Accuracy

The following parties have reviewed the information above and certify, to the best of their knowledge, that the information they have provided is true and accurate.

_____   _____
Lessor   Date

_____   _____
Lessee   Date

_____   _____
Agent   Date

RENTAL CONTRACT

Date: _____

Owner(s): _____

Address: _____

City: _____ State: _____ Zip: _____

Resident(s): _____

Address: _____

City: _____ State: _____ Zip: _____

The Landlord agrees to rent the dwelling located at

Address: _____

City: _____ State: _____ Zip: _____

to the Resident(s), known as: _____, for the period beginning on the ____day of _____ (month), 20____, and monthly thereafter until the last day of _____ (month), 20_____, at which time this Agreement will end.

Resident(s) agree(s) to the following terms:

1. Rent:

Resident(s) will pay in advance on the first day of every month the amount of $_____ as rent. Failure to pay rent on time will result in the Owner taking immediate legal action to evict the Resident from the premises and seize the security deposit.

2. Late Fee:

Rent received after the first of the month will be subject to a late fee of 10%, plus $ _____ dollars per day.

3. Bad Checks:

Resident(s) further agree(s) to pay a service charge of $10 or 5% of the amount of any dishonored check, whichever is greater, regardless of the reason.

4. Security Deposit:

Resident agrees to pay a security deposit of $_____ as a guarantee that resident(s) will fully comply with the terms of this agreement. The Security Deposit may not be applied by the tenant towards unpaid rent at any time during the tenancy. At the end of the tenancy, Owner will deduct any damages, unpaid rent, or charges, and disburse the remainder to the resident.

5. Appliances:

Appliances located at or in the property are there solely at the convenience of the Owner, who assumes no responsibility for their operation. In the event that such appliances fail to function after occupancy is started, the Resident(s) may repair them at their own expense or ask that Owner remove them.

6. Pre-Payment Discount:

As an incentive to the Resident to be responsible for all maintenance of the premises and yard each month, and to make rent payments ahead of time, a discount in the amount of $_____ may be deducted from the above rental sum each month. THIS DISCOUNT WILL BE FORFEITED IF THE RESIDENT FAILS TO PERFORM AS STATED ABOVE. If the discount is lost one month, the resident may still receive the discount in subsequent months by complying with the terms of this agreement. Discounts that are lost because a maintenance call by the Landlord was necessary during the month will be added to the amount of the next month's rent.

7. Extra Visitors:

Only the _____ adults and _____ children named below may reside in the dwelling.

_____

Resident(s) agree(s) to pay $75.00 each month for each extra person who shall occupy the premises in any capacity other than visiting.

8. Condition of Property:

Resident(s) accept(s) the condition of the property "AS IS," waives inspection of property by Owner, and agrees to notify Owner of any defects.

9. Loss or Damage:

Resident further agrees to indemnify Owner against any loss, damage, or liability arising out of Resident's use of the property, including visitors using the property with Resident's consent.

10. Cleaning:

Resident(s) accept(s) premises in its current state of cleanliness and agrees to return it in like condition.

11. Maintenance:

During the period of this agreement, resident(s) agree(s) to maintain the premises including woodwork, floors, walls, furnishings and fixtures, appliances, windows, screens doors, lawns, landscaping, fences, plumbing, electrical, air conditioning and heating, and mechanical systems. Resident is specifically responsible to replace and/or clean filters on HVAC units regularly. Any damages caused to units because of failure to change and clean filters will be paid for by the Resident. Resident will remove tacks, nails, or other hangers nailed or screwed into the walls or ceilings at the termination of this agreement. Damage caused by rain, hail, or wind as a result of leaving windows or doors open, or damage caused by overflow of water or stoppage of waste pipes, breakage of glass, damage to screens, or deterioration of lawns and landscaping resulting from abuse or neglect, is the responsibility of the Resident. Resident agrees to provide pest control if needed.

12. Vehicles:

Resident agrees never to park or store a motor home, recreational vehicle, commercial vehicle or trailer of any type on the premises; and to park only_____ automobiles described as follows: _____

Parking is allowed ONLY ON THE PAVED DRIVEWAYS PROVIDED. No vehicle may be repaired or stored on the property without a current registration and tag, except in the garage. ANY VEHICLE PARKED ON ANY UNPAVED AREAS OR WITHOUT A CURRENT REGISTRATION MAY BE TOWED AND STORED AT RESIDENT'S EXPENSE BY A TOWING SERVICE.

13. Pets:

Resident will pay a non-refundable pet fee of $_____ per month per pet. All pets found on the property that are not registered under this agreement will be treated as strays and disposed of by the appropriate agency as prescribed by law. A Resident(s) found to be harboring an undisclosed pet will pay a pet fee for the entire term of this lease, regardless of when the pet was first introduced to the premises. The Resident specifically understands and agrees:

A. No pet that is attacked-trained or vicious, or known to have bitten people or damaged property, will be kept on the premises;

B. Resident is solely responsible for any and all damage done by a pet to the owner's property including, but not limited to the premises, carpeting, draperies, blinds, wall coverings, furnishings, appliances, and landscaping, including the lawn and shrubbery;

C. Resident is responsible for any and all damage or loss to persons or property of others caused by the Resident's pet(s) and agrees to hold the owner harmless for any such damage;

D. All pet(s) will be cared for and maintained in a humane and lawful manner;

E. All pet waste shall be removed and disposed of promptly, including waste deposited in neighbor's yards by Resident's pets;

F. All pets shall be maintained so as to not cause annoyance to others.

14. Resident's Obligations:

The Resident agrees to meet all of resident's obligations; including:

A. Compliance with all applicable building, housing, and health codes.

B. Keeping the dwelling clean, and sanitary; removing garbage and trash as they accumulate; maintaining plumbing in good working order to prevent stoppages and/or leakage of plumbing, fixtures, faucets, and pipes.

C. Operating all electrical, plumbing, sanitary, heating, ventilating, A/C, and other appliances in a reasonable and safe manner.

D. Safeguarding property belonging to the owner against damage, destruction, loss, removal, or theft.

E. Conducting him/herself, his/her family, friends, guests, and visitors in a manner that will not disturb others. Resident agrees to meet the above conditions in every respect, and agrees that failure to do so will be grounds for termination of this agreement and loss of all deposits without further recourse.

15. Subletting:

Resident agrees not to assign this agreement, nor to sub-let any part of the property, nor to allow any other person to live on the premises except those named in paragraph 4 above, without first obtaining the written consent of the Owner and paying the appropriate surcharge. Resident agrees that a failure to comply with the provisions contained in the Rental Agreement cannot be corrected after the fact; and that eviction proceedings may be begun at once without notice.

16. Court Costs:

Resident agrees to pay all court costs and reasonable Attorney's fees arising from the Owner's enforcement of legal action against Resident or any of the Owner's other rights under this agreement or any state law. If any provision in this Agreement is found to be unenforceable under the law, the remaining provisions shall continue to be valid and subject to enforcement in the courts without exception.

17. Owner's Statements:

All rights given to the Owner by this agreement shall be cumulative in addition to any other laws that might exist or come into being. A one-time exercise or failure to exercise, by the Owner, of any right shall not be construed as a waiver of any other rights. No statement or promise of Owner or his agent as to tenancy, repairs, alternations, or other terms and conditions shall be binding unless made in writing and signed by Owner.

18. Partial Payment:

The acceptance by the Owner of a partial payments of rent due shall not, under any circumstance, constitute a waiver of the Owner's rights, nor affect any notice or legal eviction proceedings commenced under state law.

19. Abandonment:

Resident's absence from these premises for 15 days while rent is due and unpaid, shall be considered abandonment. In case of abandonment, this agreement gives Owner the right to take immediate possession of the property and to exclude Resident(s) from entering the property; removing at his/her expense all his/her personal property contained in the residence and placing it into storage at Resident's expense.

20. Utilities:

Residents are responsible for payments of all utilities, garbage, water and sewer charges, telephone, gas, or other bills incurred during their residency. Resident(s) specifically authorize the Owner to deduct amounts of unpaid utility bills from their deposits after termination of this agreement.

21. Personal Property:

This agreement confers no rights of storage. The owner shall not be liable for any personal injury or loss of property by fire, theft, breakage, burglary, or otherwise, for any accidental damage to persons, guests, or property in or about the leased/rented property resulting from electrical failure, water, rain, windstorm, or any act of God, or negligence of owner, or owners agent, contractors, or employees, or by any other cause, whatsoever. Resident agrees to make no claim for any such damages or loss against owner. Resident will purchase the necessary "renters insurance" or provide self-insurance in adequate amounts to cover any risk. Resident agrees to list Owner as "additional insured" on any such insurance policies.
_____ (initials)

22. Removal of Property:

Resident agrees not to remove Owner's property or make any alterations or improvements without first obtaining specific written permission from the Owner. Any removal/alteration of Owner's property without permission will be considered abandonment and surrender of the premises, and termination by the Resident of this agreement. The Owner may take immediate possession and exclude Residents from the property, storing all Resident's possessions at Resident's expense, pending reimbursement in full for Owner's loss and damages.

23. Waterbeds:

If any occupant of the premises uses a flotation bedding system, the Resident shall be required to carry an insurance policy with a loss payable clause payable to the Owner, covering personal injury and damage to the Owner, in a form standard to the industry, with a minimum limit of $100,000. If the Resident installs a flotation bed installation without securing the required insurance and providing the Owner with a copy as evidence, the Resident will be considered in default.

24. Termination:

After payment of one month's rent, this agreement may be terminated by mutual consent of the parties, or by written notice given by either party at least 15 days prior to the end of any monthly period. Owner may alter or modify any provision of this agreement by giving resident written notice at least 15 days prior to the end of any monthly period. All parties agree that termination of this agreement prior to _____ (date), regardless of cause, will constitute a breach of the tenancy and that in such case all deposits shall be forfeited in favor of the owner as full liquidated damages at the owner's option.

25. Method of Payment:

The deposit and first rent payment under this agreement must be made in cash, or with a cashier's check drawn on a local financial institution. Subsequent monthly rent payments may be paid by personal or business check until and unless a check is dishonored and returned unpaid. Whatever the reason, once a check has been dishonored, no other additional payments may afterward be made by check. Returned checks will not be redeposited. The Resident will receive 3 days' written notice and will be required to pay the amount due, including the bad check charge, in cash. Resident is aware that past rent, damages, utilities, or other costs owed by Resident may affect Resident's ability to obtain credit for future housing.

26. Delivery Of Rents:

Rents may be mailed through the U.S. mail to:
Address: _____
City: _____ State: _____ Zip: _____

Any rents lost in the mail will be treated as if unpaid until received by Owner. It is recommended that payments made by cash or money order be delivered in person to the owner's office at the above address. In order for the tenant to qualify for a discount, rents must be received by mail or in-person on or before the due date.

27. Return of Deposit:

Security Deposits will be deposited for the Resident's benefit in a non-interest bearing bank account. Release of these deposits is subject to the provisions of State Statues and according to the following terms:

A. The full term of this rental agreement has been completed.
B. Formal written notice has been given at least 15 days prior to the end of any monthly period.
C. Premises, building(s), or grounds have been inspected and there is no evident damage.
D. The entire dwelling, appliance, closets, and cupboards are clean and free of insect pests, the refrigerator is defrosted, and all debris and rubbish has been removed from the property; the carpets are cleaned and odorless.

E.   Any and all unpaid charges, including pet charges, late charges, extra visitor charges, delinquent rents, and utility charges, have been paid in full.

F.   All keys have been returned, including keys to any new locks installed while resident was in possession.

G.   A forwarding address has been left with the owner.

The balance of the deposit will be sent 30 days after termination of this agreement to the address provided by the Resident, payable to the signatories of this agreement. If Owner imposes a claim on the deposit, Resident will be notified by certified letter. If such written claim is not sent, the Owner relinquishes the right to make any further claim on the deposit and must return it to the Resident, provided Resident has given the Owner notice of intent to vacate, abandon, and terminate this agreement proper to the expiration of its full term, at least 15 days in advance.

28. Phone:

If telephone land line is required, resident is responsible to install and maintain telephone service, and agrees to furnish to the owner the phone number, and any changes, within 3 days after installation.

29. Gas, Electric, and Water:

Resident agrees to transfer the gas, electric, and water service charges to his or her name immediately upon occupancy and to make arrangements for meter readings as needed.

30. Three (3) Day Inspection:

Under the terms of this discount lease/rental agreement, Residents will be provided with an inspection sheet. Resident will inspect the premises and fill out and return the inspection sheet to the Owner within 3 days after taking possession of the premises. If no defects have been reported after 3 days have expired, it will be assumed that the property and its appurtenances are functioning in a satisfactory manner in all respects. Resident agrees that failure to submit inspection sheet shall be conclusive proof that there were no defects of note in the property. After the expiration of the 3-day period, Resident is obligated to provide for routine maintenance at his/her own expense, or to lose the discount.

31. Owner's Agents and Access:

The owner may be represented by an agent who will carry identification. Resident specifically agrees to permit the owner or Owner's agent(s) access to the premises for the purposes of inspection, repairs, or to show the property to another person at reasonable hours, on request. Resident will also allow signage in the yard.

32. Repairs:

The monthly discount is offered as an incentive to maintain the property. In the event repairs are needed, it is urged to arrange for professional assistance in performing repairs that are beyond the competence of the Resident. Resident should refrain from contacting the Owner except for emergencies, to report leaks or other urgent problems that may cause damage to the property, or for repairs costing more that the discount because such involvement by the Owner will result in the loss of the discount. Any repair that will cost more than the amount of the discount must be approved in writing by the owner or the tenant will be responsible for the entire cost of that repair. Any improvement made by the tenant shall become the property of the Owner at the conclusion of this agreement.

33. Worker's Warranty:

Resident(s) guarantee(s) that the Resident will undertake work or repairs only if he/she is competent and qualified to perform the work, and that the person performing the work will be totally responsible to assure that all activities are carried out in a safe manner that will meet all applicable statutes. Resident(s) further guarantee that they will be accountable for any mishaps or accidents resulting from work done on the property, and that they will hold the Owner free from harm, litigation, or claims of any other person.

34. Radon:
Radon is a naturally occurring radioactive gas that may present health risks to persons who are exposed to it over time when it has accumulated in a building in sufficient quantities. Levels of radon gas that exceed federal and state guidelines have been found in buildings. Additional information regarding radon and radon testing may be obtained from your county public health office.

35. Lead-Based Paint:
Houses built before 1978 may contain lead-based paint. Lead from paint, paint chips, and dust can pose health hazards if not taken care of properly. Lead exposure is especially harmful to young children and pregnant women. Before renting pre-1978 housing, landlords must disclose the presence of known lead-based paint and lead-based paint hazards in the dwelling. Tenants must also receive a federally approved pamphlet about prevention of lead poisoning.

36. Smoke Detectors:
Smoke detectors have been installed in this residence. It is the tenant's responsibility to maintain the smoke detectors by testing them periodically and replacing batteries as recommended by the manufacturer. In the event that a detector is missing or inoperative, the tenant must notify the landlord immediately.

37. Default by Resident:
If any breach or violation of any provision of this contract by Resident occurs, or any information in Resident's application is found to be untrue or misleading, Owner or Owner's agent may terminate this contract, evict the Resident and take possession of the residence. In such a case, the Resident agrees to forfeit the Security Deposit, and Owner may still purse any remaining amounts due and owing.

38. Bankruptcy:
In the event of a bankruptcy or state insolvency proceeding being filed against the Resident(s), their heirs, or assigns, the Owner, his agent, heirs, or assigns, at their discretion, may immediately declare this contract null and void, and at once resume possession of the premises. No judicial officer shall ever have any rights, title, or interest in or to the above-described property by virtue of this agreement.

39. Renewal Term:
At the end of initial term herein, Owner may elect to renew for another term at an increase of 3% to 5% of current rental rate, depending on the market index.

40. Acknowledgment:
In this agreement, the singular number will also include the plural, the Masculine gender will include the Feminine, the term Owner will include Landlord, Lessor, and the term Resident will include Tenant, Lessee. The parties signing below acknowledge that they have read and understand all of the provisions of this agreement. This contract is bound by all heirs, executors, successors, and/or assigns.

41. Right To Sign:
The individual(s) signing this Lease/Rental Agreement as Resident(s) guarantee(s) that he/she/they have the right to sign for and to bind all occupants.

LEGAL CONTRACT: This is a legally binding contract. If you do not understand any part of this contract, seek competent legal advice before signing.

ACCEPTED THIS _____ day of _____ 20_____, at _____.

_____

Resident

_____

Resident

_____

Owner

NOTICE TO CHANGE RENT

Date: _____

To: _____

_____

THIS IS A NOTICE that the terms of the lease agreement under which you occupy the premises described above are about to be changed.

Beginning _____ (Month & Day), _____ (Year), your rent will be increased by _____ ($_____) per month from _____ ($_____) to _____ ($_____), payable in advance.

Owner/Manager
This notice was served by the Owner/Manager in the following manner (check those that apply):
___ by personal delivery to the tenant,
___ by leaving a copy with someone on the premises other than the tenant,
___ by mailing,
___ by posting.

HOUSE APPLICATION

NOTE: A $20 application fee, paid by cash or money order, must be paid before this application will be processed. NO personal checks will be accepted!
This application must be filled out and signed by all adults who will be living in the house.

All information will be carefully checked and verified. False information will result in automatic rejection of this application.

Please call our office if you have questions regarding this application.

This is an application for the house located at:

_____(Address)

FIRST APPLICANT:
Full Name (First, M.I., Last) _____
Date of Birth _____ Social Security No. _____
Phone (Day) (_____) _____ (Evening) (_____) _____
# of People Who Will Live in House _____
In Case of Emergency, Contact: _____
CURRENT ADDRESS: Own _____ Rent _____
Street _____Apt. No. _____
City _____ State _____ Zip _____
Number of years at this address _____
Name of owner _____
Phone number of owner (_____) _____
WHY ARE YOU MOVING? _____
_____

PREVIOUS ADDRESS: Own _____ Rent _____
Street _____ Apt. No. _____
City _____ State _____ Zip _____
Number of years at present address _____
Name of owner _____
Phone number of owner (_____) _____
WHY DID YOU MOVE? _____
_____

EMPLOYMENT INFORMATION:
Current Employer _____
Street _____ Phone (_____) _____
City _____ State _____ Zip _____
Title_____ Type of business _____
Number of years at this job _____ Self employed _____

Previous employer _____
Street _____ Phone (_____) _____
City _____ State _____ Zip _____
Title_____ Type of business _____
Number of years at this job _____ Self employed_____
CO-APPLICANT:
Full Name (First, M.I., Last) _____
Date of Birth _____ Social Security No. _____
Phone (Day) (_____) _____ (Evening) (_____) _____
# of People Who Will Live in House _____
In Case of Emergency Contact: _____
CURRENT ADDRESS: Own _____ Rent _____
Street _____ Apt. No. _____
City _____ State _____ Zip _____
Number of years at this address _____
Name of owner _____

Phone number of owner (_____) _____

WHY ARE YOU MOVING? _____

_____

PREVIOUS ADDRESS: Own _____ Rent _____

Street _____ Apt. No. _____

City _____ State _____ Zip _____

Number of years at present address _____

Name of owner _____

Phone number of owner (_____) _____

WHY DID YOU MOVE? _____

_____

EMPLOYMENT INFORMATION:

Current Employer _____

Street _____ Phone (____) _____

City _____ State _____ Zip _____

Title_____ Type of business _____

Number of years at this job _____ Self-employed_____

Previous employer _____

Street _____ Phone (____) _____

City _____ State _____ Zip _____

Title_____ Type of business _____

Number of years at this job _____ Self-employed_____

WEEKLY INCOME BEFORE TAXES:

	APPLICANT	CO-APPLICANT	TOTAL
Base Income	_____	_____	_____
Overtime	_____	_____	_____
Bonuses	_____	_____	_____
Other*	_____	_____	_____
Total Monthy Income	_____	_____	_____

DESCRIBE OTHER INCOME:

Applicant/Co-Applicant	Type	Amount
_____	_____	_____
_____	_____	_____
TOTAL		_____

*Alimony, child support, or separate maintenance income need not be revealed if the Applicant or Co-Applicant does not wish to have it considered as a basis for repaying this loan.

MONTHLY HOUSING EXPENSES:

	APPLICANT	CO-APPLICANT
Rent/House	_____	_____
House/Renter's Insurance	_____	_____
Utilities	_____	_____
Other	_____	_____
Total Monthly Payment	_____	_____

APPLICANT AND CO-APPLICANT MUST BOTH ANSWER THESE QUESTIONS: ANSWER "YES" or "NO." If "Yes," please explain. Please call our office if you have any questions about this section.

Applicant: Yes/No

_____ Have you declared bankruptcy in the last 2 years?

_____ Have you ever been evicted or been asked to leave a property for any reason?

_____ Do you have any unpaid JUDGMENTS or COLLECTIONS?

_____ Have you ever been involved in a lawsuit as PLAINTIFF or DEFENDANT?

_____ Have you been convicted of a felony or misdemeanor in the last 5 years? (Except minor traffic violations)

_____ Have you ever had a home foreclosed on?

_____ Have you been pre-qualified to purchase a property by a bank or mortgage broker?

_____ Would you be willing to attend low-cost home buyer's classes?

_____ Do you intend to buy this home?

Please List Checking Account Numbers and Approximate Balances

Account Number	Approximate Balance
_____	$ _____
_____	$ _____

Please List Savings Account Numbers and Approximate Balances

Account Number	Approximate Balance
_____	$ _____
_____	$ _____

Please List All Types of Remodeling Work You Have Performed

Please list owner names and addresses of any major remodeling jobs you have completed

Owner's Name	Address of Remodeled Property	Type of Work Done
_____	_____	_____
_____	_____	_____

Co-Applicant: Yes/No

_____ Have you declared bankruptcy in the last 2 years?

_____ Have you ever been evicted or been asked to leave a property for any reason?

_____ Do you have any unpaid JUDGMENTS or COLLECTIONS?

_____ Have you ever been involved in a lawsuit as PLAINTIFF or DEFENDANT?

_____ Have you been convicted of a felony or misdemeanor in the last 5 years? (Except minor traffic violations)

_____ Have you ever had a home foreclosed on?

_____ Have you been pre-qualified to purchase a property by a bank or mortgage broker?

_____ Would you be willing to attend low-cost home buyer's classes?

_____ Do you intend to buy this home?

Please List Checking Account Numbers and Approximate Balances

Account Number	Approximate Balance
_____	$ _____
_____	$ _____

Please List Savings Account Numbers and Approximate Balances

Account Number	Approximate Balance
_____	$ _____
_____	$ _____

Please List All Types of Remodeling Work You Have Performed

Please list owner names and addresses of any major remodeling jobs you have completed

Owner's Name	Address of Remodeled Property	Type of Work Done
_____	_____	_____
_____	_____	_____

I certify under penalty of legal action that I have answered all of the above questions to the best of my ability. I give permission to _____ to use the provided information for purposes of verifying my qualifications to lease this property.

Applicant's Signature _____ Date _____

Co-Applicant's Signature _____ Date _____

CO-SIGNER AGREEMENT
(ADDENDUM TO RENTAL AGREEMENT)

Date: _____

Landlord: _____

Tenant: _____

This agreement is attached to and is hereby part of the Rental Agreement between the above-mentioned Landlord and Tenant, which is dated: _____.
My name is _____, and I have submitted a Rental Application in order to allow the Landlord to do a credit check on myself. I do not have any intention of residing in the unit referred to in the aforementioned Rental Agreement. I have read this Agreement and hereby promise to guarantee the Tenant's fulfillment of the financial commitment of this Agreement. I understand I will be required to pay for any unpaid rent, cleaning fees, and damages in the amount incurred by the Tenant under the Terms of this Agreement if, and only if, said Tenant(s) fail to pay.

_____   _____
Co-Signer Signature   Date

APPLICANT DISCLOSURE FORM

I hereby request that my application for the following rental property (address)_____be reviewed by _____.

Applicant Name: _____

Applicant Social Security Number: _____

Date of Birth: _____

Driver's License: _____State: _____

Applicant Address:_____

Applicant Home Phone: _____

Applicant Cell Phone: _____

Applicant Work Phone: _____

Address of Rental: _____

I give my authorization for _____to obtain and review my consumer credit report and any public records needed to come to an applicant decision. I also authorize _____to investigate any other personal information for the same purpose.

Signature_____

Date_____/_____/_____

APPLICANT DENIAL LETTER

Date: _____

Dear Applicant,

The application you placed for rental of the premises described as _____ located at _____ (street), _____ (city), ____ (state) _____ (zip) has unfortunately been denied.

The reason for our denial of your rental application was:

_____1.   Application contained incomplete or false information or the information that you provided on your application could not be verified.

_____2.   Previous rental history was reported as unfavorable for applicant.

_____3.   Did not meet income or debt qualifications.

_____4.   Information contained in your credit report.

In accordance to the Fair Credit Reporting Act, we are required to inform you where credit information was gathered from. We obtained this report from:

_____1.   Experian (TRW) Consumer Assistance, P. O. Box 949, Allen, TX 75002, 800-682-7654

_____2.   Trans Union Consumer Relations, P. O. Box 1000, 2 Baldwin Place, Chester, PA 19022, 800-888-4213

_____3.   CBI/Equifax Credit Information Service, P. O. Box 740241, Atlanta, GA 30374-2041, 800-685-1111

Insufficient credit information was obtained from the credit reporting agency marked above.

The credit reporting agency marked above was unable to provide a sufficient amount of information about you.

A person or company provided background information about you. Within 60 days of receiving this letter, you have the right to request information on the nature of the information provided. You must make this request in writing. Under federal law, we are prohibited from releasing information regarding the source of this information.

The credit reporting agency marked above may have gathered credit information on you based on reports from one of the other agencies. The agencies above serve only to provide credit information and were in no manner directly responsible for the denial of your rental application.

Under federal law, you have the right to receive a copy of your credit report, to dispute the accuracy and completeness of the report, and to insert a statement regarding specific entries on your credit report. Call the credit reporting agency marked above if you believe that there is inaccurate information contained on your credit report. You can also write the credit reporting agency at the address listed above to inform them of inaccuracies. A disclosure of the inaccuracies can be made orally, in writing, or electronically. Contact the agency marked above for specific details on filing complaints.

Within 60 days of ____/____/____, you are eligible to receive a free copy of your consumer credit report from the agency marked above.

You may have additional rights under the credit reporting or consumer protection laws of your state. If you wish, you may contact your state or local consumer protection agency or a state Attorney General's office.

Best Regards,

_____

Landlord/Property Manager

ASSIGNMENT OF RENTS FORM

Date: _____

Assignor(s): _____

Address: _____

City: _____ State: _____ Zip: _____

Assignee(s): _____

Address: _____

City: _____ State: _____ Zip: _____

Assignor, in consideration of $_____ and other valuable consideration tendered, the receipt of which has been acknowledged, hereby sells, assigns, transfers, and sets over to Assignee, his/her executors, and administrators, all the rents, issues, and profits now due and of which may become due under any lease, whether written or verbal, or

any letting of, or any agreement for the use of or occupancy of any part of the premises described as _____
_____, which may have been or may be made or agreed to, or which may be made or agreed to by the Assignee under the power granted it. The purpose of this Agreement is to establish a total transfer and assignment of all such leases and agreements and all the avails under the leases and agreements to the Assignee and in particular those leases and agreements now on hand as follows:

Date of Lease	Lease Term	Monthly Rent
		$
		$

Rents will be paid monthly in advance on the aforementioned property.

SECURITY DEPOSIT AGREEMENT

Date of Acceptance:_____
Owner: _____
Tenant: _____

Owner hereby acknowledges receipt from the Tenant of $_____ for the Security against any default and/or damages for the unit Tenant is renting located at ____
_____.

This Deposit will be refunded to the Tenant in event that all conditions of the Lease Agreement are met upon the Tenant's departure.

_____
Owner

_____
Tenant

RENTAL PROPERTY KNOWLEDGE SHEET

Information on Rental Property
Address _____
Apt/Unit #_____ City/State _____ ZIP _____
Apt/Unit(s) Square Footage _____
Apt/Unit Mix: Studio _____ 1 Bedroom _____ 2 Bedroom/1 Bath ____
2 Bedroom/2 Bath _____
Rent: 1 Bedroom _____ 2 Bedroom/1 Bath _____ 2 Bedroom/2 Bath _____
Other _____
Application Fee _____ Security Deposit _____
Concessions _____
Rental Age _____ Construction Type _____Parking _____
Recreational Facilities _____ Laundry _____ Pets _____

Storage _____ Utilities (Who Pays?) _____

AC/Heat _____

Appliances _____

Floor coverings _____

Special Features/Comments _____

Community Information

School District _____ Elem. School _____

Middle School _____

High School _____ Jr. College _____

College _____

Trade School _____

Preschool(s) _____

Childcare _____

Places of Worship _____

Police/Fire Stations/Ambulance Service _____

Electric _____ Natural Gas _____ Telephone _____ Cable _____

Water _____ Sewer _____ Library _____

Post Office _____

Hospital/Pharmacies/Vet/Medical Facilities _____

Nearby Employment Centers _____

Transportation Availability _____

Groceries/Shopping _____

Local Services _____

Restaurants _____

Notes _____

Rental Market Information

Rental Competitors/Rental Rates/Concessions _____

_____

My Competitive Advantages _____

_____

My Competitive Disadvantages _____

WEEK-TO-WEEK RENTAL CONTRACT

This week-to-week rental contract is entered into on this date, _____, 20__
by and between _____(Owner) and _____(Renter).

WITNESSETH: That for and in consideration of the payment of the rent due and the
performance of the covenants contained on the part of the Renter, said Owner does hereby demise and let unto the Renter, and Renter hires from Owner for use as a residence
the specific premises hereby described as _____ ,which are located at
_____ (street), _____ (city), ___ (state) _____ (zip) for a tenancy from week-to-week beginning on _____ (date) until _____
(ending date) at a weekly price of _____ dollars, for a total rental amount of
_____(dollars), payable in advance on the first day of tenancy.

The following are also mutually agreed upon by both Renter and Owner:
1.   Renter shall not violate any city ordinance or state law in or about the rental location.
2.   Renter shall not sub-let the rental property, or any part thereof, or assign this contract without the written consent of said Owner.
3.   Renter shall give immediate notice to the Owner or agent of same should any fire, theft, or vandalism occur on said premises.
4.   Renter must not make any alterations or improvements to said property unless prior without written consent has been given by Owner.
5.   If legal action takes place or must be initiated by Owner, Renter agrees to pay all costs, expenses, as well as all attorney's fees, as the court may affix.

Arrival Date: _____ Arrival Time: _____(__p.m./__a.m.)
Departure Date: _____ Departure Time: _____(__p.m./__a.m.)

Said premises __are / ___are not furnished with furniture, cooking utensils, kitchen equipment, linens, and bedding.

The following items are furnished: _____
_____

A non-refundable $_____ deposit is required in order to reserve said premises each week.
A deposit of $_____ for cleaning is required at time of check in. Cleaning deposit will be refunded only if said premises are left in clean condition at the time of check out.

If Owner is to incur any cleaning expenses in order to restore said premises to the condition they were in at the time of Renter's occupancy, the amount required for said restoration will be deducted from the cleaning deposit, and any remaining funds from the cleaning deposit will be refunded to the Renter.

_____
Owner Signed

_____
Owner Printed

_____
Renter Signed

_____
Renter Printed

TENANT WALK-THROUGH LIST

A walkthrough inspection of the property was completed on _____. The following items were inspected and their condition is noted with a yes if in working order and a no if it is not in working order:

- ❏ Stove
- ❏ Wall Oven
- ❏ Refrigerator
- ❏ Ice Maker
- ❏ Dishwasher
- ❏ Built-in Microwave
- ❏ Trash Compacter
- ❏ Disposer
- ❏ Freezer
- ❏ Window Fans
- ❏ Ceiling Fans
- ❏ Attic Fans
- ❏ Smoke Detectors
- ❏ Washer
- ❏ Dryer
- ❏ Electric Air Filter
- ❏ Central Vac
- ❏ Water Softener
- ❏ Exhaust Fans
- ❏ Alarm System
- ❏ Intercom
- ❏ Garage Door Openers
- ❏ Plumbing Fixtures
- ❏ Lighting Fixtures
- ❏ Window Treatments
- ❏ Storm Windows
- ❏ Storage Shed
- ❏ Wood Stove
- ❏ Fireplace
- ❏ Screen Doors
- ❏ Existing Screens
- ❏ Existing Storm Doors
- ❏ Heating and AC

Item that require repair/cleaning include:

1_____

2_____

3_____

4_____

5_____

6_____

7_____

8_____

9_____

10_____

Remarks: _____

_____

TENANT(S):

_____ / _____
Date   Signature

_____ / _____
Date   Signature

LANDLORD(S):

_____ / _____
Date   Signature

_____ / _____
Date   Signature

RENTAL MOVE IN/ MOVE OUT CHECKLIST

Date Move In: _____
Date Move Out: _____
Apartment/Unit #: _____
Tenant: _____

Condition of Room	Check In				Check Out				Comments
	New	Good	Okay	Poor	New	Good	Okay	Poor	
Entry/Halls									
Floors									
Walls									
Doorway									
Living Room									
Floors/Carpet									
Ceilings									
Walls									
Windows/Screens									
Ceiling Fan/Light Fixture									
Other: _____									

Condition of Room	Check In				Check Out				Comments
	New	Good	Okay	Poor	New	Good	Okay	Poor	
Kitchen									
Floors									
Ceilings									
Walls									
Light Fixtures									
Windows/ Screens									
Cabinets									
Oven									
Refrigerator									
Dishwasher									
Sink									
Disposal									
Faucets									
Vents									
Counters									
Other: _____									
Dining Area									
Floors									
Ceilings									
Walls									
Light Fixtures									
Windows/ Screens									
Other: _____									

Condition of Room	Check In				Check Out				Comments
	New	Good	Okay	Poor	New	Good	Okay	Poor	
Bedroom #1									
Floors/Carpets									
Ceilings									
Walls									
Light Fixtures									
Windows/Screens									
Closet									
Other: _____									
Bedroom #2									
Floors/Carpets									
Ceilings									
Walls									
Light Fixtures									
Windows/Screens									
Closet									
Other: _____									

Signed Landlord

Signed Tenant

NOTICE OF CHANGE OF RENT

Date: _____ (month/day/year)

To: _____

YOU ARE HEREBY NOTIFIED that the terms of your tenancy under which you re-side in the aforementioned property are changing effective _____ (month) _____ (day) _____ (year).

As of said date, your rental amount will be increased by _____ dol-lars ($_____) per month from your current amount of _____ dollars ($_____) to the new amount of _____ dollars ($_____) per month, payable in advance.

_____   _____
Signed Owner/Manager   Date

This change of rent notice was served by the Owner/Manager by way of:
❑ personal delivery to said tenant   ❑ certified mail
❑ post on said tenant's door

DRUG-FREE HOUSING ADDENDUM

Date: _____
Tenant: _____
Landlord: _____
Rental Address: _____

In regard to the Rental Agreement made between the abovementioned Landlord and Tenant and the property listed above, the Parties hereby make agreement that the fol-lowing addendum as of this date will hereby be in effect and part of the aforementioned Agreement.

With concern to a new Rental Agreement or renewal of a Rental Agreement and in re-gards to the aforementioned rental address, the Landlord and Tenant hereby agree to the following terms:

1.   No person, whether the Tenant, a resident of the rental property, or a guest, shall in any way engage in any type of criminal activity, including any drug-related criminal behavior/activity, on or anywhere near the property. The above-mentioned drug-related criminal activity includes the illegal manufacture, sale, distribution, use, or possession with intent to manufacture, sell, distribute, or use, of a controlled substance [as is defined in section 102 of the Controlled Substances Act (21 U.S.C.802)].

2.   No person, whether the Tenant, a resident of the rental property, or a guest, shall engage in any type of activity or behavior that intends to assist in crimi-nal activity, including anything drug-related.

3.   Tenant and residents of the rental property are not permitted to engage in the manufacture, sale, or distribution of any illegal drugs at any location whether on or near the premises or otherwise.

4.   No person, whether the Tenant, a resident of the rental property, or a guest, shall engage in any acts of violence or any threats of violence. These acts or threats of violence include, but are not limited to the unlawful possession or discharge of firearms on or near the property.

5.   Tenant hereby agrees and understands that should any search warrants by issued by the court for this aforementioned rental address/property will cause an involuntary break of the Rental Agreement and the Landlord may request eviction of the Tenant if that shall occur. Both Parties hereby understand that no arrests or convictions need to transpire prior to a breach of the Rental Agreement pursuant to this paragraph, just the judicial determination of probable cause to believe that some form of criminal and illegal activity has occurred will be deemed satisfactory for such breach.

_____

Tenant

_____

Landlord

ROOMMATE AGREEMENT
(ADDENDUM TO THE RENTAL AGREEMENT)

Date: _____

This Agreement is made by and between

_____, _____,

_____, _____,

who have, on the _____ day of _____, 20____,
signed a lease for _____ (address) for a term lasting
from _____ to _____, a copy of which is attached to
this agreement, and plan to reside on said premises; and wish to provide for the sharing of
responsibilities as tenants of the rented premises.

ALL PARTIES AGREE:

1.   That each of the parties will follow the rules and conditions set out in the attached lease.

That each of the parties agrees to One _____(1/__) of the following expenses associated with the leased premises.* (This means one divided by the number of roommates. For example, in a household with 3 roommates, each member's share would be One-Third (1/3).)

Check if applicable:
_____ rent ($_____/mo.)
_____ general maintenance and upkeep
_____ gas
_____ food
_____ electricity
_____ damages not due to the negligence identified party
_____ telephone service
_____ water
_____ other _____

If any of the parties pays more than the One _____ (1/__) share, the other parties agree to reimburse the first party.

2. Each party agrees to pay for any long-distance telephone calls he or she makes.

3. A security or damage deposit in the amount of $_____ will be paid to Owner/agent. The parties agree that the total deposit is $_____ and that each tenant's portion is $_____. Unless otherwise stated in the lease, the tenants agree that the landlord will be asked to return the deposit in the following manner:

_____

_____.

If one roommate subleases their room to a new tenant, unless otherwise stipulated in the lease, the security deposit exchange shall be conducted in the following way:

_____

_____

4. Each of the parties agrees to pay his/her share of the rent, utilities, and phone in a timely manner during the entire term of the lease unless those responsibilities are taken over by a subtenant.

5. A roommate may sublease his/her room to a new tenant if the following conditions are met:
   a. the party arranges to sublet his/her share to a subtenant at his/her expense.
   b. the subtenant is acceptable to the remaining parties, who will not unreasonably withhold their acceptance.
   c. the owner/manager gives written consent to the subtenant.

6. That repairs or improvements to the premises, the costs of which are to be shared by the parties, exceeding $ _____ shall be approved in advance.

7. If pets are permitted under the lease, each pet owner shall be solely responsible for all damages caused by his or her pet, including, but not limited to, damage to furniture, carpeting, doors, lawn, and garden.

8. Additional provisions (rules for music, smoking, housecleaning, etc.):

_____

_____

Signature of Each Roommate:

_____   _____

_____   _____

(Each roommate should be given a copy for their records and a copy should be given to the landlord).

WATERBED AGREEMENT
(ADDENDUM TO THE RENTAL AGREEMENT)

Date	Rental Address
Management/Owner	Renter

This agreement is part of the Rental Agreement dated _____
between Management/Owner and Renter for the above-mentioned residential unit. The
Renter desires to keep a waterbed described as _____
___ in the unit occupied under the Rental Agreement, and because the Rental Agreement
expressly prohibits waterbeds within the premises without written permission from the
Management, Renter hereby agrees to:

1.   Keep only one (1) waterbed approved by Management for the unit. Waterbed
     shall consist of _____.

2.   Consult with Management about the location of the waterbed on the prem-
     ises. Renter agrees to employ a qualified professional to install and dismantle
     the bed according to the manufacturer's specifications and also agrees not to
     relocate it without the consent of Management.

3.   Allow Management to inspect the waterbed installation at any and all reason-
     able times and to remedy any problems or potential problems right away.

4.   Provide Management with a copy of a valid liability insurance policy in the
     amount of $_____ , naming Owner as the insured, which will cover the
     waterbed installation, and to renew the policy as required for uninterrupted
     coverage.

5.   Immediately cover the cost for any damage caused by the waterbed and, in
     addition, to add $ _____ to the security/cleaning depos-
     it, any of which may be used for cleaning, repairs, or delinquent rent when
     Renter vacates. Within _____ days after Renter proves to
     Management that the waterbed is no longer to be found on the property,
     waterbed damages will be assessed and remainder of this extra deposit will be
     returned to Resident.

6.   Cover the additional time, effort, costs, and risks involved in said waterbed
     installation with payment of additional rent of $ _____, which
     [ ] includes [ ] does not include the premium for the waterbed liability insur-
     ance policy described in item 4.

7.   Management reserves the right to retract this permission to keep a waterbed
     should the Renter violate this agreement.

Signed Management/Owner

Signed Renter

SMOKE DETECTOR RENTAL AGREEMENT ADDENDUM

Date: _____

Tenant: _____

Landlord: _____

Rental Address: _____

Landlord hereby certifies that all smoke detectors set up in the above listed rental property are all in operating condition at the time of Tenant's move in. Smoke detectors in this unit are located in the following places:

  1. _____
  2. _____
  3. _____
  4. _____

As the Tenant you hereby agree that the smoke detectors are in operating condition. I also understand that to keep them in working condition, I will need to check and replace the batteries to each device on an as-needed basis. Replacement batteries are the Tenant's responsibilities. Each detector should be tested once a month to be sure they are in working order. If any problem arises with one or more of the smoke detectors once the monthly battery check and device test occurs, it is your responsibility to immediately notify the Landlord to guarantee these units offer the early discovery of a fire or smoke should such occur. We request serious teamwork between the Tenant and Landlord with this issue.

Tenant

Landlord

UTILITY ADDENDUM FOR RENTAL AGREEMENT

Date: _____

Tenant: _____

Landlord: _____

Rental Address: _____

This addendum is hereby made to the Rental Agreement made between the aforementioned Tenant and Landlord for the property listed above.

The Landlord hereby agrees to provide the water and sewer services for the rental property. Tenant's payment for service shall be made in one of the following manners:

1. Landlord will hold the billing for the utility service and Tenant will make a set utility payment of $_____ per month with his/her rent. This amount will be applied to the water and sewer bill.
2. Tenant will pay amount of utility bill as provided by the Landlord each quarter. This amount is due on the 1st of the month that the bill is due. Payment may be made with the rent due. Amount owed will be provided by the Landlord by the 15th of the previous month.

The Tenant and Landlord may together review the water meter at the beginning and end of the Rental Agreement period in order to pro-rate the utility fee for those months.

_____

Tenant

_____

Landlord

UTILITIES GUARANTEE LETTER

Date: _____

Landlord: _____

Property Address: _____

To Whom It May Concern:

The Landlord listed above has my permission to change all utilities, water, and cable into Tenant's name for the abovementioned property. Tenant hereby agrees to pay all bills that come from the use of those utilities at the property during the dates of tenancy corresponding with those agreed to in the Rental Agreement: _____ (start date) to _____ (end date).

Tenant 1 Name:	Tenant 2 Name:
Social Security #:	Social Security #:

_____

Tenant 1 Signed

_____

Tenant 2 Signed

NOTIFICATION OF INTENT TO VACATE RENTAL PROPERTY

Rental Address: _____

Name on Lease: _____

Vacate Date: _____

Lease Expiration Date: _____

Forwarding Address: _____

Lessee Signature(s):

Name_____Date_____

Name_____Date_____

As per the lease agreement, it is the lessee's responsibility to leave the premises clean and in good condition. All personal property is to be removed by the date indicated above. Any refund of security deposit funds will be sent to the forwarding address as stated above, as prescribed by law.

ACKNOWLEDGMENT LETTER OF NOTICE OF INTENT TO VACATE

Date: _____

Dear Tenant:

This letter is sent to you in acknowledgment that we have received your Notice of Intent to Vacate the premises that lists your plan to move out of the premises on _____ (date).

Please be aware that this is to be a firm date and may only be changed by written consent between both the Lessee and Lessor. If you have satisfied the terms and conditions of your Lease/Rental Agreement you may expect a refund of your deposit. Please keep in mind that a complete refund of your deposit will be determined based on whether you have completed the following list:

1.   Your unit must be returned in good, clean condition, including removal of all belongings and trash, and special cleaning attention to appliances and bathrooms.

2.   Return all keys. Be sure all unit, mail, and laundry keys are returned to management within _____ days of vacating the premises. You will be responsible for all rent until you return all keys.

3.   Be sure all final utility bills are paid in full and services have been transferred from your name.

4.   Your last month's rent should be paid in full. Your security deposit may NOT be used for this purpose. The deposit will be returned via check after final inspection and unit review has occurred.

5.   Leave your forwarding address with the Landlord for any mail or unit issues.

6.   Landlord will not be responsible for any items you leave in the unit after you have returned your keys (examples include telephones, clothing, cable boxes, satellite dishes, etc).

Keep in mind your liability will not be limited by the amount of your security deposit. Should charges and fees be over the amount of your deposit be required, you will be charged for these additional amounts.

We hope your tenancy with us has been a pleasant one. Please contact us with any questions or concerns you have. Thank you.

Sincerely,

_____

Landlord

RENTER EXIT INTERVIEW

Please provide the following feedback so that we may ensure the highest quality service to our lessees.

Reason for vacating: _____

Would you say that your rental unit was:
    Excellent   Good   Fair   Poor   Very Poor
Please list improvements that could be made to your unit:
_____
_____

Comments: _____
_____

Date:_____
Reviewed By:_____

RECEIPT OF RENTAL PAYMENT

Date: _____
Tenant Name: _____
Address: _____

Dear Tenant,
Your payment of $_____ was received from _____ on _____ (date). This payment is for the rent from _____ to _____ for the property address listed above.

Thank you,

_____
Landlord

REJECTION LETTER

Date: _____
Applicant Name: _____
Applicant Address: _____
_____
Rental Address: _____
_____

Dear Applicant,
We have received your application for tenancy. Unfortunately, we have to inform you that your application has been denied for the rental property listed above. The reason for this denial of your application is:

❑   Prior residency information provided was not able to be verified.
❑   Job history provided was insufficient.
❑   Poor or no credit history.
❑   Income not enough to meet rental requirements.

Due to the denial of your application in part based on your credit history, the Fair Credit Reporting Act requires the following disclosures be made to you:
The credit agency we received your information from was:

_____

_____

The credit reporting company did not make the decision to take the adverse action and is unable to provide you with the specific reasons why the adverse action was taken. Under Section 612 of the Fair Credit Reporting Act, you have the right to receive a free copy of your credit report(s) from the reporting agency within 60 days. You have the right to dispute with the credit reporting agency the accuracy or completeness of the credit report.

Should you have any other questions regarding your application or this letter, please do not hesitate to contact us during normal business hours.

Regards,

_____

Landlord/Owner

CHAPTER 9

Landlord Forms

PET AGREEMENT

Date: _____

This agreement is attached to and forms a part of the _____ Agreement dated _____, between _____, Management, and _____, Tenant, for the residential unit located at _____.

Resident desires to keep a pet/pets named _____ and described as _____ in the dwelling Tenant occupies under the Lease Agreement referred to above. This agreement specifically prohibits keeping pets without Management's permission, so the Tenant hereby agrees to:

1. Keep his/her pet under control during entire term of tenancy.
2. Never leave his/her pet unattended for unreasonable lengths of time.
3. Keep his/her pet restrained, not tethered, when outside Tenant's dwelling at any place on the property.
4. Properly and swiftly dispose of his/her pet's feces and waste.
5. Never leave any type of food or water for pet, or any other animal, outside the unit.
6. Keep his/her pet from causing any irritation or distress to other tenants, visitors, or management and quickly remedy any complaints made to the Management.
7. Remove all of his/her pet's offspring from the property within eight weeks of birth.
8. Pay immediately for any damage, loss, or expense caused by his/her pet and, add $ _____ to the security/cleaning deposit, any of which may be used for cleaning, repairs, or late rent when Tenant vacates the unit. Within

_____ days after Tenant proves said pet is no longer kept on the premises, this added deposit minus any assessed pet damages will be returned to Tenant.

9. Management reserves the right to revoke permission to keep the pet should Tenant violate this agreement.

_____

Signed   Management

_____

Signed   Tenant

TENANT'S SUBORDINATION AGREEMENT

Date: _____

_____ (Tenant/Lessee), a corpo-
ration authorized to transact business within the State of _____,
enters into this Agreement to subordinate all rights in and to its leasehold interest in the Lease, dated _____, signed by
_____(Lessor)

Address: _____

City: _____ State: _____ Zip: _____

and

_____ (Tenant/Lessee)

Address: _____

City: _____ State: _____ Zip: _____

a) This Lease (hereafter referred to as "Lease") was assigned to _____
_____ on or about _____ (Date) to the
Mortgage Deed and Note given by _____(Lessor) in
favor of _____, its successors and/or assigns ("_____
_____"), to any renewal, extension, modification, or consolidation of
such mortgage.

b) _____ (Lessor)
represents to _____ that
_____ (Tenant/Lessee) is current with all rents
due under the LEASE, as set forth in an Estoppel Certificate executed by _____
_____ contemporaneously with this Agreement, and that the sub-
ordination set forth in this Agreement shall be without counterclaims, defense, or offset.

_____

(Signature)

LESSOR: _____
(Signature)
TENANT/LESSEE: _____
(Signature)

STATE OF _____, COUNTY OF _____

The foregoing instrument was acknowledged before me, this _____ day of
_____, 20 _____.

_____ Notary Public

(SEAL) State of _____
My Commission Expires: _____

PROBLEM TENANT REPORT FORM

Landlord, please fill out this form for every violation/disturbance and place in tenant's
file.* After _____ forms are placed in file, please send a warning to the tenant. If additional reports are filed, please consider the eviction process.

Date:	Tenant Name:	Tenant's Address/ Unit Number:	Violation/Disturbance Information

Landlord, please note that a violation may include property damage, late rent payments, poor property maintenance, and/or high noise complaints.

TENANT/PROPERTY INCIDENT REPORT

Date of the incident: _____ 20_____
Time of the incident: _____ a.m./p.m.
Location of the incident: _____
Apt. #: _____

Who was involved? _____
_____

What happened? _____
_____

Any witnesses? If yes, who? _____

Where do they live? _____
_____

Insurance adjuster contacted? _____
Fire department contacted? _____
Police department contacted? _____
Action or follow up? _____
_____

Who prepared this report? _____

cc: Tenant file
Attorney
Insurance company
Section 8 leasing officer (if applicable)

30-DAY NOTICE TO TERMINATE TENANCY

To (Tenant Name)	Date
(and all occupying parties)	
Address Of Premises	

This is a notice that you are required to move from and remove all of your possessions from the aforementioned premises within thirty (30) days.

The purpose of this notice is to hereby terminate the Lease/Rental Agreement for the unit of which is described above. Failure to comply will result in legal action to ensue against you to recover possession of said property, to officially declare the Lease/Rental Agreement as terminated, and recover any rent due or fees for any damages incurred during the unlawful tenancy period.

You are hereby also advised that any rent on the above-mentioned property is due and payable up to and including the date of termination of your tenancy under this notice.

_____
Owner/Management Agent

_____
Served By

CHART OF FEES TENANT MAY BE CHARGED AFTER INSPECTION UPON LEASE TERMINATION

If tenant does not return the residence in the same condition as when tenant began renting, the following chart describes the minimum charges which will be deducted from the Security Deposit tenant paid upon signing of lease. Any cost related to cleaning, labor, repairs, removals, trash pickup, replacements, where applicable will be deducted. Any rent income loss due to the time it takes to make repairs or any of the above mentioned items, will also be deducted from the security deposit.

Minimum Charge List	
Charges for Cleaning Not Done by Tenant:	
Stove/Oven	$
Refrigerator	$
Kitchen Sink	$
Cabinets	$

Minimum Charge List	
Counter tops	$
Bathroom Toilet	$
Bathroom Shower/Tub	$
Medicine Cabinet	$
Bathroom Sink Area	$
Windows	$
Closet Areas	$
Charges for Floorings Not Cleaned by Tenant:	
Tile	$
Carpet	$
Kitchen Floors	$
Bathroom Floors	$
Bedroom Floors	$
Other: _____	$
Charges for Trash Removal:	
On Property	$
Per Room	$
For Removal of Large Trash	$
Extensive Cleaning Charges:	
Per Hour Amount	$
Charges for Damages:	
For damages to walls due to negligence (per room)	$
For removing of tenant's wall coverings (per hour fee)	$
Covering of nail holes/ other small holes (per hole fee)	$
Covering/Fixing Large Holes (per hole fee)	$
Cigarette Burns (per burn fee)	$
Carpet/Rug/Tile Replacement	$
Light Bulbs (per bulb fee)	$
Unreturned Key Fee (per key fee)	$
Lock Replacement (per replacement)	$
Lawn Maintenance (min. fee)	$

Minimum Charge List	
Screen Replacement (per screen fee)	$
Window Replacement (per pane)	$

Resident hereby agrees that besides any fees owed for these issues listed above, the deposit will be returned within _____ days after date set with Management for final vacancy.

Resident understands that any amount listed above is for the minimum cleaning and damage repair.

Tenant Signed _____

Owner/Manager Signed _____

NOTICE OF INTENT TO ENTER

Date:	Renter Name and Unit Address:

This notice is to inform you that on or about _____ ❏ a.m./ ❏ p.m. on _____ (month/day/year), the Owner, Manager, Owner's agent, or Owner's employees intend to enter the premises mentioned above which you rent and occupy. They will need to stay approximately _____ ❏ minutes/ ❏ hours.

The reason for entering the property is:

_____

_____

You are not required to be present to provide access to the unit. The party who is entering will first knock and, after determining that no one is available to answer, will enter using a passkey.

This notice is intended to notify you at least twenty-four (24) hours in advance.

This notice was personally delivered by the Owner/Manager at the following time:
_____ ❏ a.m./ ❏ p.m. on _____ (month/day/year).

_____

Owner/Manager

NOTICE OF INTENT TO ENTER VERSION 2

Dear (_____):

This is a notification that the landlord, or a representative of the Landlord, will be entering your premises on (date) _____ at (approximate time) in order to:

_____ Make the following repairs: _____
_____ Show the unit to:
            _____ Prospective renters
            _____ Contractors
_____ Other: _____

You have the right to be present during this time. Please notify the landlord immediately if the date or time is problematic. You are, of course, welcome to be present. If you have any questions or if the date/time is problematic, please notify the Landlord at (___-___-____).

Landlord Signature:_____Date:_____

APARTMENT/UNIT SERVICE CALL

Date:	
Renter:	Unit/Apartment #:

Hello. Your apartment/unit was serviced today. The following occurred:
❑ Filter Changed Today
❑ Heat Checked Today
❑ Air Conditioning Checked Today
❑ _____ Checked Today
❑ _____ Checked Today
❑ _____ Checked Today

Please be aware that the following items were not completed:
1. _____
2. _____
3. _____

If you have any questions or require additional assistance, please contact Management.

Service Call Completed By: _____

TENANT EMERGENCY/SERVICE CALL INFORMATION

NEW TENANT INFORMATION

Dear Tenant:
Welcome! This list contains the numbers that you may need to contact for emergency services or service calls while a resident at your new address. During an emergency, you

may find you are unable to reach the owner or myself. In this situation, please be sure to contact one of the numbers below for your need to be addressed after office hours. Please let us know if you have any questions. We will be sure to send you updates to any of these numbers should a change occur.

Thank you,

_____

Landlord Signature

In Case Of:	Who to Call/Action to Take:	Phone Number:
Fire		
Criminal Activity		
Ambulance/Paramedic Assistance Needed		
Water Line Break	Turn off Water Valve	----------------
Gas Leak		
Electricity Outage (Except for billing issues)		
Emergency Repair Necessary		
Utility Companies:	**Who:**	**Phone Number:**
Phone		
Electric		
Water		
Cable		
Closest Community:	**Name:**	**Phone Number:**
School		
Shopping Center		
Pharmacy (24-Hours)		
Laundry		
Furniture and Appliance Rental/Purchase Store		
Library		
Bank		

Post Office		
Public Transportation (Bus, Cab, Trolley, etc)		
Newspaper		
Other:	**Name:**	**Phone Number:**
_____		
_____		

CRIME REPORT REQUEST

Use this form to request a crime report on an address from your local police department.

Date:	From:

Dear Officer,

I am hereby requesting a crime report and a "call to service" report for the below property address:

_____

_____

I would appreciate this request be handled in a timely manner and greatly appreciate your assistance. Please send this report to my attention at the following location:

_____

_____

You may contact me at (____) _____-_____. Thank you for your assistance,

_____

Landlord Signature

REFUSAL TO RENT/LEASE FORM

Date: _____

Dear Applicant,

Your request to rent or lease property located at the following address _____

_____ has been denied. The reason for this denial is specified below.

- ❑ Your application was incomplete.
- ❑ You have insufficient credit references.
- ❑ We were unable to verify the credit references provided.
- ❑ We were unable to verify credit as no credit file available.
- ❑ Your credit file is insufficient.
- ❑ Your credit file shows delinquent accounts.

❑   Your credit file shows too many obligations.
❑   Your past rental history has been too short.
❑   We were unable to verify your current residence.
❑   We were unable to verify your employment.
❑   Your employment record has been irregular or temporary.
❑   Your employment record shows too short a time period of current employment.
❑   Your income is insufficient to handle the rent/lease amount.
❑   We were unable to verify your income.
❑   Your credit file shows bankruptcy.
❑   Your credit history shows you have been evicted from a previous residence(s).
❑   Your credit file shows you have been involved in a suit, garnishment of wages, foreclosure, or repossession.
❑   Other: _____

Due to the reason(s) marked above, we are unable to provide you tenancy. We do not rent/lease to anyone based on these issues.

Thank you,

_____

Management/Owner

We obtained information from: _____

Fair Credit Reporting Act
Under the Fair Credit Reporting Act, you have the right to make a written request, within 60 days of receipt of this notice, for disclosure of the nature of the adverse information. The Federal Equal Credit Opportunity Act prohibits creditors from discriminating against credit applicants on the basis of race, color, religion, national origin, sex, marital status, age (provided the applicant has the capacity to enter into a binding contract), because all or part of the applicant's income derives from any public assistance program or because the applicant has in good faith exercised any right under the Consumer Credit Protection Act. The Federal agency that administers compliance with this law concerning this creditor is the Federal Trade Commission, Equal Credit Opportunity, Washington, D.C. 20580.

INSPECTION FAILURE LETTER

Date: _____
To: _____
_____

Dear Tenant:
During the inspection of your unit which took place on _____ (date), the following conditions were found to be lower than the standards required by your Rental/Lease Agreement. You are hereby notified that you have _____ days from the date of this letter to correct these conditions to the standards set in your agreement. We will also

be submitting your residence to a weekly inspection for the next _____ months while we verify that the conditions are remaining in the right standards. If neglect continues, we will have no choice but to take action as specified under your Rental/Lease Agreement.

(Landlord, please fill in the precise problem in the space provided by each main problem.)

❑   Lawn Care Issues: _____.
❑   Trees/Bushes Issues: _____.
❑   Animal Dropping Issues: _____.
❑   Broken Windows/Screens/Doors/Gates: _____.
❑   Trash Removal/Pick Up: _____.
❑   Walls/Doors: _____.
❑   Paint Touch Up: _____.
❑   Leak Repair: _____.
❑   Loose Hardware Tightened or Replaced: _____.
❑   Filters/Pads Replaced: _____.
❑   Broken-down Vehicle Removal: _____.
❑   Other: _____.

Please address these areas of concern as soon as possible. Thank you.

Sincerely,

_____

Landlord/Owner

CHAPTER 10

Late Payment Forms

FIRST NOTICE: LATE RENT

Date: _____

Resident(s) include:
Resident Adult 1: _____
Resident Adult 2: _____
Resident Child(ren): _____

Rental Residence Address:

_____

Dear _____,

This is a friendly reminder that we have yet to receive your rent payment for the month of _____. We ask that you please remit by _____ (date). Payment made by this date will ensure no late penalties are assessed.

Thank you for your prompt attention to this matter.

Respectfully,

_____
Landlord Signature

_____
Landlord Printed

Should you have any questions regarding this matter, please call _____.

NOTICE OF OVERDUE RENT

Date: _____

TO: (Tenant's Name & Address)
_____
_____

FROM: (Landlord's Name & Address)
_____
_____

Your rent in the amount of $_____ was due on _____ (date) for the month of _____ in which you were occupying the premises located at _____. We ask that you please bring your payment to the landlord's address as given above or call us immediately at _____.

If you have already remitted payment, please disregard this notice.

Thank you,

_____
Landlord Signature

NOTICE OF PAST DUE RENT

TO BE SENT VIA CERTIFIED MAIL
Date _____

Resident(s) include:
Resident Adult 1: _____
Resident Adult 2: _____
Resident Child(ren): _____

Rental Residence Address:
_____

Rent Due Date: _____
Rent Amount: $ _____
Rent Amount Past Due $ _____
Late Charge Amount $ _____
Total Rent Amount Due $ _____
Estimated Amount of Potential Court Fees $_____

According to the records of _____, you are behind in your rent. We are unable to keep our rental properties maintained (including the mortgage, utilities, and taxes) if we do not receive the rental payments due to us in a timely manner. While we hope that your delinquency period is just an oversight, we will have to impose a past due rental notice and late charge. This letter hereby serves as that notice.

We are giving you three (3) days to pay this past due amount and additional late charge. Many times our tenants fail to pay the rent due to financial issues and as much as we understand and sympathize with the predicament, we cannot provide free housing without getting ourselves into financial difficulties. If you find you are unable to pay the amount past due and late charges, we do require that you move. If, after this three (3) day grace period, you have yet to pay the amount due or have not vacated the home, we will file for a court order to have your possessions removed from the premises. If this situation comes to a court suit, this will require you to pay not only the total amount due from past rent and late charges, but will also require you pay all court costs associated with this suit.

It is in the best interest of the tenant to pay the amount due before a court action is taken. This action could affect not only your credit rating, but also your attempt to rent another property. If you move out of the residence without first paying all rent and charges due, the court will grant a judgment against you that could result in the garnishment of your income or the seizing of your possessions.

PAYMENT ARRANGEMENT

I am currently renting (address) _____ from (owner) _____. I acknowledge that I currently owe $_____ in past-due rent.

I promise that I will pay the above amount owed, in full, by the date of _____, 20___.

In the event that I do not follow through with the above promise for any reason, I shall vacate said premises immediately by the above mentioned date. If I fail to do so, I give my permission to owner to change the locks and allow the owner to re-rent said premises. If said premises are unfurnished, I give said owner or agent permission to remove the furniture from said premises and set it out on the street. The owner will return all personal clothing and belongings to me.

I realize it is my responsibility to pick up my personal belongings and articles no later than 48 hours after owner has changed the locks.

Date: _____ 20_____.

_____
Signed Management

_____
Signed Resident

NOTICE TO VACATE PREMISES

The following notice will be considered VOID if rent due and all charges are paid within the time limit provided.

To _____ (Tenant) and everyone residing at said premises. You are hereby notified that _____ (Landlord) wants you to vacate the premises you are currently occupying and in which you have been renting from me (us). Premises is situated in _____ (County) and State of _____ and is described as follows: _____

Grounds: _____

Your compliance with this notice on or before the _____ (day) of _____ (month) in the year ____ will prevent any court action to be taken by me as stated previously.

YOU ARE BEING ASKED TO LEAVE THE PREMISES. IF YOU DO NOT LEAVE, AN EVICTION ACTION MAY BE INITIATED AGAINST YOU. IF YOU ARE IN DOUBT REGARDING YOUR LEGAL RIGHTS AND OBLIGATIONS AS A TENANT, IT IS RECOMMENDED THAT YOU SEEK LEGAL ASSISTANCE.

Respectfully,

_____
Landlord Printed

_____
Landlord Signed

_____
Date

_____
Address

Should you have any questions regarding this matter, please call _____.

PAST DUE LAND CONTRACT PAYMENT

Date: _____
Tenant: _____
Address: _____
City State Zip: _____

Dear _____:

As of today's date, we have not received your payment for the month of _____.
You now owe $_____ in rent, plus a $ _____ late charge. This payment is due immediately if you wish to continue living in the house.
This is the 30-day notice of default required in Paragraph ____ of your Land Contract. This paragraph states in part:

(Insert text of YOUR land contract's default payment paragraph here)

You will note that unless you correct the default by paying the money owed, the entire balance will immediately become due, and you will immediately owe the entire price of the house. If you move out on or before _____ (30 days from today), leave the house in a clean and orderly condition, and return the keys to me, I will sue you only for the unpaid back rent.

You have three options:

1.   Make a full payment of unpaid rent and late charges and continue buying the house under the land contract.
2.   Move out immediately, leaving the property clean and ready to rent. You will owe only the payments for the time you are in the house.
3.   Wait for the court to evict you and issue a judgment for the entire amount due on the land contract.

I sincerely regret that you were unable to keep up your payments. If you have questions, feel free to give me a call.

Sincerely,

_____

Contract Holder

SECOND NOTICE: LATE RENT

Date: _____

Resident(s) include:
Resident Adult 1: _____
Resident Adult 2: _____
Resident Child(ren): _____

Rental Residence Address:

_____

Dear _____,

This is a reminder that we have yet to receive your rent payment for the month of _____. We ask that you please remit by _____ (date). According to the Lease Agreement signed by you, the rent for this property is due on the _____ of every month with a late fee to be assessed after the _____ day of every month if said rent payment has not been made.

Therefore, per said Lease Agreement, we are placing a late charge on your account in the amount of $_____. We ask that you include this late fee when providing rent payment. We ask that you please remit rent and late fee payment immediately to avoid further action.

Thank you for your prompt attention to this matter.

Respectfully,

_____

Landlord Signature

_____

Landlord Printed

Should you have any questions regarding this manner, please call _____.

CHAPTER 11

Lead Paint Forms

LEAD DISCLOSURE RULES SUMMARY

Adapted from
www.epa.gov/Compliance/resources/policies/civil/tsca/lead.pdf
Please check with an attorney for the correct format and procedure for your state.

Summary of Rule and Requirement

The purpose of the Disclosure Rule is to ensure that individuals and families receive the information necessary to protect themselves and their families from lead-based paint and/ or lead based paint hazards. This information will help families and individuals make informed housing decisions to reduce their risk of exposure to lead hazards.

The Disclosure Rule requires that sellers, lessors, and agents must comply with certain requirements when selling or leasing target housing. For purposes of the Disclosure Rule, "Seller" is defined as any entity that transfers legal title to target housing, in whole or in part. The Disclosure Rule defines "Lessor" as any entity that offers target housing for lease, rent, or sublease. "Purchaser" is defined as an entity that enters into an agreement to purchase an interest in target housing under the Disclosure Rule. "Lessee" is defined as any entity that enters into an agreement to lease, rent, or sublease target housing. Finally, the Disclosure Rule defines "Agent" as any party who enters into a contract with a seller or lessor, including any person who enters into a contract with a representative of the Lessor or Seller, to sell or lease target housing.

The Disclosure Rule requires that before a Purchaser or Lessee is obligated under any contract to purchase or lease target housing, certain requirements must be met. These requirements include the following:

- Sellers and Lessors must disclose the presence of any known lead-based paint and/or lead-based paint hazards to the Purchasers and Lessees and to any Agent;
- Sellers and Lessors must provide Purchasers and Lessees with any available records or reports pertaining to the presence of lead-based paint and/or lead-based paint hazards in the target housing;
- Sellers and Lessors must provide Purchasers and Lessees with an EPA-approved lead hazard information pamphlet;
- Sellers must grant Purchasers a 10-day period to conduct a risk assessment or inspection for the presence of lead-based paint and/or lead-based paint hazards;
- Sellers and Lessors must complete a Disclosure Form certifying compliance with the Disclosure requirements;
- Sellers and Lessors must retain a copy of the Disclosure Form for at least three years from completion of the transaction; and
- Each Agent involved in any transaction to lease or sell target housing must ensure compliance with all requirements of the Disclosure Rule.

The Disclosure Rule contains exclusions for the following transactions:
- Sales of target housing at foreclosure;
- Leases of target housing that have been found to be lead-based paint free by the appropriate inspector;
- Short term leases of 100 days or less;
- Lease renewals where previous disclosure has occurred;
- The purchase, sale or servicing of mortgages;
- The sale or lease of 0-bedroom dwellings; and
- Housing for the elderly or persons with disabilities (unless any child under six (6) years of age resides or is expected to reside in such target housing).

I. Consultation with EPA Headquarters
In the implementation of this enforcement program, EPA Headquarters is requiring that EPA Regional Lead Coordinators ("Regions") consult with Headquarters on a specified number of enforcement actions to ensure consistency and to address any unique issues. Therefore, each region must receive concurrence from Headquarters on the initial six (6) civil administrative complaints and notices of noncompliance before issuance. The Regions must also contact and consult with EPA Headquarters on the use of TSCA subpoenas to enforce the Disclosure Rule. These consultation and concurrence efforts will help ensure national consistency and address issues that arise during implementation of the Disclosure Rule enforcement program.

II. Enforcement Response Policy Applicability
This Disclosure Rule Enforcement Response Policy is immediately applicable and will be used to determine the enforcement response and to calculate penalties in administrative enforcement actions concerning violations of the Disclosure Rule.

III. Applicability to Federal Facilities
As discussed in Section III below, the Disclosure Rule defines "Seller" and "Lessor" to include government agencies. Thus, when a Federal facility or government agency is the Seller or Lessor of target housing as defined in the statute and the rule, the requirements of Section 1018 and the Disclosure Rule apply to such facility or agency.

Section 1018(b)(5) makes a violation of the Disclosure Rule a prohibited act under Section 409 of TSCA and the facility or agency is then subject to EPA enforcement authority under Section 16 of TSCA. Section 408 of TSCA subjects each department, agency, and instrumentality of the executive, legislative, and judicial branches of the Federal Government to all Federal, State, interstate, and local requirements, both substantive and procedural, respecting lead-based paint, lead-based paint activities, and lead-based paint hazards. The Federal, State, interstate, and local substantive and procedural requirements referred to in Section 408 of TSCA include, but are not limited to, all administrative orders and all civil and administrative penalties and fines regardless of whether such penalties or fines are punitive or coercive in nature. The Disclosure Rule contains Federal requirements respecting lead-based paint, lead-based paint activities, and lead-based paint hazards. Therefore, Federal facilities are subject to the Disclosure Rule requirements.

EPA thus has express penalty authority over Federal facilities. In assessing penalties against Federal agencies, EPA will apply the Disclosure Rule Enforcement Response Policy. Before a penalty order becomes final, Section 16(a)(2) of TSCA requires the Administrator to provide the Federal agency with notice and an opportunity for a formal hearing on the record in accordance with the Administrative Procedures Act. 40 C.F.R. Part 22, sets forth the U.S. Environmental Protection Agency's (EPA's) general rules of administrative practice governing the assessment of administrative penalties. The Consolidated Rules of Practice also require that before a final order of the Environmental Appeals Board issued to a Federal agency becomes effective, the head of the department, agency, or instrumentality of the United States to which the order was issued can request a conference with the Administrator [40 C.F.R. § 22.31(e)].

EPA AND HUD REAL ESTATE NOTIFICATION AND DISCLOSURE RULE QUESTIONS AND ANSWERS

Adapted from
www.ct.gov/dph/lib/dph/environmental_health/lead/pdf/1018qa.pdf.
Please check with an attorney for the correct format and procedure for your state.

The Rule

What is the purpose of this rule and who is affected?
To protect the public from exposure to lead from paint, dust, and soil, Congress passed the Residential Lead-Based Paint Hazard Reduction Act of 1992, also known as Title X. Section 1018 of this law directed HUD and EPA to require disclosure of information on lead-based paint and lead-based paint hazards before the sale or lease of most housing built before 1978. The rule would ensure that purchasers and renters of housing built before 1978 receive the information necessary to protect themselves and their families from lead-based paint hazards.

When does the rule take effect?
The rule's effective date depends on the number of housing units owned.
- For owners of more than 4 dwelling units, the effective date is September 6, 1996.

- For owners of 4 or fewer dwelling units, the effective date is December 6, 1996.

Affected Housing

What type of housing is affected by this rule?

This rule applies to all housing defined as target housing, which includes most private housing, public housing, housing receiving federal assistance, and federally owned housing built before 1978.

What type of housing is not affected by this rule?

Housing that is not affected by this rule includes:

- 0-bedroom dwellings, such as lofts, efficiencies, and studios.
- Leases of dwelling units of 100 days or fewer, such as vacation homes or short-term rentals.
- Designated housing for the elderly and the handicapped unless children reside or are expected to reside there.
- Rental housing that has been inspected by a certified inspector and is found to be free of lead-based paint.

How does this rule apply to housing common areas such as stairwells, lobbies, and laundry rooms?

Common areas are those areas in multifamily housing structures that are used or are accessible to all occupants. The rule requires that sellers and lessors disclose available lead information about common areas so that families can be informed about preventive actions.

Why doesn't this rule affect housing built after 1978?

Congress did not extend the law to housing built after 1978 because the Consumer Product Safety Commission banned the use of lead-based paint in housing in 1978.

Is my home unsafe if it contains lead-based paint?

Approximately three-quarters of the nation's housing built before 1978 contains some lead-based paint. This paint, if properly managed and maintained, poses little risk. If allowed to deteriorate, lead from paint can threaten the health of occupants, especially children under 6 years old. If families and building owners are aware of the presence of lead-based paint and the proper actions to take, most lead-based paint hazards can be managed. The EPA pamphlet *Protect Your Family From Lead in Your Home* provides important information for families and home owners to help them identify when lead-based paint is likely to be a hazard and how to get their home checked.

Seller & Lessor Responsibilities

What if I'm selling target housing?

Property owners who sell target housing must:

- Disclose all known lead-based paint and lead-based paint hazards in the housing and any available reports on lead in the housing.
- Give buyers the EPA pamphlet *Protect Your Family from Lead in Your Home.*
- Include certain warning language in the contract as well as signed statements from all parties verifying that all requirements were completed.
- Retain signed acknowledgments for 3 years, as proof of compliance.
- Give buyers a 10-day opportunity to test the housing for lead.

What if I'm renting target housing?

Property owners who rent out target housing must:

- Disclose all known lead-based paint and lead-based paint hazards in the home and any available reports on lead in the housing.

- Give renters the EPA pamphlet *Protect Your Family From Lead in Your Home.*
- Include certain warning language in the lease as well as signed statements from all parties verifying that all requirements were completed.
- Retain signed acknowledgments for 3 years, as proof of compliance.

Am I required to give the EPA pamphlet *Protect Your Family From Lead in Your Home* to existing tenants?

No, but when tenants renew their leases, you must give them the pamphlet and any available reports. In other words, you must give them the same information that you are required to provide new tenants.

What if the buyers/renters don't speak English?

In cases where the buyer or renter signed a purchase or lease agreement in a language other than English, the rule requires that the disclosure language be provided in the alternate language. The EPA pamphlet *Protect Your Family From Lead in Your Home* is printed in English and Spanish and will be made available to the public. EPA and HUD are considering publishing the pamphlet in other languages as well.

Must I check my house for lead prior to sale?

No. The rule does not require that a seller conduct or finance an inspection or risk assessment. The seller, however, is required to provide the buyer a 10-day period to test for lead-based paint or lead-based paint hazards.

Is the seller required to remove any lead-based paint that is discovered during an inspection?

No. Nothing in the rule requires a building owner to remove lead-based paint or lead-based paint hazards discovered during an inspection or risk assessment. In addition, the rule does not prevent the two parties from negotiating hazard reduction activities as a contingency of the purchase and sale of the housing.

What if I know there is lead-based paint in my home?

If you know there is lead-based paint in your home, you are required to disclose this information to the buyer or renter along with any other available reports on lead.

What if the lessor knows that there is no lead-based paint in my rental housing?

If your rental housing has been found to be free of lead-based paint by a certified inspector, this rule does not apply. However, landlords seeking an exclusion to this rule must use state-certified inspectors. If your state does not have a certification program, you may use a certified inspector from another state. In addition, EPA is developing certification requirements for individuals and firms conducting lead-based paint inspections, risk assessments, and abatements.

Agent Responsibilities

What are my responsibilities as an agent?

Agents must ensure that:

- Sellers and landlords are made aware of their obligations under this rule.
- Sellers and landlords disclose the proper information to lessors, buyers, and tenants.
- Sellers give purchasers the opportunity to conduct an inspection.
- Lease and sales contracts contain the appropriate notification and disclosure language and proper signatures.

What is the responsibility of an agent if the seller or landlord fails to comply with this rule?

The agent is responsible for informing the seller or lessor of his or her obligations under this rule. In addition, the agent is responsible if the seller or lessor fails to comply. However, an agent is not responsible for information withheld by the seller or lessor.

Purchaser & Renter Rights

As a purchaser, am I required to conduct and finance an inspection?

No. The rule simply ensures that you have the opportunity to test for lead before purchase.

Can the inspection/risk assessment period be waived?

Yes. The inspection or risk assessment period can be lengthened, shortened, or waived by mutual written consent between the purchaser and the seller.

If I am renting, do I have the same opportunity to test for lead?

Under the law, the 10-day inspection period is limited to sales transactions, but nothing prevents the renter from negotiating with the lessor to allow time for an inspection before rental.

Where can I find a qualified professional to conduct an inspection?

State agencies can provide helpful information for locating qualified professionals in your area. The EPA pamphlet *Protect Your Family From Lead in Your Home* provides the phone numbers of these state agencies. It is important to verify the qualifications of individuals and firms before hiring them.

Must inspectors be certified?

Some cities and states have their own rules concerning inspector certification. These requirements, which may be administered at the state or federal level, may not be in place for several years. Once these requirements are in place, professionals who offer to perform lead-based paint inspections must be certified. The certification requirements that EPA is developing will ensure that inspectors engaged in lead-based paint activities have completed an EPA-certified training program or an EPA-approved state program. Meanwhile, EPA and HUD recommend that people inspect the qualifications and training of individuals and firms before hiring them to conduct risk assessments, inspections, or abatements.

Liability

Does this rule increase my liability for future lead poisoning on my property?

In some cases, disclosure may actually reduce the owner's liability since occupants may be able to prevent exposure from the beginning. Under this rule, however, sellers, landlords, or agents who fail to provide the required notices and information are liable for triple the amount of damages.

Are mortgage lenders liable under these rules if the seller or lessor fails to disclose?

Under the disclosure regulation, the rule does not identify mortgage lenders as liable parties. This rule does not affect other state and federal provisions regarding the obligations and responsibilities of lenders.

What if a seller or lessor fails to comply with these regulations?

A seller, lessor, or agent who fails to give the proper information can be sued for triple the amount of damages. In addition, they may be subject to civil and criminal penalties. Ensuring that disclosure information is given to home buyers and tenants helps all parties avoid misunderstandings before, during, and after sales and leasing agreements.

LEAD PAINT POISONING NOTICE
FOR OWNER OR TENANT

(This notice should be sent via certified mail with a return receipt requested or by personal delivery whereby you get a signature from the tenant or property owner).

Date: _____

Sender of Notice's Name & Address:	Name & Address of Property Owner/Tenant being served this notice:
Phone:	Phone:

This notification is to inform you that the following has occurred or requires your attention:

❑ A child under the age of _____ years, or a pregnant woman, who resides at _____ has been diagnosed with a blood lead level of _____ or more on or before _____.

❑ The following areas need your immediate attention as they may contain lead:
The following areas have been found to contain peeling, chipping, flaking paint that is may be accessible to a child:
❑ Living Room ❑ Kitchen ❑ Bedroom ❑ Bathroom ❑ Dining Room
❑ Hallway ❑ Door Frame ❑ Porch ❑ Stairway ❑ Windows
❑ Exterior Walls ❑ Other Area(s) _____

The following areas have been found to contain structural defects:
❑ Living Room & Kitchen ❑ Bedroom ❑ Bathroom ❑ Dining Room
❑ Hallway ❑ Door Frame ❑ Porch ❑ Stairway ❑ Windows
❑ Exterior Walls ❑ Other Area(s) _____

Please list other Hazardous Conditions or areas:
_____
_____

I, _____Owner/Tenant of the aforementioned property hereby acknowledge having received this Lead Paint Poisoning Notice.

Signature _____ Date_____

LESSOR'S DISCLOSURE OF INFORMATION ON LEAD-BASED PAINT AND/OR LEAD-BASED PAINT HAZARDS

Lead Warning Statement

Housing built before 1978 may contain lead-based paint. Lead from paint, paint chips, and dust can pose health hazards if not managed properly. Lead exposure is especially harmful to young children and pregnant women. Before renting pre-1978 housing, lessors must disclose the presence of known lead based paint and/or lead-based paint hazards in the dwelling. Lessees must also receive a federally approved pamphlet on lead poisoning prevention.

Landlord's Disclosure

(a) Presence of lead-based paint and/or lead-based paint hazards (check (i) or (ii) below):

    (i) _____ Known lead-based paint and/or lead-based paint hazards are present in the building (explain).

    _____

    (ii) _____ Lessor has no knowledge of lead-based paint and/or lead-based paint hazards in the building.

(b) Records and reports available to the lessor (check (i) or (ii) below):

    (i) _____ Lessor has provided the lessee with all available records and reports pertaining to lead-based paint and/or lead-based paint hazards in the building (list documents below).

    _____

    (ii) _____ Lessor has no reports or records pertaining to lead-based paint and/or lead-based paint hazards in the building.

Tenant's Acknowledgment (initial)

(c) _____ Lessee has received copies of all information listed above.

(d) _____ Lessee has received the pamphlet *Protect Your Family from Lead in Your Home*.

Agent's Acknowledgment (initial)

(e) _____ Agent has informed the lessor of the lessor's obligations under 42 U.S.C. 4852d and is aware of his/her responsibility to ensure compliance.

Certification of Accuracy

The following parties have reviewed the information above and certify, to the best of their knowledge, that the information they have provided is true and accurate.

Lessor	Date
Lessee	Date
Agent	Date

SELLER'S DISCLOSURE OF INFORMATION ON LEAD-BASED PAINT AND/OR LEAD-BASED PAINT HAZARDS

Lead Warning Statement

Every purchaser of any interest in residential real property on which a residential dwelling was built prior to 1978 is notified that such property may present exposure to lead from lead-based paint that may place young children at risk of developing lead poisoning. Lead poisoning in young children may produce permanent neurological damage, including learning disabilities, reduced intelligence quotient, behavioral problems, and impaired memory. Lead poisoning also poses a particular risk to pregnant women. The seller of any interest in residential real property is required to provide the buyer with any information on lead-based paint hazards from risk assessments or inspections in the seller's possession and notify the buyer of any known lead-based paint hazards. A risk assessment or inspection for possible lead-based paint hazards is recommended prior to purchase.

Seller's Disclosure

(a) Presence of lead-based paint and/or lead-based paint hazards (check (i) or (ii) below):

    (i)   _____ Known lead-based paint and/or lead-based paint hazards are present in the housing (explain).

            _____

    (ii)   _____ Seller has no knowledge of lead-based paint and/or lead-based paint hazards in the housing.

(b) Records and reports available to the seller (check (i) or (ii) below):

    (i)   _____ Seller has provided the purchaser with all available records and reports pertaining to lead-based paint and/or lead-based paint hazards in the housing (list documents below).

            _____

    (ii)   _____ Seller has no reports or records pertaining to lead-based paint and/or lead-based paint hazards in the housing.

Purchaser's Acknowledgment (initial)

(c) _____ Purchaser has received copies of all information listed above.

(d) _____ Purchaser has received the pamphlet *Protect Your Family from Lead in Your Home.*

(e) Purchaser has (check (i) or (ii) below):

    (i)   _____ received a 10-day opportunity (or mutually agreed upon period) to conduct a risk assessment or inspection for the presence of lead-based paint and/or lead-based paint hazards; or

    (ii)   _____ waived the opportunity to conduct a risk assessment or inspection for the presence of lead-based paint and/or lead-based paint hazards.

Agent's Acknowledgment (initial)

(f) _____ Agent has informed the seller of the seller's obligations under 42 U.S.C. 4852d and is aware of his/her responsibility to ensure compliance.

Certification of Accuracy

The following parties have reviewed the information above and certify, to the best of their knowledge, that the information they have provided is true and accurate.

_____

Seller   Date

_____

Purchaser   Date

_____

Agent   Date

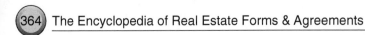
LEAD PAINT POISONING DISCLOSURE

Date: _____

This building was built before 1978 and has probably been painted with lead-based paint. Lead from paint, paint chips, and dust can pose health hazards, particularly to young children and pregnant women, if not managed properly. Lead poisoning in young children may produce permanent neurological damage, including learning disabilities, reduced intelligence quotient, behavioral problems, and impaired memory. Its effects may occur gradually and imperceptibly, often showing no obvious symptoms.

Lead-based paint that is in good condition is usually not a hazard. Children are at risk of getting lead poisoning if they ingest lead from paint chips, which are clearly visible, or lead dust, which is not always visible. Lead-based paint may also be a hazard when found on surfaces that children can chew or that receive a lot of wear-and-tear, such as windows and window sills, doors and doorframes, stairs, railings and banisters, and porches. Lead paints and primers may have been used in many places outdoors, such as on walls, fences, and porches. Lead from exterior house paint may be present in the soil around the outside of the building. The possibility of exposure to lead can be minimized by dusting window sills and other surfaces regularly with a damp cloth, and by preventing small children from chewing on painted surfaces or ingesting paint chips. Newspaper, pottery, furniture, and common household dust may also contain lead. Inform your family and any guests with small children about the danger of lead poisoning.

Your signature on this document is an acknowledgment that you understand the risk posed by lead-based paint in buildings constructed before 1978, and that you agree to hold us harmless of any possible problems that could result from lead-based paint, and any costs involved in diagnosis and treatment of such problems. This agreement includes all people who will be living with you in the building, those for whom you are responsible, and your guests.

Landlord:

____ Lead-based paint and/or lead-based paint hazards are known to be present in the building (explain):

_____

_____ Landlord has no knowledge of lead-based paint and/or lead-based paint hazards in the building.

_____ Landlord has provided the tenant with all available records and reports pertaining to lead-based paint and/or lead-based paint hazards in the building (list documents below).

_____

____ Landlord has no reports or records pertaining to lead-based paint and/or lead-based paint hazards in the building.

Tenant: (Initial below)

____ Tenant has received copies of all information listed above.

____Tenant has received the pamphlet "Protect Your Family from Lead in Your Home."

Tenant: _____

Date: _____

Landlord: _____

Date: _____

CHAPTER 12

Construction Forms and Contracts

CONSTRUCTION CONTRACT

Case Number:_____ Date: _____
Borrower Name(s): _____
Phone #: _____ Phone #: _____

THIS IS A MODEL DOCUMENT FOR USE IN RENOVATION OR CONSTRUC-
TION LOAN TRANSACTIONS. THIS FORM IS PROVIDED AS AN EXAMPLE
AND IS NOT VALID AND ENFORCEABLE IN ALL JURISDICTIONS. LENDERS
SHOULD CONSULT WITH LEGAL COUNSEL TO ENSURE THAT ALL FORMS
USED TO ORIGINATE RENOVATION OR CONSTRUCTION MORTGAGES
ARE APPROPRIATE, AND THAT ALL LEGAL INSTRUMENTS ARE COMPLET-
ED CORRECTLY AND IN COMPLIANCE WITH APPLICABLE LAW.

THIS CONSTRUCTION CONTRACT ("Contract") dated as of _____, ____
by and between _____ ("Owner")
and _____ ("Contractor").

Owner and Contractor, in executing this Construction Contract, agree as follows:

1. Work.
Contractor shall build the items identified in Exhibit "A" ("Work") in accordance with
the specifications in the Contract Documents, as identified in Article 8 of this Contract,
on property that is located at _____
_____ ("Property").

2. Contract Time.

The Work will be completed on or before _____ ("Completion Date"), subject to modifications in approved Change Orders. The Completion Date shall be the date when the Work is sufficiently complete in accordance with the Contract Documents so that Owner can occupy or utilize the Property for its intended use ("Substantial Completion"). If Owner will pay Contractor for all or part of the Work with funds advanced by a lender, Substantial Completion shall be the date as defined by the loan documents. Before starting the Work, Contractor shall submit an estimated project schedule indicating the starting and completion dates of various stages of the Work for review by the Owner.

3. Price.

Owner shall pay to Contractor $_____ ("Contract Price") for completion of the Work.

4. Change Orders.

Any increase or decrease in the Contract Price, change in the Work or change in the Contract Time must be set forth in a change order signed by Owner and Contractor and approved by the lender ("Change Order").

5. Payment Procedures.

a) Progress Payments. Contractor shall submit to Owner a request for payment in a form agreed to by Owner and Contractor and approved by lender ("Request for Advance"), which shall cover a period of at least_____ calendar days.

Within _____ calendar days after a Request for Advance is presented, Owner shall notify Contractor if Owner has any concerns about the Request for Advance that Owner believes should be resolved before Owner pays the amounts specified in the Request for Advance, and, in this event, Owner and Contractor shall promptly meet to address such concerns. Owner shall pay Contractor _____ percent (__%) of the full amount covered by the Request for Advance within _____ calendar days from the day it was presented while retaining _____ percent (__%) thereof ("Holdback") to be paid simultaneously with the final payment. Payment may be withheld for: (1) failure to perform the Work in accordance with the Contract Documents; (2) defective Work that is not corrected; or (3) failure of the Contractor to pay subcontractors or to pay for labor, materials or equipment when due.

b) Final Payment. Final payment of the balance of the Contract Price including the Holdback shall be made in accordance with the following procedures:

i)   When Contractor considers the Work substantially complete, Contractor shall notify Owner in writing. Within a reasonable time thereafter, Owner and Contractor shall inspect the Work. Promptly after such inspection, Owner shall deliver to Contractor a written punch list of the items that must be completed in order for the Work to reach final completion ("Final Completion"). Alternatively, Owner shall deliver to Contractor a written statement that Final Completion has been reached because no punch list items remain to be completed.

ii)   If Owner delivers a written punch list to Contractor, then Contractor shall deliver to Owner a written notice that the Work is finally complete when Contractor believes that the punch list items have been completed. Then Owner and Contractor shall promptly inspect the punch list items. Promptly after such inspection, Owner shall deliver to Contractor either (i) a written statement that Final Completion has been reached or (ii) another written punch list of the items that still must be completed in order for the Work to reach Final Completion in which event the punch list procedure described above shall be repeated until all punch list items have been completed.

iii)   When Final Completion has been reached and after Contractor has delivered to Owner all maintenance and operating instructions, schedules, guarantees, certificates of inspection, marked up record documents and other documents, Contractor may request final payment following the procedure for progress payments. The final Request for Advance shall be accompanied by all documentation required by the Contract Documents, together with complete and legally effective releases or waivers (approved by Owner and lender) of all potential liens arising out of or filed in connection with the Work.

6. Interest.

Payments due and unpaid to Contractor shall bear interest at the rate of _____ percent (__%) per annum or the maximum rate allowed by law at the place of the Work, whichever is lower.

7. Contractor's Representation.

In order to induce Owner to enter into this Contract, Contractor affirms that Contractor has reviewed and is familiar with the nature and extent of the Contract Documents, Work site, locality, and all local conditions and laws and regulations that may affect cost, progress, performance, or furnishing of the Work. Contractor is duly licensed to perform the Work as required by local laws and regulations.

8. Contract Documents.

The Contract Documents that comprise the entire Contract between Owner and Contractor concerning the Work consist of this Contract, Exhibit "A," the Plans and Specifications, all Change Orders and _____.

9. Contractor's Responsibilities.

a) Performance. Contractor shall perform the Work in accordance with the Contract Documents, and shall be solely responsible for the means, methods, techniques, sequences, and procedures of construction.

b) Personnel. Contractor shall provide competent, suitable personnel to survey and lay out the Work and perform construction as required by the Contract Documents. Contractor shall at all times maintain good discipline and order at the Property.

c) Furnished Items. Contractor shall supply and take full responsibility for all materials, equipment, labor, transportation, construction equipment and machinery, tools, appliances, fuel, power, light, heat, telephone, water sanitary facilities, temporary facilities, and all other facilities and incidentals necessary for the furnishing, performance, testing, start-up, and completion of the Work.

d) Materials. All materials and equipment shall be new and of good quality, unless otherwise specified in the Contract Documents. All materials and equipment shall be applied, installed, connected, erected, used, cleaned, and conditioned according to the instructions and advice furnished by the applicable supplier.

e) Subcontractors. Contractor shall be fully responsible to Owner for all acts and omissions of its subcontractors, suppliers and other persons and organizations performing or furnishing any of the Work under a direct or indirect contract with Contractor to the same extent that Contractor is responsible for Contractor's own acts and omissions. Nothing in the Contract Documents shall constitute any contractual relationship between Owner and any such subcontractor, supplier, or other person or organization, nor shall it create any lien on the Owner or any obligation on the part of Owner to pay any such subcontractor, supplier or other person or organization except as may otherwise be required by laws and regulations.

(f) Permits; Inspections. Contractor shall apply for, obtain, and pay for all construction permits and licenses. Whenever necessary and in a timely manner, Owner shall assist Contractor, in obtaining such permits and licenses. Contractor shall pay all governmental charges and inspection fees necessary for the accomplishment of the Work. Contractor shall give all notices and comply with all laws and regulations applicable to furnishing and performance of the Work.

(g) Taxes. Contractor shall pay all applicable sales, consumer, use, and other similar taxes required to be paid by Contractor in accordance with the laws and regulations of the place where the Work is being performed.

(h) Use of Premises. Contractor shall confine construction equipment, the storage of materials and equipment and the operations of workers to the Property, and shall not unreasonably encumber the Property with materials or equipment. Contractor shall be fully responsible for any damage to the Property or contiguous areas resulting from the performance of the Work. During the progress of the Work, Contractor shall prevent accumulations of waste materials, rubbish, and other debris resulting from the Work. When the Work is completed, Contractor shall remove all waste materials, rubbish, and debris from and about the Property as well as all surplus materials, tools, appliances, construction equipment, and machinery, and shall leave the Property clean and ready for occupancy by Owner.

(i) Record Documents. Contractor shall maintain in a safe place at the Property one record copy of all drawings, specifications, addenda, written amendments, Change Orders, and the like in good order and annotated to show all changes made during construction, which will be delivered to Owner.

(j) Safety. Contractor shall be responsible to initiate, maintain, and supervise all safety precautions and programs in connection with the Work. Contractor shall comply with all applicable laws and regulations relating to the safety of persons or property.

(k) Continuing the Work. Contractor shall carry on the Work and adhere to the progress schedule during all disputes or disagreements with Owner.

(l) Damage to the Work. Contractor shall repair or replace, at Contractor's sole expense, every portion of the Work that is damaged or destroyed prior to Final Completion and caused in whole or in part by the acts or omissions of Contractor. Notwithstanding the foregoing, Owner shall bear the cost of such repair or replacement if the sole cause of the damage or destruction of the Work was Owner's negligence.

(m) Warranty. Contractor warrants and guarantees to Owner that all Work will be in accordance with the Contract Documents and will not be defective. If within one year after the date of Final Completion or such longer period of time as may be prescribed by laws or regulations or by the terms of any specific provision or applicable special guarantee in the Contract Documents, any Work is found to be defective, Contractor shall promptly, without cost to Owner and in accordance with Owner's written instructions, either correct the defective Work, or if the Owner has rejected it, remove it from the Property and replace it with non-defective Work. If Contractor does not promptly comply with the terms of the Owner's instructions, or in a situation where delay would result in serious risk of loss or damage, Owner may have the defective Work corrected or the rejected Work removed and replaced. All direct and indirect costs associated with such removal and replacement (including but not limited to fees and charges of engineers, architects, attorneys, and other professionals) will be paid by Contractor.

(n) Indemnify and Hold Harmless. Contractor shall indemnify and hold harmless Owner against all loss, liability, cost expense, damage, and economic detriment of any kind whatsoever that arises out of or results from performance of the Work but only to the extent caused in whole or in part by the acts or omissions of the Contractor.

(o) Related Work at Property. Owner's employees or other contractors contracted by Owner may perform other work at the Property which is not part of the Work. Contractor shall afford Owner's employees and each other contractor who is a party to such a direct contract proper and safe access to the Property and a reasonable opportunity to transport materials and equipment onto the property, store them, and carry out such work. Contractor shall do all alteration, cutting, fitting, and patching of the Work necessary to make its several parts come together properly and to integrate with work done by other contractors. Contractor shall not cut, excavate, or otherwise act in a way that alters or endangers the work of other contractors. Contractor will only cut or alter work done by other contractors with the written consent of Owner and those whose work will be affected.

10. Insurance.

(a) Contractor's Insurance. Contractor shall purchase and maintain appropriate comprehensive general liability and other insurance, with limits and features as follows: _____.

Before any Work is started, Contractor shall deliver to Owner certificates (and other evidence of insurance requested by Contractor) that Contractor is required to purchase and maintain.

(b) Owner's Insurance. Owner shall be responsible for purchasing and maintaining Owner's liability insurance and other reasonably appropriate insurance.

11. Termination.

(a) Termination by Owner. If the Contractor breaches any of its obligations under this Agreement, then Owner may give Contractor written notification identifying such breach. If Contractor has not cured such breach within seven (7) calendar days from its receipt of Owner's written notification or if such breach cannot be cured within such seven (7) day period, then if Contractor either does not begin cure within such seven (7) day period or fails to diligently prosecute cure to completion, Owner may terminate this Contract and take possession of the Work. Alternatively, instead of terminating the Contract, Owner may cure the breach and deduct the cost thereof from amounts otherwise owed to the Contractor.

(b) Termination by Contractor. If the Owner breaches any of its obligations under this Agreement, then Contractor may give Owner written notification identifying such breach. If Owner has not cured such breach within seven (7) calendar days from its receipt of Contractor's written notification, or if such breach cannot be cured within such seven (7) day period, then if Owner either does not begin cure within such seven (7) day period or fails to diligently prosecute cure to completion, Contractor may terminate this Contract.

12. Assignment.

Assignment of any rights or interests under this Contract shall not be binding on any party to this Contract without the written consent of such party. Payments due under this Contract may not be assigned. Notwithstanding the foregoing, the Owner hereby assigns all of its rights, title, and interest in and to this Contract to the Owner's lender, _____, having an address at _____ _____, as additional security for the loan. The Contractor hereby consents to such assignment. Notwithstanding anything to the contrary in this Contract, upon a breach by the Owner of this Contract, the Contractor shall give the lender notice of such a breach, at the address set forth above, and provided that the Owner or the lender cures such default within a reasonable period and continues to pay the Contractor all amounts due under this Contract, the Contractor shall continue to perform its services under this Contract.

13. Heirs and Assigns.

The agreements contained in the Contract Documents are binding upon the Owner and Agent and their respective heirs, successors, legal representatives, and assigns.

14. Governing Law.

This Contract, and all transactions carried out in connection with it, shall be governed by, construed, and enforced in accordance with the laws of the State of _____.

IN WITNESS WHEREOF, Owner and Contractor have signed this Contract.
This Contract will be effective on _____, _____.
Owner: _____   Contractor: _____
Address for giving notices: License No._____
By: _____
Address for giving notices: _____

CONSTRUCTION CONTRACT ADDENDUM

Date: _____
The following is a legal addendum to the contract made between _____ and _____ on _____ (date).

Both parties that were part of the contract agreement hereby understand and agree that the contract agreement is not an employment contract but an agreement with the task to accomplish specific results.

Both parties agree and understand that _____ is considered an independent agent and is not an employee of _____.

_____
Signed

_____
Signed

TERMINATION OF CONSTRUCTION CONTRACT

Date: _____

It is hereby known that _____ and _____ have had a previous construction agreement of which was dated and signed on _____.

It is hereby understood that both parties would like to terminate said agreement.

Both parties agree to the following terms and conditions:
1. The aforementioned construction contract will end on _____.
2. Both of the parties equally agree to release and un-encumber each other of any liability whatsoever with regards to that agreement.
3. In all other regards, the said agreement will hereby continue in full force and effect.

Both parties hereby agree and set forth this termination agreement on the date listed above.

_____

Signed

_____

Signed

MANAGER'S CONSTRUCTION CONTRACT

1. General

This contract is entered into this the day of _____, by and between _____ hereafter Owner and _____ hereafter Manager, and provides for supervision of construction by Manager of a residence to be built on Owner's Property at _____, and described as _____. The project is described on drawings dated_____ and specifications dated_____, which documents are a part thereof.

2. Schedule

The project is to star as near as possible to _____, with anticipated completion_____ months form starting date.

3. Contract Fee and Payment

a. Owner agrees to pay Manager a minimum fee of _____ ($_____) for the work performed under this contract, and based on the next schedule

i.	Down payment due prior to commencement of the job	$_____
ii.	Framed	$_____
iii.	Roof	$_____
iv.	Ready for drywall	$_____
v.	Trimmed out	$_____
vi.	Final	$_____

b. Payments billed by Manager are due in full within 10 days of bill mailing date

c. Final payment to Manager is due full upon completion of residence; however, Manager may bill upon substantial completion the amount of the final payment less 10 percent of the value of work yet outstanding. In such case, the amount of the fee withheld will be billed upon completion.

4. General Interest of Contract

This contract treats the Owner effectively as the "General Contractor." The Manager will provide the Owner with expert guidance and advice, supervision and coordination of trades and material delivery. The Manager will act in a professional capacity and simply as agent for Owner, and he/she shall not assume or incur any pecuniary responsibility to contractors, subcontractors, laborers, or material suppliers. Owner will contract directly with subcontractors and obtain from them the certificates of insurance and releases of liens. Similarly, Owner will open his own accounts with material suppliers and be billed and pay directly for materials supplied. Owner shall pay all expenses incurred completing the project, except Manager's overhead as specifically exempted in paragraph 9. At all times, Manager shall act in a manner intended to be beneficial to the interests of the Owner.

5. General Responsibilities of Manager

Manager shall have full responsibility for coordination of trades, ordering materials and scheduling of work, correction of errors and conflicts, if any, in the work, materials, or plans, compliance with applicable codes, judgment as to the adequacy of trade's work to meet standards specified, together with any other function that might reasonably be expected in order to provide Owner with a single source of responsibility for supervision and coordination of work.

6. Specific Responsibilities of Manager

a. Submit to Owner in a timely manner a list of subcontractors and suppliers that Manager believes competent to perform the work at competitive prices. Owner may use such recommendations or not at his option

b. Submit to owner a list of items requiring Owner's selection, with scheduled dates for selection indicated, and recommended sources indicated

c. Obtain on Owner's behalf all permits required by governmental authorities

d. Arrange for all required surveys and site engineering work

e. Arrange for all the installation of temporary services

f. Arrange for and supervise clearing, disposal of stumps and brush, and all excavating and grading work

g. Develop material lists and order all materials in a timely manner, from sources designated by Owner

h. Schedule, coordinate, and supervise the work for all subcontractors designated by the Owner

i. Review, when requested by Owner, questionable bills and recommend payment action to Owner

j. Arrange for common labor for hand, digging, grading, and cleanup during construction, and for disposal of construction waste

k. Supervise the project through completion, as defined in paragraph 11.

7. Responsibilities of Owner

1. Arrange all financing needed for project, so that sufficient funds exist to pay all bills within ten days of their presentation

2. Select subcontractors and suppliers in a timely manner so as not to delay the work. Establish charge accounts and execute contracts with same, as appropriate, and inform Manager of accounts opened and of Manager's authority in using said accounts

3. Select items requiring Owner selection, and inform Manager of selections and sources on or before date shown in selection list

4. Inform Manager promptly of any changes desired or other matter affecting schedule so that adjustments can be incorporated in the schedule

5. Appoint an agent to pay for work and make decisions in Owner's behalf in cases where Owner is unavailable to do so

6. Assume complete responsibility for any theft and vandalism of Owner's property occurring on the job. Authorize replacement/repairs required in a timely manner

7. Provide a surety bond for his lender is required

8. Obtain release of liens documentation as required by Owner's lender

9. Provide insurance coverage as listed in paragraph 2

10. Pay promptly for all work done, materials used, and other services and fees generated in the execution of the project, except as specifically exempted in paragraph 9

8. Exclusions
The following items shown on the drawings and/or specifications are NOT included in this contract; therefore, Manager's supervision responsibilities are the following:
(List below)

9. Extras/Charges
Manager's fee is based on supervising the project as defined in the drawings and specifications. Should Extras or Changes occasioned by Owner, unforeseen site conditions, or governmental authorities require additional supervisory work, Manager will be paid an additional fee of 15 percent of cost of such work. The basic contract fee is a minimum fee and no downward adjustment will be made if the scope of work is reduced, unless contract is canceled in accordance with paragraphs 14 or 15.

10. Manager's Facilities
Manager will furnish his own transportation and office facilities while supervising the project at no expense to Owner. Manager shall provide, at no cost to Owner, general liability and workers' compensation insurance coverage only for Manager's direct employees.

11. Use of Manager's Accounts
Manager may have certain trade accounts not available to Owner which Owner may find it to his advantage to utilize. If Manager is billed and pays such accounts form Manager's resources, Owner will reimburse any bills and payments paid by Manager for such accounts within 10 days of receipt of Manager's bill at cost plus 8 percent of the materials or services.

12. Project Completion
a. The project shall be deemed completed when all the terms of this contract have been fulfilled, and a Residential Use Permit has been issued.

b. The project shall be deemed "substantially complete" when a Residential Use Permit has been issued, and work equivalent to less than $500 remains to be done.

13. Insurance

Owner shall insure that workmen's compensation and general liability insurance are provided to protect all parties of interest and shall hold Manager harmless from all claims by subcontractors, suppliers, and their personnel, and for personnel arranged for by manager in Owner's behalf, if any.

Owner shall maintain fire and extended coverage insurance sufficient to provide 100 percent coverage of project value at all stages of construction, and Manager shall be named in the policy to insure his interest in the project.

Should owner of manager determine that certain subcontractors, laborers, or suppliers are not adequately covered by general liability or workers' compensation insurance to protect Owner's and/or Manager's interests, Manager may, as agent of Owner, cover said personnel on Manager's policies, and Owner shall reimburse Manager for the premium at cost plus 10 percent.

14. Termination of Contract by Manager

Should the work be stopped by any public authority for a period of 30 days or more through no fault of the Manager, or work should be stopped through act or neglect of Owner for 10 days or more, or should owner fail to pay Manager any payment due within 10 days written notice to Owner, Manager may stop work and/or terminate this contract and recover form. Owner payment for all work completed as a proration of the total contract sum, plus 25 percent of the remaining to be paid if the contract were completed as liquidated damages.

15. Termination of Contract by Owner

Should the work be stopped or wrongly performed through act or neglect of Manager for 10 days or more, Owner may so notify Manager in writing. If work is not properly resumed within 10 days of such notice, Owner may terminate this contract. Upon termination, entire balance then due to Manager for that termination of work then completed, as a proration of the total contract sum, shall be due and payable and all further liabilities of Manager under this contract shall cease. Balance due to Manager shall take into account any additional cost to Owner to complete the house occasioned by Manager.

16. Manager/Owner's Liability for Collection Expenses

Should Manager or Owner respectively be required to collect fund rightfully due him through legal proceedings, Manager or Owner respectively agrees to pay all costs and reasonable attorney's fees.

17. Warranties

Manager warrants that he will supervise the construction in accordance with the terms of this contract. No other warranty by Manager is implied or exists.

Owner (Signature):_____

Manager (Signature): _____

IN WITNESS WHEREOF,

State of _____

County of_____

Sworn to and subscribed before me, a Notary Public, for the State of _____

County of _____,

This _____ day of _____ 20_____

By : _____ Notary Public
My Commission Expires: This _____day of _____, 20 _____

RENOVATION & REMODELING COSTS

(Many Line Items Will Be Blank)			Original Amount:	$
A. PRE-CONSTRUCTION COSTS:	**Total Project Costs**	**Adjusted Costs**	**Changes to Budget**	**Remaining Funds**
Testing & Inspection fees, to include asbestos, radon, lead				
Design review/Plan check fees				
Permits - City/County				
Extra insurance				
5 Utility connection fees or temporary utilities				
TOTAL PRE-CONSTRUCTION COSTS				
B. CONSTRUCTION COSTS:				
General requirements				
Special inspections/Testing geotech, structural				
Equipment rental				
Project management/Supervision				
SUB-TOTAL GENERAL REQUIREMENTS				
Site preparation				
Clearing, grading, excavation				
Demolition-removing				
Exterior and interior walls				
Roof: shingles				
Roof: rafters				
Plaster, drywall, other wall materials				
Electrical wiring				
Electrical heaters, radiators, etc.				

Plumbing				
Asbestos, lead paint, other hazardous materials				
Stakeout for new addition				
Shoring & fill				
Site retaining walls/waterproofing/backfill				
Site drainage				
Private septic system OR				
Domestic water well, pump, water system				
Pump house & pressure water system				
SUB-TOTAL SITE PREPARATION				
Foundation complete				
Underground utilities				
Foundation & building footers, retaining walls poured				
Waterproofing				
Concrete slab				
SUB-TOTAL FOUNDATION COMPLETE				
Building rough-in completion				
Rough framing materials:				
Walls				
Floors				
Ceilings				
Roof				
Addition				
Structural steel				
Trusses/components				
Rough framing labor				

Concrete interior floors				
Plumbing				
Toilet(s) - list number				
Sink, kitchen				
Sink, bathroom (#)				
Refinish tub				
Replace tub				
Water heater				
Piping				
New plumbing - kitchen				
New plumbing - bath				
Heating, ventilation, air conditioning				
Electrical- refit				
Electrical - new				
Fire protection - sprinklers				
Fireplaces and flues				
Insulation				
Security & communications pre-wiring				
SUB-TOTAL BUILDING ROUGH-IN COMPLETION				
Exterior weather-tight				
Waterproofing decks, etc.				
Sheet metal, gutters, downspouts				
Roof covering				
Windows				
Exterior doors				
Skylights				
Glazing				

Exterior siding				
Exterior trim				
Stucco				
Masonry veneer				
Garage doors				
60 Exterior painting				
SUB-TOTAL EXTERIOR				
Drywall/Finish carpentry				
Insulation				
Drywall/Plaster				
Interior stair treads, railings				
Cabinetry				
Finish materials/Millwork				
Interior doors				
Interior trim				
Finish hardware				
Finish carpentry labor				
SUB-TOTAL DRYWALL/ FINISH CARPENTRY				
Interior finish				
Counter tops				
Tub/shower/enclosures				
Interior painting/ Wall coverings				
Hard surface finish flooring				
Carpeting				
Built-in appliances				
Security system				
Intercom				

Built-in vacuum cleaner				
Plumbing fixtures				
Finish electrical				
Lighting fixtures				
Finish heating, ventilating, air cond.				
Solar backup				
Bath Accessories				
Tub, Shower Doors, Mirrors				
Finish Grading				
Pool/Spa				
Hardscape (Driveway, Walkways, Steps)				
Landscaping				
Irrigation System				
Fencing and+ Gates				
Touch-up/Final Cleaning				
Miscellaneous				
SUB-TOTAL BUILDING COMPLETION				
TOTAL CONSTRUCTION COSTS				
Loan costs - closing + interest				
TOTAL LINE ITEM COST BREAKDOWN				

CHAPTER 13

Land Forms
and Contracts

LAND CONTRACT FOR PURCHASING

Date: _____

Seller: _____

Address: _____

City: _____ State: _____ Zip: _____

Buyer: _____

Address: _____

City: _____ State: _____ Zip: _____

The Seller, on behalf of himself, his heirs, and assigns, agrees to sell to the Buyer, their heirs, and assigns, the real estate commonly known as:

_____

and further described as: _____

together with all appurtenances, rights, privileges, and easements, and all buildings and fixtures in their present condition located upon the property.

1. Contract Price and Method of Payment:

The Buyer agrees to purchase the above described property for the sum of _____Dollars ($_____), payable as follows:

a) A deposit of $_____ at the time of execution of this Land Contract.

b) The principal balance of $_____ together with interest on the unpaid balance owed by Buyer, payable in consecutive monthly installments of $_____ beginning on the _____ day of _____20____, and on the _____ day of every subsequent month until the balance and interest is paid in full, or until the _____ day of _____, 20_____ when the entire remaining balance plus accrued interest shall become due and payable. There is no prepayment penalty if the Buyer elects to pay the entire purchase price on this contract.

2. Interest Rate:

The interest on the unpaid balance due shall be (___ %) percent per year computed monthly, in accordance with a month amortization schedule during the life of this agreement. Payments shall be credited first to the interest and the remainder to the principal or other sums due to the Seller. The total amount of principal and interest unpaid after a payment has been applied shall be the interest-bearing principal amount of this obligation for the next succeeding interest computation period. If any payment is not received within _____ (____) days of payment date, a late charge of (_____%) percent will be assessed. The monthly installments shall be payable as set forth by the Seller in this contract.

3. Encumbrances:

Said real estate is presently subject to a mortgage with _____ . The Seller shall not place any additional mortgage on the premises without the prior written permission of the Buyer. To protect Buyer's interests, Buyer may elect at any time to pay any sums due under this agreement directly to the mortgagee, and any amounts remaining to the Seller. Seller understands that this transaction may permit the mortgagee to exercise their right to accelerate the loan and to call the remaining balance due. In any such event, the Seller agrees to hold buyer harmless and in no way liable for any damage to seller as a result of such action. Seller initials _____.

4. Evidence of Title:

The Seller shall be required to provide an abstract or guarantee of title, statement of title, title insurance, or other evidence of title satisfactory to Buyer.

5. Recording of Contract:

The Seller shall permit a copy of this contract to be recorded in the _____ County Recorder's Office at Buyer's discretion at any time subsequent to the execution of this Contract.

6. Real Estate Taxes:

Real estate taxes to the County Treasurer shall be in the Seller's name throughout the term of this agreement. Payment of said taxes shall become the responsibility of the Buyer upon the execution of this agreement, and [___] shall [___] shall not be escrowed and added to the payment required by Buyer herein.

7. Insurance and Maintenance:

The Seller shall insure the property with a non owner-occupant (landlord) policy against fire and extended coverage to the benefit of both parties sufficient to cover both parties' interests in the property. This insurance policy shall be for an amount no less than _____, payment of which shall be the responsibility of the Buyer, and which shall be escrowed and added to the payment due under this contract.

8. Transfer of Possession:

The Seller shall be given possession of the above described premises at the execution of this Contract and shall subsequently keep possession subject to the default provisions set forth below.

9. Delivery of Deed:

Upon full payment of this contract, Seller shall issue a General Warranty deed to the Buyer free of all encumbrances except as otherwise set forth. In addition, Buyer reserves the right to convert this contract into a note and mortgage that shall bear the same terms as the contract for the remaining balance, and receive a warranty Deed to Buyer or assigns from Seller any time the following conditions have been met by Buyer,

1. At least 20% of the purchase price has been paid to the Seller.
2. Buyer is willing to pay all the costs of title transfer and document preparations.

10. Default by Buyer:

If Buyer fails to make an installment payment within thirty (30) days of when it is due under the terms of this contract, the entire unpaid balance shall become due and collectable at the discretion of the Seller. Seller shall be entitled to all the remedies provided for by the laws of this state and/or to any other remedies. If this Contract is breached in any other respect by the Buyer, Seller shall be entitled to all relief provided for by the laws of this state now or in the future.

11. Payment of Taxes and Insurance Premiums:

If Buyer fails to maintain current the status of all real estate taxes and insurance premiums as required under this Contract, Seller may pay any such premiums, taxes, interest, or penalties, and add the amount paid to the principal amount owing under this contract, or to exercise any remedies available to the seller provided for by the laws of this state now or in the future.

12. One-time Waiver:

No waiver by Seller at any time of any of the terms of this agreement shall be construed as a permanent waiver or as a release from any of the obligations of the Buyer under the terms of this Contract.

13. General Provisions:

To the knowledge of the Seller, no government agency, or employee or official of a government agency, has given any notice to the Seller that it considers the construction on the Property or the operation or use of the Property to be out of compliance with any law, ordinance, regulation, or order, or that any investigation has been or might be initiated respecting any possible non- compliance.

14. Special Provisions:

_____

15. Entire Agreement:

This document contains the entire agreement between the Owner and the Agent. No prior agreements, verbal statements or understandings pertaining to any of the matters in this Agreement shall be effective for any purpose.

IN WITNESS WHEREOF, the parties have set their hands this _____day of _____, 20_____,

BUYER (SIGNATURE):_____
WITNESS (SIGNATURE):_____
SELLER (SIGNATURE): _____
WITNESS (SIGNATURE): _____

State of _____

County of_____

Sworn to and subscribed before me, a Notary Public, for the State of _____

County of _____

This _____ day of _____ 20_____

By: _____

Notary Public

My Commission Expires: This _____day of _____, 20 _____

CHAPTER 14

Quit-Claim
Deed Forms

QUIT-CLAIM DEED VERSION 1

This Indenture Witnesseth That _____

_____

of _____ County, and State of _____

RELEASE AND QUIT-CLAIM
To _____

_____

of _____ County, in the State of _____

for the sum of _____ Dollars

the REAL ESTATE in _____ County,

in the State of _____, described as:

_____

_____

_____
Grantor's Signature

_____
Grantor's Name

_____
Recipient Signature

_____
Recipient Name

_____
Witness

_____
Witness

IN WITNESS WHEREOF,
State of _____
County of_____
Sworn to and subscribed before me, a Notary Public, for the State of _____
County of _____
This _____ day of _____ 20_____
By:_____
Notary Public
My Commission Expires: This _____day of _____, 20 _____

QUIT-CLAIM DEED VERSION 2

Date: _____
Grantor: _____
Address: _____
City: _____ State: _____ Zip: _____
Recipient: _____
Address: _____
City: _____ State: _____ Zip: _____

The Grantor, in consideration of One Dollar ($1.00) paid by the Recipient, and for other good and valuable consideration, the receipt of which is hereby acknowledged, before these witnesses does remise, release, and quit-claim unto the Recipient, and his/her heirs and assigns, forever, all the right, title, interest, claim, and demand that the Grantor has in and to the following described lot, piece, or parcel of land:
(INSERT LEGAL DESCRIPTION)

_____
_____

The Recipient, his/her heirs and assigns shall have and hold the premises described above and all estate therein, together with all the rights, privileges, buildings and easements belonging to it, and all proceeds, title, interest, and claim whatsoever of the Grantor, either in law or equity.

IN WITNESS WHEREOF,
State of _____
County of_____
Sworn to and subscribed before me, a Notary Public, for the State of _____
County of _____
This _____ day of _____ 20_____
By:_____
Notary Public
My Commission Expires: This _____day of _____, 20 _____

QUIT-CLAIM DEED VERSION 3

Date: _____

This Quit-Claim Deed is executed this date by _____(Grantor)

who resides at _____ and _____

(Recipient) who resides at _____.

The Grantor, in consideration of the payment of $1.00 (One Dollar) paid by the Recipient, for which this agreement serves as a receipt, does hereby remise, release, and quit-claim to the Recipient, all right, title, interest, and claim which the Grantor has in and to the following described lot, piece, or parcel of land located in _____ _____ (City, County, State) to with:

_____

_____

to have and hold forever, together with all with all the rights, privileges, buildings and easements belonging to it, all interest, equity, and claim whatsoever the Grantor may have, either in law or equity, for Recipient's proper use and benefit.

IN WITNESS WHEREOF, the Grantor has signed this document on the date written above.

_____

Grantor Signature

_____

Recipient Signature

Signed, sealed, and delivered in presence of:

_____

Witness

_____

Witness

IN WITNESS WHEREOF,

State of _____

County of_____

Sworn to and subscribed before me, a Notary Public, for the State of _____

County of _____

This _____ day of _____ 20_____

By:_____

Notary Public

My Commission Expires: This _____day of _____, 20 _____

QUIT-CLAIM DEED VERSION 4

For and in consideration of the property located at_____, in the county of_____ and state of_____ bounded and described as follows *[legal description of real property]*:

_____

_____

In consideration of the compensation of _____this quit-claim deed does serve to remit and release all ownership, interest, title, and rights by grantor _____ to the above stated property unto seller_____ whose current address is _____ _____.

Witness my hand [and seal] this _____ day of _____*[month]*, _____*[year]*. This quitclaim deed is executed.

_____

Notary Public

_____

Acknowledgment of Seller

_____

Acknowledgment of Buyer

_____

Witness

CHAPTER 15

Mortgage, Title, and Bank Forms and Agreements

MORTGAGE

Date: _____

Mortgagor: _____

Address: _____

City: _____ State: _____ Zip: _____

Mortgagee: _____

Address: _____

City: _____ State: _____ Zip: _____

1. Amount of Lien: "Note"

Mortgagor is indebted to Mortgagee for the amount of $_____ (U.S. Dollars) and has agreed to pay this amount, plus interest, according to the terms of a certain note (the "Note") given by Mortgagor to Mortgagee, dated _____ (Date).

2. Description of Property Subject To Lien: "Premises"

To secure the payment of the Secured Indebtedness defined in this mortgage agreement, Mortgagor grants, sells, and conveys to the Mortgagee the property located in _____ County, in the State of _____, described in detail in Exhibit "A" attached to and made a part of this document, together with all buildings, structures and other improvements now located, or to be located in the future, on, above, or below the surface of that property, or on any part and parcel of that property; and, together with all and any of the tenements, easements, riparian, and littoral rights, and appurtenances belonging to or associated in any way with that property, whether owned currently or acquired by Mortgagor in the future, and including all rights of ingress and egress to and from adjoining property (currently existing or arising in the future) together with the reversion or reversions, remainder and remainders, rents, issues, and profits from them; and all the estate, right, title, interest, claim, and demand of any kind of Mortgagor in respect to the property and every part and parcel thereof; and, together with all machinery, apparatus, equipment, fittings, fixtures, whether actually or constructively attached to the property specified in this mortgage agreement, and including all trade, domestic, and ornamental fixtures, and articles of personal property of every kind and nature ("Equipment"), now owned or acquired in the future by Mortgagor and located now or in the future in, upon or under that property or any part of that property, and used or usable in connection with any present or future operation of the property; and, together with all the common elements shared with any parcel, unit, or lot which is all or part of the property.

ALL the foregoing is covered by this Mortgage and will be collectively referred to as the "Premises" for the purpose of this agreement.

The Premises are hereby granted to the Mortgagee to have and to hold, for the use and benefit of the Mortgagee, forever.

3. Uniform Commercial Code Security Agreement

It is agreed that if the nature of any of the property mortgaged in this agreement is such that a security interest in it can be realized under the Uniform Commercial Code, this instrument shall constitute a Security Agreement, and Mortgagor agrees to join with the Mortgagee in the execution of any financing statements and to execute any and all other documents that may be required for the completion or renewal of such security interest under the Uniform Commercial Code.

4. Redemption

If Mortgagor promptly pays or causes to be paid to Mortgagee, at its address listed in the Note, or at any other place designated by Mortgagee, Mortgagee's successors or assigns, with interest, the principal sum of _____dollars ($_____) when the note reaches maturity, as stated in said Note, or sooner, unless maturity date is amended or extended according to the terms of the Note executed by Mortgagor and payable to the order of Mortgagee, then the lien on the property shall cease and be void. Otherwise, the lien shall remain in full force and effect.

5. Agreements of Mortgagor

a) Secured Indebtedness. This Mortgage is given as security for the Note and also as security for any and all other sums, debts, obligations, and liabilities arising under the Note or this Mortgage, or under any amendments, modifications, or supplements to the Note or Mortgage, and for any renewals, modifications, or extensions of any or all of the foregoing obligations and liabilities (all of which are collectively referred to as the "Secured Indebtedness"). The entire Secured Indebtedness is equally secured with and has the same priority as any other amounts owed by Mortgagor at the date of this agreement.

b) Performance of Note, Mortgage. Mortgagor shall observe and comply with all provisions of this agreement and of the Note, and shall promptly pay to Mortgagee, in U.S. dollars, the Secured Indebtedness with interest as set forth in the Note. This Mortgage and all other documents constitute the Secured Indebtedness.

c) Payments Other Than Principal and Interest. Mortgagor is responsible to pay, when due and payable, (1) all taxes, assessments, and other charges levied on, or assessed against the Premises, this instrument or the Secured Indebtedness or any interest of the Mortgagee in the Premises or associated obligations; (2) premiums on insurance policies covering the Premises against loss from fire and other hazards, as required by this agreement; (3) ground rents or other lease rentals; and (4) any other sums related to the Premises or the indebtedness secured hereby, for which Mortgagor is responsible.

d) Insurance. Mortgagor shall keep the Premises insured at its sole cost and expense against all hazards as is customary and reasonable for properties of a similar type and nature located in _____ County, _____.

e) Maintenance. Mortgagor shall maintain the Premises in good condition and repair and shall not commit or allow any damage to be done to the Premises.

f) Prior Mortgage. With regard to the Prior Mortgage, Mortgagor hereby agrees to:

(i)   Pay promptly, when due, all installments of principal and interest and all other sums and charges payable under the Prior Mortgage;

(ii) Promptly perform and observe all of the terms, covenants, and conditions required by Mortgagor under the Prior Mortgage, within the period provided in the Prior Mortgage;

(iii) Promptly notify Mortgagee of any default, or any notice claiming any event of default by Mortgagor in the performance or observance of any term, covenant, or condition required by such a Prior Mortgage;

(iv) Mortgagor will not request or accept any voluntary future advances under the Prior Mortgage without Mortgagee's prior written consent, which shall not be unreasonably withheld by Mortgagee.

6. Defaults

a) Event of Default. Any one of the following events, if it is not resolved within _____ days after written notice of the event for a monetary default, or _____ days after written notice from Mortgagee for non-monetary defaults, shall constitute an "Event of Default":

(i)   Mortgagor does not pay the Secured Indebtedness, or any part of the Secured Indebtedness, or the taxes, insurance, and other charges, as set forth in this agreement, when these become due and payable;

(ii) Any statement of Mortgagor contained in this agreement, or contained in the Note, is found to be untrue or misleading in any material respect;

(iii) Mortgagor materially fails to observe and carry out the covenants, agreements, obligations, and conditions set out in this Mortgage, or in the Note;

(iv) Foreclosure proceedings (whether judicial or otherwise) that affect the priority of this Mortgage are instituted on any mortgage or any lien of any kind secured by any portion of the Premises.

b) Options of Mortgagee Upon Default. Upon the occurrence of any Event of Default, the Mortgagee may immediately do any one or more of the following:

(i)   Declare the total Secured Indebtedness, including without limitation all payments for taxes, assessments, insurance premiums, liens, costs, expenses, and attorneys' fees as set forth in this agreement, to be due and collectible at once, by foreclosure or otherwise, without notice to Mortgagor. Mortgagor expressly waives the right to receive such notice.

(ii) Pursue any and all remedies available under the Uniform Commercial Code. It is agreed that ten (10) days' notice of the time, date, and place of any proposed sale shall be reasonable.

(iii) If Mortgagee elects the Secured Indebtedness to be due and payable in full at once as provided for in Paragraph 2.02(a) above, or as may be provided for in the Note, or any other provision of this Mortgage, the Mortgagee may pursue all rights and remedies for the collection of such Secured Indebtedness granted by this Mortgage or by any other agreement, law, equity, or otherwise, to include, without limitation, the institution of foreclosure proceedings against the Premises under the terms of this Mortgage and any applicable state or federal law.

7. Prior Liens

Mortgagor shall keep the Premises free from all prior liens (except for those consented to by Mortgagee in writing).

8. Notice, Demand, and Request

A written notice, demand, or request, delivered according to the provisions of the Note relating to that notice, shall constitute fulfillment of those provisions.

9. Meaning of Words

The words "Mortgagor" and "Mortgagee," whenever used in this agreement, include all individuals, corporations (and if a corporation, its officers, employees or agents), trusts, and any and all other persons or entities, and the respective heirs, executors, administrators, legal representatives, successors, and assigns of the parties hereto, and all those holding under either of them.

The pronouns used in this notice refer to either gender and both singular and plural, where appropriate. The word "Note" may also refer to one or more notes.

10. Severability

If any provision of this Mortgage or any other Loan Document is found to be invalid or unenforceable under the law, the remaining provisions of the document in which that provision is contained shall continue to be valid and subject to enforcement in the courts without exception.

11. Governing Law

The terms and provisions of this Mortgage are governed by the laws of the State of _____. Interest, or payment in the nature of interest for any debt secured in part by this Mortgage, shall not exceed the maximum amount permitted by law. Any payment in excess of the maximum amount shall be applied to the Secured Indebtedness or disbursed to Mortgagor as set forth in the Note.

13. Paragraph Headings

The captions and paragraph headings in this document are used only for convenience and for reference, and shall have no effect upon the construction or interpretation of any provision in this contract or on determining the rights or obligations of the Mortgagor or Mortgagee.

14. Attorneys' Fees

For purposes of this Mortgage, attorneys' fees include, but are not limited to, fees incurred in all matters of collection and enforcement, construction and interpretation, before, during and after suit, trial, proceedings, and appeals. Attorneys' fees may also include hourly charges for paralegals, law clerks, and other staff members operating under the supervision of an attorney.

IN WITNESS WHEREOF, the Mortgagor has caused this instrument to be duly executed as of the day and year first above written.

Signature of Mortgagor: _____

Date: _____

Signature of Mortgagee: _____

Date: _____

STATE OF _____, COUNTY OF _____

The foregoing instrument was acknowledged before me, this

_____ day of _____, 20 _____.

_____ Notary Public

(SEAL) State of _____

My Commission Expires: _____

AFFIDAVIT OF TITLE TO OBTAIN A LOAN

Name: _____

Residence: _____

Owner of:

I hereby swear that:

1. I have owned the specified grounds since   .

2. My possession has been peaceful and uninterrupted.

3. The title has never been argued against, questioned, or discarded, nor insurance refused, as far as I know. I know of no reason why the possession or title might be called into question, or why any claim to any part of the grounds or any interest in it adverse to me might be set up.

4. There are no records against me entered in any court of this state or the United States regarding any judgments unpaid or unsatisfied.

5. The grounds are, as far as I know, free from all leases, mortgages, taxes, assessments, charges, and other liens and encumbrances, except _____.

6. The grounds are now occupied by _____.

7. No bankruptcy measures have ever been initiated by or against me in any court or before any officer of any state or of the United States, nor have I at any time made an obligation for the benefit of creditors, nor an assignment, now in effect, of the rents of the grounds or any part of it.

8. I am a citizen of the United States, and more than _____ years old. I am by occupation _____.

9. I am married to _____, who is over _____ years of age and is able to convey or mortgage real estate. I was married to _____ on _____. I have never been married to any other person now living.

10. I have not been known by any other name during the past _____ years.

11. There are no awaiting actions affecting the described grounds. No repairs, modifications, or improvements have been made to the premises which have not been completed more than _____ days prior to the date of this affidavit. As

far as I can recall, there are no facts relating to the title to the premises which have not been mentioned in this affidavit.

This affidavit is made to induce _____ to make a loan to me in the amount of $_____, to be protected by a mortgage on the premises.

_____
Signed

NOTARY
State of _____
County of_____
Sworn to and subscribed before me, a Notary Public, for the State of _____ County of _____
This _____ day of _____ 20_____
By:_____
Notary Public
My Commission Expires: This _____day of _____, 20 _____

AFFIDAVIT RE TITLE – CORPORATION

Date:_____
Sworn Name: _____
Sworn president of _____ (corporation)
Sworn owner of the real estate in the city of _____ located in _____ County described as _____.

Regarding the grounds, he/she swears that:
1. The corporation is the sole owner of the property described.
2. No other corporation, person, or persons have any interest or title in equity or otherwise, in or to the grounds except as later stated.
3. According to his [her] own knowledge and belief, the grounds have been held in a peaceful and uninterrupted matter without argument by the corporation and previous owners for the period of 2-20 years last past and that no argument exists between this affiant and others regarding the title to the grounds or its boundary lines.
4. The grounds are not subject to nor its use dependent upon any easement, and no conveyance has been made nor any encumbrance created affecting the grounds or any part of the grounds since the _____ day of _____.
5. No person has any official contract for the purchase of the grounds which has not been duly recorded before the last title search.
6. No requests have been made by any municipal department demanding any change or modification in and about the or improvements on the grounds.
7. No one in ownership of the above or any part of the grounds has any interest in the premises otherwise than as tenants, and if underwritten, leases then as per leases assigned to purchasers this day.
8. There are no suits or judgments, decrees, attachments, or orders against the corporation for the payment of money which remain unfulfilled of record in

any court having its records in _____ County or in the _____ court of the state of _____.

9. The transfer and sale of the within described grounds to _____ and _____ his wife [her husband] is not for the purpose of evading payment of any just debts.

10. No improvements, replacements, or repairs, nor any labor or material used in and about the assembly of improvements on the specified real estate have been made which have not been fully paid, and that there are no mechanics' lien claims of any nature outstanding and unpaid.

The statements and representations in this affidavit are made for the purpose of assuring _____ and _____ his wife [her husband], good title to the grounds and to induce the purchasers to pay the sum of $_____ by exchange of properties.

Sworn: _____
Sworn's Spouse: _____

NOTARY
State of _____
County of_____
Sworn to and subscribed before me, a Notary Public, for the State of _____
County of _____
This _____ day of _____ 20_____
By:_____
Notary Public
My Commission Expires: This _____day of _____, 20 _____

AGREEMENT TO REVISE NOTE PAYMENT SCHEDULE

Date: _____

This agreement is made on the above-listed date and is in regard to a loan evidenced by the following:
Loan Date: _____
Maker of Loan: _____
Maker's Address: _____
_____
Loan Payable to: _____ (Payee)
Payee Address: _____
_____
The Loan is secured by a ❑ mortgage/ ❑ deed of trust.
Date of Mortgage or Deed of Trust: _____
Property Address for Mortgage/Deed of Trust: _____
Mortgage/Deed of Trust Recorded: _____ (County Recorder)
County of Record: _____
State: _____
Registry Book: _____

Registry Page #: _____

Registry Volume: _____

The payment schedule of the aforementioned Mortgage/Deed of Trust is hereby revised to the following schedule: _____.

This Agreement is a revision of the aforementioned instrument. It is not a replacement or new obligation to the instrument or Mortgage/Deed of Trust. Except for the revision of the payment schedule as shown above, all terms and conditions of the Mortgage/Deed of Trust and the Instrument will remain in full force and effect.

IN WITNESS WHEREOF, both the Maker and Payee hereby sign and agree to this revision on this date.

_____

Maker Signed

_____

Payee Signed

AGREEMENT BETWEEN JOINT PROPERTY OWNERS TO TRANSFER TITLE

Date:_____

Owner A: _____

Owner A Address: _____

Owner B: _____

Owner B Address: _____

Whereas, both Owners A and B are mutually held and possessed of certain property, both real and personal, in the city of _____, county of _____, and state of _____, and are wishing for adjusting and untying their interests so that the title to such property may be held in distinctly by Owner A.

This agreement between A and B states:

1. That Owner A hereby agrees with Owner B that Owner A, during his/her natural life, will be required to compensate Owner B for the length of Owner B's natural life an annual sum of $_____.

   a. This annual fee is due in monthly increments of $_____ with the initial payment due on the date of signing of this agreement. Each additional payment shall be made each month during the natural life of Owner B.

2. Upon Owner B's death, if Owner A has survived Owner B, then the commitment outlined with this Agreement of Owner A is considered satisfied and no additional payments will be due to any of Owner B's assigns or heirs.

   a. Should Owner A die before Owner B, the due payments shall cease and Owner A, his/her heirs and assigns, in lieu of this Agreement, will leave free of all claims and burdens to Owner B real or personal property or a combination of the two in the amount of $_____ to be effective on the date of death of Owner A.

     b. Should Owner B and the heirs and assigns of Owner A be unable to agree upon the splitting of Owner A's estate, then that property in the amount of $_____ may be set aside in kind to Owner B. Then any proceeds from sales of the personal property of the estate of Owner A will be sold and the proceeds or a portion thereof will be provided to Owner B should he/she be willing to accept the payment to make up the amount due.

3.   Owner B, in consideration with all items outlined in this agreement hereby sells and conveys to Owner A, all rights, titles, and interests in and to all of the property, both real and personal, wherever situated, in which B and A are now mutually interested.

Owner A: _____

Owner B: _____

ASSIGNMENT OF MORTGAGE

Adapted from
**www.mnhousing.gov/idc/groups/public/documents/
document/mhfa_004799.rtf.**
Please check with an attorney for the correct format and procedure for your state.

Date: _____

Assignor: _____

Assignor's Address: _____

Assignee: _____

Assignee's address: _____

(hereinafter referred to as the "Assignment")

FOR VALUABLE CONSIDERATION, The Assignor under the laws of the State of _____, hereby sells, assigns, and transfers to Assignee listed above the Assignor's interest in the Mortgage dated _____ and executed by _____ as Mortgagor to _____, as Mortgagee, and filed for record _____, as _____(document number), in the Office of the County Recorder or Registrar of Titles of _____(county), _____ (State), together with all right and interest in the note and obligations specified in the Mortgage and the debt secured by it. Assignor covenants with Assignee, its successors, and assigns, that of the debt secured by the Mortgage the sum of $_____.00 with interest thereon is still due and unpaid from _____, and that Assignor has good right to sell, assign, and transfer the same.

In Witness whereof, Assignor has performed and delivered this Assignment to Assignee on the date hereof.

Assignor: _____

Assignee: _____

Witness: _____

NOTARY

State of _____

County of_____

Sworn to and subscribed before me, a Notary Public, for the State of _____

County of _____

This _____ day of _____ 20_____

By: _____

Notary Public

My Commission Expires: This _____day of _____, 20 _____

ASSIGNMENT OF JOINT OWNERSHIP WITH RIGHT OF SURVIVORSHIP

Date: _____

Assignor: _____

Address: _____

City: _____ State: _____ Zip: _____

Assignee: _____

Address: _____

City: _____ State: _____ Zip: _____

Should there be more than one Assignor or Assignee, they will be represented in the singular within this document.

In consideration for the payment of $_____ made to the Assignor by the Assignee (the receipt of which has been acknowledged), and in consideration of the Assignee providing to the Assignor the following:

_____

The Assignor hereby assigns and transfers over to the Assignee the property described below:

_____

Assignee's interest will be held:

_____

If the property has a balance owed, the current balance is $_____.

If no balance is owed, the property's next payment if one is owed will be due on _____.

WITNESSETH, Both parties have hereto signed this assignment on _____ (date) at _____ (Location).

Assignor: _____

Assignee: _____

The spouse(s) of the Assignor(s) has(have) signed below stating that in consideration of this assignment have hereby given up any claims, rights, interests, or any other rights as may currently be due to them regarding the abovementioned property.

Date: _____

Spouse: _____

Hereby witnessed by the following who are known to the Assignor(s) and Spouse(s) and have personally witnessed the signing of this Assignment.

Acknowledged and appeared before us that he/she/they signed this Assignment freely and voluntarily. We are signing below at the request of the Assignor.

Date: _____

Witness: _____

Witness: _____

NOTARY

State of _____

County of_____

Sworn to and subscribed before me, a Notary Public, for the State of _____

County of _____

This _____ day of _____ 20_____

By: _____

Notary Public

My Commission Expires: This _____day of _____, 20 _____

AGREEMENT BETWEEN LIEN HOLDER AND LENDER

Date: _____

Lien Holder: _____

Lender: _____

Owner: _____

The following Agreement is hereby made on the above listed date by and between the Lien Holder of _____ and the Lender, a corporation which was organized under the State Laws of _____. The Lender's headquarters are located at

_____.

RECITALS

Due to the reason of _____, the Lien Holder shall _____ on _____ in the service of the aforementioned Owner, Lien Holder has a lien on the property in the amount of $_____. The Owner would like to negotiate _____ from the Lender and the Lien Holder has acknowledged it is in their best interest. Lender has agreed to loan the Owner money if the Lien Holder will subordinate Lien Holder's present _____. _____

has a lien against the aforementioned property of the Owner.

For the previous reasons, the Lender and Lien Holder hereby agree to the following:

A. Subordination of Lien

The Lien Holder's lien will be considered second only to the Lender's claim on the Owner's property in accordance with the Agreement dated _____ and recorded on _____ (date). Any future loans the Lender chooses to enter into will be subordinate to the Lien Holder's claims.

B. Assignment of the Sums Owed

The Lien Holder may assign to the Lender any amount currently owed by the Owner until payment has been made in full. The Lien Holder has the right to execute any assignments that the Lender may require to put this Agreement into effect. The Lien Holder will either need to endorse or deposit with the Lender any and all notes regarding the claims of the Lien Holder. These will be held by the Lender until the payment has been made in full.

IN WITNESS WHEREOF, all parties have agreed to this Agreement and have signed below on _____ (date) at _____ (location of signing).

_____
Signature

_____
Signature

AGREEMENT REQUIRING SELLER TO ATTAIN A RELEASE OF THE MORTGAGE ON A PROPERTY

Date: _____
Seller: _____   Spouse: _____
Buyer: _____

This Agreement is hereby made on the date first listed above by and between the aforementioned Seller and his/her Spouse and the Purchaser.

RECITALS

The Sellers are the owners of the real estate located at _____ in _____(City), _____(County), and _____(State) of which they have on this date sold and transmitted to the Buyer for the agreed upon fee of $_____ of which the Buyer must make a purchase money mortgage in the amount of $_____.

Currently, the real estate property is subject to a lien from two mortgages which was made by _____ and recorded in the _____County Clerk's office of _____ state. The Sellers hereby agree according to the conveyance to obtain a release and discharge of said property from the lien of the mortgages as described above. Accordingly the Sellers have agreed to obtain the release as mentioned above in an appropriate time frame and no later than _____ (date). Should the Seller not obtain the release and discharge as required and by the date herein mentioned, the purchase money mortgage from the Buyer to the Seller will, at the decision of the Buyer, become null and void and Seller will be required to cancel and discharge the mortgage. The Buyer will then be entitled to the refund of the price paid over and above the mortgage and the Buyer will reconvey the property to the Sellers.

Should the Seller not cancel and discharge the mortgage and refund the Buyer with the amount listed above, then the Buyer has the right to hold the property and the mortgage in the amount of $_____ from the Buyer to the Sellers for the portion of the purchase price will then be null and void.

The Sellers are granted one year from _____ (date) to obtain the release and discharge previously mentioned herein.

_____
Seller Signed

_____
Seller's Spouse Signed

_____
Buyer Signed

MORTGAGE LOAN ASSUMPTION AGREEMENT

Adapted from
**www.housing.mt.gov/Includes/BOH/Singlefamily/
LoanAssumptionAgreement.pdf**.
Please check with an attorney for the correct format and procedure for your state.

BOND SERIES: _____
MBOH LOAN NO.:_____
SERVICER LOAN NO.:_____

THIS AGREEMENT is made on _____, between
_____ (hereinafter called "the Seller");
_____ (hereinafter called "the Borrower");
_____
(hereinafter called "the Mortgage Lender"); and the Montana Board of Housing (hereinafter called "the Board").

WHEREAS, the Seller is obligated to the Mortgage Lender pursuant to the terms of a promissory note in the face amount of $_____, dated _____ (hereinafter called "the Note"); and

WHEREAS, the Note is secured by a trust indenture dated _____, recorded on _____ in Book_____, Page_____, Entry Number_____, in the records of the Recorder of _____ County, Montana (hereinafter called "the Trust Indenture"); and

WHEREAS, the Trust Indenture creates a lien on the property located at
_____, Montana (hereinafter called "the Residence"); and

WHEREAS, The Note and Trust Indenture (hereinafter referred to together as "the Mortgage Loan") have been sold and assigned to the Board pursuant to its Single Family Mortgage Purchase Program; and

WHEREAS, The Seller desires to sell and convey the Residence to the Borrower, subject to the Mortgage Loan, and both the Seller and the Borrower have requested that the Mortgage Lender and the Board consent to the sale of the Residence subject to the Mortgage Loan;

THEREFORE, The Mortgage Lender and the Board hereby consent to the conveyance of the Residence to the Borrower, subject to the Mortgage Loan, and to the assumption of the Mortgage Loan by the Borrower, upon the following conditions:

1. At the time of the conveyance from the Seller to the Borrower, the payment obligations due under the Mortgage Loan shall be current.

2. The Borrower hereby assumes and agrees to pay the indebtedness evidence by the Mortgage Loan, it being agreed and understood that as of the date of this agreement the balance due on the Mortgage Loan is_____
    Dollars ($_____), that the interest rate on the Mortgage Loan shall be _____% per annum, that the monthly payments due under the Mortgage Loan shall be $_____, plus applicable taxes and insurance, and that the next payment due under the Mortgage Loan is due on
    _____.

3. The borrower agrees to assume, be liable for, and be bound by all of the obligations and covenants in the Mortgage Loan, including the Montana Board of Housing Uniform Rider to Trust Indenture appended to all standard form mortgages executed on FHA, VA, or RD forms, which provides among other things that the Lender or its assignee may, at any time and without prior notice, accelerate all payments due under the Trust Indenture and Note and exercise any other remedy allowed by law for breach of the Mortgage or Note if, without the prior written consent of the Lender or its assignee:

    a. The Borrower sells, rents, otherwise transfers any interest in the property by deed of trust, conditional sales contract, pledges, agreements to hold title in escrow and any other form of owner financing or fails to occupy the Residence as his or her permanent and principal residence; or

    b. The Borrower fails to abide by the agreement contained in the Affidavit of Borrower's.

2. Eligibility, or if the Mortgage Lender or the Board finds any statement contained in the Affidavit of Borrower's Eligibility to be untrue.

    a. The Board, at any time, in its sole discretion, determines that the requirements of Section 143 of the Internal Revenue Code of 1986, with respect to Mortgage Loans, have not been complied with, whether or not the Borrower is responsible for such noncompliance.

3.   Consent of the Board and the Mortgage Lender to the Assumption by the Borrower of the obligations of the Mortgage Loan shall in no way constitute a release of any of the Seller's obligations under the Mortgage Loan.

4.   The Seller hereby agrees that the Mortgage Lender and Board may authorize the further conveyance of the Residence, subject to the Mortgage Loan, without obtaining the consent of the Seller.

5.   Nothing contained in or done pursuant to this Assumption Agreement shall affect or be construed to affect the lien, charge, or encumbrance of the Mortgage Loan on the Residence or its priority over other liens, charges or encumbrances.

IN WITNESS WHEREOF the parties have executed this agreement on _____.

_____   _____
Seller   Borrower

_____
Mortgage Lender

By: _____   By: _____
Authorized Officer   Authorized Officer

This agreement is not valid unless signed by all parties.

AS SECURITY FOR LOAN

Date: _____

Assignor: _____

Address: _____

City: _____ State: _____ Zip: _____

Trustor: _____

Address: _____

City: _____ State: _____ Zip: _____

The   undersigned   Assignor, _____
___ (name of Assignor), the owner of _____% of the entire beneficial interest under the Trust Agreement dated _____, and known as _____ (identify Agreement), executed by _____ [name of Trustor], as Trustor, grants a security interest in and assigns to _____[name of Bank] (Bank), and to its successors and assigns, all of the interest of Assignor under the terms of the trust agreement and in the property described in the trust agreement, and to all proceeds of the property or any part of it, including, without limitation, all proceeds from rentals, mortgages, sales, conveyances, or other dispositions or realizations of any kind of or from the property or any part of it, including the right to manage, direct, and control the property and the activities of the trustee in respect to the property.

1. Warranties.

Assignor represents and warrants that Assignor has full power and authority to make the assignment provided for here and that Assignor is the owner of _____% of the beneficial interest in the collateral under the Trust Agreement, and that the collateral pledged in this Agreement is free and clear from any lien, encumbrance, security interest except for the security interest of the Bank as evidenced by the Agreement, or other right, title, or interest of any other person, firm, or corporation.

(a). Assignor is responsible for defending the collateral against all claims and demands of any person or entity that makes any claim upon the collateral that is adverse to Bank.

(b). There is no financing statement now on file in any public office covering any of the property included within this assignment or intended to be included in this assignment. If any amount remains unpaid on any indebtedness or liabilities of Assignor to Bank, or any credit from Bank to Assignor is in use by or available to Assignor, Assignor will not execute, and there will not be on file in any public office any financing statement or statements describing or attempting to describe the collateral pledged here.

2. Obligations Secured.

This assignment is given as collateral security for payment in full of
(Description of obligation) _____

3. Remedies on Default.

On nonpayment at maturity, whether by acceleration or otherwise, of the principal of or interest on the debt secured here, or at any time or from time to time in the future:

(a). Bank may exercise any one or more of all of the rights or remedies set forth in the trust agreement described above or set forth in any other debt contract secured by this document. Bank shall also have full power and authority to exercise all of any one or more of the remedies, and shall have all the rights of a secured party, under the Uniform Commercial Code of the State of _____. Any requirement of the Code for reasonable notice shall be considered to be met if notice is mailed, postage prepaid, to Assignor at the address of Assignor as shown on this document at least five days prior to the time of the sale, disposition, or other event giving rise to the requirement of notice. The right of Bank to purchase the collateral for its own account at any sale or other disposition of the collateral shall not be affected by the fact that at the time of sale, Bank is the trustee under the trust agreement described in the first paragraph of this document. The fact that the Bank is trustee not affect in any manner the rights of Bank to sell, dispose of, or otherwise deal with the security interest granted here.

(b). Bank may proceed immediately to exercise each and all of the powers, rights, and privileges reserved or granted to Assignor under the trust agreement described in the first paragraph of this document to manage, direct, control, and deal with the property or any part of it covered by the trust agreement, including, without limitation, the right to collect and receive the proceeds from rentals and from mortgages, sales, conveyances, or other dispositions or realizations of any kind of or from the property or any part of it.

(c). Bank may protect and enforce this conveyance by suits or proceedings in equity, at law, or otherwise, for the foreclosure or for the appointment of a receiver of the property covered by the trust agreement or any part, and for the enforcement of any other proper, legal, or equitable remedy available under applicable law.

4. Application of Proceeds.

After first deducting all legal or other costs and expenses incurred by the above-mentioned proceedings, the Bank will apply any and all net proceeds realized through such proceedings to pay any or all of the secured debt as Bank deems proper, with any surplus to be returned to Assignor. On full payment of all indebtedness secured by this agreement, this assignment and the lien or charge created by or resulting from this agreement shall cease to exist.

5. Nonliability of Assignee.

Regardless of anything to the contrary appearing in the trust agreement, interest in the property as described above is assigned and transferred to Bank only as collateral security. By its acceptance of this agreement, Bank shall not become liable for any of the Assignor's obligations or liabilities under the trust agreement described in the first paragraph of this document, whether under the terms of the trust agreement or arising from legal action, or otherwise. Assignor acknowledges that Assignor remains liable to the same extent as if this assignment had not been made.

6. Interpretation.

In the event that this assignment is executed by more than one Assignor, the word "Assignor" shall be construed to include all or any of them, and all of the obligations contained in this agreement shall be the joint and several obligations of Assignors and each of them.

Executed on _____ (Date)

Signature of Assignor: _____

Acceptance: _____ (Bank) acknowledges receipt of the above assignment on _____ (Date), and accepts the same.

Authorized signature of Bank representative: _____

Trustee's Endorsement _____, as trustee under the trust agreement dated _____, and known as ____
_____, acknowledges receipt of the above assignment on _____ (date), and accepts the same.

Authorized signature of trustee:
_____

BALLOON MORTGAGE NOTE

Date: _____

Holder: _____

Address: _____

City: _____ State: _____ Zip: _____

Maker: _____

Address: _____

City: _____ State: _____ Zip: _____

Payee: _____

Address: _____

City: _____ State: _____ Zip: _____

For the value received, the Maker promised to pay to the Payee listed above the principal amount of $_____ at an interest rate of _____% annually on the unpaid balance. Payment must be tendered in U.S. currency and be paid in the United States. Maker agrees to the following payment terms:

Monthly Payment of $_____ payment of Principal and Interest

Payment due date: _____

Beginning date of payments: _____

Number of Payments due at this amount: _____

After the number of payments above have been reached, on _____(date), along with the monthly payment listed above, the entire unpaid principal balance as well as any accrued interest, will then balloon and become due without delay.

This Note and the interest associated with it is secured by a mortgage on the real estate property and was made by the aforementioned Maker to the Payee and is to be enforced according to the laws of the state of _____.

Should the Maker default on any payment as described above or within the mortgage, then the entire balance of the mortgage will be due and payable immediately to the Holder. The unpaid balance will accrue interest at the highest rate allowed under the state laws of _____. Should the Holder fail to implement this option, it will not represent a waiver of his/her right to implement it in the event of any subsequent default by the Maker.

Maker or Endorser or any person liable for this shall hereby waive any objection or protest and hereby agrees that to pay any costs and reasonable legal fees should any legal action be taken in order to collect on this Note or to protect the security of the Mortgage herein mentioned.

_____
Signed Maker

AGREEMENT TO ESCROW DEED AND PURCHASE PRICE

Date: _____

Seller: _____

Buyer: _____

Escrow Agent: _____

It here is hereby agreed between the Seller and Buyer listed above having made an agreement between them in regard to the purchase and sale of the real estate property described within the attached deed from the Seller to the Buyer. The following payment terms are as follows:

Buyer shall pay Seller: $_____

Payment Start Date: _____

Payment End Date: _____

Payment Due Date: _____

Seller should then be in a position to deliver to the Buyer a free and clear title to the property described in the attached deed and Seller having accordingly signed and carried out the attached warranty deed turning over the property to the Buyer as was provided for in the contract agreed to and signed on _____ (date). Seller deposits the warranty deed with the aforementioned Escrow Company, hereby known as the Escrowee, to provide the warranty deed to the Buyer after Seller, now being at the point to provide a free and clear title to the property and the Buyer deposits with the Escrow Agent, as Escrowee, a sum in the amount of $_____, which will then be paid by the Escrowee to the Seller as soon as the Seller has shown clear title to the property.

_____
Seller

_____
Buyer

_____
Escrow Agent

BY DEED

Date: _____
Grantor: _____   Company: _____
Grantee: _____

This deed is made on the above-listed date by and between the aforementioned Grantor and Grantee.

By the deed dated _____ and recorded in the State of _____, Book _____, Page Number _____, between the aforementioned parties, the Grantee did grant to the Grantor the following: _____

Grantor has agreed to surrender _____ to the Grantee for a payment in the amount of $_____.

In consideration of this payment that has been acknowledged, paid to the Grantor by the Grantee, the Grantor hereby discharges and forever quitclaims to the Grantee all of the _____ and his/her rights thereof. Grantor understand that the release of the _____ is forever released from him and the Grantee has all rights to enter into free and clear from all easements which belong to the Grantor on the property.

_____
Signed Grantor

_____
Signed Grantee

NOTARY
State of _____
County of_____

Sworn to and subscribed before me, a Notary Public, for the State of _____
County of _____
This _____ day of _____ 20_____
By:_____
Notary Public
My Commission Expires: This _____day of _____, 20 _____

CASH PAYMENT PLUS ASSUMPTION OF THE EXISTING MORTGAGE

Date: _____
Seller: _____
Purchaser: _____

The purchase price of $_____, subject to the pro-rations, will be paid by a payment in the amount of $_____ (including any deposits already paid) in cash, cashier's check, or a certified check. The balance will be paid by the Purchaser who is taking the title. The title is subject to and will be assumed as of the date of the closing and the Purchaser hereby agrees to pay the debt that is secured by the current mortgage or deed of trust that was signed and dated on _____ and recorded in _____ County, _____ Document Number. This is evidenced by the note that is currently held by _____ and has an un-paid balance as of the date listed above in the amount of $_____ with an interest rate of _____% annually on any unpaid principal as long as the note is not in default at the time of closing. The payments of the notes are as follows:

_____ payments per year
$_____ per payment
_____ date final payment is due

All parties hereby agree to sign an assumption agreement with and in a form that satisfies the holder of the note. The purchaser is required to pay the assumption expense, as long as the fee does not exceed $_____. Should the fee exceed this amount, the remaining balance will be paid by the Seller.

_____
Signed Purchaser

_____
Signed Seller

CONTRACT AS TO POSSESSION OF PROPERTY WITH DELAYED CLOSING

Date: _____
Seller: _____
Buyer: _____

This Agreement is made this date by and between the above-listed Seller and Buyer.

RECITALS:

In regard to the contract which was signed by both the Buyer and Seller on _____ (date), the Seller agreed to sell to the Buyer and the Buyer agreed to purchase from the Seller the property described as _____ _____. Delay is expected in completing this sale and the Buyer would like to take immediate ownership of the property.

Therefore, the Seller has agreed to deliver full possession of the property on _____ (date) as if the conveyance has been completed. The Buyer will be free to make any modifications and/or additions to the property as so desired. These modifications are subject in all respects to the approval of the Seller and should not make it so that the value of the property is hindered. Both parties understand that the Buyer's taking possession of the property does not waiver the sales contract or in any manner affect the rights of either parties under it; that such taking of possession shall not be deemed an acceptance of the title to the property; but that the same shall be considered as taken in the interim upon, and without prejudice to, the due completion of the contract in all regards.

_____

Signed Seller

_____

Signed Buyer

NOTARY

State of _____

County of_____

Sworn to and subscribed before me, a Notary Public, for the State of _____

County of _____

This _____ day of _____ 20_____

By:_____

Notary Public

My Commission Expires: This _____day of _____, 20 _____

TITLE SEARCH FORM

Date of Search: _____

Title search for the Property located at:

Address: _____

Address: _____

City: _____ State: _____ Zip: _____

Legal Description of Property: _____

Acreage: _____

No. of Bedrooms:_____

No. of Bathrooms: _____

Other _____: _____

Other _____: _____

Current Owner(s): _____

Address: _____

City: _____ State: _____ Zip: _____

Taxes and Special Assessments.

Include the year due or each year due and the amount owed.

County: _____

School: _____

City: _____

Special Assessments: _____

Water: _____

Sewer: _____

Other Taxes: _____

Other Assessments: _____

Potential Other Assessments for future improvements: _____

Mortgages, Deeds of Trusts, Financing Statements:

_____

_____

Any Possession Rights or Claims other than Owner? (Explain)

_____

_____

Any Easements, Right-of-Ways, Recorded Leases, Contracts, Encroachments, Party-Wall Agreements, and others:

_____

_____

Any Other Exceptions, Defects, Survey Defects:

_____

_____

CHAPTER 16

County & Community Forms

Agreement is made this _____, 20__, between _____ and _____, husband and wife, residents of the county of _____, state of _____.

Recitals:

The parties are now married each to the other.

Husband is possessed of certain property that is owned and held by him as his sole and separate estate.

It is the desire of husband to change and convert the legal status of the property from his sole and separate estate to the status of community property of himself and _____, his wife.

Therefore, in consideration of the premises and of the love and affection which husband has for his wife, it is agreed between the parties that the certain property described in "schedule A" attached to and made a part of this agreement, is declared to be owned and held by the parties in community, in the same manner and to the same effect as if acquired by the parties during coverture from the joint earnings of these parties, as contemplated in section _____ of the _____ revised statutes of _____.

By: _____
Husband

By: _____
Wife

State of _____

County of_____

Sworn to and subscribed before me, a Notary Public, for the State of _____

County of _____

This _____ day of _____ 20_____

By: _____

Notary Public

My Commission Expires: This _____day of _____, 20 _____

CHAPTER 17

Design and Decorating Forms and Checklists for Professionals and Homeowners

CLIENT CONTACT FORM FOR INTERIOR DESIGNERS

Name: _____

Spouse and/or children's names and ages: _____

Address: _____

How did you hear of us? _____

Home Number: _____

Office Number: _____

Fax Number: _____

Cell Number: _____

E-mail: _____

Why are you calling today? _____

How do you like to be contacted? _____

Notes: _____

CLIENT STATISTICS FORM FOR INTERIOR DESIGNERS

Time call came in: _____ a.m./p.m.

Was a message left? _____

How quickly was the call returned? _____

Was message left to customer? If so, when? _____

How quickly was the call returned by customer? _____

Who referred the customer? _____

Was a thank-you sent to referral? _____

How did customer hear of service? _____

Visit date: _____

Written estimate date: _____

Date permission was granted: _____

Estimated time for project: _____

Date completed: _____

Date billed: _____

Date collected: _____

Actual time spent on project: _____

Follow-up date: _____

- In what way did I follow-up? _____
- What did I send? _____
- Did I get a response? _____

CONTRACT SUMMARY SHEET
FOR INTERIOR DESIGNERS

Client Name:
Address:
Telephone:
Cell Phone or Regular Phone:
Fax:
E-mail:
Contact Person for Client:
Designer:
Detailed Description of Project:
Project Beginning Date:
Schedule of Project:
How will merchandise purchased and construction costs be handled?
How will request for additional work be handled?
Estimated budget to be included with design concept:
Are revisions billable and what expenses are billable?
How long do you allow clients to pay bills after receipt of invoices?
Will you charge interest on overdue invoices?

What are the specific terms of the agreement?
Does the client want you to restrict publicizing the project?
Who will sign the agreement for the client?
Does the agreement have following standard provisions for this design firm?
The quality and completion of merchandise is responsibility of construction, supplier, or contractor? Yes or No
If delays are cause by client suppliers or other acts the time line will be extended to finish the job? Yes or No
The designer shall have no liability for lateness, failure, or negligence of suppliers or contractors to perform duties? Yes or No
The clients will be responsible for payment of sales tax, packing, shipping, and related charges on such purchases? Yes or No
Client must sign and approve changes? Yes or No
The designer will own all rights to the designs? Yes or No
Is there an arbitration provision or problems that arise? Yes or No
Person Completing Contract Summary Sheet
Date

CONTRACTOR LOG FOR INTERIOR DESIGNERS

Client:
Name:
Project:
Name:
Location:
Job Number:

Item	Contractor	Contact in Organization

Bid Documents Spec	Drawings	P.O. Number	P.O. Total

Pricing Change Orders	Invoice Total	Schedule Start	Inspection	Delivery Date	Completed

DESIGN AND DECORATING CHECKLIST

- ❑ Determine your design needs and the purpose of the room
- ❑ Take before pictures
- ❑ Break down the room and create a holding area
- ❑ Determine the focal point of the room
- ❑ Evaluate the shape of the room
- ❑ Place the largest piece of upholstery first
- ❑ Shop the home for items from other rooms
- ❑ Place the area rug
- ❑ Finish placing the furniture, working down in size
- ❑ Place lighting
- ❑ Place tall plants or trees
- ❑ Place artwork
- ❑ Begin to accessorize on focal wall
- ❑ Take "after" photos
- ❑ Create shopping list

DESIGN AND DECORATING SUPPLIES CHECKLIST

- ❑ Furniture movers for both carpet and hardwoods
- ❑ Mark-it level
- ❑ Hammer, nails, picture hanging wire, wall anchors, and picture hanging kit
- ❑ Rechargeable cordless drill and batteries
- ❑ Screwdriver
- ❑ Scissors
- ❑ Wire cutter
- ❑ Step stool
- ❑ Permanent marker
- ❑ Straight and safety pins
- ❑ Rubber bands
- ❑ Museum or poster putty
- ❑ Furniture touch-up sticks or pens
- ❑ Floral sheers and tape
- ❑ Painters tape
- ❑ Lint brush and wrinkle release spray
- ❑ Flashlight
- ❑ Masking tape and Scotch tape

- ❑ Pencil and chalk
- ❑ Other items for decorating: greenery, floral foam, plate stands, old books, fabric scraps, small accessories, curtain rods and rings, sheer drapes

DESIGN MASTER ROOM SHEET

Client:
Room Worked On:
Date:
Floor Details
Walls Details
Ceilings
Window Treatments
Furniture
Appliances
Floors
Hardware
Lamps and Lighting Fixtures
Accessories
Art and Photography

INITIAL SURVEY FORM FOR INTERIOR DESIGNERS

Client:
Name:
Project:
Job Name:
Location:
Job Number:

Site Dimensions and Conditions

Room or Site	Items	Drawing Number	Photographs Number	Notes
Inventory				

Room or Site	Items	Drawing Number	Photograph Number	Notes

Date:
By:

JOB INFORMATION SHEET
FOR INTERIOR DESIGNERS

Name of Company:
Job Name and Number:
Location including Town and State:
Client Name:
Address:
Phone:
Cell:
Fax:
Any Other Contact Information:
Bill to Address:
Ship to Address:
Project Team:
Designer:
Assistant Designer:
Architects:
Contractor or Subcontractors:
Consultants:
Bill Information:
Rate:
Time and Materials:

Tax Percent:	
Total Cost:	
Design Development:	
Presentation Dates:	
Project Implementation Dates:	
Contract Document and Bids:	
Final Project Completion Items:	
Work Change Order:	
Date:	
Number:	
Items:	
Hours and Rate:	
Expense:	
Totals:	

Items	Estimated Labor	Estimated Total	Actual Labor	Actual Material Expenses	Discount	Total
Floors						
Wood						
Tile						
Ceramic						
Carpeting						
Other						
Window Treatments						
Shades/Blinds						
Louvers						
Draperies						
Fixtures						
Bath						
Kitchen						
Lighting						

Wall/Door							
Furniture purchased							
Furniture made or reupholstered							
Linens							
Rugs							
Appliances							
Insurance							
Storage							
Shipping							
Project Total							

PRE-APPOINTMENT QUESTION FORM FOR INTERIOR DESIGNERS

Can you tell me a bit about what you are looking for?

Did you just move into town? If so, from where?

Have you ever had redesign/redecorating/real estate staging work done before?

What kind of concerns do you have?

What are you thinking of investing in this project?

When do you anticipate making your decision?

When would be a good time for you and your spouse to meet with me?

PROJECT DRAWING LOGS FOR INTERIOR DESIGNERS

Client:
Name:
Project:

Job Name:							
Location:							
Job Number:							

Room or Site	Item	Phase of project	View of Drawing	Number	Location	Date	Notes

PROPOSAL FORMS FOR INTERIOR DESIGNERS

Date:
Person Filling in Form:
Client Information:
Name:
Address:
City, State, Zip:
Phone:
Cell:
Fax:
Project:
Name:
Location:
Fee Information:
Detailed description of the project:

Work Plan Schedule	Start and End Dates	Budget	Notes	Cost
Program Development				
Design Phase I				
Design Phase II				
Contacts and Documents				
Project Implemented				

Construction				
Installation				
Project Completion				
Work Plan Detail				
Wall and Ceilings	Notes	Budget	Total Time	Costs
Painting				
Wall coverings				
Moldings				
Other				
Floor/Stairways				
Wood				
Ceramic				
Stone				
Carpeting				
Moldings				
Other				
Window Treatments				
Shades/Blinds				
Louvers				
Drapery				
Other				
Millwork				
Fixtures and Hardware				
Bath				
Kitchen				
Lighting				

Wall/Door				
Other				
Furniture				
Furniture Purchase				
Furniture Commission				
Reconditioned Furniture				
Re-upholstery				
Electronic Devices				
Spa/Exercise Furnishings				
Linens				
Rugs				
Decorative Items				
Miscellaneous				
Travel				
Messengers				
Insurance				
Storage				
Shipping and Handling				
Total				

ROOM SPECIFICATION FORM FOR INTERIOR DESIGNERS

Room Specification:	
Client Name:	
Room Specified:	
Name of Project:	
Date:	

Carpet: Detail type and plan of installation:
Walls: What treatment of wall paint, type, wall paper, time schedule, and methods used:
Ceilings: Paint used or work to be done:
Window and Treatments:
Floors:
Furniture:
Built Ins:
Lighting
Room Layout Dimensions:
Approval:

WORK CHANGE ORDER FOR INTERIOR DESIGNERS

Client Name:
Project:
Order Number:
Person Requesting Changes:
Date:
Job Number:
Phase of Change:
Program Development:
Design Development Drawing and Schematics:
Design Development Final Phase:
Contract Documents and Bids:
Implementation:
Work Change Description Detailed:
Cost Changes and Schedule Change Details:
This is not an invoice, but a work change order. It represents changes from the original contact or order due to circumstances and must be based on the client's approval.
Authorized Signature:
Print Name:
Date:

CHAPTER 18

Miscellaneous Real Estate Forms

GENERAL WARRANTY DEED

For good consideration, we_____of_____
_____, County of_____ State of_____
_____, hereby bargain, deed, and convey to_____ of _____
County of _____, State of_____, the following
described land in _____county, free and clear with the following
WARRANTY COVENANTS:

Grantor, for itself and on behalf of its heirs, covenants with Grantee, its heirs, and assigns, that Grantor is the lawful fee simple owner of the above-described premises and has a good right to convey ownership; and that the premises are free from all liens and encumbrances. Grantor and its heirs, and all persons having any interest in the property described above, through or for Grantor, will, at the request and at the expense of the Grantee, or its heirs or assigns, execute any reasonable instrument necessary to further guarantee the title to the premises. Grantor and its heirs will forever warrant and defend all of the property so granted to Grantee and its heirs against every person who lawfully claims interest in the above-described property or in any part thereof.

These Warranty Covenants apply to the same property conveyed to the Grantors by deed of _____, dated_____19____.

WITNESS the hands and seal of said Grantors this____day of_____, 20____.

_____
Grantor

_____
Grantee

STATE OF _____, COUNTY OF _____
The foregoing instrument was acknowledged before me, this
_____ day of _____, 20 _____.
_____ Notary Public   State of _____

DEED OF SALE

Deed made this ___ *day of*_____*[month]*, _____*[year]*, between _____, of _____, referred to as the Grantor, and _____, of _____, referred to as the Grantee.

In consideration of $_____ (dollars) paid by the Grantee, the receipt of which is acknowledged by the Grantor , the Grantor has agreed to grant to the Grantee the property located at_____.

In consideration of $_____ (dollars) [or other consideration] paid by the Grantee to the Grantor, the Grantor grants to the Grantee, his [her] heirs and assigns, full and free right and authority to _____.

The Grantee covenants with the Grantor that he [she], his [her] heirs, or assigns will _____.

In witness the grantor has signed [and seal] the day and year first written above.

_____

[Signature of Grantor]

STATE OF _____, COUNTY OF _____
The foregoing instrument was acknowledged before me, this
_____ day of _____, 20 _____.
_____ Notary Public
State of _____

SIMPLE HOME INSPECTION CHECKLIST

Home Interior	Poor	Average	Excellent
Bedrooms			
Bathrooms			
Floor Plan			
Closet Space			
Fireplace/Stove			
Cable Satellite			
Living Room			
Dining Room			
Den/Study			
Media Room			
Kitchen			
Laundry Room			
Walls and Ceilings			

Carpets and Floors			
Basements/Attics			
Garage			
Bonus/Storage			
Plumbing			
Electrical			
Insulation			
Heating/Cooling			
Paint/Stain			
Sound Barriers			
Overall Interior			
Home's Exterior	**Poor**	**Average**	**Excellent**
Fencing			
Yard Area			
Gutters			
Roofing			
Patio/Deck			
Screened Porch			
Siding			
Windows			
Landscaping			
General Curb Appeal			
Garden			
Crawl Space			
Foundation			
Driveway			
Sidewalk			
Paint/Stain			
Overall Exterior			

INVESTOR'S HOME INSPECTION CHECKLIST

Address: _____

Agent contact information: _____

Seller contact information: _____

Sale price: _____

Check the following items. Make notes as to condition, and rate on a scale of one to five, with five being excellent, and one being poor.

Exterior:	*Rating*	*Notes*
Foundation	_____	_____
Paint	_____	_____
Siding	_____	_____
Windows	_____	_____
Screens	_____	_____
Outbuildings	_____	_____
Porch	_____	_____
Deck	_____	_____
Steps	_____	_____
Roof	_____	_____
Driveway	_____	_____
Fencing	_____	_____
Gutters/downpipes	_____	_____
Landscaping	_____	_____
Location	_____	_____

Kitchen:		
Tile/wall	_____	_____
Appliances	_____	_____
Floor	_____	_____
Cabinets	_____	_____
Sink/plumbing	_____	_____
Mold	_____	_____

Bathrooms:		
Toilet	_____	_____
Tub/shower	_____	_____
Sink	_____	_____
Mold	_____	_____
Electric	_____	_____
Ventilation	_____	_____

Other details:		
Number of bedrooms	_____	_____
Carpet	_____	_____
Electrical outlets	_____	_____
Living area	_____	_____

Extra rooms   _____   _____
Storage   _____   _____
Lot size   _____   _____

SELLER'S OPEN HOUSE CHECKLIST

Tasks to do when preparing for an Open House

_____1.   Survey the house for necessary general repairs
_____2.   Repair holes in the walls
_____3.   Replace old or dulled pain
_____4.   Clean or replace stained or heavily soiled carpeting
_____5.   Clean dusty window coverings and furnishings
_____6.   Get rid of unwanted items stored in garages and basements that create clutter.
_____7.   Clean thoroughly
_____8.   Arrange for a babysitter

Tasks to do immediately before an Open House

_____1.   Heat or cool the building as needed
_____2.   Pick up and put away clutter
_____3.   Put the toilet seats down
_____4.   Close the shower curtains
_____5.   Remove used towels
_____6.   Air out the house
_____7.   Take out the trash
_____8.   Make sure the buyers have adequate parking

GLOSSARY

A

Abandonment An owner or renter gives up their property & leaves without passing ownership or tenancy rights to anyone else. The abandoner still owes any debts related to the property, unless the owed party cancels them. Abandoned properties are reclaimed by lenders or other entities with a prior interest.

Abatement A lowering of rent fees or another reduction benefiting the tenant, such as free rent, early move-in, or removal of a harmful substance, like asbestos.

Abnormal sale A house or property sells for more or less than its current market value — for instance, 25 percent less than comparable homes nearby. Appraisers can ignore abnormal sales when comparing similar properties for value.

Absentee owner Someone who owns a property without managing it or living on-site, who might hire another person to oversee it.

Absorption rate How quickly homes sell or rental spaces gain occupants. Calculate this percentage by dividing the total number of homes or square feet of rental space in an area by the number purchased or filled during a given time period.

Abstract of title The summarized history of a piece of real estate. It describes each time the property changed hands & notes all encumbrances that have lessened its value or use. This document is certified as complete & truthful by the abstractor.

Abut To be adjacent. A property can abut — border — landmarks such as roads & easements. When one property meets or joins another, the line between is an abutment.

Acceleration clause Part of a rental contract saying a lender can insist that a borrower pay the balance of the loan right away under certain circumstances. A lender might invoke this clause if the renter defaults on the loan or seriously delays payments.

Acceptance Completion of a sales contract, when someone offers to buy a property under specific terms & the owner accepts.

Accessory building Serves a different function from the main building on a lot. Accessory buildings include garages, but they do not include separate structures for commercial use.

Accord & satisfaction An agreement settling a debt. A creditor considers the debt repaid after accepting a different or smaller compensation than the debtor originally promised. Such an accord can end a dispute.

Accrued depreciation (accumulated depreciation) The current sum of all depreciation expenses.

Accrued items, active Expenses paid early for things in the next business year. For example, people can pre-pay rent for buildings they will occupy the following year.

Accrued items, passive Expenses incurred that cannot be paid yet, such as taxes on real estate & interest on loans.

Acknowledgment Someone formally declares that they have signed a document before a notary public or another appropriately authorized person.

Acquisition appraisal A government agency determines how much to pay a property owner after acquiring his property via negotiation or condemnation.

Acquisition cost The total price someone pays for a property, with all fees added in.

Acre Equal to 43,560 square feet (4,840 square yards), an acre is the standard area unit for measuring property.

Acreage zoning (large-lot or "snob" zoning) Zoning calling for large lots, meant to make commercial or residential areas less dense.

Act of God In contracts, a natural disaster humans cannot control, such as an earthquake, severe storm, or flood. Contracts can include provisions relieving all those involved from obligation when such a disaster strikes a property.

Actual cash value The cash value of an improvement for insurance purposes. It equals the cost of replacing something minus the wear & tear.

Actual damages (and special damages) Actual damages are legally determined costs for repairing something wrongfully harmed or destroyed. Special damages include indirect effects of the property destruction, such as lessened income to a business in a damaged building.

Ad valorem Latin for "according to value." A tax based on the value of a property, particularly as determined by local government.

ADC loan The letters stand for acquisition, development, & construction. Developers use ADC loans to buy property, install utilities & roads, & erect buildings.

Addendum An amendment or revision to a contract both parties consent to & sign.

Addition Making a building larger through further construction. Additions do not include improvements such as finishing unfinished rooms.

Adjudication A decision made in court.

Adjustable-Rate Mortgage (ARM) Unlike a fixed-rate loan, this home loan has a changing interest rate, which fluctuates to stay current with rates of mortgage loans. It can also change with indexes of the government or financial market.

Adjustment date On this day, the interest rate changes for an adjustable-rate mortgage.

Adjustment period For an adjustable-rate mortgage, this is the time period between changes in interest rate.

Advance fee Money clients pay before receiving services. Real estate agents can charge homeowners an advance fee to foot advertising bills while selling the property.

Adverse financial change condition This provision lets a lender cancel a loan agreement if the borrower loses his job or has other serious financial troubles.

Adverse possession Blatantly & aggressively occupying another person's land & claiming entitlement without permission from the owner. Adverse possession does not include leasing property with an owner's consent or occupying property of unknown ownership.

Adviser An investment banker or a broker representing a property owner during a real estate transaction. The adviser collects a fee when transaction or financing ends.

Aesthetic value Worth of a property determined by its beauty.

Affidavit of title A statement written under oath by a real estate grantor or seller & recognized by a notary public. The person gives his identity, confirms that the title has not changed for the worse since it was last examined, & officially declares that he possesses the property (if appropriate).

Affirmation A way to declare a statement true without swearing an oath, if someone has religious reasons or other objections to giving oaths.

Affordability index A measure designed by the National Association of Realtors® to describe how affordable houses are for residents buying in a given area.

Affordable housing Public or private programs helping low-income people afford houses. These efforts can provide low-interest home loans, smaller down payments, & less demanding credit terms.

Agency A relationship in which principal brokers — leaders of brokerage firms — allow agents to represent them in specific transactions.

Agency disclosure An agreement most states require; real estate agents who serve sellers & buyers must disclose whom they are representing.

Agent Someone acting on another's behalf under the law of agency. Property owners authorize licensed real estate brokers to be their agents.

Agreement of sale A legal document giving the terms & price of a property sale, which both parties sign.

Alienation Property going to a new owner by sale, gift, adverse possession, or eminent domain.

Alienation clause Found in a deed of trust or a mortgage, this clause prevents the borrower from selling the property — & transferring the associated debt — to another person without the lender's permission. If the borrower sells, the lender can immediately demand full repayment of the debt.

Alluvion Soil deposit that builds up on a property & is considered the owner's possession.

Amenities Advantages to owning a property not related to money, or features that make it more desirable.

Americans with Disabilities Act (ADA) Designed to ensure that disabled people have equal access to public accommodations & transportation, jobs, telecommunications, & government services. Covers design of public buildings.

Amortization Paying off a debt & its interest in gradual installments.

Amortization schedule A charted timetable for paying off a loan, showing how much of each payment goes toward interest & toward the debt itself.

Amortization term Amount of time needed to pay off (amortize) a loan.

Anchor tenant The person or business that draws the most visitors to a commercial property, such as a supermarket among other stores.

Annexation A city expanding its borders to encompass a certain area. Most states require public approval first, demonstrated by holding votes in the city & the area it will annex. Annexation also denotes personal property becoming part of real property.

Annual debt service The yearly payments a person must make on a loan, comprising the principle & interest added over 12 months.

Annual percentage rate (APR) The actual interest rate of a loan for a year, which might be higher than the rate advertised. It must be disclosed, in accordance with the Truth in Lending Act.

Appointments Items in a building that may enhance or lessen how valuable or functional the property is. Examples include furniture, equipment, & fixtures.

Apportionment Dividing yearly costs associated with a property between the seller & the buyer. Each party pays expenses like insurance or taxes for the portion of the year they owned the property.

Appraisal report The report an appraiser writes describing a property's value & summarizing how it was determined.

Appraised value The monetary value of a property given in an appraisal report.

Appreciation The process of a home or property gaining value, which can stem from several factors, including additions to the building, changes in financial markets, & inflation.

Appropriation Reserving land for public access, which might be required before development projects can progress.

Appurtenance A privilege, right, or benefit tied to a piece of land without being physically part of the property. One example is the right to access someone else's land.

Appurtenant easement The right, belonging to a parcel's owner, to use a neighbor's property.

Arbitration When two parties use an impartial third entity to resolve a dispute instead of going to court. Real estate contracts can require arbitration, preventing lawsuits.

Architecture All facets of building construction, from materials, tools, & methods to elements of design & style.

Area A space defined by two dimensions: length & width. Multiplying length by width yields the area of a lot or floor.

ARM (adjustable-rate mortgage) index An openly published number that guides how adjustable-rate mortgages change.

Arm's length transaction A deal in which each party protects its own interests above all.

Arrears A payment made "in arrears" is given at the end of a month or other term. Late or defaulted payments can also be described as in arrears.

Artesian well A vertical tunnel to access water naturally springing from underground.

"As is" condition A term in real estate contracts meaning the buyer or renter accepts the property & its flaws just as they are, giving up the right to insist on repairs or renovations.

Asbestos This mineral, formerly common in insulation & other building materials, is now prohibited because it causes lung disease.

Asbestos-containing materials (ACM) Prohibited because of health hazards since the early 1980s, materials containing asbestos still are found in some old buildings.

As-built drawings Illustrations showing exactly how a building was constructed, including alterations to the original plans & the position of utilities & equipment.

Asking (advertised) price The amount a property owner hopes a buyer will pay, which may change with negotiation.

Assessed value The value a tax assessor determines a home to have; used for computing a tax base.

Assessor A public official responsible for valuing properties for tax purposes.

Asset A valuable possession or property.

Asset management All aspects of handling real estate assets from when someone first invests in them until they sell them.

Assignment Handing over the responsibilities & rights associated with a property to another, as a landlord does to a paying tenant. If that recipient fails to pay, the original party absorbs the debt.

Assignment of lease Passing off the rights to use a leased property from one renter to another. For instance, those who occupy an apartment for part of the year may recruit someone else to live there when they are gone.

Assignment of rents A contract saying a tenant's rent payments will go to the owner's mortgage lender if the owner defaults.

Assignor Someone who passes a property's interests & rights to a new recipient.

Associate broker (broker-associates, affiliate brokers, or broker-salespersons) A real estate broker supervised by another broker. This manager holds the associate broker's license.

Association of unit owners An organization of condominium owners who oversee the property where they live.

Assumable mortgage This mortgage loan can be shifted from one borrower to another.

Assumption Buying another's mortgage.

Assumption clause Part of the contract drawn when a mortgage changes hands — it makes the party buying the mortgage loan responsible for it.

Assumption fee Money one must pay when buying another's mortgage, to cover costs for processing the paperwork.

Attachment A person's possessions that legal authorities seize when the person fails to pay a debt. For example, landlords attach items their tenants own to unpaid rent.

Attest To observe an event & sign a document certifying that you witnessed it.

Attic Space between the top story's ceiling & the roof that people can access. Conversely, a structural cavity is a similar space that people cannot enter.

Attorney-in-fact Someone who can legally act on another's behalf, which can mean selling the other party's property.

Attorney's opinion of title A summarized history of a piece of real estate that an attorney has scrutinized & declared valid, in his opinion.

Attornment A legal agreement in which tenants formally accept a new landlord by signing a letter of attornment.

Auction Selling personal property or land to the highest bidder, which states can do with foreclosed property. Bidders can make public or private offers, in writing or speech.

Auctioneer Licensed person who carries out auctions of real estate or other property.

Authorization to sell Contract licensing a real estate agent to sell one's property. The agent can advertise the property & collect a fee for selling it, but cannot make the final agreement to sell.

Automated underwriting These computer systems allow lenders to approve loans faster & reduce the costs of lending.

Automatic extension A clause found in a listing agreement — an accord a property owner makes with a real estate broker, saying the owner will pay the broker to lease or sell property for a given price. An automatic extension makes the listing agreement persist after it expires, for a specified time. Certain states forbid or discourage using automatic extensions.

Average occupancy The percentage of time a property was occupied in the last year. To calculate, divide the number of months it was occupied by 12.

B

Backup offer A second buyer offers to purchase or lease property if the current buyer cannot follow through. When the first buyer backs out, the backup offer takes effect.

Balance Debt unpaid. Appraisers also use balance to describe a situation in which a property's improvements are proportional to the land & to each other, making the property's value peak.

Balance sheet A list of someone's net worth, assets, & liabilities.

Balloon loan A mortgage with monthly payments followed by a large final payment, which covers the remaining debt.

Balloon payment The large, final payment in a balloon mortgage loan, which covers the debt not paid in earlier installments.

Bankruptcy Occurs when someone cannot pay their debts on time. Declaring bankruptcy may lead to court decisions to ease or obliterate debts.

Bargain & sale deed Gives the grantor the right to convey title without making warranties against encumbrances or liens, but the grantor can attach warranties if desired. See definitions of "lien" & "encumbrance" for further information.

Base loan amount Sum of money forming the basic payments on a loan.

Base principal balance Version of the original loan sum adjusted based on principal payments & later fundings. It excludes other unsettled debts & accumulated interest.

Basis point A term financial markets use to mean 1/100 of a percent.

Below grade A building or part existing below the ground surface.

Bench mark A permanent mark carefully measured to show height, which surveyors use to begin their surveys or measure the elevation of a site.

Beneficiary Someone who gets or is entitled to benefits, such as a person receiving income from a trust fund. A beneficiary can also be the lender of a deed of trust loan.

Bequeath To leave possessions to certain recipients in one's will. For passing on real estate in a will, use the term "devise."

Betterment Any actions improving a piece of real estate.

Bill of sale This document legally transfers personal property — not real estate title — to a new owner.

Binder An agreement signifying that a buyer wants to join a real estate contract. The buyer might also make a payment to show earnest desire & ability to purchase the property

Biweekly mortgage A plan to make payments on a mortgage every two weeks. When debtors pay half the monthly fee every two weeks, they end up supplying 13 months' payment over a year, settling the debt faster.

Blanket loan This mortgage covers multiple pieces of real estate but partially frees each parcel from the mortgage lien when certain fractions of the debt are repaid.

Blighted areas Part of a city or other area where the buildings are rundown or needing repair.

Blueprint Working set of thorough guidelines for a construction project.

Board of Realtors® Licensed real estate professionals belonging to the state & National Association of Realtors®

Bona fide Considered free from fraud, like a contract verified by a notary public.

Book value A property's worth as determined by its purchase price & upgrades or additions, minus any depreciation. Corporations use it to indicate their properties' values.

Boundary The border around a property.

Branch office An outlying arm of a real estate business — separate from the main office — where licensed brokers work on behalf of the headquarters.

Breach of contract Breaking terms of a contract in a legally inexcusable way.

Bridge loan (gap loan, swing loan, or interim financing) A short-term loan taken out between mortgages, or used by those still looking for a more enduring loan. It can be useful for buildings under construction.

Broker Someone paid to liaise between sellers & buyers.

Brokerage A group or corporation of brokers. Also means the broker industry.

Brownfield A property where people once used hazardous substances, such as a vacant gas station or closed factory.

Brownstone A row house adjoining other buildings that stands three to five stories tall.

Budget mortgage The debtor pays extra money for insurance, real estate taxes, or other fees beyond the basic payments — principal & interest. Not paying these added fees can bring foreclosure. The lender sets this money aside in an escrow account (see "escrow" definition) until the taxes or other fees need to be paid. Budget mortgages are used for conventional residential mortgages as well as loans guaranteed by the Department of Veterans Affairs or the Federal Housing Administration.

Buffer zone A piece of land separating two properties with different purposes. Buffer zones are parks or are used in similar ways.

Build-out Upgrades made to real estate following a tenant's orders.

Build to suit A landowner pays to construct a building suited to a tenant's needs, then the tenant leases it. Used for tenants who want to do business in specific type of building without owning it.

Buildable acres Proportion of land buildings can occupy, considering how much space will go to roads, open areas, setbacks, or spots not suitable for construction.

Building code Local laws describing how people can use a given property, including what types of construction, building materials, & improvements are legal. Building inspectors make sure people comply.

Building line (setback) A border set a certain distance from a lot's sides, showing where people may not construct buildings.

Building permit Document giving permission for people to build, alter, or demolish improvements to buildings. It abides by zoning laws & building codes.

Building restrictions Specify what sizes, locations, & appearances a building can legally have, as part of a building code.

Building standards Themes the developer or owner of a building uses in its construction, like certain types of windows or doors.

Bulk sale A buyer purchases an entire group of real estate assets in different locations.

Buy-back agreement A contract term saying the seller will purchase a property back if certain events occur.

Buy-down Lowering a buyer's interest rate on their mortgage during the loan's beginning years. To do this, the seller or builder gives the buyer "discount points," which he pays the lender, & the lender lowers his monthly payments.

Buy-down mortgage A home loan in which the seller or builder pays a lender to lower mortgage payments for the party who bought the property.

Buyer's agent This real estate agent acts on behalf of someone looking to purchase property, & owes that party common-law or statutory agency duties.

Buyer's broker This broker represents someone looking to buy residential real estate, & owes that party common-law or statutory agency duties, as a buyer's agent does.

Buyers' market A situation in which buyers can be choosy about real estate & shrewd about pricing because there are more properties than buyers. That happens when economies slow, when too many buildings are constructed, or when population numbers fall.

Buyer's remorse Anxious feeling someone has after purchasing a home.

C

Cancellation clause A contract term saying that, if certain things happen, the contract becomes void. For instance, if someone sells property he has been renting out, this clause cancels the lease.

Cap Prevents the interest rate on an adjustable-rate mortgage from growing past a certain amount. It guards the borrower against skyrocketing monthly payments.

Capital To a real estate agent, capital means cash or the capacity to exchange assets for money.

Capital appreciation Growth in a property's value once partial sales & capital improvements are accounted for. It differs from a capital gain, which one receives by selling the property.

Capital gain Extra money gained when someone sells a property for more than they paid to buy it.

Capital improvements Bouts of spending that improve or preserve a property, such as adding useful buildings.

Carryback financing A seller helps a buyer finance the purchase of property — for instance, by loaning the buyer money to pay the mortgage lender.

Cash flow How much income an investment pays, minus expenses. Cash flow is negative if expenses are larger than the income.

Cashier's check Preferable for real estate deals, a cashier's check guarantees the recipient gets paid, pulling money directly from the bank instead of someone's account.

Cash-out refinance Refinancing a mortgage for more money than it originally covered, to use the extra money for personal purposes.

Caveat emptor "Let the buyer beware" in Latin. The buyer purchases property at his own risk, shouldering the responsibility of examining it for defects.

Certificate of completion Paperwork an engineer or architect issues, saying a construction project is complete, meeting the terms in its blueprint. Signing this document can signal that a buyer must now make the final payment.

Certificate of insurance Insurance companies issue this document to confirm that they cover someone, & people show the certificates to their lenders to prove they have enough insurance for their property.

Certificate of occupancy (CO) A document stating that a structure complies with health requirements & building codes. These certificates come from building agencies or local governments.

Certificate of sale Document one receives when purchasing a building foreclosed for tax reasons. It proves that the buyer paid the necessary taxes for the redemption period & claimed the property title afterward.

Certificate of title An attorney's official opinion on who owns the title to a property, or other aspects of its status. The attorney makes this statement after scrutinizing public records.

Certified check Draws on money in a bank customer's account, not the bank's own funds — unlike a cashier's check. These less-secure checks are prohibited in certain real estate transactions.

Chain of title All the times a title has moved from owner to owner, until the present. Attorneys use this history to evaluate the title's status.

Chattel Tangible personal property, such as jewelry or clothes.

Circulation factor Space allowing internal circulation in an office, not part of net square footage.

Class "A" High-quality or nicely located property that will bring in a lot of rent money.

Class "B" Desirable property that falls short of bringing in the highest rent price possible.

Class "C" Low-rent property with acceptable living conditions but sparse amenities.

Clear title Title free from potential problems or hassles, such as legal encumbrances, defects, & liens.

Clearance letter The written results of a termite inspection, provided by a licensed inspector. Mortgages backed by the Department of Veterans Affairs or Federal Housing Administration, along with certain other home loans, cannot progress without this letter.

Closing The end of a sale, where buyer pays the seller, both parties or their representatives sign necessary documents, & the buyer receives the title & loan.

Closing costs Money spent when closing a real estate deal, including fees for appraising property & for the loan & title, but not the actual property.

Closing statement (HUD-1 Settlement Statement) A thorough account of how people spent, gained, & loaned money or started loans, when parties buy & sell real estate.

Cloud on title Any circumstance or document making it uncertain who holds the title to real estate. Sometimes hard to remove, clouds on title may be cleared up by a suit to quiet title or a quitclaim deed, after a title search reveals the cloud.

Cluster housing Closely grouped homes with tiny yards where residents share a common recreation spot.

Co-borrower See "cosigner."

Collateral Something a borrower stands to lose by not paying a debt. The property is collateral in the mortgage loan financing its purchase.

Collection When a borrower does not repay a debt, the lender seeks payment & prepares for a possible foreclosure, sending notices to the borrower.

Commercial leasehold insurance Insurance that pays rent if a tenant cannot. Lenders might require businesses in shopping centers to carry this insurance.

Commercial mortgage Money loaned for businesses to buy their properties or buildings.

Commercial mortgage broker Specializes in brokering mortgages for businesses.

Commercial mortgage lender Specifically funds mortgage loans for commercial uses.

Commercial property Slated for businesses, not homes or residential buildings.

Commingling A real estate agent illegally mixes his own money & a client's in one account, instead of keeping the customer's funds in an escrow or trust account.

Commission Money clients pay brokers for selling or buying property, consisting of a certain percentage of the property's price.

Commitment fee Those applying for loans pay this price to lenders, & the lenders agree to follow certain terms on a loan.

Common area assessments (homeowner's association fees) Money condominium owners or planned unit development (PUD) residents give their homeowner's association, which spends it to maintain the building or property.

Common area maintenance (CAM) Fees tenants pay beyond their rent for the upkeep of common facilities, such as parking lots & halls.

Common areas Used by all condominium residents or unit owners in planned unit developments (PUDs). These spaces are maintained by homeowners' associations using residents' money.

Common (or party) wall Separates units in a duplex, condominium, or similar building.

Community property Purchased by a married couple and, in specific states, owned by both people.

Comparable sales (comparables or comps) How much money similar properties nearby sold for — sellers assume another such property in that area will fetch a comparable price.

Comparative unit method A way to appraise properties by examining them in chunks of a certain size, such as square feet or acres.

Competent party Those who can legally partake in a contract because they are old enough, mentally stable, & not influenced by drugs or alcohol.

Competitive market analysis (competitive market analysis or CMA) Comparing the price on a seller's home to costs of other houses sold recently that have similar amenities, styles, & locations.

Completion bond Legal guarantee that a project will be finished as specified.

Compound interest Additional interest one pays for their mortgage, besides the accrued interest.

Concessions Money or other benefits landlords give tenants to encourage them to sign leases.

Condemnation When the government seizes private property without permission from its owner & renders it public through eminent domain.

Conditional commitment A lender's pledge to loan money if the borrower satisfies specific terms.

Conditional sale A real estate contract stating that the seller owns the property until the buyer fulfills all the contract's conditions.

Condominium Building where the many residents jointly own common areas & hold titles to private living spaces, called "units."

Condominium conversion A rental property changes from one form of ownership to become a condominium.

Condominium hotel (condotel) Condominium that works as a commercial hotel, where people live for short terms, use a registration desk, & have cleaning, food, & telephone services. But tenants own their living units.

Condominium owners' association Group of people who own units in a condominium, manage its common spaces, & enforce its rules.

Conforming loan A mortgage that Freddie Mac or Fannie Mae find acceptable to purchase.

Construction documents Illustrations & notes an engineer or architect makes to specify how a construction project will proceed & what materials it requires.

Construction to permanent loan A loan to finance construction that can transform into a mortgage later — but certain ones do not become mortgages.

Consumer price index (CPI) A way to measure inflation based on the prices of things

specific populations purchase at over certain time periods.

Contiguous space Divided spaces over one floor or connecting floors that can combine, so a tenant in the building can rent them all simultaneously.

Contingency Circumstances that must exist for a contract to bind the parties. If a contract is contingent on something that never happens, parties are free from it.

Contour map Displays the physical features of a site — topography — using contour lines for different elevations.

Contract Legal document binding one or both parties involved to fulfill their promises. If a party breaks its promise in the contract, there is a legal remedy.

Contract for deed/land contract Under this contract, a party pays for property in installments. The buyer can live on the property & use it, but does not own the title before paying the full price in monthly fees.

Contract for sale See "purchase agreement."

Controlled business arrangement A situation in which consumers are offered a bundle of services, such as real estate agents' aid, mortgage brokerage, & home inspection.

Conventional loan A borrower uses this long-term loan from a non-government lender to buy a house. Conventional loans include fixed-term & fixed-rate mortgages, but not loans backed by the Federal Housing Administration or Department of Veterans Affairs.

Conversion Assigning property a new use or type of ownership — changing a large house into an apartment complex, for instance.

Conveyance The document stating that a title passes to a new owner. Also means transference of titles between parties ("closing").

Cooling-off period Time period when parties can legally abandon a contract & not be bound. For contracts involving private residences, a cooling-off period is mandatory, stated by the Truth in Lending Act.

Cooperative (co-op) A complex made of residents who own shares in a corporation, which owns the property. Each resident has rights to one unit in the building.

Co-ownership Two or more people own a title.

Corporation Legally considered a single body, registered by the secretary of state. Some features of corporations include unending life, shares that can be traded, central leadership, & limits on their liabilities.

Cosigner Someone who agrees to pay a debt if the borrower cannot. This party or person signs the loan agreement or promissory note alongside the borrower, but does not own the title or appear on the deed.

Cost approach appraisal Approximating a property's value by adding the land's worth to the cost an appraiser says one would pay to replace the building, minus depreciation. This approach does not use prices of nearby homes to estimate a building's value.

Cost approach land value The value basic interest in land would carry if the land could be developed for ideal usage.

Cost of living index Numbers showing how much certain basic commodities cost compared to their prices in a baseline year — how these goods & services have become cheaper or pricier.

Counteroffer When someone makes an offer & the recipient makes a new offer back, refusing the original.

Courier fee Cost for delivering documents to all those involved in a real estate deal, which they pay when the transaction closes.

Courtesy to brokers Act of splitting pay between cooperating brokers & listing brokers.

Covenant An agreement binding at least two parties, it appears in documents such as leases, deed contracts, & mortgages. Parties in the covenant promise to act certain ways toward a property.

Covenant not to compete (non-compete clause or non-compete covenant) One party promises in writing not to make or distribute the same products as the other party within a certain area.

Creative financing A non-traditional mortgage from a third-party lender, such as a balloon payment.

Credit Borrowing money to purchase something valuable & agreeing to repay the lender afterward.

Credit history A record of someone's debts — past & present — & how reliably the person settled them.

Credit rating Number describing how much someone deserves a loan, determined by current finances & credit history.

Credit report A record of someone's prior residences, jobs, & credit — used to determine if the person is worthy of further credit.

Credit score (credit risk score or FICO score) A calculated summary of the data on someone's credit report.

Creditor A party owed money.

Curb appeal A property or home's good looks, as noted by viewers on its street.

D

Damages Amount of money someone gets through legal means because someone harmed them in any fashion. This includes damaging an owner's building.

DBA "Doing Business As." Used to note someone's invented business name or trade name, but not meant to deceive clients.

Debt service Total money one needs to pay all the principal & interest of a loan for a certain amount of time.

Debt-to-equity ratio How much unpaid mortgage a property has, compared with its equity. The ratio would be 1:2 if a property had $100,000 of unpaid debt & $50,000 of equity.

Debt-to-income ratio What percent of monthly income someone spends re-paying a debt. To calculate, divide the monthly money paid toward the debt by that month's gross income.

Declaration of restrictions Rules people must follow if they live in a given condominium or subdivision.

Decree A government- or court-issued order.

Deed This document legally transfers property to a new owner. That buyer gets the deed after negotiating with & paying the seller.

Deed in lieu of foreclosure Returning one's property to a lender without foreclosure proceedings, to avoid their negative effects & costs.

Deed in trust A relationship in which a land trust gives the trustee authority to mortgage, subdivide, or sell real estate. How the trustee can use these powers is up to the beneficiary who provided the trust. A deed in trust is also a loan term stating that, if a debtor defaults, the lender can foreclose on the property.

Deed of trust Replaces a mortgage in certain states. It gives one or more trustees legal title to real estate, & they pay off the loan. Should they default, the lender can repossess the property.

Deed restrictions Restrictions given in a deed on how property can be used. They can limit what kind of new structures people can build there, or what activities or objects are allowed on the property.

Default A borrower defaults by failing to pay their mortgage or perform some other obligatory duty.

Deferred maintenance Appraisers using this term refer to property defects the owner has not repaired, such as chipped paint or broken windows.

Deferred payment method Strategy of delaying the date when someone will begin repaying a loan.

Deficiency judgment A borrower is charged with a deficiency judgment when his property is foreclosed, but selling it does not produce

enough money to cover the remaining unpaid mortgage.

Delayed exchange A party trades property for a second piece of real estate but does not receive it right away. This delay lets that party defer all taxable gains on the first piece of property.

Delinquency Situation in which a borrower misses mortgage payments. If continued, it brings foreclosure.

Delivery Someone's real estate or other possession passing to a different person.

Demand loan In this type of loan, lenders can call for buyers to fully repay them for whatever reason, any time.

Demising wall Separates a tenant's unit from a hall, common area, or another tenant's living space.

Density How concentrated the buildings are in a certain spot; buildings per unit area.

Density zoning These zoning ordinances limit the number of houses each acre of land can contain, on average, for a certain area.

Department of Housing & Urban Development (HUD) This government agency works to provide clean & safe living spaces without discrimination. It executes plans for community development & federal housing.

Deposit (earnest money) Money one pays when offering to buy a property.

Depreciation Appraisers use this term to mean lessened value of a property because it grows old, obsolete, or has other defects. For real estate investors, this term means a tax deduction taken while owning income property.

Description See "land description."

Designated agent Someone who holds a real estate license & has authority to be another's agent, backed by a broker.

Design-build Situation in which one person manages the construction & design of a building. Also see "build to suit."

Development loan (construction loan) Borrowed funds to buy real estate, prepare it for construction, & erect buildings.

Devise Act of awarding someone real estate through a will. The devisor, or donor, leaves the property to the devisee.

Direct sales comparisons approach (market comparison approach) An appraiser places a value on property by examining the prices on recently purchased estates nearby with similar qualities.

Disbursement Money someone loans, invests, or otherwise pays out.

Discharge in bankruptcy Occurs when a bankrupt party is freed from the debts that were assigned during bankruptcy proceedings.

Disclaimer Statement that someone is surrendering property they owned or washing their hands of responsibilities.

Disclosure A document listing all the relevant positive & negative information about a piece of real estate.

Discount broker A broker whose fees are lower than most. These costs might be a flat rate instead of a percentage of the sale.

Discount points Fees the lender can charge with lower interest rates than typical loan payments. Discount points represent percentages of the loan, with one point equaling one percent of the loaned money.

Dry closing Both parties have made their agreement, but have not exchanged money or documents. The escrow will finish the closing.

Dry mortgage (non-recourse loan) A mortgage for which the borrower pledges property for collateral, but stands to lose nothing else to the lender & is not personally liable.

Due diligence Actions by someone looking to purchase real estate — checking the property for defects or hazards & verifying that a seller represents it.

Due on sale clause A mortgage provision stating that, if borrowers sell the property the loan covers, they must immediately pay the lender the rest of the mortgage debt.

Duress Circumstance in which someone is illegally coerced or threatened to act unwillingly. If someone joins a contract under duress, it can be canceled.

E

Earnest money Money a buyer deposits under a contract & loses if he backs out of purchasing the property. But if he buys the real estate, the money goes toward that sale.

Easement A party's right to use a portion of a property it does not own, for defined purposes such as accommodating telephone or power lines.

Easement in gross An easement tied personally to its owner, not meant to benefit any of the owner's land. One example involves someone granting another person rights to access part of his property for life.

Economic life How many years an improvement will continue giving property value.

Economic obsolescence (environmental or external obsolescence) Decrease in a property's value as changes to surrounding areas render it obsolete or less desirable.

Effective gross income How much gross income a property can bring in, after subtracting an allowance for vacancy & collection.

Effective age An assessment of a building's condition an appraiser presents.

Effective date Date when securities can initiate, once a registration statement takes effect.

Efficiency unit Small, one-room living space in a building housing several families. These units might lack full bathroom & kitchen facilities.

Egress Way to exit a property via a public road or other means.

Elevation drawing An illustration showing property from the front, side, or back, to demonstrate how it is situated without including perspective.

Eminent domain Government ability to buy property at market price & render it public.

Encroachment Part of a building or other structure illegally intruding on another's land or an alley or street. Encroachment includes any upgrade or improvement extending onto someone else's lot unlawfully.

Encumbrance Anything that diminishes a property's worth or makes it less useful or enjoyable. Examples include taxes, mortgages, easements, judgment liens, & rules restricting how the property is used.

Endorsement Signing the back of a check one pays; also means supporting a statement or making it more credible.

Entitlement Being owed something with legal backing. Entitlement also refers to protection of the lender by the Department of Veterans Affairs, in case a veteran cannot pay.

Entity A legally recognized corporation or person.

Environmental audit Examination of a property for hazards.

Environmental Impact Statement Document stating the negative effects of a major project on the environment, as required by law.

Environmental Protection Agency (EPA) Federal agency that works to prevent pollution & enforces national laws against it.

Equalization Factor A number by which one multiplies a property's value to align it with state tax assessments. This adjusted value provides a basis for the ad valorem tax.

Equity A property's value minus its liabilities, such as unpaid debts

Equity buildup Equity gradually accumulating as the borrower repays the loan.

Equity mortgage See "home equity line" & "home equity loan."

Equity of redemption The owner's right to recover property before the foreclosure sale, providing he comes up with enough money for loan payments & real estate taxes.

Errors & omissions insurance Protects against errors by a builder or architect.

Escalation clause A lease term stating that the landlord can raise rent if his own expenses grow.

Escalator clause A lease term requiring tenants to pay higher rent as costs increase.

Escape clause Releases parties from the sale contract if something expected does not happen — for instance, if a buyer cannot secure a loan to purchase the property.

Escrow Closing of a deal by an escrow agent — a neutral third party. Escrows are also sums of money or valuable possessions passed to a third party, who delivers them when certain conditions are met.

Escrow account (impound account) Used by mortgage lenders & servicing businesses to store money that will pay real estate taxes, homeowner's insurance, & other items.

Escrow agent (escrow company) A third party who neutrally ensures that those having a real estate transaction meet the necessary conditions, such as putting valuables in an escrow account, before any money or property changes hands.

Escrow disbursement Paying out the money from an escrow account for property expenses due, such as mortgage insurance or taxes.

Estate Someone's property & all other assets after he dies.

Estate in land Details on how much interest someone holds in real estate, & the nature of that interest.

Estimated closing costs Approximately how much it costs for a real estate sale to occur.

Ethics Moral code that guides professional behavior.

Eviction Removal of a property's occupant by law.

Evidence of title A certificate of title or other proof that one owns a property. Examples include title insurance, a Torrens registration certificate, or an abstract of title along with a lawyer's opinion.

Examination of title An inquiry & report revealing who has owned a property through its history — performed by title companies.

Exception Something an insurance policy does not cover.

Exchange A swap of similar property. For example, trading two pieces of real estate.

Exclusive agency listing An owner exclusively contracts & pays a real estate broker to sell a property during a certain time period under the owner's terms. The owner can still sell the property himself without paying the broker if he finds a buyer the broker has not claimed or approached.

Executed contract An accord for which each party has completed its duty.

Executor (executrix for females) The person a will names to manage an estate.

Exhibit A secondary document used in support of a different, main document.

Expansion option A lease provision allowing a tenant to lease bordering areas, expanding their rented space, after a certain amount of time. This provision shows up in commercial leases.

Express agreement A written or verbal contract allowing parties to declare their intentions & contract terms in speech.

Extended coverage Extra insurance against problems that homeowner's policies do not typically cover, for uncommon hazards a property faces.

Extender clause This rarely used clause makes a listing agreement renewable automatically until involved parties decide to end it.

Extension When both parties agree to lengthen a time period given by a contract.

F

Fair Credit Reporting Act (FCRA) Federal laws governing the procedures credit reporting agencies use.

Fair Housing Act Federal legislation stating that someone providing housing cannot discriminate against people because of religion, gender, disability, appearance, race, nationality, or familial status.

Fair market value Price determined by how much a buyer will agree to pay & how little a seller will accept. In a competitive market, properties would sell at certain times for market value.

Fannie Mae See "Federal National Mortgage Association."

Fannie Mae Community Home Buyers Program In this type of community lending meant to help low- to medium-income families buy homes, Fannie Mae & mortgage insurers provide flexible guidelines for participating lenders to underwrite loans & decide who has enough credit to receive them.

Farmer's Home Administration (FMHA) Part of the U.S. Department of Agriculture, this agency gives farmers & rural people access to credit.

Feasibility study Determines how well a proposed development will achieve an investor's goals. It appraises income, expenses, & how the property can be used or designed to greatest effect.

Federal Deposit Insurance Corporation (FDIC) An independent part of the U.S. government, this agency insures commercial banks' deposits.

Federal Emergency Management Agency (FEMA) Provides flood insurance for property owners at risk & performs other similar functions.

Federal Housing Administration (FHA) This government agency works to make housing available by providing loan programs, as well as guarantee & insurance programs for loans.

Federal National Mortgage Association (FNMA) Nicknamed Fannie Mae, this shareholder-owned company is congressionally chartered & leads the nation in supplying mortgage funds. Fannie Mae purchases lenders' mortgages & sells them in another form — as securities — in secondary mortgage markets.

Federal Reserve System Supplies the country with money & sets interest rates, acting as nation's primary banking system.

Federal tax lien A debt set against a piece of real estate when someone neglects to pay federal taxes. The Internal Revenue Service uses this lien to encourage the owner to pay income taxes.

Fee appraiser (independent fee appraiser or review appraiser) Someone a prospective property buyer pays to appraise real estate.

Fee for service Money a consumer pays someone holding a real-estate license for his services.

Fee simple The greatest interest in real estate that laws recognize. It entitles the interested party to all possible property rights.

Feudal system In this system, a sovereign ruler controls all rights & allows people to own property only during life. When someone dies, the king or other ruler gets the title back. Pre-colonial England used a feudal system.

FHA loan Given by a lender approved by the Federal Housing Administration. The FHA insures this loan.

Fiduciary relationship A confident & trusting relationship between principal & agent or another two parties.

Filled land Land artificially raised with piled rocks, gravel, or dirt. If a property has filled land, sellers disclose that fact to buyers.

Financing gap Portion of a property's price the buyer cannot afford. For example, a buyer might have funds & loans covering 90 percent of a $100,000 real estate sale, leaving a $10,000 gap.

Fire insurance Covers property lost or damaged in a fire. It can include related water or smoke damage.

Fire wall Made of fire-resistant substances meant to slow spreading flames.

Firm commitment In this document, a lender agrees to loan a borrower money needed to buy property.

First mortgage A property's original mortgage, which must be paid before any others. When a property has more than one lien, the first mortgage is most important, & it is the earliest debt settled for a foreclosed property.

Fiscal year The 12-month calendar of financial reports, typically starting the first day of January.

Fixed costs & fixed expenses Fees that do not change with productivity, sales success, or a property's occupants. Unlike utility bills, which depend on how much water or electricity one uses, fixed costs like fixed-rate mortgage payments remain steady.

Fixed-rate mortgage A home loan with a constant interest rate.

Fixture A possession one fixes permanently to a property, making it part of the real estate.

Flag lot Skirting a subdivision's rules by dividing property into distinct parcels.

Flat An apartment on one story only.

Flex space A structure with offices or showrooms that also contains space for factory work, laboratories, storage, & other purposes. The arrangement of these different spaces can change.

Flexible payment mortgage (adjustable-rate mortgage) A home loan with a variable interest rate, which changes while allowing the borrower to repay the debt.

Flip To profit by purchasing & quickly reselling property.

Flood certification Determination of whether property falls within a designated flood zone.

Flood insurance Required for properties in designated flood zones, this policy protects against losses caused by floods.

Flood-prone area A place with a 1-percent chance of one flood per century, where chances remain that high each year.

Floor plan Describes how rooms are positioned in a home or other building.

Flue The cavity that guides soot & smoke from a fireplace into the chimney.

Footing A grounded concrete support beneath a foundation that bears another structure & distributes its weight evenly. Footings are wider than the things they support.

For Sale By Owner (FSBO) An owner sells property without using a real estate broker. This owner works directly with the buyer or the buyer's real estate agent.

Forbearance Granting someone time to fix a problem — such as a loan default — before making any legal moves.

Force majeure An unstoppable external force that causes parties to breach a contract.

Foreclosure Someone loses property to settle a mortgage debt they cannot pay. This legal procedure turns the property title over to the mortgage lender or allows a third party to buy the property — without any encumbrances that would lessen its value — in a foreclosure sale.

Forfeiture Losing valuable possessions or money by failing to follow a contract.

Foundation drain tile A pipe that drains water from a foundation. It can be made of clay.

Foundation walls Underground walls providing a building's main support. These concrete or masonry walls can also define a basement.

Franchise Agreement in which a company lets offshoot offices use its name & services for a fee. Franchises in real estate include brokerages working for a national business.

Free & clear title See "clear title."

Free-standing building A structure separate from others, such as a shed by a house.

Front-end ratio A lender's comparison of how much a person pays each month to finance their housing & how much money they earn.

Front footage Length, in feet, of the front edge of a piece of land.

Front money Money someone needs to buy land & prepare it for development.

Frontage The foremost part of a lot, which can border a road or body of water.

Full disclosure Keeping nothing secret that could influence a sale; for example, telling the buyer a property's defects.

Full recourse This means that if the borrower stops repaying the loan, full responsibility goes to its endorser — the person who backed the loan.

Functional obsolescence A state of lowered value when an improvement is badly designed or loses function, such as a sliding window that sticks & will not open.

Funding fee Payment for mortgage protections, like the fee to secure a loan backed by the Department of Veterans Affairs.

G

Gambrel roof A roof with two sloping sides. From its top, the slopes descend gently, then each side takes a steeper angle for its lower part.

Gap in title A missing link in the history of who has held a title, resulting when records are incomplete.

Garden apartment A building in which at least a portion of the tenants can use a common lawn yard.

Garnishment Resulting from a legal judgment, garnishment means automatic deductions from a borrower's paycheck to repay the lender for outstanding debts.

Gazebo Small structure found in gardens, backyards, & parks. Gazebos are partially open but roofed.

General contractor The primary person in charge of a construction project, who is contracted to oversee it & can hire subcontractors to handle it.

General (or master) plan Used by governments to grow communities in an organized way. This long-term program dictates how property will be developed & used.

General real estate tax Sum of municipality & government taxes on a piece of property.

General warranty deed The most common & safest deed used when people transfer real estate. The party granting it guarantees sure & clear title to the property.

Gift letter States that money someone will use for a down payment or other purpose came from a friend or relative's gift, creating no debt. People send gift letters to lenders & government agencies.

Ginnie Mae See "Government National Mortgage Association."

Good Faith Estimate (GFE) Total cost of getting a home loan as estimated by a broker or lender, summing all fees the borrower must pay.

Government loan A mortgage loan insured or backed by the Department of Veterans Affairs, the Rural Housing Service, or the Federal Housing Administration.

Government National Mortgage Association (GNMA or Ginnie Mae) Like Freddie Mac & Fannie Mae, this federally-owned corporation funds lenders who make home loans. It also buys loans, but only if they are government-backed.

Government survey method A standard way of describing land features used in the majority of U.S. states, especially in the west.

Grace period A set amount of time when someone can make an overdue loan payment before suffering any consequences.

Grade The height of a hill or slope compared to level ground, including how steeply it angles. To calculate grade, divide the raised area's elevation (in feet) by the number of horizontal feet you would travel to get there on flat ground. If a slope reaches 30 feet high by the time one travels 100 horizontal feet, its grade is 30 percent.

Grandfather clause Idea that something built or made under an old set of rules is allowed to stay as it is, even when new rules take over. A building might not comply with new legal codes, but if it was grandfathered in before those rules came, it might be left alone.

Granny flat (in-law apartment) A small space someone rents in a home zoned for a single family.

Grant Passage of property to a new owner, which people can do using deeds.

Grant deed Grantors of these deeds give recipients their word that they have not passed the real estate to anyone else before. They affirm the property has no encumbrances lessening its use or value except what the deed lists. California is known for deals using grant deeds.

Gratuitous agent Services clients for free.

GRI Graduate, Realtors® Institute. GRIs are people trained in finance, investing, appraisal, law, & sales as prescribed by the Realtors® Institute.

Gross building area Summed area of all floors in a building, excluding projecting pieces of architecture or other things not part of the house's bulk. It includes penthouses, basements, & mezzanines that are part of an outer wall's main surface.

Gross income A household's income minus expenses & taxes.

Gross income multiplier A number used to estimate a property's value. One multiplies the property's yearly gross income by this figure.

Gross leasable area Total amount of space meant for rent-paying tenants & no one else.

Gross rent multiplier (GRM) A number used in gauging a property's value. One multiplies the property's monthly gross income by this figure.

Ground lease A lease in which a tenant only rents land, not a building. The tenant may own or construct a building on the land following the lease's rules. Ground leases can last a long time, & they can be net leases, meaning the tenant pays the property's maintenance fees & taxes.

Guaranteed sale program Brokers can offer this option, agreeing to give a property owner a set amount of money if that person's listed real estate does not sell within a certain time period. The owner is free to buy another house because his previous building is guaranteed to sell.

Guarantor Someone making a guarantee.

Guaranty Interaction in which someone agrees to settle another's obligations or debt if the other cannot.

Guardian Person a court selects to manage the property & affairs of a child or someone else who cannot do it alone.

H

Habitable room Living spaces, which one counts when summing a home's number of rooms. They exclude corridors & bathrooms.

Handicap A disability that hinders one's mental or physical functions, limiting at least one life activity described in the Fair Housing Act.

Hard cost Money spent to build improvements on a property.

Hard-money mortgage Secured by cash from a borrower rather than real estate. The borrower pays money or pledges the equity of property.

Hazard insurance (homeowner's insurance or fire insurance) Covers property damage by wind, fire, & other destructive forces.

Heirs & assigns People designated to receive another's property by a deed or will. Assigns receive the interest to a piece of real estate & heirs inherit a deceased person's property. Heirs & assigns can will the property they receive to someone else, or they can sell it.

Hiatus Missing information in a property's ownership history. Also, a hiatus is a gap created between two pieces of land because the legal description is inaccurate.

High rise A structure exceeding 25 stories tall in a business district or six stories in a suburb.

High-water mark Property line separating a public waterway & a land parcel. Also, a line showing how far a medium tide comes up a shore.

Highest & best use The most legal & sensible way one can use property or land, to give it peak value in a financially realistic, well-supported way.

Historic structure A building given special status for tax purposes because it is officially deemed historically important.

Hold harmless clause One party pledging in a contract to guard another against legal actions & claims. Rent contracts may include this term to protect a building owner from lawsuits by a tenant's customers.

Holdover tenant This tenant holds onto a property once the lease ends.

Holdback A chunk of loaned money the lender withholds until a certain event happens, such as builders finishing a house.

Holding company Owns or manages one or more other companies.

Holding escrow A situation in which a third party (escrow agent) holds onto a deed's final documents of title.

Home equity conversion mortgage (HECM or reverse annuity mortgage) Allows homeowners to turn their home's equity into monthly cash payments, which a lender provides.

Home equity line Open-ended credit for loans that homeowners get by building up their property's value — its equity.

Home equity loan A loan someone takes out using his house as collateral.

Home inspector A person authorized to assess how operational & structurally sound a property is.

Homeowners' association (HOA) A group enforcing rules or restrictions the developer sets on a neighborhood, condominium, or community. This group collects payments each month for the community's expenses & upkeep.

Homeowner's insurance policy See "hazard insurance."

Homeowners' warranty Insures devices & systems for heating, cooling, & other purposes over a certain period, guaranteeing that they will be fixed if needed.

Homestead Land that a family owns & lives on. Parts of this land or its value are safe from legal action relating to debt, in certain states.

Hostile possession See "adverse possession."

House rules They govern the behavior of condominium occupants. Members of the condominium owners' association create these rules to foster peaceful relations between owners & residents.

Housing expense ratio (HER) What portion of gross monthly income someone spends on housing costs, expressed as a percent.

Housing for the elderly Living space designed to accommodate people 55 or older, with common access areas.

Housing starts The approximate number of construction projects for housing units beginning during a certain time period.

Department of Housing & Urban Development (HUD) This U.S. government agency manages the Federal Housing Administration & various programs for developing houses & communities.

HUD median income An estimate from the Department of Housing & Urban Development (HUD) of how much money families in a given area earn, on average.

HUD-1 Settlement Statement (settlement sheet or closing statement) A detailed list of the funds parties pay when their transaction completes.

Hundred-percent location The spot in a city where land is most valuable, which can mean the rent is highest & vehicle & foot traffic is heaviest.

HVAC Stands for heating, ventilating, & air conditioning.

Hypothecate To back a loan by pledging property, but not surrendering it.

I

Illiquidity Difficulty converting something to cash. Real property is deemed illiquid because turning it into money is not easy.

Impact fee Private developers pay this fee to the city for permission to start a project. The money helps the city build infrastructure, such as sewers, for the new development.

Implied agency When a party acts like another party's agent & both show that they accept this relationship, they form an implied agency.

Implied listing An agreement in which parties show their concurrence by how they act.

Implied warranty of habitability In this legal theory, landlords imply that property for rent is fit to live on & use for its intended purpose.

Impound Portion of a mortgage payment set apart & saved to cover private mortgage insurance, pay real estate taxes, & insure property against hazards.

Improved land Land with some development or construction, whether people can live there or not.

Improvement Any construction that boosts a property's value, including private structures like buildings & fences, as well as public structures like roads & water piping.

Improvements Changes that make a building or property more valuable, useful, or enjoyable.

In-house sale A kind of sale made solely by the broker in the listing agreement, with no other brokers involved. This kind of sale includes situations in which the broker finds the buyer, or in which the buyer approaches someone working for the broker.

Income approach A way to estimate how much a money-making property is worth. One predicts how much net income the property will make each year through its entire life & capitalizes that income, determining its present value.

Income property A piece of real estate the owner uses to earn money without residing there.

Income statement A document reporting someone's financial history, including the amounts of money made & expenses paid, where that money came from & went, & how much the subject profited or lost. It can report on cash or accruals.

Incorporation by reference Adding terms to a given document by referencing the other documents where they appear.

Incurable obsolescence A flaw on a property that cannot be fixed or is too expensive to merit repairs.

Indemnify Guard another against harm or loss.

Indenture An agreement on paper between at least two people whose interests differ. An indenture can also be a deed with reciprocal commitments the parties agree to fulfill.

Independent contractor Someone hired to achieve a result through means they choose & control. Independent contractors pay their own expenses & taxes & receive no employee benefits. Real estate brokers are known to operate this way.

Index A table of financial information lenders use to determine how much interest a borrower will pay on an adjustable-rate mortgage.

Index loan A long-lasting loan for which payment amounts change in tune with a certain index.

Indicated value How much a piece of real estate is worth, depending on its land value & its cost minus depreciation; the net income it makes during yearly operations; & how much similar properties currently sell for.

Indirect costs Money spent on development for things besides the labor & materials going directly into structures on the lot.

Indoor air quality Degree of pollution in a building from smoke, radon, or other gaseous contaminants.

Industrial park A zone meant for manufacturing & for related projects & entities.

Informed consent Choosing to permit something after learning enough details to inform one's decision.

Infrastructure Utility lines, roads, sewers, & other public developments meant to meet peoples' basic needs in a subdivision or city.

Initial interest rate The starting interest rate for an adjustable-rate mortgage. It can fluctuate over time, changing the borrower's monthly mortgage payments.

Initial rate duration How long an adjustable-rate mortgage is set to keep the interest rate it started with.

Injunction When a court compels someone to do a certain act, or not to.

Innocent misrepresentation When someone lies accidentally.

Innocent purchaser A party that buys contaminated property without knowing it is tainted, despite having it investigated beforehand. This buyer bears no obligation to clean it up.

Inquiry notice The notice that laws suppose a reasonable individual would gain if he inquired into a property.

Inside lot Surrounded on three sides by other lots & fronted by a road, unlike a corner lot with two sides bordering roads.

Inspection report A document prepared by a licensed inspector that describes the condition of a property.

Installment contract (contract for deed or articles of agreement for warranty deed) This contract lets a buyer make gradual payments for real estate. Meanwhile, the buyer possesses the property, but its title remains with the seller for a time, possibly until the buyer finishes paying.

Installment note It calls for the buyer to pay for the property in specific amounts over time.

Institutional lenders Entities that invest in loans & other securities as a business, using others' funds they manage or their own money. The law regulates the loans institutional lenders make.

Instrument A legal statement in writing establishing parties' rights, relationship, or required duties, such as a contract.

Insulation disclosure Open sharing of details about the insulation in a house required of real estate brokers & anyone building or selling new homes. They disclose the insulation's thickness, components, & effectiveness (R-value).

Insurable title Can get coverage from title insurance companies.

Insurance binder Provides coverage temporarily until one can set up a permanent policy.

Insured mortgage Guaranteed through private mortgage insurance or the Federal Housing Administration.

Interest A fee borrowers pay lenders alongside loan repayments. Lenders charge debtors interest for using their loaned money.

Interest in property A share owned in a property, by law.

Interest-only loan In this type of mortgage, the borrower pays the monthly interest on a loan, making no payments against the debt itself.

Interest-rate buy-down plans See "buy-down."

Interim financing See "bridge loan."

Interstate Land Sales Full Disclosure Act A nationwide law governing how real estate transactions among states will work.

Interval ownership See "time-share ownership plan."

Intestate If the owner of a property dies without a functioning will, he is intestate. Here, the state laws of descent determine who inherits the property.

Intrinsic value The worth a piece of real estate has because it is a type of property the buyer happens to favor.

Inventory The amount of real estate on the market, not taking into account its quality or availability.

Investment property Real estate used to earn money.

Investment structure Strategic doling out of investment money to different entities that will manage it via loans, joint ventures, leveraged acquisitions, participating debt, triple-net leases, & convertible debt.

Involuntary conversion When a property's status or ownership changes without the current owner's consent. A house destroyed by a flood or condemned is involuntarily converted.

Involuntary lien A lien against a property made without the owner's consent. For instance, governments can lay involuntary liens on properties if owners fail to pay taxes.

Ironclad agreement Unbreakable by anyone taking part.

Irrevocable consent Approval a party gives that it cannot take back or cancel.

J

Joint liability & joint several liability Owners each bear total liability for all damages.

Joint tenancy (tenancy in common) People equally sharing ownership of a property. If one of them dies, the others receive his share.

Judgment lien Claim laid via legal judgment against property owned by someone in debt.

Judicial foreclosure A civil lawsuit turning over real estate to a lender or third party because the property owner fails to pay debts. Using civil lawsuits for foreclosure is standard in certain states.

Jumbo loan A massive mortgage that Freddie Mac & Fannie Mae cannot take on.

Junior lien A second mortgage or other obligation that will not be the first claim a property owner addresses. The owner must satisfy a more important lien before addressing the junior lien.

Just compensation Fair price the government pays a property owner when using eminent domain to render the land public.

K

Key lot Property desired for its location, which can allow the owner to use adjacent lots to their full potential. Also, a key lot is a property with its front on a secondary street & one side bordering the rear of a corner lot.

Key tenant An important renter who leases copious space in a shopping center or other complex.

Kicker Additional fee a debtor pays beyond a mortgage's interest & principal.

Kitchenette Measuring less than 60 square feet, this area is for handling & cooking food.

Knockdown Unassembled, premade building materials sent to a construction site for assembly & installation.

L

Land banker Entity that develops land for future construction & inventories improved pieces of land for later uses.

Land description Legal account of what a piece of property is like.

Land grant Land the government provides for colleges specializing in agriculture, or for other developments such as roads & railroads.

Land leaseback Deal in which an owner sells land & becomes a renting tenant, leasing from the new owner. This lease covers the land but not construction upon it. When the lease ends, any structures built on the property go back to party who originally owned it.

Land trust A trust a landowner creates, which recognizes only one asset: real estate.

Land use map A map displaying different uses of land in a certain area, along with how much is used & to what degree.

Landlocked A property bounded by other lots, not directly bordering a road.

Landlord A person who leases property to someone else.

Landlord's warrant Legal permission for a landlord to take a tenant's property & publicly sell it, to drive the tenant to pay late rent or other fees.

Late charge Additional money a lender demands when the debtor misses due payments.

Late payment Money a borrower pays a lender after it was due.

Latent defect A structural flaw an inspection misses, which can pose a hazard to residents. Certain states require licensees & sellers to check for latent defects & reveal any they find.

Leaching cesspool Its contents leak into the soil.

Lead poisoning Dangerous illness from lead building up in body tissues.

Lease A verbal or written agreement that a tenant will pay for exclusive access to a landlord's property over a certain time period. State laws require long-term leases to be written out, such as agreements exceeding one year.

Lease option/purchase Allows a person to rent a home & apply part of their lease payments toward purchasing it later.

Leasehold improvements Fixtures a tenant installs or buys for a property. The tenant can legally remove them when the lease ends if doing so leaves no damage.

Leasehold state Situation where someone holds a real estate title by leasing the property long-term, not owning it.

Legal age How old people must be to bear legal responsibility for their actions. One must be 18 to enter real estate agreements or contracts.

Legal description An account of what a certain parcel looks like, detailed enough that an independent surveyor could find & recognize it.

Legal notice Giving legal notice means making others aware of something in whatever fashion the law requires. A tenant gives a landlord written legal notice before ending a lease.

Legatee Someone given property through a will.

Lessee Someone renting property through a lease.

Lessor Someone leasing property to another person.

Let To lease real estate to a tenant, unlike subletting, which involves the tenant renting the property to someone else.

Levy To set the tax rate on a piece of property after assessing it. To levy is also to collect or take. Seizing property to settle a debt is called levying an execution.

Liabilities Debts to repay or obligations to fulfill.

Liability insurance Guards owners against claims of property damage, negligence, or personal injury.

LIBOR (London Interbank Offered Rate) One kind of index lenders use to set & change interest rates on adjustable-rate mortgages, known for its use with interest-only mortgages.

License The right to broker real estate, given by a state. A license can also mean any right a person holds & cannot sell, or permission — which can be withdrawn — to use land for a time.

Lien A claim laid on property, which can encourage the owner to settle a debt or obligation. Liens allow lenders to sell property if owners do not repay their debts.

Lien statement (offset statement) Statement describing how much debt remains to be paid against a lien on real estate, its due date, interest to be paid, & claims declared.

Lien waiver Document contractors sign giving up the right to make claims on a property once they have been paid for their work.

Life-care facility A home for senior citizens that gives medical care.

Light industry Zoning name for manufacturing companies that are not loud, polluting, or otherwise disruptive.

Limitations of actions Window of time to take a legal action before it becomes prohibited.

Limited liability company Joint ownership in which individuals are protected because they do not bear full liability. The participants are considered partners for tax purposes.

Limited referral agent A licensed real estate salesperson who refers sellers & buyers to brokerages, getting paid when a deal closes.

Limited warranty deed Its warranties only cover the time period the last person held a title before passing it on — not time with its previous owners. Any problems that arose when those earlier owners had the property do not fall under warranty.

Line of credit Credit a financial institution grants a borrower for a specific time period, with a set maximum limit.

Line of sight easement A right stating that one cannot block the view on an easement's land.

Line stakes Stakes marking the edge of a piece of land.

Lineal foot A horizontal line across the ground measuring one foot long.

Liquid asset Any asset easily exchanged for money.

Listing agreement A relationship in which the owner of real estate pays or otherwise compensates a broker to lease or sell property under certain conditions & for a specific price.

Listing broker The person whose office makes the listing agreement, who can also work directly with the buyer.

Loan application fee Fee borrowers pay lenders to review their applications for loans.

Loan officer Someone who officially represents a lending institution, with limited power to act for it.

Loan servicing The steps lending institutions take with each loan. They include managing borrowers' payments & issuing statements; collecting on loans past due; making sure owners pay their taxes & insurance on a property; handling escrow/impound accounts; managing assumptions & payoffs; & other tasks.

Loan-to-value ratio (LTV ratio) Comparison between the sum loaned as a mortgage & the value of the collateral property securing the loan.

Location, location, location An expression stressing how much a property's location influences its value.

Lock box Holds the key to property being sold, locked away. Only agents holding the code or key can open the box.

Lock in A lender's promise to charge a borrower a certain interest rate for a specific time span.

Lock-in period The time span for which a lender promises a borrower a certain interest rate.

Loft Unfinished building space. Also, open area on the two lowest floors that accommodates retail or manufacturing.

Long-term lease Rental contract lasting three or more years before ending or being renewed.

Lot & block (recorded plat) system A way to identify plots of land in a subdivision, using numbers for lots & blocks as they appear on a map, called a subdivision plat.

Low-documentation loan A mortgage for which borrowers provide only fundamental proof of their assets & income.

Low rise A structure standing four stories or less above ground.

M

Maggie Mae (Mortgage Guarantee Insurance Corporation, MGIC) Provides insurance for those investing in mortgage loans.

Maintenance fee Monthly fee paid by people in homeowner's associations to maintain & mend common parts of the property where they live.

Maps & plats Surveys showing the features of land parcels, including area measures, landmarks, property lines, who owns them, & more.

Margin A number added to the index determining interest rates on adjustable rate mortgage. It adjusts the numbers in the index to create the interest rate a borrower gets. A margin can also be a percentage tacked onto that index through the term of the mortgage.

Market conditions Marketplace traits such as demographics & rates of interest, employment, vacancies, property sales & leases.

Market data approach (Sales comparison approach) Gauging a property's value by comparing it with similar real estate sold recently.

Market study Estimation of future demand for particular real estate projects, including possible rental fees & square feet sold or leased.

Marketable title Legitimate, clearly held title at low risk for lawsuits over flaws.

Master deed Used by condominium developers to record development on the whole property, broken down into units people own.

Master lease The main lease controlling all following leases. It may encompass more real estate than the entire group of subsequent leases.

Maturity The date a loan becomes due or a contract ends.

Maturity date The day by which a borrower must fully repay a loan.

Mechanic's lien Used by contractors & others involved in building on property to ensure they get paid. This claim lasts until the workers are compensated for services & supplies rendered for construction, improvement, or repair.

Merged credit report Combines data from Experian, Equifax, & TransUnion — three major credit bureaus.

Merger The uniting of at least two investments, companies, or other interests.

Mezzanine A floor midway between a structure's major stories, or between the ceiling & floor in a single-story building.

Mezzanine financing A blend of equity & debt that takes second priority behind a primary loan. It allows lenders to possess property if the borrower does not pay the debt.

Mid-rise A structure four- to eight-stories tall, or as many as 25 stories in business districts.

Mile 5,280 feet (1,760 yards).

Minimum lot area Lowest lot size a subdivision permits. Such small lots would not suit acreage zoning, which calls for spacious properties.

Minimum property requirements Conditions property must meet before the Federal Housing Administration will underwrite a mortgage. The home must be reliably built, habitable, & up to housing standards in its location.

Mixed use A multi-purpose part of a property, such as space for business as well as residency.

Mobile home A manufactured home delivered somewhere, able to relocate.

Model home A home exemplifying others that are being developed. Model homes are furnished & displayed for buyers as part of an effort to sell other homes in a development.

Modular housing Housing manufactured off-site & delivered to a site in pieces.

Month-to-month tenancy Someone paying rent month by month, with no longer commitment. This is the default situation if the landlord & tenant make no rental agreement. Month-to-month tenancy can take over after a lease expires.

Monument A natural or man-made landmark used to create property lines for a surveyor's description of real estate.

Moratorium Time period during which payments are not required or certain acts are prohibited.

Mortgage Borrowed money for buying real estate, with the purchased property for collateral.

Mortgage banker An institution that uses its own funds to make home loans, which mortgage investors & insurance companies can buy.

Mortgage broker Someone who pairs loan-seekers with mortgage lenders. Brokers are approved to work with certain lenders.

Mortgage Insurance (MI) Protects lenders from particular consequences if borrowers fail to repay loans. Lenders can require mortgage insurance for certain loans.

Mortgage Insurance Premium (MIP) The price of mortgage insurance, paid to private companies or governments.

Mortgage interest deduction A tax deduction home owners get for paying yearly interest on mortgages.

Mortgage pre-approval A lender determines that a borrower has the finances & credit to merit a particular loan with specified terms.

Mortgagor One who borrows money from a mortgage lender.

Mud room A small chamber opening to a play place or yard. Mudrooms can house laundry machines.

Mudsill A building's lowest horizontal part — possibly laid in or on the ground.

Multi-dwelling units Collected properties housing more than one family but covered by one mortgage.

Multiple listing Sharing of information & profit between real estate brokers. They agree to give one another details about listings, & to split commissions from the sales.

Multiple listing clause A clause requiring & authorizing a broker to share a listing he manages with other brokers.

Multiple Listing Service (MLS) A group of brokers who share listing agreements, hoping to find suitable buyers quickly. Acceptable listings include exclusive-agency & exclusive-right-to-sell types.

Municipal ordinances Laws by local governments regarding standards for subdivisions & buildings.

N

Narrative report An appraisal written in explanatory paragraphs — not a letter, table, or form.

National Association of Realtors® A group of real estate agents working toward best practice in their field.

Negative amortization Happens when a borrower makes monthly payments smaller than the interest rate on an adjustable-rate mortgage. The leftover interest builds up & adds to the unpaid balance.

Negative cash flow Occurs when a property makes too little income to pay for its own operations.

Net after taxes Income a property makes minus its operating costs & taxes.

Net lease It calls for a tenant to pay taxes, insurance, utilities, & upkeep expenses for a property, along with rent.

Net Operating Income (NOI) A property's income before taxes, with expected vacancies & operating costs factored in.

Net sales proceeds Money made by selling part or all of an asset, minus costs from closing the sale, paying a broker, & marketing the property.

Net usable acres Part of a plot appropriate for construction, minus land that cannot be built on because of building code restrictions, such as zoning or density rules.

Net worth A company's value, determined using the worth of its total assets minus all liabilities.

No cash out refinance (rate-and-term refinance) Refinancing of a mortgage designed to cover only its remaining debt & fees for getting a second loan.

No-cost loan Has a higher interest rate, but no associated fees.

No deal/no commission clause A contract clause stating that a broker gets paid only if the property title changes hands as the contract specifies.

No-documentation loan Given for a large down payment to people with good credit. Applicants need not verify their assets or income.

Nominee Someone who represents another, within limits. This can include buying real estate for someone else.

Noncompete clause Part of a lease stating that only a certain tenant's company can do business on a property.

Nonconforming loan A loan too large or otherwise unsuitable for Freddie Mac or Fannie Mae to buy.

Nonconforming use A way of utilizing property prohibited by zoning laws but allowed because it began before those ordinances existed.

Nondisclosure Keeping a fact hidden, whether purposefully or accidentally.

Non-judicial foreclosure Selling property because its owner fails to pay the mortgage, but not working through a court of law. This form of foreclosure might deter title insurers from providing a policy later.

Non-recourse loan Does not hold the borrower personally responsible if he fails to pay.

Normal wear & tear Normal degradation of property with time & usage. It involves things such as small scratches on counter tops or tramping down of carpet.

Notary public Someone legally approved to witness & certify that deeds, mortgages, & other contracts or agreements are carried out. A notary public can also give oaths, take affidavits, & perform other duties.

Notice of default A document sent to notify people that they have defaulted on their loans & are open to legal action.

Notice to quit Tells a tenant to leave rented property by a certain date, or to remedy a problem, such as overdue rent. This document is also called an eviction notice.

Nuisance Actions on a property that keep others from using nearby land to the fullest. Examples include making loud noises, letting pets wander, or producing pollutants in subdivisions that do not allow these things.

O

Observed condition A way to appraise how much value a property has lost by assessing how much it has degraded, lost function, or grown obsolete relative to surrounding areas.

Obsolescence Lessened value in property because it is outdated, whether because its components functions less well or it cannot compare with surrounding property.

Occupancy agreement Allows the buyer to use a piece of real estate before the escrow closes. The buyer gives the seller money for rent.

Occupancy permit A permit signifying that a property meets safety & health standards necessary for it to be habitable. Local governments issue occupancy permits.

Occupancy rate Percent of space in a building currently being rented.

Off-site management Administration of property from a distance.

Off-street parking Found on private land.

Offer Stated wish to sell real estate or buy it at a certain cost; also, a selling price for securities or loans.

Offer & acceptance Needed for a successful real estate sale contract.

Offer to lease Document meant to lead to an official lease. This offer is made to help the owner & renter agree on lease terms.

Office exclusive A listing handled by one real estate office only, or kept from a Multiple Listing Service by the seller.

Offset statement See "lien statement."

On or before An expression meaning something is due by a specific date.

On-site management Duties a property manager must perform while present at the property.

One-hundred-percent commission An agreement between salesperson & broker in which the salesperson pays the broker administrative fees & keeps all the commission from certain sales.

Open-end loan Can increase to a certain amount, keeping the original mortgage as its backing.

Open listing In this contract, the seller pays a broker only if the broker finds a suitable buyer before the seller or another broker does.

Open space Area of water or land devoted to people's enjoyment or use, whether private or public.

Operating budget A financial plan for money-making property, based on logically predicted spending & income.

Operating expense Normal expenses of running operations on a piece of real estate.

Opinion of title A certificate giving an attorney's opinion of whether someone has valid title to the property for sale.

Option ARM loan An adjustable-rate mortgage that gives the borrower several alternative ways to make monthly payments.

Option listing Listing a property for sale & allowing the listing broker the choice to buy it.

Option to renew A provision in rental contracts stating that, under certain terms, the tenant can lengthen the lease.

Oral contract A verbal agreement, which cannot be enforced in real estate matters.

Ordinance Civic regulation of land uses.

Orientation How a building is situated in relation to prevailing winds & sun angles. The right orientation can give the building a heating or cooling advantage.

Origination fee The price a borrower pays a lender to prepare a loan.

Out parcel A piece of land near another property that once included it. Also, a single retail property in a shopping center.

Outside of closing (paid outside closing, POC on settlements) Directly paying closing fees without following normal procedures.

Outstanding balance Unpaid debt, which is a borrower's duty to address.

Over-improvement Using the land too intensively. This includes spending money excessively to improve the property.

Overage Additional money beyond rent paid for leasing retail property, determined by sales success.

Overhang Roof edge sticking out past an outer wall.

Owner financing Occurs when a seller lends the buyer needed money to purchase his property.

Owner occupant One who owns & inhabits property.

Ownership in severalty Possession of property by one person, who is considered "severed" from additional title-holders.

P

Pad A spot for one mobile home among others. Also, a pad is a site or foundation suitable to be improved — built upon or used — in a certain way.

Paper A deed contract, mortgage, or note someone retrieves from the buyer after selling property.

Parapet Part of a house's wall reaching higher than the roof.

Parcel A lot, part of a tract.

Parking ratio A figure comparing the leasable square feet in a building to its number of parking spots.

Partial sale Selling a portion of a property.

Participating broker Finds a buyer for property listed with a different brokerage firm. Participating brokers can split payment with listing brokers.

Parties Central or primary entities in legal processes or transactions. Parties buy & sell real estate.

Partition Court procedure to divide real estate between co-tenants when they do not agree to end shared ownership.

Payment bond Assures a building owner that construction costs will be covered, & no one will file a mechanic's lien.

Payoff statement A document reporting how much money a debtor must repay, in total. This statement, which the lender signs, protects the interests of both parties.

Penthouse A luxurious dwelling on a high-rise building's uppermost floor.

Per diem interest Due or added to each day.

Percentage lease Used for business properties, this rental contract calls for tenants to pay a percentage of their profits to the owner, when sales exceed a specific amount.

Percentage rent Rent payments that grow or shrink, depending on how successfully a commercial property makes money.

Percolation test A way to determine if someone can use a septic system to remove waste. It tests how well soil soaks up & draws off water.

Perfecting title Clearing a real property title of claims or clouds.

Performance bond Posted by a contractor. Its proceeds go toward fulfilling the contract & ensures that the contractor will fulfill all contract duties, or pay the owner for losses if not.

Periodic tenancy Rental of a building one month or year at a time, which does not necessarily give the tenant any right to extend the rental period.

Permanent financing A lasting loan not meant to fund construction or other short-term needs.

Permissive waste (negative waste, passive waste) Occurs when tenants do not maintain their property & fix problems as realistically expected.

Personal property (chattel) Possessions that people can carry with them — not real property.

Personal representative (executor, administrator) Someone appointed to carry out the will of a person who dies. This representative is chosen by the will itself or by the probate court.

Phase I Audit The first check for negative environmental effects on a property. Having this audit allows buyers to avoid responsibility for fixing problems they find after purchasing the real estate.

Physical life Predicted time period that buildings or other structures on real estate will last or remain livable.

Pier A column holding up some edifice.

Piggyback loan A multi-lender mortgage with one lender in charge. Also, a pledged long-term loan combined with a construction loan.

Pipestem lot (flag lot) A slender lot forming a corridor for nearby residents to reach a road, used in places where lots fronting roads are not always available. The pipestem lot fronts the road on its short side.

Pitch Angle, such as a roof slope. Pitch is also a black, viscous material used to patch roofs or pavement.

PITI (Principal, Interest, Taxes, Insurance) The parts of each payment on mortgage insurance or impounded loans.

Planned unit development (PUD) Has common areas & living units owned by an association, unlike a condominium, in which people own their individual units & the association owns common spaces.

Planning commission (zoning commission, zoning board, or planning board) Citizens who local governments authorize to collectively create zoning laws & hold hearings.

Plat An illustration mapping borders of roads, easements, & pieces of property.

Plans & specifications Illustrations specifying all details of a development project, including its electrical & mechanical features, as well as orders for design & use of certain materials.

Plat book This public record shows how tracts of land are broken down, providing the size & shape of each parcel.

Plat map Shows property lines in a given area, such as a subdivision.

Plaza A central public gathering space or courtyard amid a shopping center or other area.

Plot plan A map of how a parcel is used or will be used. It details where it is, how large it is & how it is shaped, & what parking spaces & landscaping it has.

Pocket listing Kept private by the listing broker for a time before entering the Multiple Listing Service. Delaying its entry gives that broker time to find a buyer before other brokers do.

Point See "discount points"

Potable water Safe to drink.

Power of attorney Written permission for someone to act as another's agent, under specific terms. The agent is called an attorney-in-fact.

Pre-approval letter Tells a buyer how much money a lender will loan.

Pre-qualified loan A lender's opinion that a borrower is eligible for a given loan. Lenders interview possible borrowers & examine their credit histories to decide pre-qualification, but lenders must formally evaluate people's finances before loaning them money.

Preliminary report Given by a title insurer before the insurance itself to show that the company is willing to insure a title.

Premium Extra worth beyond the face value of a bond or mortgage, or extra money paid beyond market price for something excellent or desirable. Premiums are also prices of insurance coverage.

Prepaid expenses Money handed over early, for scheduled payments such as insurance & taxes.

Prepayment Money repaid to a lender before it is required, to shrink a debt.

Prepayment penalty Fee borrowers must give lenders for repaying the entire debt prematurely. Lenders charge this penalty because a buyer who pays off a loan early pays less interest & other fees.

Presale Allows people to buy homes or other structures that are planned but not yet built.

Preservation district Zoned to conserve wildernesses & beaches, as well as managed forests, grazing sites, & historic or picturesque spots.

Prevailing rate The average amount of interest borrowers are paying on mortgages.

Price An expression of value in money — how much cash something is worth, not value itself.

Prime rate Cheapest interest to pay. It comes with short-term loans to banks' favored clients.

Principal broker Licensed & in charge of everything a brokerage firm does.

Principal residence Where a person mainly resides.

Principle of conformity States that properties are worth more if they resemble others nearby in their dimensions, appearance, functionality, & age.

Priority Sequence of importance. High priority liens are those made first & addressed first, but tax liens beat all others in priority.

Private Mortgage Insurance (PMI) Insurance from private companies that guards lenders against losing money if a borrower fails to repay a loan. When a borrower takes a loan for more than 80 percent of a home's price, the lender must have this insurance.

Pro forma statement Describes financial outcomes predicted, not necessarily realized.

Pro rata Amount of operating & upkeep costs each tenant pays, based on the proportions of property rented.

Probate Court decision of who is heir of an estate & what assets are included.

Processing fee Money borrowers pay lenders for collecting needed information to set up their loans.

Profit & loss statement Describes the money a business earns & spends along with ensuing losses or profits over a certain amount of time.

Progress payments Funds loaned to builders in installments as a construction project progresses.

Promissory note A pledge on paper to pay off a debt by a certain date.

Property manager A person paid to oversee another's property. This manager handles upkeep & accounting, & takes rent payments.

Property reports Government documents that describe properties for prospective buy-ers. Developers & sub-dividers compile these mandatory papers.

Proration Costs assigned proportionally to the seller & the buyer when a transaction closes. These expenses are prepaid or paid at the end of a term.

Prospect Someone expected to purchase.

Public auction A meeting where the public gathers to buy property seized from a borrower to pay off a defaulted mortgage.

Public land Federally owned. Someone can buy it if the government no longer needs it.

Punch list A list of problems to fix or features to complete for a nearly finished construction project.

Purchase agreement Contract giving the conditions & terms of a property sale, signed by both parties.

Purchaser's policy (owner's policy) Insurance the seller provides the buyer as required by their contract. This policy guards against problems with the title.

Q

Quadraplex A building with four private home units.

Qualification A borrower's eligibility for a loan based on credit history & ability to repay.

Qualified acceptance Occurs when someone takes an offer under specific conditions, adjusting or changing its terms.

Qualifying ratio A comparison between a borrower's income & the debt payments that would be handled after getting a loan of a certain size. It helps lenders decide how much money to loan.

Quarter section 160 acres.

Quitclaim deed A document that erases someone's ownership of real property & transfers it to another without any obligations & without guaranteeing that the person giving it up had certain ownership.

R

Radon A natural gas implicated in lung cancer.

Range of value The spectrum of prices a piece of real estate might be worth on the market.

Rate lock Guarantee a lender makes not to change a borrower's interest rate for a certain time.

Raw land Undeveloped, untouched property.

Ready, willing, & able buyer Someone who can & will accept the sales terms a property owner gives, & will do what is needed to close the deal.

Real estate agent Someone with a license to coordinate sales of real property.

Real estate fundamentals Factors that determine property's value.

Real estate investment trust (REIT) A group of people who share ownership in a trust that invests in real estate. They receive profits from the trust & get tax breaks on income from the property.

Real estate license law Governs who can broker real estate in a given state, to guard buyers & sellers against scams & ineptitude.

Real estate owned (REO) Real property a lender or savings institution receives because of a foreclosure.

Real estate recovery fund Created in certain states to pay parties claiming losses caused by someone holding a real estate license. Licensees contribute money to it.

Real Estate Settlement Procedures Act (RESPA) This federal law states that lenders must give borrowers a reasonable estimate of what costs they will incur before they get a loan. It forbids lenders from giving or getting kickbacks & certain fees for referrals to agents specializing in real estate settlements.

Real property Real estate & the associated rights, benefits, owned land, & improvements upon it.

Realtist Someone part of the National Association of Real Estate Brokers (NAREB).

Realtor® Trademarked name for an active member of the National Association of Realtors®.

Reasonable time Amount of time that can realistically be expected for something to occur, such as parties fulfilling duties for a contract. Not including reasonable times in contracts can leave them vulnerable to legal challenges.

Recapture clause A contract term allowing a party to take back rights or interests previously granted to others.

Recapture rate To an appraiser, this means the rate at which someone recovers invested money.

Reciprocal easements They restrict how subdivision or development land is used, in all the owners' best interests. Also, they are easements pertaining to everyone involved.

Reclamation Altering land so it can support construction, natural resource use, or other operations, such as priming wetlands for agriculture by draining off water.

Reconveyance Occurs when a borrower gets a title back from the lender or the lender's trustee after paying off the mortgage.

Record owner Someone who owns a real estate title, noted in a public record.

Record title Publicly recorded title.

Recording An action necessary to render a deed effective as a public notice. Deeds & other documents are filed at the recorder's office for a given county. Also, a recording (noun) is information from correctly implemented legal papers, documented by the registrar's office.

Recording fee Price one pays a real estate agent for making a property sale part of public records.

Recreational lease A lease allowing the tenant to use property for recreation. Used, for example, in large subdivisions pools or sports facilities.

Rectangular (government) survey system Surveying that uses markers called base lines & principal meridians as references to describe land. The U.S. government created this method in 1785.

Redlining A lender discriminating illegally against borrowers in specific areas, making them no loans even if they are eligible.

Reentry A landlord's legal prerogative to repossess property when a tenant's lease ends.

Referral agency Finds possible sellers & buyers & refers them to real estate agencies, which handle other tasks surrounding a sale. A referral agency comprises a group of licensed salespeople who earn money for each referral.

Refinance To substitute a new loan for an old one. Refinancing also means using money gained from a loan to repay another loan.

Registered land Property documented within the Torrens system.

Registrar An official record keeper who works with documents like mortgages & deeds.

Regulation A rule applying to procedures or management activities, which can function as a law.

Regulation Z Obliges lenders to share all the terms & costs of a mortgage with borrowers, to clarify the agreement they are undertaking. This federal legislation applies the contents of the Truth & Lending Act.

Rehab (Rehabilitation, Rehabilitate) A major restoration to help a structure last. To rehabilitate is to improve the condition of a building.

Rehabilitation mortgage Pays for fixing up a building.

Reinstate Restore something's previous status. A property owner is reinstated by getting the property back after selling it.

Reissue rate A lowered fee from a title insurer for insurance on a property recently covered by another policy.

Release (release of lien) Liberates real property from being collateral in a mortgage.

Relocation clause A lease provision stating that the landlord can transfer a tenant to a different part of the building.

Relocation company Helps an employee move to a new city, performing services such as buying the person's new home & selling the old one. It contracts as needed with other companies to smooth the moving process.

Remaining term The term or payments remaining before a loan is paid off.

Remediation Clearing a property of environmental contaminants or lowering them to a tolerable amount.

Rendering An artistic illustration of how an undeveloped structure will look when finished.

Renegotiation of lease Occurs when tenant & owner discuss new terms different from what is in their existing contract.

Renewal option A rental contract clause giving a tenant the choice to make a lease last longer.

Rent control Caps how much rent landlords can ask for. These government regulations are meant to control housing costs so people can afford to rent.

Rent escalation Changes in rental fees reflecting upkeep costs for the property or living expenses.

Rent roll Lists each tenant, their rent, & when their lease ends.

Rent schedule Created by a landlord to give a tenant predictions of rent payments— as determined by market forces, expected expenses for the building, & the owner's future plans regarding the property.

Rental agency Receives compensation to co-ordinate the dealings between potential tenants & landlords.

Rental agreement A spoken or documented agreement that someone will inhabit & use a landlord's building under specific conditions & terms.

Rental growth rate Expected changes over time in how high rental rates will be, based on market forces.

Repairs Fixing up features of a property, but not trying to lengthen its useful life as a capital improvement would.

Replacement cost Expectation of how much money it will take to build a new structure equal to a current one.

Replacement reserve fund Money saved by a Planned Unit Development, condominium, or cooperative project to replace shared parts of a building.

Reproduction cost The current expense of building a precise double of an existing structure.

Request for proposal (RFP) Document from potential clients formally asking investment managers to describe their business records, investing tactics, fees charged, current chances for investing, & other information.

Rescission One party voiding a contract, leaving both parties situated as they were before making the agreement.

Reserve account Paid into by a borrower for the lender's protection.

Reserve fund Holds money in escrow for a building's expected maintenance costs.

Resident manager Someone living in an apartment building while managing it.

Resort property Has the natural beauty or built structures for vacation & enjoyment. Examples include golf courses & resorts associated with beaches & theme parks.

Restriction Legal constraints on how people can use a piece of land.

Restrictive covenant A limitation on how an owner can use property, included in the deed by the party granting it.

Re-subdivision Further breaking down a subdivision to form more lots.

Retainage Payment for a contractor's work, delayed until a certain time, such as when construction finishes.

Retaining wall An upright barrier against moving soil or water.

Revenue stamp Placed on a deed to show that parties have paid state taxes for transferring a title.

Reverse mortgage Allows people with valuable property to get payments from lenders, drawn from the equity of their real estate.

Review appraiser Someone from the government, a bank, or another authority who examines the contents of appraisal reports.

Revolving debt Situation in which the debtor pays back a loan & borrows against that loan while continuing to repay it.

Rider Something added to a contract, such as an amendment.

Right of first refusal Given in a lease, it states that the tenant gets the first chance to purchase the rented property. It can also allow the tenant to rent more property if he matches reasonable terms someone else has offered the landlord for that space.

Right of way Permission for another to build roads on an owner's land or pass through without owning the land.

Right to rescission Allows borrowers to back out three days or fewer after signing for a loan.

Right to use Prerogative to inhabit or use real estate, given by law.

Rollover risk Chance that renters will leave once their current lease ends.

Roof inspection clause Included in certain sales contracts, it requires the seller to disclose what kind of roofing a home has, & any possible defects. The seller must handle repairs.

Rooming house A home where guests pay to occupy bedrooms. Rooming houses can also let guests use their kitchens.

Row house Homes attached to others on either side, meant to support one family each.

Rules & regulations Orders describing what real estate licensees can or cannot do. They can carry the weight of law.

Runs with the land A rule or privilege that runs with the land stays connected to the property no matter who owns it.

Rural Not part of the heavily populated areas in & around cities.

R-value A measurement of how well something provides insulation — blocks or conducts heat.

S

Sale & leaseback Involves an owner selling property then renting it from the new owner via a long-term lease.

Sales comparison approach (market data approach) Gauging a property's worth by studying the values of similar properties sold recently.

Sales contract A document the seller & buyer sign to agree on the details of a property purchase.

Salesperson Someone working for or with a licensed broker on real estate business.

Satellite tenant Other renters in a mall or similar complex besides the anchor tenant — an important business using much space.

Scarcity Low availability of something desired. Scarcity of real estate can drive up prices if many buyers are looking.

Schematics Sketches of project plans, without final touches.

Seasoned loan Partially paid off.

Second mortgage Another home loan after the first one. It takes second priority for repayment.

Secondary financing Another mortgage beyond the first one taken out to help purchase a house. Government lenders allow junior mortgages, within limits.

Section 8 housing Private rental spaces subsidized by the Department of Housing & Urban Development, so tenants only pay part of the rent.

Security deposit Money that tenants give a landlord when the lease begins & get back when it ends, unless they fail to damage the property or fail to pay rent.

Seller carryback A situation in which the party selling the house lends the buyer money to purchase it.

Seller financing See "seller carryback."

Seller's market Occurs when demand for real estate rises or supply drops, allowing sellers to charge more.

Selling broker Real estate licensee who locates a buyer.

Semi-detached dwelling A home attached to another structure by a single, "party" wall.

Servicer Collects loan payments from borrowers & handles their escrow accounts, acting for a trustee.

Setback Required space between the edge of a building & a landmark or property line, in a given zone.

Settlement See "closing."

Settlement fees See "closing fees."

Shell lease Allows a tenant to rent an incomplete building & finish construction.

Sherman Anti-Trust Act Federal legislation restricting trade relationships between states or with foreign countries. It aims to prevent monopolies or focus points of economic force that might harm the economy or consumers.

Short sale Occurs when an owner sells property but the proceeds do not pay off his mortgage. The lender lets the remaining debt go, opting for less money & avoiding a foreclosure.

Sick building syndrome A problem of contaminated air in industrial or business buildings. People exposed may suffer irritated skin & eyes, upset stomachs, & headaches.

Sight line A direction or plane of vision.

Silent second A second mortgage the borrower does not disclose to the lender of the first.

Site Where a piece of real estate is. A site is also land beneath a structure, or ground ready for construction.

Site analysis A judgment of a parcel's usefulness for a certain purpose.

Site development Preparation of a site for construction.

Site plan Describes precisely where a parcel is & where builders will make improvements.

Situs Traits of a location driving the market value of a piece real estate, including nearby properties & their effects on its worth.

Slab The uncovered horizontal surface forming a floor, which rests atop support beams.

Slum clearance (urban renewal) Removing dilapidated buildings to make space for more beneficial land uses.

Small-claims court Handles minor disagreements involving claims less than $1,000.

Soft money Tax-deductible contributions to development projects, or money used for fees supporting construction but not the act of building. For instance, soft money might pay architects or cover legal expenses.

Solar heating Harnessing sunlight energy to heat water or rooms in a house.

Sole proprietorship A situation in which one person owns a business, including no other owners.

Space plan A map of required room configurations for tenants. Space plans can describe the dimensions & layouts of rooms, including where doors are.

Spec (Speculative) home Built by a contractor who has yet to find a buyer, but expects to locate a single family to purchase the home.

Special assessment A selective levy or tax relating to a road, sewer, or other public improvement. It applies only to people whom the improvement helps.

Special conditions (contingencies) Must be fulfilled before the real estate contract containing them can bind parties involved.

Special damages See "actual damages."

Special use permit (conditional use permit) Allows people to use land in ways a given zone normally would not permit.

Special warranty deed A guarantee for buyers against flaws in a property that originated under the last owner, but not other previous owners.

Specifications Specific details on the construction materials, techniques, dimensions, & other elements workers must use in a project, accompanying blueprints & plans.

Spite fence Built to irritate a neighbor. Spite fences may be abnormally high, so certain states legally limit fence heights.

Split level A house with floors staggered so that rooms in one part sit about halfway between stories in an adjacent part.

Splitting fees Dividing up money earned, which real estate brokers can do only with one another, or with sellers & buyers.

Spot loan Made to condominiums or other properties a lender has not funded before. For condominiums, securing such a loan for individual units can be difficult, & lenders might require extra payments for services like legal costs.

Spot zoning Designating one parcel of land for different uses than other zoned property around it — an act courts might prohibit.

Square-foot method Approximating the cost of improvements by counting the proposed square feet & multiplying by the price for one square foot of the type of construction planned.

Staging A scaffold that supports construction materials & workers, removed when no longer needed. Staging is also an informal term for readying homes to impress potential buyers.

Staking Using pins, stakes, or paint marks to show property boundaries, but not encroachments.

Standard metropolitan statistical area A county containing one or more major cities housing at least 50,000 people.

Standards of Practice The ethical code licensed members of the National Association of Realtors® are required to adopt.

Starts See "housing starts."

State-certified appraiser Someone authorized by state government to appraise property.

Statute A law the legislature enacts.

Statute of frauds State law saying that certain contracts, deeds, & other agreements affecting title cannot be legally enforced unless they are written out & signed.

Statute of limitations The law specifying how much time can pass before it becomes too late to bring an issue to court.

Stigmatized property A property where something occurred to give it a negative reputation. Certain states limit disclosure of these events, which include illness, violence, & other tragedies.

Straight lease (flat lease) Tells a tenant how much rent is due each period during the entire lease. The rent will not change.

Straw man One who buys property & sells it to someone else, whose identity is kept secret.

Strip center (strip mall) A line of stores too small to house an anchor tenant, such as a major department store.

Structural alterations Modification of the parts supporting a building.

Structural defects Harm to the parts of a house bearing its weight. Structural defects make property less habitable, & they arise from earthquakes, sinkholes, & other forces shifting the ground.

Structural density Comparison between how much floor space a building has & the lot's area. A typical industrial building has a structural density of 1 to 3, meaning its land area is three times its floor space.

Studio A living space built for efficiency, having a kitchenette, bathroom, & one main area.

Subagency found in Multiple Listing Service agreements, subagencies involve real estate salespeople trying to sell other agents' listed properties.

Subprime loan A loan with elevated fees & interest, given to someone with a lower credit score.

Subagent In real estate, a salesperson authorized to work for the broker in a listing agreement. More generally, someone employed under an agent.

Subcontractor A contractor hired for part of a construction process by the main contractor. Subcontractors often specialize in doing certain jobs.

Subdivision Land broken down into sections by an owner — subdivider — following a plan called a plat, which meets local land use laws. Subdivisions contain streets, blocks, & plots for buildings. Housing developments are a familiar type of subdivision.

Subdivision & development ordinances See "municipal ordinances."

Subjective value (personal value) The price a certain person would pay for a piece of real estate.

Sublease, subleasing, subletting A lease contract between someone renting a space & one who rents it from the original renter. "Sublessee" is the term for a secondary renter.

Subordinate financing A loan second to another in priority, taken out after the first loan.

Subordinate loan A subsequent mortgage using the same real estate for collateral as the original loan.

Subordinated classes Last to be paid from mortgages underlying it.

Subordination Having a lower class of security that shares the risk of losing credit with a security of a superior class. In general, subordination means placing a right, security, or something else at a lower priority or status.

Subordination clause Gives a mortgage priority over another mortgage recorded earlier.

Subpoena duces tecum A court's command for someone to provide certain documents, such as records or books.

Subscribe To sign a document at the bottom.

Subsidized housing Living spaces partially paid for by the government, including single-family homes, apartments, & assisted-living facilities.

Substantial improvement Increases the building's value by more than 25 percent within two years. Also, substantial improvements are any made after the building has been used for at least three years.

Subsurface rights Authority to own water, oil, gas, & other materials in the ground below a parcel of real estate.

Summary possession (eviction) Occurs when an owner takes back leased property because the tenant stays after the lease ends or breaks the rental contract.

Super jumbo mortgage Depending on the lender, a super jumbo mortgage exceeds $650,000 or $1,000,000.

Superfund Refers to the strict federal law requiring entities to clean up environmental hazards on property they once owned. The Superfund list includes those obligated to remove such hazards.

Surcharge An extra fee a tenant must pay for using more electricity or other utilities than a lease allows.

Surety Someone who knowingly becomes involved in another's debt or commitment.

Surety bond Formed when a bonding or insurance firm promises to bear responsibility for debts, defaults, or other burdens. Surety bonds regarding real property can guarantee a contract will be fulfilled or a construction project finished on time.

Surface water Storm water in the ground, not channeled into streams.

Surrender Voiding of a rental contract by agreement of the landlord & tenant.

Survey Method of measuring the area & borders of land. Surveys note a house's position & size, the boundaries of a lot, easements affecting property, & any structures intruding on a lot — encroachments.

Survivorship The right for a person sharing home ownership to continue possessing the property if the second owner dies.

Sweat equity A nickname for the labor an owner invests to improve property.

T

Takeout financing Required by construction lenders, takeout financing is a pledge to finance a construction project permanently once it is complete. To receive it, the building must have a certain number of units bought or meet other requirements.

Tangible personal property Not real estate — any possession one can touch, move, & see.

Tangible property Visible & touchable like tangible personal property, but including immovable possessions like real estate.

Tax base The summed worth of all the property a taxing authority manages.

Tax certificate Given to someone to prove he paid property taxes, & to show his right to receive the deed, with proper timing & circumstances.

Tax deed Transfers a property to a new buyer after the owner loses it for neglecting tax payments. Properties are transferred using tax deeds if the previous owner does not pay the due taxes during a certain redemption period.

Tax deferred exchange (tax-free exchange or 1031 exchange) Trading of a property for the pledge to supply a similar one later, allowing someone taking part to avoid taxes on the first piece of real estate.

Tax lien A claim the federal government makes against a piece of real estate to induce its owner to pay neglected taxes.

Tax map A record kept by courthouses & tax offices that maps a parcel's size, shape, location, & other details relevant to taxation.

Tax rate The proportion of something's value one must pay as tax.

Tax sale Selling of real property because the owner fails to pay taxes. Courts decide if tax sales occur.

Teaser rate A temporary, cheap interest rate meant to entice people to take out mortgages.

Tenancy at sufferance Occurs when someone holds onto a property without permission after a lease ends.

Tenancy at will Living on an owner's property with permission, which can be revoked whenever the owner chooses. The tenant is also free to leave at will.

Tenancy by the entirety Shared property ownership by married couples when they wed. One spouse gets full ownership if the other dies. Not every state recognizes tenancy by the entirety.

Tenancy in common Involves a group of people owning property, with each person having a separate — not shared — interest & the ability to leave it to an heir. Each person is the exclusive owner of one part of the property.

Tenant (Lessee) Someone with rights to buildings or land through renting or ownership.

Tenant at will Someone a landowner permits to occupy the property.

Tenant contributions Money or service a tenant provides beyond paying rent, mandatory under the lease.

Tenant improvement (TI) Positive changes to property made by renters or the people working for them.

Tenant improvement allowance Money a landlord provides for tenants to repair & upgrade rented property.

Tender To provide something — such as money or materials — or fulfill an obligation or contract requirement.

Tenement Items permanently affixed to buildings or land. Tenements are also long-standing apartments.

Termite inspection A professional check for signs of invading termites. Loans backed by the FHA necessitate these inspections, & real estate contracts might suggest them.

Termite shield A metal barrier meant to bar termites from a house.

Testimonium An ending clause stating that parties have officially transferred property by signing the contract on the date given.

Thin market (limited market) Has low sales rates & a few people buying & selling.

Third party Someone indirectly involved in or related to a transaction, contract, or other interaction.

Time is of the essence A contract expression meaning that something must be done as soon as possible.

Time value of money Means that money brings more enjoyment & use in the present than the future, & has more value now.

Time-share ownership plan Involves tenants sharing property but using it at different times of year.

Title Ownership of real estate, or proof thereof.

Title company A company that insures titles & resolves who owns them.

Title exam Investigation verifying that a seller's ownership of property appears in public records. It reveals any encumbrances the property bears.

Title insurance It protects property buyers against flaws or legal problems that come with their real estate, if the policy mentions them.

Title report An early description of a title, not including its ownership history.

Title search A search of public records to reveal any potential problems that might hinder passing property to a new owner.

Topography The shape & elevation across a piece of land.

Torrens System A way of resolving conflicts over land ownership. Only certain states require brokers to work using the Torrens System.

Total expense ratio It compares the money one owes each month to one's earnings with expenses & taxes subtracted.

Total inventory Entire area of usable space at a property.

Total lender fees Payment a lender requires for putting together a loan.

Total monthly housing costs Monthly mortgage payments plus home-related insurance, real estate taxes, & any other monthly expenses of owning a home.

Townhouse A dwelling — not a condominium — joined to others.

Township A square containing 36 square miles used for government surveying.

Township lines East-west survey lines separated by six miles, running parallel to the edge of a piece of land.

Township tiers Land strips between township lines, given numbers showing how far south or north they are.

Tract Land subdivided — broken down.

Tract house Has a similar layout & style to surrounding homes.

Trade fixture A possession affixed to a commercial property that one can detach when the rental contract ends.

Transfer tax Taken by state or federal officials when real estate changes hands.

Treasury Index Serves as a basis for changing interest rates on adjustable-rate mortgages.

Treble damages Tripled from their original amount by legal processes allowed in particular states.

Trespass Taking or coming onto land illegally.

Triple net lease ("NN") Necessitates that the renter pay taxes, insurance, & utilities in addition to rent.

Triplex Contains three dwellings.

Truss A frame supporting a roof with widely-spaced beams.

Trust account The same as an escrow account in certain states. It contains all the money a broker gathers for customers, holding it back for specific uses.

Trust deed (deed of trust) Involves a borrower entrusting a title to a lender, who can publicly sell it if the borrower fails to repay the loan.

Truth in Lending Act U.S. government law saying that lenders must provide documents honestly describing the details of a mortgage.

Turnkey project Has someone besides the owner in charge of building or improving a structure — for example, a project the developer finishes to the last detail. Also, a purchased property already stocked with furnishings or other objects is a turnkey property.

Turnover How quickly properties sell, or how often people leave their rented homes or jobs.

U

Under contract When a seller is under contract, it means he is committed to the transaction with a certain buyer & unable to choose another.

Under-floor ducts Passages for phone & electricity wires beneath a floor, allowing businesses or offices choices of how to arrange devices using these lines.

Underground storage tank Holds water, gasoline, unwanted substances, or other liquids underground.

Under-improvement Something constructed that does not take full advantage of the property where it is.

Undersigned One whose name appears at the end of a document he signed.

Underwriting Involves lenders determining what terms & conditions to set on loans, based on the risks each borrower presents.

Underwriting fee Covers the expenses mortgage lenders pay to validate borrowers' personal information & choose who receives a loan.

Undisclosed agency Only allowed in certain states. It involves one real estate agent representing both parties in a transaction & not revealing the double allegiance.

Undivided interest Shared property on which no co-owner gets any part all to himself.

Unencumbered Free from anything making property less useful or enjoyable, such as legal claims.

Unenforceable contract Unsigned or otherwise useless for starting a lawsuit.

Unfair & deceptive practices Intentional lies, misleading statements, & other harmful or unethical acts.

Uniform Building Code (UBC) Provides national building standards. It is known for its use in the western United States.

Uniform Commercial Code (UCC) Set of legal rules about commerce that standardize financial transactions between states. This code governs warranties, doing business, selling property or entire businesses, loaning money, & other commercial doings. Every state except Louisiana uses a version of UCC.

Uniform Residential Appraisal Report (URAR) A form for presenting appraisal results for a certain building, which can be crucial for purchasing secondary mortgages.

Uniform Settlement Statement Given to the buyer & seller in transactions involving federal loans. It shows the amounts of money both parties will pay in closing their deal.

Unmarketable title A seriously flawed title.

Unrecorded deed Undocumented transfer of property ownership.

Unsecured loan Given based on a borrower's good credit, not any collateral property.

Upgrades Improvements or alterations made before a sale's closing date & paid for by the buyer.

Upside down A nickname for the situation where a borrower accumulates more debt than his property is worth.

Up-zoning Classifying property as having higher usage than it was considered to have before.

Urban renewal (slum clearance) Destroying dilapidated city buildings & constructing new ones.

Urban sprawl Development spreading from a city. It is sparser than the urban center, & it can house people who work in the city.

Usable square footage All the area within a tenant's living unit.

Use tax Taken from those who import or buy tangible possessions.

Useful life The time period before a building depreciates or stops making money.

Usury Requiring illegally high interest payments.

Utility easement Allows water, sewage, electric, or other utility lines to pass through someone's property.

V

VA loan Made through a lender authorized by the Department of Veterans Affairs. A VA loan provides a safe way for financing veterans who qualify.

Vacancy factor Percentage of future gross income expected to be lost because living spaces remain empty.

Vacancy rate The proportion of total rental spaces that are vacant.

Valid contract Can be legally enforced because it has all the necessary parts of a working contract.

Valuable consideration Allows someone receiving a promise to make claims on the money or time of a person who does not their pledge.

Value-added The worth a property is expected to gain after improvement or repair.

Variable payment plan A schedule for repaying a mortgage with varying monthly payment.

Variable rate See "adjustable-rate mortgage."

Variance Like a special uses permit, variance allows someone to improve or use property in ways the current zoning rules forbid.

Vendor's lien A claim on land the seller holds until the buyer fully pays for the property.

Veneer A layer of brick, wood, or other material hiding a less preferred surface.

Verification Made when parties swear that their contract or other document contains no lies. Verification requires a qualified witness.

Verification of deposit (VOD) A statement of a borrower's account history & current status, given by banks.

Verification of employment (VOE) A document confirming that a loan recipient works at a given job. The employer signs this statement.

Vestibule An entryway opening into a larger room.

Veterans Administration (VA) Designed to provide affordable loans to eligible U.S. veterans who serve on active duty for more than 120 days. Veterans can get loans without down payments from this federal agency.

Villa A living unit having one story, a yard, & parking spots. Villas can group in twos & fours, or form condominiums.

Visual rights The right to preserve pleasing views, keeping them free of large signs or other obstructions.

Voluntary lien A claim on a piece of real estate that the owner allows & recognizes.

W

Wainscoting A surface along the bottom of an inner wall.

Walkthrough A visit to a home by the buyer just before closing the deal. The buyer makes sure the property is unoccupied & free from unexpected defects.

Walk-up A tall apartment complex where people must use the stairs for lack of an elevator.

Warehouse fee Paid at closing, it is charged by a lender for keeping a borrower's mortgage before selling it to secondary buyers.

Warranty deed Guarantees that the person giving the deed will guard the recipient against all possible claims.

Waste line Drains the water from sinks, showers, & other plumbing fixtures besides toilets.

Water rights Possessed by people living on bodies of water, these rights describe how owners can & cannot use nearby water sources.

Water table The higher levels where water rests in the ground over a certain area.

Way A passage for vehicles or pedestrians, such as an alley or street.

Wear & tear Weathering of property from the elements, its age, or from people using it.

Weep hole Small drains in walls for extra water.

Weighted average rental rates Averages & compares the different rental rates of at least two buildings.

Wetland Swamps, marshes, & other water-filled lands protected from development by environmental laws.

Will A document that transfers property to another (the testator) when the will's creator dies.

Without recourse A phrase meaning a borrower cannot appeal to a borrower after failing to pay debts; rather, the lender can take the property.

Work letter Given to a tenant by a landlord. It details which improvements the landlord will take care of & which ones the tenant must handle.

Workers' compensation acts Require employers to insure their employees against injuries at work.

Working drawings Exact illustrations & details of how a construction project will progress.

Wraparound debt Involves a specific agreement by the lender & borrower: a borrower pays debts on a mortgage using loaned money from the mortgage lender, which is then called a wraparound lender. The loan used to pay mortgage debt "wraps around" the mortgage itself. A promissory note & mortgage document are needed to secure this type of loan.

Writ of execution Allows real estate to be sold based on a court decision.

Write-off In accounting, this means an asset lost because it cannot be collected.

XYZ

X Can replace a signature of an illiterate person, if witnessed & affirmed by a notary.

X-bracing Bracing across a panel or divider.

Year-to-year tenancy Involves renting property one year at a time, which can also be called periodic tenancy.

Yield Money regained from an investment through interest & dividends.

Yield spread Variation in money earned by commercial mortgages as compared to standard values. Yield spread also compares wholesale mortgage rates with retail mortgage rates. Maintaining this spread allows mortgage brokers to earn money.

Zone condemnation Clearing out areas by knocking down structures, leaving space for new buildings.

Zoning Dividing cities or towns into areas meant for different kinds of buildings or uses, which laws & regulations dictate.

Zoning ordinance Laws & regulations specifying how people can use or build upon land in a certain zone.

BIBLIOGRAPHY

Connecticut Department of Public Health
www.ct.gov/dph/lib/dph/environmental_health/lead/pdf/1018qa.pdf

Iowa Real Estate Commission, **http://www.state.ia.us/irec**

Minnesota Housing Finance Agency
www.mnhousing.gov/idc/groups/public/documents/document/mhfa_004799.rtf

Montana Department of Commerce, Housing Division
**www.housing.mt.gov/Includes/BOH/Singlefamily/Loan
AssumptionAgreement.pdf**

State of Delaware,
**www.dpr.delaware.gov/boards/realestate/documents/Management
Agreement_Reside**ntial.doc

United States Environmental Protection Agency,
www.epa.gov/Compliance/resources/policies/civil/tsca/lead.pdf

Washington Department of Natural Resources,
www.dnr.wa.gov/Publications/psl_og_sample_lease_oct06.pdf

INDEX

449-452, 454-455, 457, 461-462, 464, 469, 471

Intent to Enter, 342, 10

Intent to Vacate, 311, 333-334, 10

Interest, 15-16, 20-22, 24-25, 30, 35, 38-39, 44-46, 50, 53, 56-59, 62, 64, 66, 68-69, 72-77, 80-81, 86-87, 92, 94-95, 97-98, 100-101, 103-104, 113, 119, 136, 140, 154, 158-159, 173, 175, 179, 183, 185, 189, 193-194, 201, 203-204, 208, 210-212, 214-216, 218, 220, 222, 224, 232-233, 235, 238-239, 243, 245-247, 252-253, 257, 260-262, 264-265, 272-273, 275-276, 281, 312, 338, 351, 355, 362-363, 367, 370, 372, 374, 379, 381-383, 386-394, 397-399, 402-406, 408, 414, 425, 431-433, 436-437, 440-441, 443-444, 446-447, 449, 451-458, 460-461, 463, 468, 470-474, 5-6, 8

Interior Design, 2

Invoice, 115, 117, 139, 176, 416, 424, 6

L

Lead Paint, 355, 361, 364, 376, 11

Lease Cancellation, 271, 9

M

Material Men, 125, 133, 199, 213, 257, 266, 271

Month-to-month Lease, 277, 9

O

Office Lease, 195, 251, 8-9

Open House, 429, 12

Overhanging Eaves, 28, 5

P

Pet Agreement, 280, 282, 337, 10

Promissory Note, 14, 22, 33-34, 58, 62, 103-104, 222-223, 401, 441, 462, 474, 6

Property Management, 160, 163, 8

Property Rights Agreement, 31, 5

Q

Quit-Claim Deed, 385-388, 11

R

Radon, 20, 216, 268, 312, 375, 451, 463

Real Estate Agent, 25, 37, 141-142, 145, 152, 168, 170, 230, 435, 437, 439, 447, 463, 472, 7, 9

Referral, 89, 111, 143, 152, 413, 455, 464, 6, 8

Rejection Letter, 335, 10

Remodel, 176, 191

Renovation, 365, 375, 11

Rent, 20-21, 75, 84-85, 150, 156-157, 164, 174-175, 177-180, 182-185, 189-190, 193-194, 196-197, 199-204, 206-212, 214, 216, 218, 220, 226-227, 231, 235, 238, 241, 245-248, 251-254, 257, 259-263, 265, 268, 273, 275, 277-279, 281-289, 291-292, 294-297, 299, 301, 304, 306-307, 309-310, 313-316, 318, 320-322, 327, 329, 331-332, 334-335, 337, 339-340, 342, 345-346, 349-355, 358, 431-432, 434-435, 438-440, 444, 449-450, 453-454, 456-460, 462, 464-466, 468, 470-471, 9-11

Restaurant, 203, 206, 213, 8